Communitarian Foreign Policy

Communitarian Foreign Policy

Amitai Etzioni's Vision

Nikolas K. Gvosdev

Routledge
Taylor & Francis Group

LONDON AND NEW YORK

First published 2016 by Transaction Publishers

Published 2017 by Routledge
2 Park Square, Milton Park, Abingdon, Oxon OX14 4RN
711 Third Avenue, New York, NY 10017, USA

Routledge is an imprint of the Taylor & Francis Group, an informa business

Library of Congress Catalog Number: 2015016248

Library of Congress Cataloging-in-Publication Data

Gvosdev, Nikolas K., 1969-
    Communitarian foreign policy : Amitai Etzioni's vision / Nikolas K. Gvosdev.
        pages cm
    Includes index.
    ISBN 978-1-4128-6260-8 (acid-free paper) 1. United States--Foreign relations--1989- 2. World politics--1989- 3. International relations--Philosophy. 4. International cooperation. 5. Human rights--International cooperation. 6. Etzioni, Amitai--Political and social views. I. Title.
    JZ1480.G86 2015
    327.101--dc23
                                                                    2015016248

ISBN 13: 978-1-4128-6260-8 (hbk)

Contents

Acknowledgments

First and foremost, I would like to thank the Fund for Public Voices for a generous grant that enabled me to take the time to focus on this topic. I also extend my gratitude to Amitai Etzioni, who provided a good deal of assistance—first, in getting this project off the ground, and especially in locating material and answering questions that helped round out the documentary record. In addition, he scrupulously avoided anything that might even remotely be construed as an effort to influence my conclusions or assessments. Etzioni will read this work for the first time only after it has appeared in print. Needless to say, the interpretations of his writings are entirely my own, and I alone bear full responsibility for what appears in these pages.

I worked on this project in a private capacity, using my own time and resources. The opinions in this work are entirely my own and in no way represent the views of the US Naval War College, the Department of the Navy, the Department of Defense, or the US government. I wish to extend my appreciation to the Naval War College for creating an environment conducive to free academic expression and the study of national security affairs.

Any major intellectual endeavor rests upon the support and assistance of countless others. My thanks go to Jonathan B. Imber, the editor in chief of *Society*, who asked me to write an overview of Etzioni's views and recommendations in terms of U.S. foreign policy. This piece served as the basis for the proposal that became this volume. I am grateful to *The National Interest*, *World Politics Review*, and *Ethics and International Affairs* for the ability to test out ideas and put forward concepts in their pages that have found their way into this book. My deepest appreciation goes to Mary E. Curtis and Transaction Press for agreeing to publish this work. I would also like to express my thanks to the Watson Institute at Brown University for providing me a perch where a good deal of this book took shape.

This work benefited tremendously from the suggestions and comments of a number of colleagues, including Thomas Nichols, Derek Reveron, Paul Smith, David Cooper, Christopher Marsh, Colin Dueck, Ray Takeyh, and Damjan de Krnjevic-Miskovic. Any and all errors in this book are my responsibility alone.

Finally, I want to acknowledge the support and understanding of my family—especially my wife, Heidi Kranz, and my son, Adrian, particularly during those times when I was consumed by this project.

Preface

I first encountered the foreign policy writings of Amitai Etzioni in 2004. As the executive editor of the journal *The National Interest*, I had received an advance copy of his book *From Empire to Community*. I was already well-acquainted with Etzioni's work in domestic policy matters, in framing communitarianism as a third-way approach to navigate the divide between big-government statism and a laissez-faire approach. I knew that his ideas helped to provide an intellectual foundation for a number of the policy initiatives undertaken by the Clinton administration in the areas of education, welfare reform, law enforcement, health care, and public service.

Yet communitarianism did not seem to offer much guidance in terms of how the United States (or any other nation) should conduct foreign policy. The landmark November 1991 statement, the "Responsive Communitarian Platform," focused most of its attention on the state of affairs within society. At the same time, it expressed a hope that the "multiplication of strongly democratic communities around the world" might lay the groundwork for the emergence of a global community to deal with pressing transnational issues. Yet, given his prominence as one of the leading members of America's corpus of public intellectuals,[1] I was curious about what he would have to say about international affairs and America's role in the world.

There were criticisms that Etzioni's domestic prescriptions amounted to middle-of-the-road triangulations between liberal and conservative views. I therefore assumed that his book would be classed with a growing number of works that attempted to square the circle between Kissingerian Realpolitik and Wilsonian idealism—the latest iteration of an effort to create a "realistic liberalism" or a "liberal realism."[2] Alternatively, I imagined that it would offer a compelling philosophical justification for a pragmatic approach to foreign policy. Instead, *From Empire to Community* presented a unique argument and perspective.

Etzioni agreed with liberal internationalists that the Westphalian order in world affairs was being eroded and that a new set of global norms was required. However, he maintained that a stable global architecture could not be indefinitely maintained by the fiat of even a global hegemon like the United States, and would only endure if it appealed to the interests of different nations. Etzioni's emerging global community was not an idealistic association of nations bound by shared values. Instead, it would come about through the voluntary coordination of states that could not, relying solely on their own resources, combat an increasing array of transnational threats to their security and prosperity. This cooperation would, over time, help to engender the trust that would lay the foundation for forming closer associations. Moreover, a joint effort among states would generate a dialogue on differences in values, as opposed to the imposition of Western preferences on the rest of the world. Cooperation was also something realizable and achievable. It would provide a contrast to the post-Cold War euphoria in which American policymakers were being encouraged to take on "very ambitious foreign policy goals and commitments, while assuming that these goals can be met without commensurate cost or expenditure on the part of the United States."[3]

This argument appealed to me. As a graduate student in the 1990s who focused on the politics of the post-Soviet Eurasian states, I was initially caught up in the optimism that accompanied "11/9" (the fall of the Berlin Wall in 1989). Along with others, I anticipated that the end of the Cold War would lead to a world defined by the spread of liberal democracy and a (Western-derived) rules-based international order. However, close (and, in some cases, direct personal) observation of the problems encountered in the successor states of the former USSR—and those resulting from the outbreak of the Yugoslav wars of succession—led me to a renewed appreciation of the importance of stability and sustainability. This observation also engendered a growing suspicion of vast, even utopian, projects of transformation, which invariably fell far short of the stated objectives and sometimes even made conditions worse. All of this led me to put a greater emphasis on the "morality of results" rather than "the morality of intentions."[4] Over time, I began to embrace the thinking outlined by the school of the American realists, starting with Hans Morgenthau. It placed the concept of "national interests" at the center of any successful and viable foreign policy approach, and maintained that the most moral approach was one based on the values of prudence and pragmatism. Yet criticism that the realist school led to an amoral approach to decision making, as well as the question of whether seeking a stable balance of power in the international system was a means or an end in itself, continued to nag at me. In addition, American realists for the most part did not make the case for the desirability of closer international cooperation and engagement (in the absence of a compelling threat). They seemingly accepted the idea that there could be no basis for nation-states coming together in a sustained manner for a common good.

Etzioni's arguments in *From Empire to Community* filled in that gap. Morgenthau had already argued that nothing in the realist view "militates against the assumption that the present division of the political world into nation states will be replaced by larger units of a quite different character."[5] Yet many realists remained suspicious of proposals for larger associations and unions, in part because of the liberal internationalist belief that such institutions could be made binding and lasting by proclamation and fiat. Etzioni made the argument for why an idealist end-state—a community of nations—could come about only by applying realist tenets, such as the need to appeal to national interests and to achieve stability. In several reviews of his book, I termed Etzioni's approach "communitarian realism" based his proposition that the emergence of a true international community would arise out of concrete concerns for security and protection of interests. The approach also postulated that there could be a moral purpose to a realist-based foreign policy beyond simple maintenance of the balance of power.

This was my introduction to Etzioni as a foreign-policy thinker. After the release of *From Empire to Community*, he would publish additional tomes—*Security First* (2007) and *Hot Spots* (2012) that further developed his ideas. I also went back to examine Etzioni's first forays into this area, at the height of the Cold War, starting with *The Hard Way to Peace* (1962) and *Winning Without War* (1964). Increasingly, I found a unique method of inquiring into international affairs that blended liberal and realist precepts and that drew on a gradualist framework to achieve change in the international system. Etzioni attempted to avoid the utopian naïveté of the former but also to move beyond the amorality of the balance of power of the latter. Indeed, the gradualist approach—of breaking apart complex policy goals into small, discrete steps—seems to be a better way of promoting sustainable change within the international system than the "forcing the spring" approach often embraced by US policymakers.

While there has been a good deal of research and commentary published on the influence of Etzioni and the communitarians on domestic policy, there is no broad-based scholarly analysis of his work on foreign affairs, apart from commentary on and reviews of individual books and articles that he himself wrote. Beyond this, there has been no sustained effort to examine whether a coherent communitarian view on foreign policy exists, and has and would have any long-lasting influence on US foreign policy. A preliminary perusal suggests that policymakers and various presidential administrations have tended to adopt bits and pieces of Etzioni's platform for conducting international affairs. This has made it more challenging—although not impossible—to assess the influence of Etzioni's ideas on the conduct and practice of US foreign policy. At the same time, some of his warnings about possible failures were not heeded by policymakers but ultimately were vindicated by events. This is particularly true of the overly optimistic expectations as to how quickly and easily Afghanistan or Iraq could be remolded along the lines of a secular Western liberal democracy.

Hence, this present volume attempts to establish Etzioni's communitarian approach to international relations as a distinct and separate school of American foreign-policy thought, and to provide a more systematic evaluation of his ideas and proposals by examining their strengths and weaknesses.

Notes

1. Andrew Stark, "Why Political Scientists Aren't Public Intellectuals," *PS: Political Science and Politics* 35:1 (September 2002), 577.
2. See, for instance, Andrew Rosen, "Richard Holbrooke: A Self-Described 'Idealistic Realist, or Realistic Idealist,'" *Huffington Post*, December 15, 2010, http://www.huffingtonpost.com/andrew-rosen/richard-holbrooke-a-selfdb796844.html.
3. Colin Dueck, "Hegemony on the Cheap: Liberal Internationalism from Wilson to Bush," *World Policy Journal* 20:4 (Winter 2003/04), 1.
4. Nikolas K. Gvosdev, "Assessing the Ethics of Intervention," *Ethics and International Affairs*, January 16, 2014, http://www.ethicsandinternationalaffairs.org/2014/assessing-the-ethics-of-intervention/.
5. Hans Morgenthau, *Politics Among Nations: The Struggle for Power and Peace*, 5th ed.,Rev. ed. (New York: Alfred A. Knopf, 1978), 9.

Introduction

"Success has a thousand fathers" was the first part of the aphorism found on the desk of Ambassador L. Paul "Jerry" Bremer, the head of the Coalition Provisional Authority in Iraq.[1]—These words could just as easily describe any effort to plumb the intellectual sources of a particular US foreign policy. In the aftermath of success, everyone wants to claim credit by proffering the articles, attendance at high-level meetings, television appearances, or classroom encounters that show how they shaped a particular initiative. (The second part of the saying—"Failure is an orphan"—is equally true, as very few step forward to claim intellectual custody of the ideas that are associated with grand strategic failure.)

Many of those who are active as foreign policy "pundits" are influential commentators, which is important, as they react to and offer informed, expert commentary about proposals on the table—but have less influence in "setting the agenda" or impacting "the way people think."[2] In other cases, an individual may have played a critical role surrounding a specific event or set of events—one thinks of Suzanne Massie and her influence in shaping Ronald Reagan's perceptions of Russia, including teaching him the famous proverb he was so fond of quoting ("Trust but verify")[3]—but had no impact on any other administration or set of issues.

There is a much smaller group of people who could be said to have helped shape and steer the long-term conversation about the US role in the world and the type of global order best suited to meeting America's values or interests (or some combination of the two). Measuring a person's influence (and the influence of their ideas) within what is often termed the "foreign policy community" can be more difficult. This designation expands beyond serving government officials—and in some cases, military officers—to encompass academics, former officials, business leaders, think-tanks scholars, experts, and activists "who may influence foreign affairs and security policy."[4] Sometimes there can be direct confirmation, for instance, when a president waves around a copy of a person's book (or aides leak to the press that a particular author has exercised a deep influence on a chief executive's thinking).[5] Perhaps a member of the foreign policy community will be presented as a tutor to a senior figure who is said to need expert guidance in making sense of the world,[6] or will form part of a brain trust brought in to advise senior statesmen.[7] In some cases—Henry Kissinger and Zbigniew Brzezinski being among the most well-known—an academic counselor-advisor may be entrusted with operational responsibilities for policy execution as well—getting the opportunity to put his perspectives into practice.[8]

More often, a person influences policy through an indirect process of transmission of ideas by vocalizing and popularizing concepts that are then taken up by government. These concepts may also be put into practice by a teacher's "disciples"—former students who then go out to populate the national security apparatus. In this wider scope, a person can make "useful contributions to policy, either directly or at arm's length" by "framing, mapping, and raising questions" that then influence how policy executors approach foreign policy issues.[9] A person can be influential, even without having served in senior foreign-policy positions within government, because "policy impact can be successfully achieved even if policy prescriptions are not directly translated into actual policy."[10]

Of particular importance are public intellectuals who can serve as "informal intellectual brokers" between policy and academic communities.[11] Through their writing and public outreach, they set the parameters for debate, and establish the "mental models" through which policy is filtered, as well as help to shape the agenda that policymakers must address.[12] As part of this work, and one for which they may receive little overt credit, public intellectuals may move ideas and proposals from the fringe—from Daniel Hallin's so-called "sphere of deviance" where they would receive no coverage or consideration—into the realm of legitimate controversy or even consensus.[13] At various points, for instance, radical cuts in the stockpile of nuclear weapons or support for the creation of a Palestinian state were proposals beyond the pale of mainstream conversation in the US foreign policy community; today, both are accepted as legitimate policy aspirations. Public intellectuals helped to prepare the ground for the shift in both elite and public opinion on these and other matters.

What metrics can we then use to determine whether someone is an "agenda-setter"[14] rather than simply a commentator on the events of the day? James McGann offers three baskets of criteria: (1) utilization indicators (for instance, whether a person or institution is called to brief policymakers, offer testimony, and provide expert commentary in the media); (2) output indicators (the "paper trail" of books, articles, and briefings produced); and (3) impact indicators (for example, the extent to which recommendations are "considered or adopted" by those in government).[15] Of course, visibility does not always translate into influence, and trying to assess impact can be more difficult still. Nevertheless, we can use these criteria as rough benchmarks to ascertain whether a particular figure is having an impact on the policy process.

Where does Amitai Etzioni fit in this grand scheme of things? Of course, the American foreign policy community has no formal mechanism for elevation to its ranks akin to being elected to occupy one of the forty slots of the "immortals" of the French Academy. (The closest analogue would be an invitation to join the Council on Foreign Relations, an organization to which Etzioni has belonged as a member.) Instead, in very much the same way as the judge in the 1964 trial of the Russian Jewish poet Joseph Brodsky inquired, "Who has recognized you as a poet? Who has enrolled you in the ranks of poets?"—membership in the foreign policy community is based on a mixture of self-identification, governmental solicitation, peer recognition, and public acceptance. Certainly others considered to be members in good standing of the foreign policy community recognize Etzioni as a peer and are willing to engage his ideas in serious consideration.[16] Using McGann's criteria, Etzioni would certainly be considered to have met the standards for having his credentials as a bona fide member of the foreign-policy community validated. This validation is based on his involvement in activities—ranging from providing service on task forces and commissions (for instance, the Markle Foundation's Task Force on National Security in the Information Age and the Atlantic Council of the United States) to being consulted on policy issues by both the executive branch and Congress, and tapped as an advisor to US government agencies (such as the Arms Control and Disarmament Agency).[17] Etzioni's service, as a "senior advisor to the White House" during the Carter administration, focused mainly on domestic policy issues. But matters of foreign policy could not be easily and neatly separated, and service in a senior advisory capacity to a president, in the eyes of many, conveys credibility to Etzioni's musings on foreign policy matters.[18] Certainly, there is also the prodigious output of books, articles, and lectures, which one observer characterizes as "not only powerful academic pieces of work but [creations that] have been incredibly influential in . . . shaping public debate and political discourse."[19] Labeled "the everything expert" by *Time* which explicitly noted his work in the foreign-policy arena[20], and included by Richard Posner in his list of the leading one hundred public intellectuals in the United States,[21] Etzioni has a strong claim to make in terms of being seen as an agenda-setter, particularly because as the *Time* article noted, he tended to produce "hard-nosed, workable programs that politicians like."

How influential, important, and useful his ideas on foreign policy and international relations are is, in the end, in the eye of the beholder. Certainly, one can argue that other members of the foreign-policy community may be assessed as having more impact on America's conduct of its foreign relations. Yet, a strong *prima facie* case can be made that it is worth evaluating Etzioni's ideas and recognizing him as an independent thinker in his own right.

Notes

1. Patrick E. Tyler, "After the War, the Overseer," *New York Times*, July 13, 2003, A1, http://www.nytimes.com/2003/07/13/world/after-the-war-the-overseer-overseer-adjusts-strategy-as-turmoil-grows-in-iraq.html.
2. Alberto Mingardi, "How to Measure the Influence of Think Tanks," *EconLog*, January 31, 2014, http://econlog.econlib.org/archives/2014/01/how_to_measure.html.
3. Mary Elizabeth Malinkin, "Reagan's Evolving Views of Russians and their Relevance Today," Kennan Institute brief, December 1, 2008, http://www.wilsoncenter.org/publication/reagans-evolving-views-russians-and-their-relevance-today.
4. See, for instance, the definitions and discussion provided in The National Committee on United States-China Relations, "Survey of Programs on United States-China Relations and Security Issues," *China Policy Series* no. XXIII (March 2007), 3, http://www.ncuscr.org/files/7.%20Survey%20Final%20Report%20for%20Ford-Publication%20Version.pdf.
5. Michael T. Kaufman, "The Dangers of Letting a President Read," *New York Times*, May 22, 1999, http://www.nytimes.com/1999/05/22/books/the-dangers-of-letting-a-president-read.html.
6. Elaine Scoliano, "The 2000 Campaign: The Advisor; Bush's Foreign Policy Tutor: An Academic in the Public Eye," *New York Times*, June 16, 2000, A1, http://www.nytimes.com/2000/06/16/world/2000-campaign-advisor-bush-s-foreign-policy-tutor-academic-public-eye.html
7. For instance, consider the meetings Vice-President Dick Cheney would have with outside experts (cf. Barton Gellman, *Angler: The Cheney Vice Presidency* (New York: Penguin Press, 2008), 72, 261) or Secretary of State Hillary Clinton's dinners during her tenure in office (cf. Laura Rozen, "Dinner with Secretary Clinton: Afghanistan on the Menu," *Foreign Policy*, February 3, 2009, http://thecable.foreignpolicy.com/posts/2009/02/03/dinner_with_secretary_clinton_afghanistan_on_the_menu).

8. Patrick Tyler, *A World of Trouble: The White House and the Middle East from the Cold War to the War on Terror* (New York: Farrar, Straus and Giroux, 2009), 180.

9. Joseph S. Nye, "Bridging the Gap Between Theory and Policy," *Political Psychology* 29:4 (August 2008), 596.

10. James G. McGann, *2012 Global Go To Think Tank Report*, report of the Think Tanks and Civil Societies Program of the University of Pennsylvania (Philadelphia: University of Pennsylvania, 2013), 30, http://gotothinktank. com/dev1/wp-content/uploads/2013/07/2012_Global_Go_To_Think_ Tank_Report_-_FINAL-1.28.13.pdf.

11. Alexander L. George, *Bridging the Gap: Theory and Practice in Foreign Policy* (Washington, DC: United States Institute of Peace Press, 1993), 17.

12. See the discussion of the role of public intellectuals, and Etzioni's own role in this process, in the introduction written by Michael Nisbett, the codirector of American University's Center for Social Media at the School of Communication, in Mike Hulme, *Exploring Climate Change Through Science and in Society* (Abingdon, Oxon: Routledge, 2013), x.

13. Daniel Hallin, *The Uncensored War: The Media and Vietnam* (New York: Oxford University Press, 1986), 116–18; see also his comments, "Does NPR Have A Liberal Bias," *On the Media*, National Public Radio, September 14, 2012, http://www.onthemedia.org/story/235596-does-npr-have-liberal- bias/transcript/.

14. Mingardi, op. cit.

15. McGann, 29–30.

16. See, for instance, G. John Ikenberry's review of Etzioni's *Hot Spots: American Foreign Policy in a Post-Human-Rights World* and his characterization of Etzioni as a "referee" in charting the debates over foreign policy, in *Foreign Affairs* 92:2 (March/April 2013), http://www.foreignaffairs.com/ articles/138900/amitai-etzioni/hot-spots-american-foreign-policy-in-a- post-human-rights-world.

17. A copy of Etzioni's vita can be accessed here: http://www.gwu.edu/~ccps/ etzioni/general_biography_information.html.

18. See, for instance, Ido Oren, "Why Has the United States Not Bombed Iran? The Domestic +Politics of America's Response to Iran's Nuclear Programme," *Cambridge Review of International Affairs* 24:4 (2011), 660.

19. See the introduction made by Matthew Taylor, the chief executive of the Royal Society for the Arts, prior to Etzioni's June 4, 2007 lecture, "Foreign Policy After Bush," in London. A transcript is available at http://www. thersa.org/__data/assets/pdf_file/0016/646/Foreign-Policy-after-Bush- etzioni-040607.pdf.

20. "The Everything Expert," *Time*, February 17, 1975, 68.

21. The tabulations for Etzioni are found in Richard Posner, *Public Intellectuals: A Study of Decline* (Cambridge, MA: Harvard University Press, 2001), 197, 213, 437.

1

The Intrusion of Reality: The Genesis of the Etzioni Approach

Amitai Etzioni is known primarily as the "godfather" of the communitarian movement and one of America's leading sociologists. Thus, although usually viewed primarily as a domestic-policy public intellectual, Etzioni has also produced a considerable body of work addressing foreign-policy issues during his career. However, his initial career trajectory did not suggest that he was particularly interested in these matters.

Etzioni served in the *Palmach*, the "strike forces" of the *Haganah*, and the underground army of the Jewish community (*Yishuv*) prior to the establishment of the State of Israel and during the subsequent 1948 War of Independence. However, not much in his subsequent collegiate and graduate education or his early academic and professional career would suggest an intensive focus on or interest in foreign policy or national security matters. The undergraduate and graduate work of many of those now considered to be members of the broad foreign-policy community focused on law, history, and international relations. In contrast, Etzioni's studies in social philosophy with Martin Buber, who developed the "philosophy of dialogue"; his academic work in sociology at the Hebrew University; and his doctoral research at the University of California at Berkeley (under the tutelage of Seymour Martin Lipset, a leading political sociologist) were not natural conduits into the study of world affairs and international politics nor a path into the national security bureaucracy. Instead, his focus was on the domestic community, for, as Etzioni himself was to note, "If I was to participate in the deliberations about the remaking of society, sociology seemed to be the best tool."[1] From his perch as a sociologist in the academy, he could contribute ideas to the policy discourse.

Upon receiving his doctorate in 1958 and accepting an appointment to teach at Columbia University, Etzioni focused his efforts on the field of organizational sociology. He examined the dynamics between how organizations used power (force, incentive, or normative) and how its members oriented to the organization (from hostile to involved). In addition, he observed that similar patterns existed whether the organization was governmental, industrial, commercial, educational, or religious in nature. This research was published in 1961 (*A Comparative Analysis of Complex Organizations: On Power, Involvement, and Their Correlates*) and secured for Etzioni the status of a rapidly rising star in the field. But it did not position him to be seen as an authoritative voice on international affairs and US policy; indeed, the professor who hired him to join the Department of Sociology at Columbia, William J. "Si" Goode, bluntly noted, "You are a sociologist; what do you know about foreign policy?"[2]

For one thing, Etzioni had fought in a struggle for independence and had seen firsthand the realities of the use of force. State-building was not an abstract concept but something he had witnessed firsthand. Just as Zbigniew Brzezinski, another practitioner-academic, had observed that his formative experiences as a teenager during World War II "made me much more sensitive to the fact that a great deal of world politics is a fundamental struggle,"[3] Etzioni had made the decision "to take up arms and put lives—ours and all those we loved—on the line for the Jewish state."[4] Yet he would never romanticize violence. He took from his experiences as a combat veteran

> . . . a feeling that one ought to do everything in one's power to work out differences that exist within and among communities and to avoid resorting to violence. Violence is the ultimate degradation. It leaves those subject to it no choices, deprives them of all liberty and rights . . . Coffee shop revolutionaries, who glamorize violence, have never experienced the pain and grief it inflicts, the deep scars it leaves, the vengeance it invites.[5]

What drew Etzioni into the US foreign-policy debate was the belief that the United States, by the late 1950s, was locked into a dead-end approach to world affairs and its own security. The optimism felt in liberal and academic circles at the close of the Second World War—based on the notion that the United Nations system envisioned by Franklin D. Roosevelt would be able to secure international peace and security, and to hold together the wartime alliance between the United States and the Soviet Union[6]—had been replaced by superpower rivalry. The US strategy shifted from cooperation with the Kremlin to containment of the Soviet state and its spreading influence—a policy initially envisioned by George Kennan as relying on diplomatic and political pressure that soon took on a decidedly military cast, especially after the Korean War.

In addition, the United States expanded its defense perimeters beyond the Western Hemisphere to encompass a good portion of the Old World[7] in what Robert Jervis has termed the "globalization of US commitments."[8] This was accompanied by the deployment of American military forces to forward positions in Europe, the Middle East, and Asia to serve as a visible and tangible sign of the US security pledge against possible Soviet aggression or pressure.[9] Moreover, American interests around the world increasingly were seen as indivisible, committing the United States to consider responding to any Soviet challenge wherever it might occur.[10] Attacks that might take place in Europe or East Asia that did not immediately threaten the US home land would nonetheless bring about a response.

Initially, the United States hoped that its status as the sole possessor of nuclear weapons would help deter Josef Stalin from making any aggressive moves. When the Soviet Union broke the US monopoly on atomic weapons, however, this new reality meant that any clash between the two powers could quickly escalate to a nuclear war. A number of US strategists accepted this as a necessary risk. In 1956, Paul Nitze, who had served in the Truman administration as Director of Policy Planning for the State Department, bluntly concluded:

> We do not wish or intend to use means beyond those which are necessary for the achievement of any given objective. It is obviously to the interest of the West that war, and especially atomic war in any form, be avoided if that is possible without submitting to even greater evils. Furthermore, it is to the West's interest, if atomic war becomes unavoidable, that atomic weapons of the smallest sizes be used in the smallest area, and against the most restricted target systems possible, while still achieving for the West the particular objective which is at issue.[11]

To dissuade the Soviets, Nitze recommended that the United States and its allies "maintain indefinitely a position of nuclear attack-defense superiority versus the Soviet Union and its satellites," and advised maintaining the "geographic advantage" of the West (in terms of being able to encircle the Soviet bloc with bases). The hope, of course, was, as Thomas Schelling later noted, that "by arranging it so that we might have to blow up the world, we would not have to."[12] Yet US officials acknowledged that such an approach carried with it the risk that even a limited atomic war might be possible and that the United States should take steps to prepare for it. Admiral Arthur Radford, chairman of the Joint Chiefs of Staff during the Eisenhower administration, expressed his belief that the use of nuclear weapons "would become accepted" over time—that is, they would be seen as just another weapons system to be used, while Secretary of State John Foster Dulles fretted, "Somehow or other we must manage to remove the taboo from the use of these weapons."[13]

This was the context in which Etzioni, who had moved to the United States from Israel in 1957, began to consider foreign-policy questions. Among some of his academic colleagues, in reaction to the strategic situation, an antinuclear peace movement emerged that combined elements of the traditional pacifist community with scientists, intellectuals, and religious figures concerned that nuclear weapons threatened the very existence of the human community. New grassroots organizations—the Council for a Livable World (created by Leo Szilard, the scientist and coauthor with Albert Einstein of the letter to President Roosevelt that had started the Manhattan Project), the National Committee for a Sane Nuclear Policy, the Committee for Nonviolent Action, and Physicians for Social Responsibility, among others—emerged to oppose further nuclear tests and stockpiling of atomic weapons, as well as to advocate for deep cuts or even unilateral disarmament.[14] Etzioni's opposition to the nuclear buildup associated with these emerging Western strategies led him to join the emerging peace community and to engage in antinuclear activism.

Etzioni had firsthand experiences with violence in the conflict with the British and the subsequent struggle for independence. In addition, he was increasingly concerned about the possibility, and even likelihood, of a situation breaking out that would result in the use of atomic weapons—and, in Etzioni's own words, turn us "into ashes in the ovens of some horrible nuclear mega-burners."[15] Consequently, the young sociology professor found himself quite sympathetic to the aspirations of the peace movement. His personal experiences—both as someone who had escaped the Holocaust in Germany and who had to deal with the realities that the infant state of Israel might end up extinguished, strangled in its cradle—gave him a particular insight into the question of annihilation. Yet he also was aware of the importance of deterrence and accepted that force might have to be used to preserve peace—but needed to be done in a calculated, prudent fashion.

Nitze's strategy of laying down redlines for nuclear war seemed extraordinarily risky. Nitze had explicitly called for US policymakers to make it clear that "the Soviets must be left in no doubt that if there were to be an outbreak of massive military aggression . . . and if the situation could not be restored by mobilization of the non-atomic strengths available, rather than accept defeat without fighting, we will fight and from a superior nuclear attack-defense position,"[16] all in the hopes that rational decision makers in Moscow would avoid provoking conflict. Added to this was the perception—shared by both the US government and its Western allies—that, by the mid-1950s, the United States was prepared to risk nuclear war over even minor matters, in part to compensate for an unwillingness to pursue a massive buildup of its conventional forces.[17]

Many in the activist community during this time wanted to focus on stopping the immediate nuclear threat and rallied behind a series of distinct policy measures (such as an immediate ban on testing atomic weapons and an end to any further construction of new systems). There was much less consensus as to what a preferred long-term solution ought to look like, beyond a general commitment to an ideology of "non-nuclear defense,"[18] although many did advocate partial or even total unilateral disarmament in order to reduce the risks of an even accidental nuclear clash. Many activists focused primarily on calling attention to the threat posed by the nuclear arms race, and left the formulation of policy positions (the sausage making of how disarmament might actually take place) to others.

Had Etzioni also been less interested in such questions, it is likely he would not have taken his first steps into staking out a position in the debate over US foreign policy. But Etzioni's distaste for the nuclear arms race between the superpowers did not lead him to embrace unilateral disarmament as a solution. He recognized that naïve idealism, even in the service of peace, could be just as risky for the survival of the United States as a free society.[19] He wanted to sketch out an approach that would be not utopian but practical.

The conventional view widely shared in both Democratic and Republican circles during this time was that containment, despite its attendant risks of a nuclear conflict, remained "the most sensible and effective Western response to Communism."[20] A corollary to this view was that any failure by the United States to demonstrate its resolve to combat and check Soviet probes would lead to the gradual erosion of containment, and to a major shift in the global balance of forces, to the detriment of US interests and those of the "free world." This view rested on the assumption that the Soviet Union would respond in kind to Western steps to disarm and so reduce global tensions. Etzioni, however, took up the challenge to devise a workable policy alternative that would avoid the unacceptable binary choice of either nuclear war or surrender to the Soviet Union.

Starting in 1961, Etzioni took up a secondary appointment at Columbia University's Institute of War and Peace Studies. His foreign-policy research and his proposed policy solutions—outlined in *The Hard Way to Peace* (1962) and the follow-up volume, *Winning Without War* (1964)—marked Etzioni's first efforts to conceptualize a practical approach to foreign-policy matters, one that espoused idealist goals but was willing to work through a gradual, pragmatic process to achieve them. These books positioned Etzioni beyond the role of a leading professor of sociology at an Ivy League university into the role of someone who could begin to articulate an intellectually compelling yet politically feasible course for policy action.

In particular, Etzioni's work found a receptive audience in the center-left of the US political spectrum, particularly in organizations like Americans for Democratic Action. The members of this group were uneasy with the course and direction of US policy during the first decade of the Cold War, but were also skeptical of the Soviet goodwill proclaimed as a matter of course by many peace activists.

Writing in the *Bulletin of the Atomic Scientists*—in the October 1962 issue that subscribers would have received just prior to the outbreak of the Cuban Missile Crisis—Owen Chamberlain saw Etzioni's proposals as the basis for a "peace movement of the political center" that "lies between the alternatives of deterrence through nuclear armament and complete unilateral disarmament" in laying out a practical, feasible path to reducing global tensions without undermining US security.[21] Etzioni was invited to testify about his proposals at a hearing convened by the Senate Foreign Relations Committee in February 1965 to debate the future course of the Arms Control and Disarmament Agency.[22] In addition, his ideas were reviewed and assessed by Senator Hubert Humphrey, who was to serve as Lyndon Johnson's vice-president and who was the Democratic nominee for president in 1968.[23]

Etzioni thus emerged as a new voice in the American foreign-policy debate. But what was it about Etzioni's ideas that sparked interest in his perspective? What made his proposals distinct from what was already on offer from other voices in the foreign-policy community?

Etzioni's musings on war and peace might not have found as much of an audience outside the specialized halls of the ivory tower had it not been for the Cuban Missile Crisis, that "volcanic event" in American foreign-policy history.[24] It was not simply that the world came to the brink of an all-out nuclear war in 1962 between the two superpowers; it was also the realization that the strategic logic of containment as defined in the 1940s and 1950s had created conditions by which the partial destruction of the world could be seen as a logical policy choice, an outgrowth of a posture that left little room for maneuver.

In his seminal 1957 work *Nuclear Weapons and Foreign Policy*, Henry Kissinger argued that the United States needed to develop a strategy of fighting "limited" nuclear wars in order to show resolve, on the grounds that US diplomacy would be far less effective if opponents did not believe that the United States would use atomic weapons. Kissinger sought to include nuclear weapons as part of the acceptable range of means to achieve political ends.[25] What the Cuban Missile Crisis succeeded in accomplishing, however, was to give "the world's fear of nuclear war an edge of terror to concretize it."[26] In the immediate aftermath of the crisis, there was an openness in the US national security establishment to considering a "new approach" to dealing with the Soviet Union.[27]

Etzioni's New Approach

Etzioni was part of a group of scholars and practitioners that included some of his colleagues at Columbia University who, in the late 1950s and early 1960s, began to challenge the conventional wisdom about what motivated governments to act in the international system and how they arrived at their policy decisions.[28] Realism was the dominant theory for explaining international relations that saw states as billiard balls interacting with one another on the pool table of international affairs. Governments would seek to maximize their defined national interests—with security ranked at the top of the list, because, in "an anarchic international system, power rules the day, and states have little choice but to protect themselves."[29]

Realism assumed that a state would more or less react in the same way to the same set of external stimuli, and Realism as an explanation for international affairs was usually paired in the immediate post-World War II period with the rational actor model for understanding how states made policy.[30] The rational actor model was premised on an assumption that governments have a process in place that considers all possible courses of action and that weighs all the costs and benefits of each approach.[31] In turn, as James Blackwell has observed, "Cold War deterrence was built on the rational actor model, which emphasizes the intellectual nature of deterrence. It holds that the threat by an opponent to use nuclear weapons, resulting in sure destruction of the other, would be so risky that no one—regardless of cultural or behavioral attributes or institutional decision-making processes—would ever conclude they could prevail in such an ultimate nuclear contest."[32]

This mind-set, augmented by the writings of strategic theorists like Herman Kahn, Thomas Schelling, Bernard Brodie, and Albert Wohlstetter, fed into a preoccupation with deterrence and thus a tendency to overestimate what was needed to offset the Soviet threat, whether in terms of arms or deployments. American politicians had an almost palpable fear of showing anything that could be constituted or understood as weakness by the USSR and its allies (or that might be characterized as such by their political opponents). Since the Korean War, US policymakers had been concerned about what I have termed the "Acheson effect"—a fear (founded or otherwise) that a 1950 speech by Secretary of State Dean Acheson, in which he seemed to exclude the Korean Peninsula from the American defense perimeter, was a proximate cause of triggering the Soviet-backed North Korean invasion of South Korea that occurred in June of that year. (In reality, Stalin's willingness to countenance the invasion was based more on the successful Communist takeover in China and an assessment that, with no US troops stationed in Korea, the North Koreans could quickly take the peninsula and present the world with a *fait accompli*). However, the "Acheson effect" fed an unwillingness on the part of US statesmen to "to rule out any possible threat or to declare any part of the world off limits to American intervention."[33]

The Acheson effect also raised the stakes because it fed the "tenacious, unshakeable belief that nuclear force is integral to the national security of any major power"; since the United States could not possibly defend all of its global commitments with its existing conventional forces, and did not want to allow the Soviet side to dictate the terms of engagement, it opened up the possibility that nuclear weapons might have to be employed.[34] Indeed, in a speech on January 12, 1954, Secretary of State Dulles noted:

> Local defense will always be important. But there is no local defense which alone will contain the mighty landpower of the Communist world. Local defenses must be reinforced by the further deterrent of massive retaliatory power. A potential aggressor must know that he cannot always prescribe battle conditions that suit him. Otherwise, for example, a potential aggressor who is glutted with manpower might be tempted to attack in confidence that resistance would be confined to manpower.[35]

This mind-set contributed to an approach to policymaking that was extremely risk-averse, particularly in terms of offering the possibility of compromises or disengagement, for fear that this would stimulate further aggression and losses. Indeed, Kahn worried that a hesitation to stand firm against the USSR, particularly out of the fear of a nuclear conflict, might lead to a series of Munich-style compromises where aggressors would be appeased and the long-term strategic position of the United States would be compromised.[36] Throughout much of this period, there was fear that the Soviet Union was on the verge of surpassing the United States and would become the world's leading power—and so be able to dictate changes in the global order which the United States would have to accept.[37]

To prevent this from occurring, the United States needed to be able to respond at all levels (up to and including the use of nuclear weapons) and at any point in the world to prevent the Soviet Union from gaining any sort of advantage. To the extent this view dominated the domestic policy discourse, it left decision makers with little margin to take chances by considering unilateral steps (such as disengagement from a region or an initial compromise on a pressing security issue) that might be interpreted as weakness. There was little interest in scaling back America's greatly expanded commitments or in defining interests more selectively, if either would create perceived vacuums that would be exploited by the Soviets.[38] There was greater debate over whether to adopt what John Lewis Gaddis has described as "two distinct styles of containment"—symmetrical (a direct, proportional response in the immediate geographic area) or asymmetrical (a response that might be in a different area and at a different level of intensity)—but were designed to counter any Soviet threat and to avoid humiliation or escalation.[39]

How—and under what conditions—the US government might be able to adopt a more flexible approach to the Cold War helped to spur Etzioni's own research. His 1961 work *A Comparative Analysis of Complex Organizations* had helped to establish the field of organizational sociology and concluded that different types of organizations, even governments, "behaved (and misbehaved) following the same sociological laws."[40]

Such observations helped to challenge the assumption that, "for all intents and purposes, states behave as rational unitary actors"[41] by calling attention to the fact that large bureaucracies would be driven more by their conception of their organizational interests than by a more abstract and general "national interest" in how they executed the decisions of senior political leaders—and in fact might even try to drive decisions based on their own preferences. The study of bureaucratic politics thus emerged as a way to assess how government institutions—and their leaders—might constrain and shape possible options made available to policymakers, in contradistinction to the rational actor model's expectations that all options and course of action were equally open to consideration. Yet this approach could not always explain policy decisions taken by governments that the rational actor model also failed to anticipate.

Etzioni, along with other colleagues like Charles Osgood and Robert Jervis, then opened up yet another area for analysis by arguing that much more attention needed to be paid to social, psychological, and cognitive influences on policymakers, including recognizing the impact of such influences as fear and misperception in driving policy.[42] The realism of the rational actor model assumed that decision makers both had access to complete information and were able to process it in the cold light of pure rationality. Instead, Etzioni might have agreed with the sentiments expressed by Rajan Menon, namely, that oftentimes critical global events "are not shaped by the calculations of accountants. Honor, prestige and hubris—all emotions not easily factored into equations and hence predictions, but no less real for that—take center stage."[43] (These observations, of course, had initially been codified by the Greek historian Thucydides.)

The psychological-cognitive dimension of policymaking was one of the areas that the rational actor model (and its version of realism) discounted or ignored altogether, a flaw that Etzioni sought to correct. After all, a sober cost-benefit analysis might point to the desirability of a particular policy choice (say, disengagement from a regional conflict) that the country's leadership might still be unable to embrace due to its own cognitive limitations or to concerns about how the change might be received. Even more risky was that the core assumption of US foreign policy during this time—a reliance on nuclear weapons "to create uncertainty in the minds of potential adversaries as to what the United States might do if aggression took place, thereby making the risks appear to outweigh the benefits"[44]—rested on the assessment that Soviet leaders perfectly understood American intent, motivation, and resolve and thus would take no precipitous action that might provoke the United States. There was little provision for the possibility that different leaders might have different tolerances for risk, which might lead to miscalculation.

Thus, alongside the traditional military, political, and economic influences on foreign policy, Etzioni felt it was just as important to examine the "psychological-symbolic forces" which could also impact how choices were evaluated and made.[45] He called attention to factors such as rigidity (continued adherence to a particular policy even after conditions had changed), as well as other forms of triggering behavior that might constrain or even invalidate the assumptions of the rational actor model.[46] It was therefore critical, in his assessment, to pay attention to creating the psychological space that was the precondition for policy change to break out of the nuclear stalemate, the necessary "symbolic steps that create an atmosphere that will support its general purpose."[47] Small unilateral gestures could create momentum leading to larger multilateral and simultaneous steps that could reduce tensions and the possibility of an accidental or unwanted clash.[48]

One practical result of this newfound emphasis by Etzioni and his colleagues on psychological factors was to increase the importance of so-called "confidence building measures" (CBMs)—steps taken to give civilian and military leaders greater confidence that moves they (or the other side) make would not be misinterpreted as a prelude to an attack. In particular, by encouraging states to make their behavior—particularly in military matters—predictable, transparent, and regularized (for instance, through a system of prior notification for military maneuvers and movement of naval, land, and air forces, thereby creating demilitarized zones and allowing for the exchange of observers), CBMs were intended to reduce uncertainty and prevent the escalation of tensions.

The first, halting steps toward creating CBMs in the late 1950s between the Western and Soviet blocs accelerated after the Cuban Missile Crisis, guided in part by the understanding that such measures served both political and psychological purposes in helping to create space for dialogue and substantive negotiations on security issues.[49] While some CBMs were initially proffered on a unilateral basis, over time diplomatic efforts were undertaken to institutionalize them in reciprocally binding agreements. They formed a critical part of the so-called "first basket" of items covered during the talks of the Conference of Security and Cooperation in Europe (CSCE) and enshrined in the 1975 Final Act. Subsequent CSCE meetings sought to move CBMs from voluntary measures to mandated procedures enshrined in treaty commitments designed "to promote military as well as political confidence."[50]

Despite his exploration of psychological and cognitive factors in foreign-policy decision making, in these initial writings, Etzioni did not dispute the core realist tenet that the search for security is a prime motivator for a state's foreign policy. But he argued that the United States already had such a preponderance of deterrent power at its disposal that Washington could afford to take risks in offering even unilateral steps to try and decrease tensions with the Soviet Union without risking its long-term security or those of its core allies. Etzioni was prepared to challenge what Robert Osgood was later to describe as the "inertia of [the] settled axioms of containment" that tended to dominate the official US perspective on foreign policy.[51]

In particular, Etzioni stressed the feasibility of "remote deterrence": US forces did not need to be forward deployed in order to deter the Soviet Union but could be pulled back from frontline states where they were ranged, in some cases, eyeball to eyeball against Soviet forces, and instead withdrawn to staging areas and countries not directly bordering the USSR.[52] While not using the term, he argued that advances in technology, both in terms of detection as well as in rapid delivery of firepower and forces, had created, in effect, a revolution in military affairs that reduced the need for frontline bases.[53]

In order to maintain its security, Etzioni argued the United States did not need to obsessively secure the entire line of the "Free World," and so a rigid US defense posture could be relaxed to become more flexible and adaptable. Such a posture would also reduce the need for the United States to attempt to manage political developments in other countries, which was usually resented by local populations as unwarranted interference in their affairs and a major contributing factor to the rise of anti-Americanism.

Creating breathing room and buffer zones, Etzioni maintained, could create the psychological space needed to decrease tensions between the superpower blocs. At the same time, however, improved US rapid-response capabilities were sufficient to guard against the possibility of Soviet treachery and the risk that the USSR might seek to take advantage of US gestures to markedly improve its geopolitical position, since troops could rapidly be surged back to the front line areas if there was a breach of the peace. Thus, if the gamble that a relaxation of tensions could be achieved through pulling back from forward confrontation proved to be a failure, the United States would not have risked its survival as a great power. It was this belief that the risks of his strategy were in fact manageable—through possessing sufficient rapid reaction capabilities, for instance—that gave Etzioni the hope that this type of proposal could be acted upon even by a risk-averse leadership.

In contrast to some of the more idealistic elements within the peace movement, who proposed grand, sweeping gestures, Etzioni, aware that this could create intense worries about insecurity, proposed breaking apart major initiatives "into numerous limited steps" implemented over a long period of time.[54] He termed his approach a "gradualist strategy for peace." He argued that the United States (or the Soviet Union) could start the process by offering a series of limited, unilateral gestures, without any requirement for immediate reciprocity on the part of the other party, to begin building the basis for communication and trust. A relaxation of tensions could then lay the basis for a more explicit round of reciprocal concessions offered by each side. Over time, Etzioni felt that this gradualist strategy would bear fruit in terms of the elimination of entire categories of weapons from the arsenals of both superpowers, and of the structuring of new mechanisms for dispute resolution.

Many of Etzioni's proposals were not in and of themselves new. But what made his strategy of gradualism different from what was already on offer from the US foreign-policy community of the time was the "persuasive rearrangement of many old ideas into a new priority list."[55] Gradualism—which will be discussed in much greater detail in the following chapter—was an effort to take various proposals for reducing Cold War tensions and to formulate them into a coherent strategy.

Etzioni, in contrast to those who fretted that the United States and its allies were under siege from the Soviet bloc, was confident that this strategy could be pursued without jeopardizing the core security of the United States. This confidence came out of his assessments that economic and technological advancements in the West would undermine some of the appeal of Soviet ideology. The prevailing "if you are not with us you are against us" mind-set, which viewed the efforts—primarily of newly independent states in Africa and Asia—to eschew bloc affiliation in favor of a neutral, nonaligned posture as a problem for US foreign policy.[56] In contrast, Etzioni envisioned strengthening the capacity of the nonaligned states to maintain their neutrality, as part of the process of constraining Soviet expansionism. Most controversially, he discounted fears that local revolutionary movements that leaned toward Marxist ideology would automatically affiliate to the Soviet bloc. Instead, Etzioni maintained that many, following the path already blazed by Josip Broz Tito of Yugoslavia (following his break with Stalinism), would embrace nonalignment.

Etzioni also applied the realist pragmatism of his gradualist approach to another core vision of the progressive foreign-policy community: the push for supranationalism leading toward more effective regional and global governance. Following World War I, Teilhard de Chardin had expressed the view that "The age of nations is past. The task before us now, if we would not perish, is to build the Earth." In the 1950s, this hope seemed as if it might yet be realized as states, particularly those produced as a result of the decolonization of the old European empires, explored the possibility of mergers and federations.

In Africa, Ghana's first postcolonial leader, Kwame Nkrumah, reached out to other regional governments in the so-called "Casablanca bloc" in an effort to create a federation of African states. The Organization of African Unity was created in 1963 as a partial response to this movement. Egypt and Syria had attempted to create a United Arab Republic with Yemen and the United Arab States, while Iraq and Jordan endeavored to create an Arab Federation. Former British possessions in the Caribbean tried to forge the Federation of the West Indies, while halfway around the world the Association of Southeast Asia was established in 1967. Of course, several Western European states had already taken significant steps to forge a more viable economic union, culminating in the Treaty of Rome (1957), which in turn laid the foundation for the European Community.

While many were confidently predicting the emergence of a series of new powerful regional federations, Etzioni was more circumspect. Any idealistic rush to union that ignored the painstakingly slow process of building viable institutions and, more importantly, was unable to get the commitment of key stakeholders in each country would not be successful. Many of these projects collapsed after only a few years or were significantly reduced in scope; only the European experiment, in part because of its gradualist approach to community building, was to endure.

Gradualism remained Etzioni's primary, overarching contribution to the US foreign-policy discussion for the rest of the Cold War era.[57] While the gradualist program was never adopted wholesale by American decision makers—in part because it bluntly made clear that there was "no gimmick for the rapid solution of the world's problems"[58]—bits and pieces of the approach to international affairs did find their way into US policy.[59]

While Etzioni continued to comment on foreign-policy matters, the bulk of his attention returned to domestic issues. After his service in the Carter administration (1979–1980), Etzioni accepted a professorship at George Washington University. He focused on drawing together the various strands of his work on domestic and foreign policy into an overarching framework, a distinct policy "school." A series of symposia and conferences, which featured contributions from such thinkers as Mary Ann Glendon, William Galston, Benjamin Barber, Robert Bellah, and others, laid the foundations of a new approach to policy.

The search for a "third way"—an attempt to strike a balance between laissez-faire individualism and the demands of the collective, especially the state—was dubbed "responsive communitarianism." In domestic affairs, it represented a search for ways to achieve social welfare goals without relying on an overly bureaucratized, impersonal, and unresponsive government bureaucracy but. The new approach sought to do this without blindly trusting that the free market would automatically provide solutions. It aimed to balance individual rights and social obligations in a manner that would enhance personal freedom and individual rights without undermining social stability and cohesion.

Responsive communitarianism debuted as the Cold War was drawing to a close. The dismantling of the Soviet bloc after 1989 and the collapse of the USSR itself in 1991 raised hopes that this might lead to the realization of many of the aspirations of earlier generations, such as a rules-based international community that could promote integration among nation-states to solve global problems. The end of superpower conflict was expected to remove the barriers that had impeded progress toward a more peaceful global community—from the arms race to deadlock at the United Nations. It seemed to herald, if not the end of history, at least a long-term holiday in "which we imagined that the existential struggles of the past six decades against the various totalitarianisms had ended for good."[60] The text of the "Responsive Communitarian Platform," released in 1991, reflected that optimism. In it, the endorsers expressed their hope that in

> the multiplication of strongly democratic communities around the world lies our best hope for the emergence of a global community that can deal concertedly with matters of general concern to our species as a whole: with war and strife, with violations of basic rights, with environmental degradation, and with the extreme material deprivation that stunts the bodies, minds, and spirits of children. Our communitarian concern may begin with ourselves and our families, but it rises inexorably to the long-imagined community of humankind.[61]

This hope was reflected as well in a change of emphasis in U.S. foreign policy—a shift from containment to "democratic enlargement"—starting with the George H.W. Bush administration and becoming quite pronounced during the presidency of Bill Clinton.[62] Preserving the freedom of the Western bloc and saving it from Soviet domination was no longer the defining task for ensuring the security of the United States. Now, the goal was to encourage the spread of Western liberal political and economic institutions throughout the world. It was assumed that states that adopted democratic forms of governance and free-market economics would also support US leadership of the international system and endorse an American global security agenda.[63] A global community would emerge by simply expanding the Western community of nations and converting (or, if necessary, compelling) other states to accept its precepts and norms.[64]

This newfound expansion was not expected to encounter much resistance or to require a great deal of effort or resources on the part of the American government. The popularization of Francis Fukuyama's argument that the end of the Cold War represented the "end of history" (in ideological terms) was translated by "American intellectuals and officials" into the assessment "that some combination of liberal capitalist economics and liberal political values is carrying the world swiftly and smoothly toward the triumph of Anglo-American values."[65]

The initial communitarian manifesto contained a critical caveat, often overlooked at the time, that progress toward any sort of global community would be "affected by important material, cultural, and political differences among nations and peoples. And we know that enduring responsive communities cannot be created through fiat or coercion, but only through genuine public conviction." Others agreed, warning that "despite the claims of liberal triumphalism, the question of what constitutes the most important defining elements of democracy is not a settled matter in the West. And when considering democracy in non-Western contexts, the task of definition becomes much more complicated, especially where cultural factors are concerned."[66]

In addition, the democratic community expressed concerns that the apparent superficiality of the US approach was leading not "to the promotion of democracy but to the inadvertent promotion of illegitimate governance" which could feed and sustain threats to the security of the United States.[67] Moreover, the celebration of globalization—the lowering of barriers to trade and commerce around the world—masked a darker side of convergence, in which a variety of illicit activities could be facilitated using these emerging global networks.[68]

While the breakdown of the authoritarian state caused by globalization was celebrated as a liberation and empowerment of the individual, in many areas it eroded the capacity of governments to cope with new environmental, security, and criminal challenges.[69] In turn, weak states became incubators for conflict and resentment. They were now unable to provide law and order or to secure a consistent level of public goods for their citizens. Moreover, they could no longer rely on the generosity of superpower patrons to help close the gaps as they had during the Cold War.[70]

The terrorist attacks of September 11, 2001, jolted the United States and, by extension, much of the rest of the world. They were a sobering reminder that, even after the end of the Cold War, the world could be a dangerous place and progress toward democracy and a global community would occur neither rapidly nor seamlessly.

A Changed World: Foreign Policy After 9/11

"A new reality was born [on September 11], a reality that linked terrorists, weapons of mass destruction, and rogue or failed states." Some might dispute then-Secretary of State Colin Powell's assertion that the world order had undergone a fundamental change as a result of the terrorist attacks of 9/11. But there was no question that these tragic events marked as significant a shock to the American foreign-policy establishment as did the Cuban Missile Crisis a generation earlier.[71]

Just as the Cuban Missile Crisis led to calls for a "new approach" to world affairs, the events of September 11th led to a similar search for a new paradigm for international affairs. The post-Cold War approach to policy was no longer sustainable.[72] Concerns about the fragility of the liberal order, and the fear that nonstate actors might be able to obtain weapons of mass destruction, highlighted anxieties about the inadequacy of post-Cold War approaches to world affairs. Chief among these was the charge, particularly by those who became styled as "neo-conservatives," that Americans—in searching for a "peace dividend" after the Cold War—had invested too little in securing the peace. Instead, they trusted in the inexorable triumph of democracy to solve critical problems of global security.[73]

A new existential threat had emerged—not that of a totalitarian superpower, but the confluence of a new world "disorder," especially the breakdown and collapse of states. The proliferation of dangerous technologies and capabilities culminated in the possibility that a terrorist organization might be able to gain access to nuclear devices.[74] Melvyn Leffler laid out what the parameters of a post-9/11 US foreign policy ought to encompass, starting with

> the recognition that the community that came into existence after the Second World War is endangered both from within and from without. If it is to survive, its core values must be collectively reaffirmed; if it is to survive, new norms and rules must be designed multilaterally, including those allowing for the collective and pre-emptive use of force; if it is to survive, the hegemonic role of the United States must be relegitimized.[75]

For many in the U.S. foreign-policy establishment, the solution was to unleash the full force of American power, especially military power, in support of an agenda of democratic transformation. It was time to move past the mistakes of the 1990s and the assumption that the world's evolution toward a democratic future was now irreversible.[76] Under this assumption, there was no requirement for a major, sustained effort on the part of the United States; many perceived that it was American timidity that had encouraged Al-Qaeda to believe that the West was weak and vulnerable. The time had come to take forceful action to secure the fruits of victory from the Cold War, and to ensure global reconstruction along Western liberal-democratic lines and in support of the Western-led global order. As Joshua Muravchik noted:

> This leads to the question of whether America can be the instigator of that change. Intuitively, since democracy means self-rule, it would seem that this is something people must do for themselves, not something that can be introduced by outsiders. But history contradicts this intuition. America, the first modern democracy, has been a powerful engine spreading democracy elsewhere. At its most active, America has done this by force of arms; at its most passive, simply by setting an example from which others have borrowed. In between these two extremes, the United States has intervened on behalf of democracy by nonviolent means: with diplomacy, foreign aid, international broadcasting, and even covert political manipulations.[77]

Coupled with a more robust strategy of intervention—based on the assessment that the "United States will have immense power resources it can bring to bear to force or entice others to do its bidding on a case-by-case basis"[78]—the expectation shared by the Bush administration and some portions of the Democratic congressional establishment was that Washington would be able to root out safe havens for terrorists, to deprive hostile and rogue regimes of access to weapons of mass destruction, and to increase the number of countries prepared to align with the United States.[79]

There were, of course, a number of major tactical differences of opinion as to how to carry out such a strategy. Should the United States act unilaterally or work only in concert with other powers, seeking mandates from international institutions like the United Nations and key regional organizations? What was the appropriate mix of "hard" (e.g., military) and "soft" (e.g., economic and cultural) power that ought to be employed? At what point should diplomatic efforts be abandoned in favor of unsheathing the sword? What priority ought to be given to pressing for "regime change" in countries that were ruled by nondemocratic forms of governance and/or were hostile to US initiatives?[80]

These differences became more pronounced after the George W. Bush administration decided to proceed with forcible regime change in Iraq for the stated purpose of pursuing a deproliferation strategy—without an explicit mandate from the United Nations in 2003. They intensified as the initial military successes in both Afghanistan and Iraq turned into much more problematic campaigns to secure the peace.

19

Those who called for strategic disengagement, for the United States to reduce its footprint around the world, pitted themselves against the proponents of a proactive use of American power (in its neoconservative and liberal interventionist variants). The events of 9/11 seemed to be a vindication of their assertion that continued US meddling around the world was ultimately detrimental to the country's national security.[81] The argument about the risks of overextension among those who endorsed disengagement gained increased salience as the costs of operations in Iraq and Afghanistan spiraled. In addition, as the initial burst of confidence in the efficacy of American power to transform the global order—particularly in the Middle East—began to wane, these arguments started to gain more traction in the foreign-policy discourse. The start of military operations, first in Afghanistan and then in Iraq, also rejuvenated the antiwar movement, with all of its suspicions about the legitimacy of nearly any American use of force in the world.

Etzioni did not fit comfortably into any of these camps. He had concentrated most of his attention on the domestic-policy implications of communitarian thought during the 1990s—notably, the possibility of creating a coherent "third way" between more laissez-faire and statist approaches to social problems. He now returned to a more in-depth examination of foreign-policy issues in the aftermath of the 9/11 attacks and the policy responses they had generated, particularly in the United States.

Etzioni was a prominent signatory of an open letter ("What We Are Fighting For: A Letter from America") released in February 2002 that laid out the moral case for using military force against Al-Qaeda and their Taliban hosts in Afghanistan. Released under the umbrella of the Institute for American Values, the missive took square aim at the re-emergent antiwar movement by declaring that "waging war is not only morally permitted, but morally necessary, as a response to calamitous acts of violence, hatred, and injustice" and, however reluctantly, was a burden that would have to be assumed by "legitimate authority with responsibility for public order."[82]

The language used in the open letter, however, was broad and open to interpretation, and its signatories espoused a variety of different approaches to how the United States ought to conduct foreign affairs.[83] Etzioni thus embarked on a more detailed and systematic exposition of his opinions on what ought to be done, drawing upon the dialogues and observations of the communitarian school and tying it together with his older foundational work outlining the gradualist approach.

These observations and recommendations formed the basis of his three major post-9/11 works dealing with foreign policy and international affairs: *From Empire to Community* (2004), *Security First* (2007), and *Hot Spots* (2012).

For Etzioni, his continued preference for finding ways for the peaceful resolution of disputes did not rule out the possibility that force might have to be employed (in a judicious manner) for national self-defense or to protect the international order. Nor could the United States effectively wall itself off from the rest of the world and its problems. While accepting some of the critiques made by pacifists and noninterventionists, particularly about the dangers of conflict and the inability of military force to provide long-term solutions, Etzioni could not align himself with their overall recommendations.

At the same time, however, he did not share the overly optimistic appraisals of either the efficacy of U.S. military power to force change or of the degree to which non-Americans would accept American preferences for how the international order ought to be structured. He agreed with the proposition that the United States ought to play a leading role in the creation of a new global architecture, but maintained that Washington, or even the West as a whole, could not impose it by fiat.

Etzioni argued that the 9/11 attacks served to dramatize existing vulnerabilities in the international system brought about by globalization and insufficient cooperation among states. Transnational threats like terrorism, climate change, or systemic economic disruption posed clear and present dangers to the stability and prosperity of most states around the world. Without a base level of security, there was no possibility for states—or the international system as a whole—to evolve along more liberal lines. Rather than searching for short-term "victories" (against terrorism or for democracy) that would end up being ephemeral, he called for a long-haul effort to build up new partnerships among states that would gradually develop into true global communities able to cope with the challenges that no single state on its own could tackle. This process would occur not by imposition of a hegemonic power but by "a convergence of interests for the various actors involved."[84]

Etzioni did not dispute a central assertion often put forward by those who wanted to scale down the use of the US military. This assertion called into question the efficacy of most US military interventions, beyond the immediate defeat of an opponent's armed forces, to bring about fundamental transformation. He also questioned the ability of the United States to "police the world" relying only on its own resources.[85]

Etzioni agreed with the assessment that national interests—especially the search for security—was a bigger component of a country's policy than an idealistic commitment to peace and cooperation, and that the effort to promote stronger partnership among states would not succeed unless it could ensure a "convergence of interests for the various actors involved."[86] American action needed to be perceived as legitimate and to gain not merely the support but the active cooperation and participation of other states and societies.

Etzioni's post-9/11 work proposed two grand bargains (the details of which will be discussed in greater detail in the chapters that follow). The first was for the United States to temper its desire to "force the spring" of liberalization around the world—a project that would only engender serious resistance in many quarters. Instead, he advocated a more limited, security-based agenda that would win support from nearly every state in the world. This agenda would inculcate the habits (and then the institutions) of interstate cooperation, starting with the threat of transnational terrorism and the spread of the technologies to create weapons of mass destruction.

The second grand bargain was to prioritize, while reconstructing failed and failing states, the restoration of order and stability. Etzioni accepted in the short-term even illiberal or authoritarian results, in return for laying the foundations for longer-term, evolutionary, and sustainable reform. Both propositions would require US policymakers to accept compromises with regard to their stated goals and the promotion of values deemed to be universal around the world. Therefore, Etzioni stressed the importance of a results-based approach to policy rather than justifying failures by making references to America's good intentions.

Etzioni's approach was meant to capture and prolong into a more lasting institutional format the ad hoc periods of close international cooperation that often occurs after major disasters among major powers. This was evidenced in the months following 9/11 and in the elevation of the G-20 after the 2008 financial crisis. His approach was also designed to find a way to ensure a continued and sustainable role for US leadership of the global community of nations by avoiding the "boom and bust" cycle of American interventionism: the promise of low-cost, rapid transformation giving way to the reality of a "long, hard slog" and thus fueling calls for outright disengagement.

Etzioni's method was also meant to disabuse members of the US foreign-policy community that solutions to twentieth-century problems would be quick and easy, or would not require prioritization and trade-offs between short-term preferences and long-term outcomes. By 2006, it was increasingly clear that requiring adherence to Euro-American prescriptions for liberal democracy and to US foreign-policy preferences as the basis for sustained global partnerships was not realistic. Major powers and important social movements were not interested in being "converted" to the Western perspective.[87] However, there was evidence to suggest that they would be open to moderating their behavior or seeking workable compromises regarding global policy with the United States.[88]

Etzioni accepts the reality of less-than-perfect partners (from the perspective of adhering to liberal values) to achieve important global objectives. He believes the US experience in Iraq and Afghanistan made it clear that overambitious reconstruction plans were not sustainable. Etzioni stressed the necessity of considering what he termed as "second-worst" policy options. These included working with authoritarian regimes to curtail the threat of nuclear proliferation—or accepting that nondemocratic institutions might need to remain intact—in order to guarantee a basic level of security within a society emerging from the shock of war or some other cataclysm, thereby "allowing considerable time for new and more liberal forces to grow."[89]

This approach dovetailed well with research that demonstrated the so-called "J curve" effect. This outcome is based on the idea that when formerly closed or authoritarian societies begin to open up and pursue reforms rapidly, the subsequent instability and dislocation that can follow can generate a backlash that discredits the reform process and leads to a restoration of the *ancien regime*. This is especially true if the ground for a successful transition has not been laid.

In Iraq, for instance, the desire to bring about a full-scale transformation of society along US models did not make sense at a time when basic services had not been restored, the ability and willingness of locals to sustain such changes was unclear, and the country was falling into the grips of an insurgency.[90] Examples of such transformation would be focusing time, energy, and resources on things like revamping the Iraqi stock exchange along American lines (and with the most advanced technology), or rewriting the Iraqi traffic code to conform to US standards.

Beyond 9/11 and the Return of Great-Power Politics

Etzioni's work appealed to constituencies that wanted a more pragmatic, cost-effective approach to American involvement in world affairs. He presents a balance that tries to avoid maintaining what would in the long run be an unsustainable primacy, but also addresses the concerns that feed the propensity for Americans to fall back into isolationism.[91] Moreover, there was a revival of interest in his earlier gradualist approach among those disillusioned with the prospect that sudden, dramatic changes in the international system were possible or desirable. The new threats—terrorism (now epitomized by the Islamic State of Iraq and Syria rather than Osama bin Laden's Al-Qaeda), pandemics (highlighted by the recent Ebola outbreak in West Africa and the emergence of respiratory syndrome coronavirus in the Middle East in 2014), and the continuing risk of state fracture and failure—remain potent challenges. But the second decade of the twenty-first century has also been characterized by the return of great-power politics.

While the United States retains a preponderance of the world's military, economic, and political power, rising and resurging powers like Russia and China now have a greater propensity to challenge aspects of the post-1991 global settlement that are not to their liking. This was demonstrated by the 2014 crisis over Ukraine and by the annexation of Crimea by Russia. Heading off the prospect of a clash between two major world powers has again returned as a pre-eminent challenge for foreign-policy thinkers and strategists.

In the 1960s, gradualism was a strategy to mitigate an already existing Cold War between the United States and the Soviet Union. As the Obama administration began to announce a rebalance of US attention and resources to Asia, especially after 2011, Etzioni began to address the question of what steps might be taken to prevent a new Cold War—this time between the United States and the People's Republic of China.[92]

Etzioni advocates a proactive approach he has labeled "Mutually Assured Restraint" (MAR). This concept focuses on ways to tamp down areas of possible conflict, rather than relying on both military and economic forms of "Mutually Assured Destruction" as a way to discourage clashes. This idea seemed to Etzioni a better way to avoid a permanent rupture. MAR, along with the strategy of encouraging joint action on a common-security agenda, was his answer to the plans announced by the Obama administration to begin a "pivot to the Pacific" in order to counter the growth of Chinese power. As with earlier projects, in January 2014, after articulating an initial framework, Etzioni released the concept of MAR into the larger U.S. foreign-policy community for debate and discussion among scholars and practitioners.[93]

Etzioni's musings on foreign affairs usually occur in the aftermath of a major crisis and are part of an effort to provide a "third way," in contradistinction to existing alternatives that seem both unworkable and unpalatable. The individual elements of his recommendations will be examined and tested in greater detail in subsequent chapters. This then leads to the assessment of whether, in the final analysis, Etzioni's different pieces of work—spanning the scope of US presidential administrations and foreign-policy challenges, from John F. Kennedy to Barack Obama—do in fact coalesce into a recognizable, internally consistent, and coherent approach to foreign policy. This appraisal also considers whether this approach, which might be termed a "communitarian" one, has anything of value to offer to future generations of US and international policymakers.

Notes

1. Amitai Etzioni, *My Brother's Keeper: A Memoir and a Message* (Lanham, MD: Rowman and Littlefield Publishers, Inc., 2003), 42.
2. ibid, 57.
3. Brzezinski made the remark in an interview with Riz Khan, "One on One," Al Jazeera, December 11, 2010.
4. Etzioni, *My Brother's Keeper,* 26.
5. *ibid,* 35.
6. See, for instance, Frederick W. Marks III, *Wind Over Sand: The Diplomacy of Franklin Roosevelt* (Athens: University of Georgia Press, 1988). Excellent insight into Roosevelt's frame of mind can be found in a letter sent to Josef Stalin during the Yalta Conference; cf. the "Attachment to Notes, Fourth Formal Meeting of Crimean Conference, 4 P.M., February 7, 1945," which is part of the cache of documents released by the National Security Archive related to the Yalta Conference on October 4, 1998, archived at http://www. gwu.edu/~nsarchiv/coldwar/documents/episode-2/06-01.htm.
7. Robert E. Osgood, "The Revitalization of Containment," *Foreign Affairs* 60:3 (1981), 466, 468.
8. Robert Jervis, "The Impact of the Korean War on the Cold War," *The Journal of Conflict Resolution* 24:4 (December 1980), 574, 585.
9. George Stambuk, "Foreign Policy and the Stationing of American Forces Abroad," *Journal of Politics* 5:3 (August 1963), 473.
10. John Lewis Gaddis, "Containment: Its Past and Future," *International Security* 5:4 (Spring 1981), 82.
11. Paul H. Nitze, "Atoms, Strategy and Policy," *Foreign Affairs* 34:2 (January 1956), http://www.foreignaffairs.com/articles/71230/paul-h-nitze/atoms-strategy-and-policy.
12. Thomas C. Schelling, *Arms and Influence* (New Haven: Yale University Press, 1966), 43.
13. Quoted in Nina Tannenwald, "Stigmatizing the Bomb: Origins of the Nuclear Taboo," *International Security* 29:4 (Spring 2005), 5, 23.

14. Paul Boyer, "From Activism to Apathy: The American People and Nuclear Weapons, 1963–1980," *Journal of American History* 70:4 (March 1984), 823; Tannenwald, 21.

15. Etzioni, *My Brother's Keeper*, 55.

16. *Atoms, Strategy and Policy.*

17. Gaddis, 81.

18. Paul Wehr, "Nuclear Pacifism as Collective Action," *Journal of Peace Research* 23:2 (1986), 107.

19. Etzioni, *My Brother's Keeper*, 68–69.

20. Erin R. Mahan and Jeffrey A. Larsen (eds.), *The Ascendancy of the Secretary of Defense: Robert S. McNamara, 1961–1963* (Washington, DC: Office of the Secretary of Defense, 2013), 2.

21. Owen Chamberlain, "Gradualism," *Bulletin of the Atomic Scientists* 18:8 (October 1962), 31.

22. Etzioni testified before the Senate Foreign Relations Committee on February 23, 1965, in the context of the debate over Senate bill 672 and its authorization of long-term funding for the US Arms Control and Disarmament Agency. Cf. "To Amend the Arms Control and Disarmament Act," Hearings before the Committee on Foreign Relations, United States Senate, Eighty-Ninth Congress, First Session, esp. 72–80. The testimony is also referenced in the "Report by the Senate Foreign Relations Committee on Amendment to Arms Control and Disarmament Act, March 5, 1965," which is included in the US Arms Control and Disarmament Agency, *Documents on Disarmament 1965* (Washington, DC: Government Printing Office, 1966), 27.

23. Hubert H. Humphrey, "After Containment," *The New Leader* 47:14 (July 1964).

24. Mark J. White, *Missiles in Cuba: Kennedy, Khrushchev, Castro and the 1962 Crisis* (Chicago: Ivan R. Dee. 1997), 149.

25. Henry Kissinger, *Nuclear Weapons and Foreign Policy* (New York: Harper and Brothers, 1957).

26. Wehr, 104.

27. G. Matthew Bonham, Victor M. Sergeev, and Pavel B. Parshin, "The Limited Test-Ban Agreement: Emergence of New Knowledge Structures in International Negotiation," *International Studies Quarterly* 41:2 (June 1997), 221.

28. See, for instance, Robert Jervis, "Hypotheses on Misperception," *World Politics* 20:3 (April 1968), 455.

29. Amy Zegart, *Flawed by Design: The Evolution of the CIA, JCS, and NSC* (Stanford, CA: Stanford University Press, 1999), 4.

30. Niel Ross, "The Rational Decision-Making Model and Leadership Behaviour in International Crises," *E-International Relations*, December 22, 2007, http://www.e-ir.info/2007/12/22/the-rational-decision-making-model-and-leadership-behaviour-in-international-crises/.

31. Valerie Hudson, "Foreign Policy Analysis: Actor-Specific Theory and the Ground of International Relations," *Foreign Policy Analysis* 1:1 (March 2005), 2.

32. James Blackwell, "The Growing Complexity of Deterrence," *ISN*, September 25, 2012, http://www.isn.ethz.ch/Digital-Library/Articles/Detail/?lng=en&id=153100.

33. Nikolas K. Gvosdev, "Politics, Strategy and U.S. Defense Budgets," *World Politics Review*, October 26, 2012, http://www.worldpoliticsreview.com/articles/12452/the-realist-prism-politics-strategy-and-u-s-defense-budgets. Excerpts from Acheson's remarks to the National Press Club on January 12, 1950, can be found at http://web.viu.ca/davies/H323Vietnam/Acheson.htm.
34. Thomas N. Nichols, *No Use: Nuclear Weapons and U.S. National Security* (Philadelphia: University of Pennsylvania Press, 2014), 6, 19.
35. Quoted in Cynthia A. Watson, *U.S. National Security: A Reference Handbook* (Santa Barbara, CA: ABC-CLIO, 2002), 164.
36. See Herman Kahn, *The Nature and Feasibility of War and Deterrence* (Santa Monica, CA: The RAND Corporation, 1960), esp. 1–4.
37. Joseph S. Nye, "The Future of Russian-American Relations," *Horizons* 2 (Winter 2015), 34.
38. Osgood, 467.
39. Gaddis, 80.
40. Etzioni, *My Brother's Keeper*, 62.
41. Zegart, 4.
42. Jervis, "Hypotheses on Misperception," 454–56.
43. Rajan Menon, "A Game of Russian Roulette? The West's Dangerous Sanctions Play against Russia," *National Interest*, August 14, 2014, http://nationalinterest.org/feature/game-russian-roulette-the-wests-dangerous-sanctions-play-11075.
44. Gaddis, 81.
45. Amitai Etzioni, *The Hard Way to Peace: A New Strategy* (New York: Crowell-Collier Press, 1962), 13.
46. See, for instance, Amitai Etzioni, "The Kennedy Experiment," *Western Political Quarterly* 20:2 (Part I) (June 1967), 361–63.
47. Amitai Etzioni, *Winning Without War* (New York: Doubleday and Company, 1964), 220.
48. Etzioni, "Kennedy Experiment," 371–72.
49. Zdzislaw Lachowski, *Confidence- and Security-Building Measures in the New Europe (SIPRI Research Report No. 18)* (Oxford: Oxford University Press, 2004), 11.
50. John Fry, *The Helsinki Process: Negotiating Security and Cooperation in Europe* (Washington, DC: National Defense University Press, 1993), 74.
51. Osgood, 467.
52. Etzioni, *Winning Without War*, 90–91.
53. Etzioni, *Hard Way to Peace*, 253.
54. Etzioni, *Winning Without War*, 219.
55. Chamberlain, 31.
56. See, for instance, Leo Mates, "Nonalignment and the Great Powers," *Foreign Affairs* 48:3 (April 1970), http://www.foreignaffairs.com/articles/24165/leo-mates/nonalignment-and-the-great-powers.
57. See, for instance, Alan R. Collins, "GRIT, Gorbachev and the End of the Cold War," *Review of International Studies* 24:2 (April 1998), 202–203.
58. Chamberlain, 31.
59. Amitai Etzioni, "From Zion to Diaspora," *Society* 15:4 (1978), 96–97.
60. Charles Krauthammer "In Defense of Democratic Realism," *The National Interest* 77 (Fall 2004), 15.

61. A copy of the platform is archived at http://www.gwu.edu/~ccps/platfor-mtext.html.
62. Robert H. Dorff, "Failed States After 9/11: What Did We Know and What Have We Learned?" *International Studies Perspective* 6:1 (February 2005), 25.
63. See, for instance, the discussion among Bruce Russett, Christopher Layne, David E. Spiro, and Michael W. Doyle, "Correspondence: The Democratic Peace," *International Security* 19:4 (Spring 1995), 164–184.
64. See, for instance, the point made by Ido Oren, "The Subjectivity of the 'Democratic' Peace," *International Security* 20:2 (Fall 1995), 180.
65. Walter Russell Mead, "The End of History Ends," *The American Interest*, December 2, 2013, http://www.the-american-interest.com/wrm/2013/12/02/2013-the-end-of-history-ends-2/.
66. Miyume Tanji and Stephanie Lawson, "'Democratic Peace' and 'Asian Democracy," *Alternatives: Global, Local, Political*, 22:1 (January–March 1997), 136.
67. Dorff, 25.
68. James Stavridis, "How Terrorists Can Exploit Globalization," *The Washington Post*, May 31, 2013, http://www.washingtonpost.com/opinions/how-terrorists-can-exploit-globalization/2013/05/31/a91b8f64-c93a-11e2-9245-773c0123c027_story.html; see also Moises Naim, "The Five Wars of Globalization," *Foreign Policy* 134 (January-February 2003), 29–37.
69. Willem van Schendel and Itty Abraham, "Introduction: The Making of Illicitness," in *Illicit Flows and Criminal Things: States, Borders and the Other Side of Globalization*, Willem van Schendel and Itty Abraham, eds. (Bloomington, IN: Indiana University Press, 2005), 2; this entire edited volume examines these questions in much greater detail.
70. Derek Reveron, *Exporting Security: International Engagement, Security Cooperation and the Changing Face of the U.S. Military* (Washington, DC: Georgetown University Press, 2010), 18.
71. Testimony of Secretary of State Colin L. Powell before the House Committee on International Relations, September 19, 2002, archived at http://www.state.gov/secretary/rm/2002/13581.htm.
72. Stephen M. Walt, "Beyond bin Laden: Reshaping U.S. Foreign Policy," *International Security* 26:3 (Winter 2001/02), 56.
73. See, for instance, William Kristol and Robert Kagan, "Toward a Neo-Reaganite Foreign Policy," *Foreign Affairs* 75:4 (July/August 1996), 18–32.
74. Graham Allison, "How to Stop Nuclear Terror," *Foreign Affairs* 83 (January/February 2004), 64.
75. Melvyn P. Leffler, "9/11 and the Past and Future of American Foreign Policy," *International Affairs* 79:5 (October 2003), 1062.
76. See, for instance, Timothy Stanley and Alexander Lee, "It's Still Not the End of History," *The Atlantic*, September 2014, http://www.theatlantic.com/politics/print/2014/09/its-still-not-the-end-of-history-francis-fukuyama/379394/.
77. Joshua Muravchik, "Bringing Democracy to the Arab World," *Current History* 103 (2004), 9.
78. Stephen G. Brooks and William C. Wohlforth, "American Primacy in Perspective," *Foreign Affairs* 81:4 (July-August 2002), http://www.foreignaffairs.com/articles/58034/stephen-g-brooks-and-william-c-wohlforth/american-primacy-in-perspective.

79. Paul D. Miller, "American Grand Strategy and the Democratic Peace," *Survival* 54:2 (2012), 56.

80. See, for instance, Max Boot, "Neocons," *Foreign Policy* 140 (January–February 2004), 24; and Anne-Marie Slaughter, "A Chance to Reshape the United Nations," *Washington Post*, April 13, 2003, B07, for a sense of some of these divisions.

81. As Patrick Buchanan summed up in 2000, "Interventionism is the incubator of terrorism." Patrick Buchanan, *Where the Right Went Wrong: How Neoconservatives Subverted the Reagan Revolution and Hijacked the Bush Presidency* (New York: Thomas Dunne, 2004), 15.

82. A copy of the open letter is archived at http://avalon.law.yale.edu/sept11/letter_002.asp.

83. Claudia Winkler, "American Values Abroad," *The Weekly Standard*, October 28, 2002, http://www.weeklystandard.com/Content/Public/Articles/000/000/001/826ekedk.asp.

84. Amitai Etzioni, *From Empire to Community* (New York: Palgrave Macmillan, 2004), 4.

85. Nikolas Gvosdev, "The Communitarian Foreign Policy of Amitai Etzioni," *Society* 51 (2014), 374.

86. Etzioni, *From Empire*, 4.

87. This process was identified and charted in depth in Naazneen Barma, Ely Ratner, and Steven Weber, "A World Without the West," *National Interest* 90 (July–August 2007), 23–30.

88. For instance, in 2008, Xie Feng, deputy chief of mission of the Chinese embassy in Washington, told an American audience that the People's Republic wanted to be one of the "constructive partners" of the United States in forging the global order. But because Washington and Beijing "do not see eye to eye on everything," he expressed the hope "that the United States will meet us halfway" in crafting solutions. Quoted in Nikolas K. Gvosdev, "Obama: Wilsonian Idealist or Progressive Realist," *World Politics Review*, November 8, 2008, http://www.worldpoliticsreview.com/articles/2898/obama-wilsonian-idealist-or-progressive-realist.

89. Stanley Crossick, "Security First," *Blogactiv.eu*, March 16, 2008, http://crossick.blogactiv.eu/2008/03/16/security-first/.

90. Rajiv Chandrasekaran, *Imperial Life in the Emerald City: Inside Iraq's Green Zone* (New York: Alfred A. Knopf, 2006), 98–99, 229–232, 236–239.

91. In recent years, there has been a noticeable trend among the American public to embrace the sentiment that the United States should focus more on domestic matters and let other countries "get along the best they can on their own." Cf. "U.S. Foreign Policy: Key Data Points from Pew Research," *Pew Research Center*, January 6, 2014, http://www.pewresearch.org/key-data-points/u-s-foreign-policy-key-data-points/.

92. The ideas began to be laid out in a series of articles, beginning with Amitai Etzioni, "China: Making an Adversary," *International Politics* 48:6 (November 2011), 647–666.

93. The position paper is available at http://communitariannetwork.org/endorse-mutually-assured-restraint-position-paper.

2

Navigating Out of the Cold War: The Gradualist Proposal

In 1962, Etzioni noted, "Every generation believed its war to be just . . . and that its war would be the last."[1] The victors of World War II were no different. They hoped that the arrangements reached at the conferences at Dumbarton Oaks, Bretton Woods, Tehran, Yalta, and Potsdam would prove to be lasting. The principal weakness of the postwar international system, however, was summed up by the Mexican delegate to the founding conference of the United Nations in San Francisco in 1945: it might be quite successful in keeping order among the "mice" but would be unable to restrain the "lions."[2] There was no provision for settling possible disputes among the great powers; it was assumed that the "Big Four"—the United States, Britain, the USSR, and then-nationalist China—would always be able to come to some sort of accord in a concert-of-powers setting in the Security Council. In addition, once both the American and Soviet superpowers that emerged after the Second World War achieved nuclear status, any conflict between them that spiraled out of control risked the destruction of the world, not merely the wreckage that would be produced in the wake of any "conventional" conflict. Thus, a tenuous peace—or, more accurately, the absence of a direct "hot war" between the United States and the Soviet Union—rested upon an unstable and unpredictable balance of terror.[3]

Neither the United States nor the USSR opted for isolationism, which would have implied a Swiss-style policy in international affairs in which they prepared to defend their borders by all necessary measures but were otherwise content to let the rest of the world go along its way. This was, in part, because both states were committed to ideologies that were held to be universal in applicability.[4] Instead, both sides extended their defense perimeters and alliance commitments far beyond their own frontiers, in what Robert Jervis has described, on the US side, as the "globalization" of American defense commitments beyond protection of the territorial homeland.[5]

For the United States, this meant not simply concluding alliances with other powers, but also deploying large numbers of forces and equipment beyond the US homeland to various points around the globe—including countries that lay in close proximity to Soviet satellite states or the USSR itself.[6] In turn, the Soviet Union, particularly after the 1962 Cuban Missile Crisis, began to expand its capabilities and its deployments in an effort to match American global power projection abilities.[7] This raised the possibility of direct clashes between Soviet and American forces (or those of their allies and proxies), highlighted first by the crisis of the Berlin airlift in 1948 and then by the outbreak of the Korean War in 1950.[8] Even if there was no particular desire to utilize nuclear weapons in these Cold War clashes, there was always the risk of inadvertent escalation if the situation on the ground got out of hand.[9]

Moreover, the particular logic of Cold War confrontations—particularly the concern that any sign of retreat or compromise might signal weakness that would encourage further testing and probing—raised a further possibility. Even if a nuclear clash was not intended or welcomed, the willingness to consider escalation to show determination and resolve might lead to the transformation of a relatively minor incident or crisis into a major superpower conflict and ultimately to a nuclear exchange.[10] Thus, a way had to be found to create the necessary psychological breathing room. This would encourage the major powers not to take the first steps on the "ladder of escalation,"[11] to move both Washington and Moscow away from keeping forces on a hair-trigger alert, and to develop an approach to create sufficient space and separation between the blocs—both geographically and politically—to reduce the likelihood of accidental collisions that might snowball into all-out conflict.

In works like *The Hard Way to Peace* (1962) and *Winning Without War* (1964) and related journal articles, public speeches, and congressional testimony, Etzioni proposed what he termed a strategy of "gradualism" to address these concerns.

The Gradualist Proposal

The first measures of any "gradualist strategy for peace" would be a series of limited, unilateral gestures offered by one side without any requirement for reciprocity by the other in order to begin building the basis for communication and trust.

Initial steps might be to withdraw forces from a frontline position; release personnel taken captive in espionage operations; permit a trade or business deal to go forward without opposition; or announce a policy shift (such as bringing down the threat level). Because these initiatives would not be linked to demands for an equal and reciprocal response from the other side, they could be undertaken unilaterally. Etzioni's gamble was that the confidence in taking such measures would provide the necessary psychological reassurance for the opposing superpower to take reassuring steps of its own. The subsequent relaxation of tensions would then lay the basis for a more explicit round of more substantive, reciprocal concessions offered by each side.[12]

Over time, those concessions might include the creation of entire neutral zones where the military forces of one or the other superpower would no longer be based. Both sides would freeze additional buildups of conventional and nuclear weapons, and then create a process to negotiate the gradual elimination of entire categories of weapons from the arsenals of both superpowers and their allies. This would be accomplished not simply by making declarations but by creating a comprehensive and intrusive process of inspection to create and maintain confidence in the process. Arms control was thus a necessary but incomplete step in the gradualist strategy, a way station allowing for freezing further acquisition of weapons, but as part of an overall effort at their ultimate abolishment.[13]

Finally, both the United States and the Soviet Union would begin to codify binding codes of conduct regulating their interaction, with an eye to promoting transparency and removing any bases for misunderstanding or misreading the actions of the other side that might lead to an accidental conflict. These codes and procedures might then habituate both countries to greater cooperative action and might even lead to more positive developments, such as joint research and development projects (for example, outer-space exploration). Once the danger of superpower conflict had been addressed, conditions for peaceful competition—or even convergence—could be created.

Etzioni maintained that these initial steps, including the pulling back of US forces from the frontlines and flash points of the Cold War—allowing a good portion of the world to be defined as "non-aligned areas"—could be undertaken without any fundamental risk to Western security. He was thus forced to grapple with the same question that beset the Truman administration (and subsequent U.S. presidents): "How far did the American sphere of responsibility have to extend in order to ensure American security?"[14] He maintained that the ongoing advances, especially "in the technology of weapons, military tactics, and organization, and increased mobility of troops and arms" made perfectly feasible a stance he labeled "remote deterrence." Such a position could keep US forces (and the militaries of America's core allies) "in a high degree of readiness and mobility (if necessary, even on ships cruising in the area during tense periods)" in the event of a Soviet thrust into the neutral zones deployed to check and reverse Soviet actions.[15]

In the absence of a direct and immediate Soviet threat, however, Etzioni believed the forward deployment of forces and equipment was unnecessarily provocative. Moreover, remote deterrence would eliminate the need for "trip wires"—the forward deployment of American forces meant to "demonstrate the United States' commitment" to the defense of partner nations.[16] Instead, the growing capacity of the United States to rapidly surge military forces to any portion of the globe—a capacity Etzioni recognized had not existed two decades prior—could reassure allies and partners of the reliability of American security guarantees, while lowering tensions with the USSR by pulling US forces away from close proximity to the Soviet bloc and reducing the possibility of any accidental clash.

Etzioni differentiated his approach from what might be termed a disarmament-and-disengagement approach: the recommendation that by withdrawing from its overseas commitments and eliminating its weapons capabilities, the United States could demonstrate that it was no threat to the USSR and thus induce reciprocal gestures. Gradualism called for an extended series of very limited steps, with the first ones taken by either side being ones that could be easily reversed at the first sign of treachery without any significant compromise to US or allied security (or to the security of the USSR and its cohorts).

The gamble was that by taking forces to a lower alert status and pulling them back, the necessary psychological space for reducing tensions could be created, giving leaders the political cover to offer further compromises and concessions, as well as giving both sides additional breathing room in terms of both time and space.[17] If it worked, "it might lead to a negotiated settlement." If not, the deterrent position of both sides remained intact. Etzioni concluded that gradualism was a "maximum gain, minimum regret" strategy.[18]

Over time, if the gradualist program was to be adopted, Etzioni hoped that the Cold War would be not just relaxed but eventually overcome. While gradualism could deal with the geopolitics, he also expected a lessening of ideological tensions as both sides found greater points of convergence. Under new conditions of greater trust, Etzioni hoped that the major powers, as well as a number of growing region-ally based unions, would be able to forge more effective institutions for dealing with truly global challenges that threatened the interests of all states—and that these challenges would form the basis of new alliances rather than superpower rivalries.[19] Some of Etzioni's confidence that gradualism could be pursued without causing significant damage to Western security came out of his assessments about the fluidity of the Soviet gains and the centrifugal forces within the Soviet bloc, at least along its periphery. This, in his assessment, made possible a strategy of neutralization more possible, as well as the emergence of middle powers that were prepared to stake out a more independent position vis-à-vis the superpowers. Thus, he believed that the Soviets could enjoy some confidence that they, too, would not be surrounded by a belt of American client-states.

On the one hand, by the late 1970s the Soviet Union had registered impressive gains in Angola, Vietnam, Ethiopia, Yemen, and Afghani-stan. These advances had been offset by the "defection" of China and its emergence as an independent pole more closely aligned with the United States, as well as the movement of key regional states such as Indonesia and Egypt into the US camp. Moreover, highlighting Etzioni's admonition to be less concerned with the possibility of Communist parties playing heightened roles in the domestic politics of other states, Moscow found its influence reduced among the Communist parties of Western Europe.[20] Yet while Etzioni saw these developments as validating his predictions about the essential fluidity of both blocs, the "losses" experienced by each side contributed to a feeling of insecurity in both capitals.

Moreover, both the United States and the Soviet Union found that their alliances and bloc relationships did not always translate into automatic support. By the 1970s, both the United States and the USSR "had to face new situations as they arose without the backing of their allies. In the war in Vietnam, the United States lacked the moral support and troop contributions from its allies which it had had in the war in Korea. The Soviet Union had to face China without the unwavering assistance of its allies in the Warsaw Pact."[21]

Etzioni argued that his proposals were not so revolutionary as to be unrealistic or unattainable, an assessment shared by some who reviewed his work.[22] Indeed, he noted that elements of the gradualist strategy had already been applied in an ad hoc fashion by the Eisenhower and Kennedy administrations. As proof of the concept that both sides could create effective neutral zones between the two major superpower blocs, Etzioni cited two major occurrences. The first was the process that led to the conclusion in 1955 of the *Österreichischer Staatsvertrag* (Austrian State Treaty) which, in turn, led to the end of the occupation of Austria as a liberal democracy but that deliberately left it outside of the Western security bloc. The second occurrence was the *de facto* recognition by the Soviet Union of Yugoslavia's "non-bloc" status.[23]

Other unilateral gestures taken by Washington and Moscow—such as the release of prisoners that then led to temporary thaws in superpower relations—were also seen as confirmation that a relaxation of tensions was possible. Given this, Etzioni called for such measures to be "more consistently employed," but noted that moving ahead with such a strategy by introducing "other supporting measures" could only take place "if the wider context is more explicitly taken into account."[24]

Moreover, there were other voices in the American public-policy arena that promoted similar ideas. Etzioni's gradualist strategy overlapped with and complemented another approach—Charles Osgood's "graduated reciprocation in tension reduction" (GRIT)—that was also being discussed at the same time as a way out of the dead end of Cold War logic.[25] Like Etzioni, Osgood called on both superpower governments to demonstrate their willingness to consider peaceful resolution by offering a unilateral conciliatory gesture (or for matching that initial gesture with an appropriate response). This action could then lay the basis for a series of reciprocal steps, creating a basis for trust and moving the Cold War standoff away from a negative tit-for-tat spiral toward one that favored peace via tension reduction.[26]

The ideas behind gradualism and GRIT began to find their way not only into the public discourse but also into the policy debate within the US government.[27] In addition to indirect transmission, both Osgood and Etzioni found direct conduits into the national security policy-making apparatus of the US government via work with the Arms Control and Disarmament Agency.

The gradualist approach was criticized on a number of different grounds. Herman Kahn, debating Etzioni at Columbia University in January 1963, described gradualism as "wishful thinking," and reiterated his view that retaining the nuclear balance would be more effective in preserving both American security and global peace than the risk of pursuing gradualism.[28] Kahn and others focused on whether the long-term gradualist goal of disarmament (after tensions had been reduced) was also desirable. A consistent position expressed by the arms control community during the Cold War was that "the reduction of arms . . . was not necessarily desirable unless it could be shown as likely to promote the primary goal, reducing the risk of war."[29] By tinkering with both the conventional and nuclear balances between the superpowers, proponents of the gradualist school might end up encouraging rather than preventing conflict. Freezing and regulating arms on both sides was seen as more stabilizing by the proponents of arms control, who argued that a too-rapid push for dismantling weapons systems might increase the risk of conflict.[30]

Etzioni's riposte was to suggest that continued developments in weapons technology might make the status quo untenable by undermining the basis on which deterrence was based. Etzioni expressed misgivings that foreshadowed the concern that was to lead to the Anti-Ballistic Missile (ABM) Treaty a decade later, and which some fifty years later nearly torpedoed efforts to conclude and ratify the so-called "New START" agreement. He considered what could happen if there was an effective breakthrough in missile defense technology that might make the guaranteed retaliation upon which deterrence rested no longer feasible or possible in the absence of significantly improved superpower relations.[31]

Walter C. Clemens, who then specialized in arms control and superpower relations at the Massachusetts Institute of Technology, raised two additional objections. The first was that gradualism, with its focus on preventing major state-on-state conflict, did not address the problem of Soviet-backed guerilla movements "nibbling" away at pro-Western states. He believed that gradualism subverted them from within but without sufficient overt action by the USSR to justify a US military response or a threat of nuclear retaliation. (This issue was once again raised following Russia's 2014 annexation of Crimea and the creation of armed separatist movements in southeastern Ukraine). Clemens's second concern was that gradualism, by its very nature and its long-term timetable, might be too slow in bringing about peace to prevent an accidental nuclear conflict from occurring in the short-to-medium term.

On a related note, Clemens also questioned whether the setup and political structure of the US government was amenable to faithfully implementing and executing a long-range gradualist plan of the type outlined by Etzioni across a series of different presidential administrations.[32] Likewise, Robert A. Levine of the RAND Corporation echoed that concern and added two more objections. The first was the risk that if Soviet intentions were incorrectly assessed, meaning that "reciprocity is illusory or insincere," then continuing along the gradualist path "might well be dangerous, particularly in their [its] cumulative effects."[33] Indeed, others argued that the Soviet Union was not truly committed to genuine tension reduction and that any supposed sign of conciliation was but a tactic to gain advantage over the West.[34]

Levine's second concern was that the adoption of a gradualist mindset by the US government might undermine the commitment needed to make deterrence credible.[35] Building on this argument, there was a major strain within American foreign-policy thinking that looked askance at any proposal that suggested offering compromises and concessions to the Soviet Union. The objection was that the end goal of US policy ought not to be to coexist with the USSR, but to defeat it; or, at least to keep up the pressure to force the Soviets into adjusting their policies.[36] In the final analysis, Philip Green of Haverford College argued that the policy proposals advanced by Etzioni, Osgood, and others were impractical and divorced from actual US national security considerations.[37]

Given their assessment of Soviet doctrine and tactics, the gradualist concept of relying on remote deterrence in place of forward US deployments was especially problematic for the US national security policy establishment. Etzioni's assertions that remote deterrence would be an effective way to maintain alliance commitments—in the absence of any forward-deployed US forces—ran up against the position originally expressed by General Omar Bradley asserted that the United States could not count on friends and partners in other parts of the world "if our strategy dictates that we shall first abandon them to the enemy with a promise of later liberation."[38] Any further diminishment of the

US military presence overseas might send the wrong signals to both the Soviets and US allies.

Indeed, a consistent objection to Etzioni's approach was that gradualism, and, in particular, the remote deterrence provisions, would be viewed by US allies as an effective abandonment of their security—and, in turn, would cause partners to defect from supporting the overall US global agenda. European commentators, in particular, were concerned about any withdrawal of US forces from the continent back to the American home land as part of any unilateral gesture to induce the Soviet Union to also take steps to reduce tensions, with many preferring a simultaneous pullback negotiated by treaty.[39] In particular, there were always concerns that the lack of a sufficient conventional deterrent based in Europe would be more destabilizing, because Washington might have to choose between following through on its threats of nuclear retaliation to deter a Soviet conventional invasion, or be forced to acquiesce to Soviet gains in order to avoid a global nuclear conflict.[40]

This was especially worrisome if the gradualist approach, with its prescriptions for creating space between the superpowers, ended up being read by the Soviet adversary not as a way to relax tensions but as a sign of weakness. Concessions offered in small matters might lead an opponent to conclude it could insist upon and receive even further concessions.[41] There was little appetite in many US policy circles, particularly in the military, to embrace a course of action that might cause allies to desert the American standard and to embolden the Soviets to press their advantage onward.

If anything, Western strategists viewed forward deployment of US forces in exactly the opposite way as did the gradualist approach: such deployments were seen as a precondition for preventing war and conflict, and as an absolute necessity for ensuring alliance solidarity.[42] US military strategists often argued that a robust frontline American presence was critical not only to protect allies in the event of war, but to nurture them in times of peace while dispersing equipment and personnel to allow for rapid responses to regional crises.[43]

In addition, Etzioni's proposals of facilitating the emergence of a belt of neutral states to separate the Western and Soviet blocs was recognized, even by Etzioni himself, to be a gamble. On the one hand, it "could help diminish the confrontation between East and West by increasing the political space between the blocs."[44] On the other hand, it might increase the prospect for conflict if instead of taking these areas off the geopolitical chessboard, the attempt to set up such neutral zones heightened competition for influence. Again, however, Robert Jervis and others warned that pushes for neutralization might not be reciprocated but might be interpreted as weakness.[45]

Despite these objections, there were those inside the US government who seemed interested in pursuing these types of ideas—whether they were directly influenced by Etzioni's writings and testimony or had come to them independently—and perhaps even utilizing them as part of a new approach to US-Soviet relations.[46] Even at the height of the Cuban Missile Crisis in October 1962, there were some officials who raised questions about steps the United States might take to both avoid sparking an accidental clash (particularly that stemming from concerns that US defensive measures might be misinterpreted by the Soviets) and give Nikita Khrushchev the maneuvering room to negotiate a settlement.[47]

The "Kennedy Experiment"

In the aftermath of the Cuban crisis, the Kennedy administration appeared to be ready to try a different approach to dealing with the USSR. Etzioni is quite clear in noting that he had no evidence that his ideas played a direct role in the change of strategy and approach undertaken after the Cuba crisis.[48] Yet what has been termed the "Kennedy experiment"[49] tracked closely with Etzioni's proposals (as well as those of Osgood) for using a series of discrete, unilateral gestures to encourage the necessary psychological space for Soviet leaders to offer concessions of their own, and thus to initiate a process of détente. It was thus characterized by some as a real-world test of the possible applicability of Etzioni's ideas, even if that had not been the stated intent of President Kennedy and his advisors.[50]

The "Strategy for Peace" address, delivered by John F. Kennedy at American University on June 10, 1963, in which the president sought to chart a new path that would avoid "the peace of the grave or the security of the slave,"[51] is usually considered to be the start of the "Kennedy experiment." In that speech, Kennedy announced that the United States would unilaterally discontinue nuclear atmospheric tests (and called for the negotiation of a treaty-based permanent ban). The Voice of America broadcast of Kennedy's speech to the USSR was not blocked, and five days later Nikita Khrushchev responded positively to the president's remarks and in turn took a unilateral step—an announced halt to further production of strategic bombers.

The Soviets also shifted their position on the creation of a United Nations observer mission to be sent to try and facilitate an end to the civil war in Yemen, a step that the USSR had opposed. In the aftermath of the Kennedy speech, the Soviet Union chose to abstain rather than veto the Security Council resolution authorizing the mission. In turn, the United States assented to the full recognition of the rights of the Communist regime in Hungary to seat their delegation at the United Nations. In these initial steps, the unilateral actions taken by Kennedy and Khrushchev did not make either side vulnerable. The United States already had an extensive working stockpile of weapons, so the unilateral cessation of testing did not immediately open up any US strategic vulnerabilities.

For his part, by the time Khrushchev had chosen to terminate the Soviet bomber line, it was already on the verge of being phased out. Yet these were unilateral measures: the United States, for example, did not require the USSR to also immediately cease nuclear testing, nor did the Soviets demand that an equivalent platform be withdrawn from US arsenals. These moves created the opening needed for both sides to start a more sustained dialogue. During this time, the deadlock that had prevented the establishment of any sort of agreement on banning nuclear tests was broken, in part because of the concessions offered in Kennedy's speech. The path was then cleared for the conclusion of the Limited Test Ban Treaty in July 1963.

The creation of the "hotline" that allowed for direct communication between Soviet and American leaders (in part to avoid future crises from getting out of hand) was concluded during this time. A process was also started that led to the Outer Space Treaty, signed in 1967, that banned the orbiting of nuclear weapons. Building on the Yemen precedent, there were moves toward finding more common ground at the United Nations. Moreover, the improved atmosphere brought a modest uptick in commercial ties, including a major sale of American wheat to the Soviet Union.[52]

But the objections that critics had raised to Etzioni's program also were heard within the Kennedy administration. After several months of progress in reducing tensions, the initial burst of energy dissipated as the fears generated by the Cuban Missile Crisis receded. Echoing the public ripostes to the gradualist approach found in journals and in debates, concerns were raised in policy circles about whether US eagerness to relax tensions with the Soviet Union would demoralize allies and weaken the vigilance needed to guard against possible Soviet treachery.[53] By fall 1963 the momentum of new initiatives had slowed considerably. Kennedy's assassination in November and Khrushchev's overthrow the following year effectively brought the first round of the "experiment" to an end.

Khrushchev's ouster was a particularly problematic development. As a number of observers have commented, to be optimally successful, an Etzioni-style approach needed to be "implemented coherently, with continuity and consistency."[54] The Kennedy administration was also under pressure to produce immediate results in order to sustain support for such an approach, yet this kind of strategy has to be conducted over a continuous period of time even if there are no immediate breakthroughs.[55] While the several months of the "Kennedy experiment" could be taken as proof of concept of the gradualist approach, it also made clear that the administration—and any of its subsequent successors—would not adopt the policy provisions of gradualism *in toto*.

Other planks of Etzioni's gradualist program were also subjects of debate within the US government. Etzioni had argued that the emergence of more neutral/nonaligned states in the world would be a net benefit for US security. This development would provide zones of separation between American and Soviet allies. In addition, it would work to block any efforts on the part of either superpower to use their territories as jumping-off points for an attack on the other. Etzioni cited as precedent of Austria's neutralization by the 1955 treaty, which he argued had paved the way for both Western and Soviet forces to leave the country. Etzioni maintained that Austria thus served as a guaranteed barrier for the Warsaw Pact from being directly threatened by NATO, and vice versa. (However, it should be noted that both the Warsaw Pact and NATO military planners never took the neutrality of states like Austria for granted and had contingencies in place for having their forces occupy or transit neutral countries.[56])

Not everyone within the US national security establishment, however, shared Etzioni's assessment. A number of voices in both parties worried that "neutralism" was, in reality, disguised anti-Americanism. Others has misgivings that "neutral status" would, in reality, simply be a halfway house on the way for countries to be eventually absorbed into the Soviet bloc. There were also concerns from those who, guided by the precepts of balance-of-power realism, argued that if the United States promoted the emergence of neutral, nonaligned states, it would only be creating vacuums that the Soviet Union would be tempted to fill.[57] Still others argued that it would be impractical to expect states to maintain equidistance from both the USSR and the United States, and that sooner or later a country would be drawn into the orbit of one (and to the detriment of the other's security).

Conversely, even some senior US political figures of the time had made the case for supporting neutrals. In 1958, then-Vice President Richard M. Nixon had defended US support for countries that showed no inclination to become American allies. He noted that US interests were served by aiding states, particularly those in the Third World, to develop genuine independence and to "toughen their economic and political fiber to a point where they can be independent of any foreign domination," and so be able to resist Soviet expansionism and to further block its abilities to project power around the world.[58] Indeed, there was a recognition that countries truly aspired to neutral status would be inclined to develop capabilities—including military ones—to protect their positions and to prevent their territories from being used as transit zones or bases.[59] In some instances, a country (for example, Yugoslavia) did not have to join the Western alliance (or give up its own homegrown Communist regime) to nonetheless be a *de facto* strategic asset for the West (in Yugoslavia's case, in blocking Warsaw Pact access to the Adriatic and frustrating Soviet efforts to project power into Central Europe).[60]

At the time Etzioni was writing *A Hard Way to Peace*, another test of the applicability of his ideas was also underway—the attempt to defuse the crisis in Laos by promoting neutralization as an alternative to conflict between pro-Soviet and pro-Western forces. Laos had become a battleground, in part due to the conflict in neighboring Vietnam (since pro-Soviet forces in the North hoped to use Laos as a transit point to supply and support an insurgency against the US-backed government in the South). The United States backed the royal Lao forces, while the USSR and the North Vietnamese aided the Pathet Lao movement. Initially, neither Washington nor Moscow wanted to "lose" Laos, and the Eisenhower administration hoped to "create a strong anti-Communist bastion in Laos."[61]

However, when it became clear to the Kennedy team that the pro-Western factions could not deliver on any promise of defeating the

Pathet Lao (and that, in reality, a victory of pro-Soviet forces might be in the cards), they turned to talks designed to broker a settlement. After nearly a yearlong set of negotiations, the International Agreement on the Neutrality of Laos was signed on July 23, 1962. This accord enshrined formal neutrality for Laos and enjoined the signatories—both the two major superpowers as well as their clients and the immediate neighbors of Laos—to refrain from either direct or indirect interference in the country's internal affairs.

More importantly, all parties were to withdraw any military forces or advisors and to commit to establish no facilities on Laotian territory or to bring Laos into any military alliance system. In theory, Laos would emerge as a buffer zone between pro-Western governments (in places like Thailand) and Communist states. Etzioni and others hoped that the Geneva accords on Laos could serve as a model for ending other superpower conflicts. It served a significant test as to whether a country that, left to its own devices, might opt for a closer association with the Soviet bloc or could successfully maintain neutral status. This was in contrast to the earlier examples of Austria and Finland, two Western states the United States was prepared to leave outside the Euro-Atlantic security community.[62]

Unfortunately, the Laos test failed. The Geneva agreement proved to be too unworkable, in part because it assumed that the United States and the Soviet Union could exercise near-total control over their clients.[63] A particular weakness that had not been foreseen in the gradualist approach, which assumed that superpower intervention was the main reason for such conflicts, was that clients might defy their superpower patrons yet suffer no particular consequence. In the case of Laos, the North Vietnamese were not inclined to honor the agreement, seeing in a neutralist government a threat to their own ability to engage in operations in South Vietnam. Even though the Soviet Union itself was prepared to honor the Geneva accords and in fact ceased direct support to the Pathet Lao, North Vietnam continued to interfere in Laotian affairs—in part urged onward by the National Liberation Front, operating in South Vietnam, which demanded secure supply lines transiting Laos. Because the Soviet Union did not wish to lose influence over the Saigon regime, it was not prepared to sanction North Vietnam for its violations of the terms of the Geneva settlement.[64] Indeed, the degree to which the Communist coalition was fissured—with no common position on policy shared by the Soviets, the Chinese, and the Vietnamese—raised serious questions as to whether neutralization could ever work as a strategy if either "bloc" could not guarantee full compliance with any settlement.

In turn, the United States resumed military assistance to Laos and engaged in air campaigns designed to interdict North Vietnamese supply routes, and to prevent the Pathet Lao from making further advances. Instead of the Geneva talks on Laos providing a model for de-escalating the crisis in Vietnam, "Southeast Asia, by the end of the decade, had become the center of Cold War tensions."[65] The failure of the Laos experiment in neutralization soured both sides on trying to apply the Austria model in other parts of the Third World; from this point on, the Lyndon B. Johnson administration focused on beating back the Communist challenge in Vietnam and competing for influence with the USSR in other areas of the world.[66]

The leadership team that took over from the deposed Nikita Khrushchev in the Soviet Union, although seeking policy stability after dealing with Khrushchev's "hare-brained schemes," was nonetheless not inclined to find points of compromise. Instead, it focused on a push to achieve nuclear parity with and conventional superiority over the United States.[67] Moreover, the Soviet invasion of Czechoslovakia in August 1968 to depose a reformist Communist government made it clear that the Soviet leadership was not interested, at least in Europe, in pulling back to allow for a larger bloc of neutral states to emerge. Writing in the organ of the Soviet Communist Party *Pravda* one month later, political theoretician Sergey Kovalev laid out the rationale for the operation—the right and indeed the duty of "Socialist countries," led by the Soviet Union itself, to intervene in the affairs of other Socialist states in the Soviet bloc to combat forces that would be hostile to Socialism (as the Soviets defined it).

This view was formally endorsed by General Secretary Leonid Brezhnev at the Fifth Congress of the Polish Workers' Party in November 1968.[68] These theses, soon popularized in the West under the style of "the Brezhnev doctrine," made it clear that the Soviet leadership would not accept the Yugoslav model of a nonaligned neutral state as an acceptable compromise for any state in Europe they considered to be within their sphere of influence.[69] It seemed that even though a gradualist-style approach might be intellectually appealing, it was not going to be readily embraced by policymakers.[70]

Yet it would be a mistake to then write off the gradualist approach as a failure, and to conclude that it had no lasting influence on policy because of the immediate outcome of the "Kennedy experiment" and the "Laos test." By raising the issue of psychological factors in foreign policy decision making, Etzioni, Jervis, and others focused attention on how actions taken by states could create (or inhibit) momentum toward trust and toward relaxing tensions—or how they could be misinterpreted and create a negative spiral toward conflict. Etzioni's proposals for using a series of small, discrete steps as a way for reducing tensions by removing uncertainty about a state's intentions fed into efforts to formalize tension-reduction measures and so-called "confidence building mechanisms" (CBMs).[71]

Some have argued that the ideas promoted by Etzioni and his colleagues during the 1960s helped to provide the intellectual groundwork for efforts, particularly starting in the 1970s, to formalize arrangements for building confidence in a Europe divided by the Cold War.[72] Etzioni, for example, emphasized the importance of inspections and observers as part of the process of reassurance.[73] Indeed, CBMs were very much in line with Etzioni's recommendations to create "psychological space" by taking measures to reduce the fear of sudden attack by making a state's behavior, particularly in military matters, predictable and transparent.

Such steps included: (1) giving prompt notification of military exercises; (2) having observers be present at maneuvers; (3) allowing access to facilities; (4) creating communication protocols for movement of military equipment; (5) launching of space vehicles, and any other activity that might be misconstrued as the start of hostilities; (6) creating demilitarized zones; (7) pulling forces back from contested areas or borderlines; and (8) facilitating exchanges of personnel to build not only contacts but to also have both sides observe processes and procedures. These types of measures, which Etzioni and others had helped to conceptualize and had discussed and debated in academic formats, were incorporated into diplomatic exchanges between the West and the Soviet bloc.[74] Many were formally recognized and incorporated into the first "basket" of the accords reached as a result of the Conference on Security and Cooperation in Europe (CSCE) in 1975 in Helsinki. Subsequent CSCE meetings sought to move CBMs from voluntary measures to mandated procedures enshrined in treaty commitments designed "to promote military as well as political confidence."[75]

Even though the gradualist approach did not become the guiding force for US policy in coping with the Soviet Union, it was also not dismissed out of hand as having nothing to offer. Bits and pieces of its proposals did find their way into the policy process.[76] Indeed, Vice President Hubert Humphrey attempted to make the case in 1965, particularly in the liberal wing of his own Democratic Party, that Lyndon Johnson's administration was already crafting policy along such lines.[77] Efforts to move ahead with negotiating treaties to ban specific categories of weapons continued, with some of the heavy lifting being undertaken by the Johnson administration.[78] Ideas proposed during the initial "Kennedy experiment" were realized, among them the Outer Space Treaty (banning the deployment of nuclear weapons in space) and the Nuclear Non-Proliferation Treaty (NPT), committing the major powers to work together to prevent the spread of nuclear weapons while, in theory, embracing the obligation to work toward eventual nuclear disarmament.

The June 1967 summit meeting between Johnson and Soviet premier Alexei Kosygin, held in Glassboro, New Jersey, was an effort to regain the momentum in moving Soviet-American relations forward. Despite the positive tone of the meetings, no superpower compromise over Vietnam was reached. Nor was there any progress in reaching an agreement on halting the development of ABM systems. The Soviet invasion of Czechoslovakia the following year helped to diminish the impact of the "spirit of Glassboro." In addition, it torpedoed any chance of a major summit meeting between President Johnson and General Secretary Leonid Brezhnev that was designed to lay the basis for a major new arms control agreement and general relaxation of tensions.[79]

The 1968 elections brought Richard Nixon to the White House, with Henry Kissinger as his national security advisor. Etzioni's opposition to the Vietnam War and other political stances was generally at odds with the positions of the new administration; Etzioni was even placed on a blacklist in 1972 that was designed to prevent him from receiving government contracts or speaking as part of any US Information Agency program. At a more fundamental level, the ultimate policy goals of gradualism differed from the Nixon-Kissinger hope of reinvigorating containment and attempting to induce the Soviet Union to take its place within a US-led international order.[80]

Nevertheless, some aspects of the Nixon administration's policy of détente with the Soviet Union, based on the assessment that a reduction in tensions was needed to pursue diplomatic initiatives, corresponded with gradualist recommendations because both sets of policies required creating conditions for diplomacy and compromise. A relaxation of tensions with the Soviet Union was designed to pave the way for limits on arms, to facilitate greater cooperation to solve (or at least manage) pressing regional issues, and to open up prospects for greater economic interchange.[81] Even the first joint US Soviet endeavor in space, the Apollo-Soyuz mission, which was planned during the Nixon years and carried out during the presidency of his successor Gerald Ford, aligned with earlier Etzioni recommendations that called for collaborative scientific efforts as a way to build up trust between the superpowers.[82]

Yet there were also some important differences between the Etzioni proposal and the Nixon-Kissinger program. Gradualism was a strategy for winding down the Cold War, whereas détente as envisioned by Nixon and Kissinger was about managing rather than solving the Cold War, and finding ways to temper superpower rivalries rather than overcome them.[83] The goal was to maintain a stable international equilibrium[84] rather than laying the groundwork for a stronger global community. As Henry Kissinger himself noted, "Détente defined not friendship but a strategy for a relationship among adversaries."[85] For the Soviets, meanwhile, détente was about taking a pause in superpower competition. Nevertheless, détente shared some features with the gradualist approach, namely in the effort to relax tensions and start a diplomatic process.[86]

Stability, in part, was to be maintained by freezing the status quo in Europe in terms of the bloc arrangements. Yet superpower competition remained active throughout the rest of the world. Raymond Garthoff identifies a critical weakness in the Nixon-Kissinger approach to détente with Brezhnev's Soviet Union as the "unrealistic commitment" on both sides not to press for advantage in the hopes of gaining more adherents and clients.[87] In other words, détente in the 1970s did not lead to an embrace of Etzioni's vision of an expanding group of "neutrals" that would separate and insulate the two superpowers. Instead, it led to increased efforts—by attempts that were short of all-out war—to detach countries from alignment to one side in order to cross into the other camp. Examples of this include the defection of Egypt from the Soviet camp to becoming a leading American ally in the Middle East, and to Soviet gains in Africa and Latin America as revolutionary movements overthrew established pro-American governments and forged stronger links with Moscow.

Many of the arguments that had been advanced as critiques of the gradualist program were again deployed in opposition to détente. Paul Nitze deployed a number of them in an influential piece penned for *Foreign Affairs* in 1976. Arms control, he warned, would not necessarily curb Soviet attempts to achieve "war-winning capabilities" nor preclude the USSR from finding other ways to "increase the prospect of Soviet expansionism through other means." The expected US-Soviet collaboration to tamp down crises in Southeast Asia and the Middle East had not materialized. Nitze argued that, in the end, the Soviets understood détente not as a way to manage a balance of power, but as a way to pursue victory in the Cold War with diminished risk of a hot war (conventional or nuclear) erupting.[88]

Ultimately, the attempt at détente during the 1970s failed because neither the Soviets nor the Americans embraced the essential precondition for success—the need for "reciprocal restraint and consultation"[89]— that also defined the gradualist approach. The 1979 Soviet invasion of Afghanistan, designed to replace a tottering pro-Soviet regime with a more reliable set of partners, seemed to validate the concerns expressed by opponents of détente that Moscow was searching not for compromise but dominance. The US assessment was that the Soviet Union had taken the conciliatory offerings of the Nixon, Ford, and early Carter administrations and had, in turn, pushed to expand its own military establishment and sphere of influence at the expense of the U.S. position. This appraisal, in turn, led to a growing acceptance in American policy circles that the Soviet Union "could be restrained and rendered harmless only by determined confrontation."[90] This view crystallized in the new posture taken by the United States during the first term of Ronald Reagan's presidency.

Ironically, during this period Etzioni had become part of the White House staff, in the latter part of the Carter administration. Gradualism might have had some appeal to the candidate Jimmy Carter in his campaign to win the White House in 1976, yet, upon taking office, Carter and his Secretary of State Cyrus Vance found difficulties in advancing an agenda of promoting human rights and pursuing a negotiated decrease of tensions with the Soviet Union.[91] Over time, the growing influence of the harder-line National Security Advisor, Zbigniew Brzezinski, who assumed more influence over the shaping of foreign policy, meant that any inclination to adopt gradualist proposals was giving way to a policy of responding more forcefully to Soviet actions. While efforts to gain a final agreement on a second arms-control package (the Strategic Arms Limitation Treaty–II) persisted, Soviet decisions to continue with trials against internal dissidents and to expand support for guerilla movements in the Third World meant that Carter, by the end of 1978, was increasingly siding with those in his cabinet who wanted to take a stronger stance against the USSR.[92] Etzioni, who was brought in to help the White House handle domestic policy issues, does not appear to have been consulted on any foreign-policy issues or to offer any exposition of how gradualism might apply to the Carter administration's foreign policy efforts vis-à-vis the USSR.

Nevertheless, the work of the 1970s in both the arms control measures and CBMs left an important "foundation for future cooperation"[93] that could be built upon once conditions—and the right set of leaders—were in place to renew efforts to wind down the Cold War confrontation.

The "Gorbachev Experiment"

Although it was not apparent at the time,, the accession of Mikhail S. Gorbachev as General Secretary of the Communist Party of the Soviet Union in March 1985 set in motion a process whereby some of Etzioni's recommendations from the early 1960s were put into practice. There is no evidence that Gorbachev or his advisors consulted or were influenced by any of the gradualist texts or that they sought the counsel of any US academics in forming policy options.[94] Yet some of the steps taken by Gorbachev, even in the run-up to his first summit meeting with Ronald Reagan in 1985, approximated recommendations made by Etzioni in his gradualist writings.[95] What we might term the "Gorbachev experiment" provided a second opportunity to test the feasibility of the gradualist approach as a way to diminish superpower tensions.

At various points during his tenure as General Secretary and then as President of the Soviet Union, Gorbachev undertook a series of policy initiatives that he made clear would take place even if the United States took no immediate reciprocal action but that were designed to establish his good faith, and to create conditions to induce talks with and concessions from the West.[96] Starting in 1985, for example, Gorbachev announced a unilateral cessation of all nuclear testing and promised a moratorium on further deployments of the RSD-10 intermediate range missile (known as SS-20s in the West).[97]

Yet long-standing distrust of Soviet motives on the part of the Reagan administration led to a cautious response, and there was no immediate rush to embrace the new Soviet leader or his proposals. Although the Geneva summit of 1985 led to no immediate policy changes or breakthroughs, it did give both leaders a chance to evaluate each other and to begin to build a personal connection. This proved to be critical, because Gorbachev and Reagan discovered that they both shared a commitment to nuclear abolitionism. The apparent sincerity of both men helped to inspire trust. Moreover, the confidence that began to develop, slowly and haltingly at first, between Reagan and Gorbachev and their teams and advisors allowed them to improvise and move forward on an agenda of winding down the Cold War.[98]

The challenge facing Gorbachev was to build the confidence needed to advance the superpower agenda.[99] However, a number of roadblocks including fallout from a series of spy scandals, interfered with gestures designed to ease tensions. Moreover, Gorbachev's first, halting efforts at using unilateral gestures to promote tension reduction and reassurance ran up against both significant resistance from within the Soviet national security establishment and forty years of entrenched suspicion of Soviet motives within the US government.[100]

However, another major breakthrough came in the summer of 1986, when, after long-time opposition, Soviet delegates at the Conference on Confidence- and Security-Building Measures and Disarmament, held in in Stockholm, Sweden, reversed their position. They accepted the proviso that all major Soviet military exercises should have on-site Western observers—an important concession given the Soviet military's preoccupation with secrecy. Jack Matlock, then serving as Senior Director for European and Soviet affairs at the National Security Council, recognized that, having made concessions on these questions, other parts of the US-Soviet agenda might now be open for substantive negotiations.[101]

In his first years in office, Gorbachev zigzagged in his first years in terms of what he sought to accomplish. In addressing Eastern European Communist leaders, he called for an intensification of efforts to more tightly connect the Soviet bloc states with the USSR and to strengthen their political, military, and economic connections; he certainly gave no hint that he would be prepared to let the bloc go its own way just a few short years later.[102] At the same time, hoping to build on the psychological momentum of his first year-and-a-half in office, Gorbachev proposed to Reagan that they hold a "working meeting" at an appropriate halfway point to discuss a series of issues that might advance the US-Soviet relationship.[103] The two leaders met at Reykjavik in October 1986, and to the surprise (and dismay) of both delegations, began to make serious headway in addressing arms-control matters, though a major breakthrough was stalled over serious differences over missile defense. Nevertheless, despite being initially cast as a failure, the meeting convinced Gorbachev that Reagan was indeed interested in ending the arms race. It presaged concessions both sides would be prepared to make to reach agreements.[104] Thus, as a Russian arms analyst later noted, "the Reykjavik summit addressed very practical issues of ongoing arms control negotiations and in so doing paved the way for the 1987 INF (Intermediate Nuclear Forces) and the 1991 START I (Strategic Offensive Arms Reductions) Treaties, as well as limitations on nuclear testing."[105]

Gorbachev also followed the gradualist principle of breaking down a security problem into smaller, discrete steps when he made the decision to "de-link" progress on an agreement to eliminate all INFs from the issue of strategic defenses.[106] This cleared the way for rapid progress on completing the INF Treaty, signed by both leaders during a December 1987 summit in Washington.

In hailing the accord, Reagan echoed many of the themes that Etzioni had propounded two decades earlier. The treaty, Reagan noted, was not simply about "controlling an arms race" but about eliminating a specific category of weaponry: "For the first time in history the language of arms control was replaced by arms reduction." To provide a firmer foundation of trust between the superpowers, it provided for the "most stringent verification regime in history, including for inspection teams actually residing in each other's territory" and laid the basis for greater openness between the military establishments of both superpowers. The treaty could be reached without endangering the security of the United States and its allies, and Reagan hoped that it would be a first step along the way in tackling other Cold War problems.[107]

In 1988, in the aftermath of the Washington summit, Gorbachev announced several more unilateral measures that would have been in keeping with a gradualist approach. In January, he made a pledge that Soviet forces would be withdrawn from Afghanistan by May 1989 even if no (face-saving) agreement was in place. In his December address to the United Nations, he announced a unilateral 500,000-person cut in the size of the Soviet armed forces, reaffirmed a commitment to nuclear abolition, and took the first steps in renouncing the Brezhnev doctrine by committing never to use military force in Eastern Europe.[108]

Gorbachev also announced large cuts in the posture of Soviet forces in Eastern Europe (50,000 troops, 10,000 tanks, 8,500 artillery systems, and 800 combat aircraft). He did so without waiting for any reciprocal commitment from the United States to pull back any of its forward-deployed forces in Europe, which had previously been a Soviet demand. Gorbachev himself had instructed his advisors that he wanted his UN speech to be "anti-Fulton" (in contrast to Winston Churchill's famous 1946 speech announcing the fall of the "Iron Curtain"), and hoped that his remarks would be the spur for continued progress in conflict reduction.[109]

Thus, in addition to pursuing progress on arms-limitations agreements, Gorbachev showed an increased willingness to settle Cold War proxy conflicts in different regions of the world on the basis of neutralization, harkening back to the Laos precedent. The March 1988 ceasefire between the Soviet-backed Sandinista regime in Nicaragua and the US-supported contra rebels occurred on the basis of informal arrangements: the Sandinistas would agree to negotiate the transition to a more open political system, while the United States would no longer seek to use the contras for the outright overthrow of the Sandinistas. A more permanent agreement would rest on the *quid pro quo* that there would be no Soviet bloc bases permitted in Nicaragua, and Moscow, and that its Cuban ally would cease all military aid to the regime in return for an end to US support for lethal assistance to the contras.[110] This was expected to pave the way for political settlements in the other conflicts in the region. One of the great unknown questions is whether such arrangements would have lasted and been stable in the absence of the implosion of the Soviet Union.[111] The Sandinistas were pushed to accept such a settlement because it was soon clear that they could not rely on a blank check of support from Moscow; Gorbachev signaled that he wanted to get such conflicts resolved.

A similar process was underway with regard to Afghanistan. Gorbachev dropped efforts to get the United States and other countries to recognize and respect Afghanistan's "socialist choice," and thus to cease efforts to get support for the Afghan *mujahideen* as a precondition for

Soviet withdrawal. By May 1987 the Soviet government was grudgingly accepting the need for power-sharing between the Soviet-backed
Marxist-Leninist *Hezb-e dimūkrātīk-e khalq-e Afghānistān* (People's
Democratic Party of Afghanistan) and the Afghan opposition, and
that the composition of such a government of national reconciliation
would move Afghanistan out of the "socialist bloc" into a more neutral
position.[112] Talks would thus be sought with the United States to find
a solution that would end the fighting but guarantee that Afghanistan
could remain, not as a forward outpost of Soviet power, but a neutral
state shielding Soviet Central Asia.

By February 1988, the Reagan administration was signaling, in
theory, its openness to such a settlement. Robert A. Peck, deputy
assistant secretary of state, testified before the Asian and Pacific affairs
subcommittee of the House Foreign Affairs Committee: "We and the
Soviet Union would agree to the same basic commitment regarding
noninterference and nonintervention. We would be prepared, if completely satisfied with the overall agreement, to prohibit U.S. military
assistance to the Afghan resistance. We would expect the Soviet Union
to show reciprocal restraint under the Geneva accords in stopping
military support for the Kabul regime . . ."[113] The Geneva agreements
signed in April 1988 were then reiterated by a unanimously passed
United Nations Security Council resolution in September, committing
the USSR to a complete withdrawal of its forces by February 1989. There
was no political settlement between the Soviet-backed regime in Kabul
and the *mujahideen*, and both the Soviet Union and the United States
continued to support their respective sides in the Afghan civil war. (The
Soviet-backed government was to survive until a post-Soviet Russian
Federation under Boris Yeltsin terminated all support, and several of
its leading commanders thereupon defected.)

During this time, the Soviets also helped to induce their Vietnamese allies to begin a withdrawal of their forces from Cambodia, where
they were ranged against a loose coalition of pro-Chinese and pro-
Western groups, including the former Khmer Rouge, and to start a
peace process that would create a coalition government. With Soviet
encouragement, the Vietnamese fully withdrew their forces by 1989
and facilitated a dialogue between the government they backed and
opposition elements, leading to several informal meetings (starting in
Jakarta in 1988) and moving to formal conferences in Paris, where a
final settlement was signed in 1991.[114]

Finally, one of the major success stories of the US-Soviet collaboration in ending regional conflicts was the Tripartite Agreement, which was reached to settle South African and Cuban intervention in the Angolan civil war and to provide for full independence for Namibia (South West Africa). In March 1988, the Soviets indicated their support for the broad parameters of a settlement that would see the Cubans withdraw from Angola in return for Namibian independence. Even if the Soviets were motivated by the desire to extricate themselves from a series of overseas adventures that were draining the USSR of resources, the improved atmosphere in US-Soviet relations helped to facilitate such settlements.

In May 1988, the U.S. Assistant Secretary of State for Africa, Chester Crocker, invited Angolan, Cuban, and South African negotiators to London—and invited the Soviets to play a role as mediators and counselors. The Soviets also engaged in direct contacts with all three parties to provide reassurances about their willingness to uphold any negotiated settlement. The Tripartite Agreement that was concluded in December 1988 focused on creating neutral barriers between the various parties.[115] In all of these areas, Gorbachev transformed the Soviet Union from an entity that sought dominance by incorporating countries into a Soviet bloc into a body that promoted coalition governments and neutral alignments, and that turned to the United Nations to supply peace-keeping forces to monitor settlements.[116]

It is important to consider Gorbachev's motives in this pursuit of his own version of a gradualist strategy. It was his hope to bring the United States into a lasting process that would lead first to verifiable arms control and then to major reductions and even the possibility, in some categories, of disarmament. At the same time, he wanted to withdraw the Soviet Union from expensive and draining involvement in conflicts throughout the Third World, but to do so in a way that would not lead to the growth of the American/Western bloc at the expense of the Soviet sphere.[117] In so doing, the burdens of sustaining the Cold War on an increasingly sclerotic Soviet economy could be lifted, yet the position of the USSR as an equal partner with the West in determining the global agenda could be preserved.[118]

As with the initial "Kennedy experiment," the US domestic elections calendar played a role in slowing down the process. The new George H.W. Bush administration undertook a "pause" in making further progress in US-Soviet relations in the first months after taking office in January 1989, in part because a new administration wanted to take stock of policy.[119] Yet the steps that had already been undertaken in the Reagan years, and the dramatic nature of the unilateral steps outlined by Gorbachev at the United Nations in December, helped to set the stage for eventual reciprocation.

Gorbachev's speech helped to convince Western governments that progress could be made on concluding a binding treaty that would limit the size of conventional forces in Europe and help create increased stability and security.[120] Formal negotiations for drafting the treaty governing conventional forces in Europe begin in Vienna in March 1989. At several points, the Bush administration proposed accelerating the negotiations and began to offer caps on how many US (and Soviet) forces would be allowed to be deployed in Europe outside of national boundaries, first offering a limit of 275,000 and then, in January 1990, reducing that figure to 195,000.[121] The final agreement, signed in Paris in November 1990, placed strict ceilings on the numbers of troops and equipment that could be deployed, reassuring all parties that no country would be able to amass an overwhelming advantage and that both blocs would retain sufficient defensive capacity. Gorbachev's willingness to offer (and enact) unilateral concessions also led to movement on promulgating a convention that would ban further production and then start destruction of Soviet and American chemical weapons. The main stumbling block in years past had been concerns about whether Soviet compliance with such an agreement could be verified. But in 1989, "in a very significant indicator of the new level of trust, the Bush administration began to press for an accord on chemical weapons without the usual emphasis on verification."[122] Gorbachev's willingness to accept the principle of "snap inspections" of Soviet sites helped to generate reciprocal trust on the US side for the talks to move forward.[123] The bilateral accord was signed during the June 1990 Washington summit.

By 1991, the "Gorbachev experiment" had morphed into the "Bush experiment," when the United States began to take the lead in taking unilateral steps in the hopes that the Soviets would follow suit. In September 1991, Bush started the Presidential Nuclear Initiatives by unilaterally demobilizing all tactical nuclear weapons deployed on US naval vessels and announcing that the United States would withdraw from Europe all US short-range missiles and nuclear shells back to depots in the United States, as well as lower the alert status of US nuclear forces. In October, Gorbachev followed suit by—pledging to eliminate Soviet nuclear artillery munitions and begin a similar withdrawal of tactical nuclear weapons from Soviet ships. These two unilateral gestures—not part of any formal treaty commitment—at a stroke removed up to 17,000 nuclear weapons from deployment, yet "were carried out without controversy or major opposition."[124] In particular, the removal of tactical nuclear weapons from US ships was a step that many in the navy had urged.

The collapse of the USSR ended the second experiment as to whether the gradualist strategy that had been proposed by Etzioni provided a workable model for regulating superpower relations. National Security Directive 23, adopted by the George H.W. Bush administration on September 22, 1989, offers a qualified endorsement. It committed the US government to a "step by step" approach in responding to Soviet initiatives, looking to move "beyond containment" toward greater integration of the Soviet Union into the international order. However, it did so with the clear recognition that "The U.S.-Soviet relationship may still be fundamentally competitive, but it will be less militarized and safer."[125] The Persian Gulf crisis the following year tested this new model of relations. On the one hand, now hoping for direct US economic aid to their faltering economy, the Soviets were much more accommodating of US preferences in how to handle Saddam Hussein's invasion of Kuwait. On the other hand, certain Soviet equities were respected by the Bush administration. Gorbachev was given the opportunity to conduct a diplomatic effort designed to get Iraq to withdraw from Kuwait before the start of military action, and the Bush administration pledged that once the conflict was over the United States and the Soviet Union would cochair a major Middle East peace conference.[126] Whether this mode of cooperation would have continued, with US leadership but also some degree of consideration given to Soviet concerns, is unknown.

An important question to pose, however, is whether the policy elements that had been taken straight out of the gradualist playbook had been embraced because of the expectation that the USSR was on the verge of disintegration and thus there was no particular danger . If so, what has been labeled as the "Gorbachev experiment" cannot be cited as confirmation that the gradualist approach had any particular salience as a useful guide to effective national security decision making. Indeed, several critiques specifically of the gradualist approach have concluded that it was the collapse of the Soviet bloc, not Gorbachev's earlier efforts at reassurance, that led to the agreements on nuclear and conventional arms control and on ending regional conflicts.[127] Thus, the end of the Cold War should not be seen as giving any sort of empirical credence to the propositions made by Etzioni, Osgood, or others.

Perhaps one can argue that by September 1991 and in the aftermath of the failed *coup d'etat* against Mikhail Gorbachev, with the Soviet Union clearly teetering on the brink of economic collapse and dissolution, Bush's decisions could be seen as largely risk-free. However, the earlier stages of unilateral action and negotiated concessions, starting first with Reagan and Gorbachev after 1985, took place under the general expectation that the USSR remained a formidable power and a fact of life of international politics for the foreseeable future. By the mid-1980s, it was clear that the Soviet Union was under strain, but even through 1989 there was little expectation of the imminent collapse of the Warsaw Pact or even of the Soviet Union itself, either on the part of Soviet or American analysts.[128]

To be sure, Ronald Reagan believed that Soviet Communism had no future. (Herb Meyer, deputy director of the Central Intelligence Agency and vice chairman of the National Intelligence Council, penned a memorandum in 1983 that argued that the Soviet bloc and the USSR itself would not survive into the twenty-first century.)[129] But there is no evidence that either the Reagan or the George H.W. Bush administrations took any national security actions vis-à-vis the USSR on the basis of an expected imminent Soviet collapse.[130] In fact, the weight of prevailing opinion in US foreign and defense policy circles was toward viewing the Soviet threat as a clear and present danger to the United States, not one that was on the verge of self-destructing.

Some of America's recollections about the dynamics of Soviet-American interactions during the mid-to-late-1980s are colored by our hindsight of the forthcoming collapse. It is easy to forget that Reagan was forced to confront and overcome conservative opposition at the time to secure ratification of the INF Treaty in 1988 on the grounds that the agreement represented major and dangerous concessions to a still-powerful and hostile Soviet Union, and that it would weaken the American strategic position in Europe.[131] This political amnesia allows for a certain discounting of the real political risks that were taken by both American and Soviet leaders during this time.

A related argument is that Gorbachev was not inclined to end the Cold War but had been forced to do so by economic pressures and other symptoms of Soviet structural weakness, and that he would not have been interested in following a gradualist-style program to wind down the Cold War in the absence of that crisis.[132] Certainly, these problems played a major role in convincing otherwise recalcitrant members of the Soviet national security establishment to go along with Gorbachev's concessions; Gorbachev also fired many members of the Old Guard as he secured control over the Communist *nomenklatura* by 1989), Yet this alone is insufficient to explain the vast sweep of Gorbachev's initiatives. There were different and feasible options in 1986 and 1987 for a Soviet leader to deal with some of those challenges without offering the same sets of initiatives that Gorbachev proffered.[133] Thus, as Andrew Kydd concluded, "Although some retrenchment was mandated by economic constraints, the nature and extent of Gorbachev's reforms are not predicted by economic factors alone. Gorbachev's apparent final goal for the Soviet Union—a socialist, democratic, multinational state participating fully in the global economic system—was not dictated by economic decline (nor, as it turned out, was it feasible)."[134]

The last decade of the Cold War, however, did verify Etzioni's contention about the critical importance of creating psychological space in order to advance negotiations and to reduce tensions. As Alan Collins concluded, "It is difficult to imagine how the Cold War could have ended if neither superpower had been prepared to take an initial conciliatory step."[135] Gorbachev was prepared to send signals, even costly ones, to reassure the United States of the Soviet Union's good intentions and to create an atmosphere for trust in which both sides could back away from the precipice of the Cold War.[136] In his own way, he embraced a "hard way to peace." In turn, Gorbachev found in Reagan an interlocutor who himself had been sending signals since January 1984 that he would be interested in finding ways to improve relations with the USSR.[137] The Reagan-Gorbachev partnership created the necessary space for a gradualist approach to take root.

Legacies

"Gradualism" remained Etzioni's principal contribution to the American foreign policy debate during the Cold War period. His work in elucidating the psychological factors that influence foreign policy decision making and the importance of integrating conflict reduction efforts along with deterrent measures influenced American strategic thinking.[138] His optimism that the Cold War could be transformed into a more peaceful competition was reflected by those who pushed ahead with efforts at détente.

Other aspects of Etzioni's approach, however, did not have as much resonance. The American national strategy community has never been comfortable with the idea of finding ways to regulate competition with a rising or near-peer competitor, and in the aftermath of the Cold War Americans sought ways to prevent a new challenger from replacing the Soviet Union.[139] In particular, Etzioni's concept of remote deterrence has never caught the imagination of the US national security establishment. Even when the Cold War came to an end and the Soviet Union disintegrated, the call for America to "come home" and to rely in the future on some form of remote deterrence did not gain broad acceptance.

While absolute numbers of personnel stationed overseas may have been reduced, the overall network of bases and installations remains in place. With the start of the so-called "War on Terror" following the 9/11 attacks, the number of countries where a US presence (via security assistance) or installations may be found has actually expanded.[140] It remains a bipartisan US article of faith that forward engagement, utilizing a global "network of alliances and partnerships" backed by overseas US military deployments, is essential "to secure American interests in critical regions."[141] In turn, many US allies in Europe and Asia "have been determined to maintain the pattern of engagement that characterized the Cold War" and to find ways to "reinforce and even deepen" US commitments, including the retention of a forward-based US military presence.[142]

Global deployment of US forces has become ingrained in US strategy. When he was chairman of the Joint Chiefs of Staff, General Colin Powell insisted that the American "forward presence is a given—to signal our commitment to our allies and to give second thoughts to any disturber of peace."[143] Of all the elements of the gradualist strategy, this proposal continues to have the least resonance as a guide for policy within the US government.

The 1990s were often characterized as a "unipolar moment" where there was no prospect of a near-peer challenger emerging, and little concern that groups of other powers might seek to bandwagon against the United States. Gradualism seemed to have scant immediate relevance to post-Cold War US foreign policy. Yet no unipolar moment lasts forever—and even though the United States remains the world's preeminent power, changes are occurring in the global balance of power.[144] The test will be whether the United States can convince a rising power to work with it to preserve the existing international order rather than moving into opposition.[145] Two decades after the end of the US-Soviet Cold War, gradualism is once again become relevant.

Notes

1. Amitai Etzioni, *The Hard Way to Peace: A New Strategy* (New York: The Crowell-Collier Press, 1962), 11–12.

2. Noted in Gary Wilson, *The United Nations and Collective Security* (New York: Routledge, 2014), 29.

3. James M. Goldgeier and Michael McFaul, "A Tale of Two Worlds: Core and Periphery in the Post–Cold War Era," *International Organization* 46:2 (Spring 1992), 469.

4. See, for instance, Detlev F. Vagts, "Switzerland, International Law and World War II," *The American Journal of International Law*, 91:3 (July 1997), esp. 466, 469.

5. Robert Jervis, "The Impact of the Korean War on the Cold War," *The Journal of Conflict Resolution*, 24:4 (December 1980), 585.

6. For instance, at the first meeting of the North Atlantic Treaty Organization Council after the start of the Korean War, the United States pledged to enact "substantial increases in the strength of the United States forces to be stationed in Western Europe in the interest of the defense of that area," per the commitment of President Truman in September 1950. Cf. Phil Williams, *The Senate and U.S. Troops in Europe* (New York: St. Martin's Press, 1985), 24.

7. Michael MccGwire, "Soviet Military Doctrine: Contingency Planning and the Reality of World War," *Survival* 22:3 (1980), 107–13.

8. The Korean War also raised the possibility of nuclear weapons being introduced into a "conventional" conflict; at various points during the fighting, senior military officers urged the use of atomic weapons and plans were in the works to employ nuclear weapons as part of a major attack on China to force Beijing to end the conflict. See Nina Tannenwald, "The Nuclear Taboo: The United States and the Normative Basis of Nuclear Non-Use," *International Organization* 53:3 (Summer 1999), esp. 448–449.

9. See Barry Posen, *Inadvertent Escalation: Conventional War and Nuclear Risks* (Ithaca, NY: Cornell University Press, 1991), esp. 18–20.

10. Frank C. Zagare, "NATO: Rational Escalation and Flexible Response," *Journal of Peace Research* 29:4 (1992), 436, 452.

11. Herman Kahn laid out his "escalation ladder," with its multiple rungs of action, which was of course meant as a methodological exercise rather than a step-by-step plan of action. But conveying the sense that states would have to think through their responses—and thus be prepared to continue to escalate or else risk losing their position if the other side, by matching the response—negated any advantage or increase gained by the first state.

Cf. Herman Kahn, *On Escalation: Metaphors and Scenarios* (New York: Frederick A. Praeger, 1965).

12.   Etzioni, *Hard Way*, 84–108.

13.   Ibid, 141.

14.   John Lewis Gaddis, *Surprise, Security and the American Experience* (Cambridge, MA: Harvard University Press, 2004), 39.

15.   Amitai Etzioni, *Winning Without War* (New York: Doubleday and Company, 1964), 103.

16.   Ibid, *Winning Without War*, 104.

17.   Amitai Etzioni, "Social-Psychological Aspects of International Relations," in *The Handbook of Social Psychology*, ed. Garnder Lindzey and Elliot Aronson (Reading, MA: Addison-Wesley, 1970), 547–49.

18.   Etzioni, *Hard Way to Peace*, 110.

19.   Etzioni, *Winning Without War*, 224–29; *Hard Way to Peace*, 191–202.

20.   Robert E. Osgood, "The Revitalization of Containment," *Foreign Affairs* 60:3 (1981), 491.

21.   Leo Mates, "Nonalignment and the Great Powers," *Foreign Affairs* 48:3 (April 1970), http://www.foreignaffairs.com/articles/24165/leo-mates/nonalignment-and-the-great-powers.

22.   Senator Hubert Humphrey found Etzioni's proposals to be a new and more creative reworking, reordering, and extension of existing policies (Hubert H. Humphrey, "After Containment," *The New Leader* 47:14 [July 1964]) while Nathan Keyfitz discerned an evolution already in place regarding the plan Etzioni laid out (Nathan Keyfitz, "Winning Without War by Amitai Etzioni," *International Journal* 20:1 (Winter 1964/65), 115–17.

23.   Etzioni, *Winning Without War*, 91–94.

24.   Ibid, xiii.

25.   Cf. Charles E. Osgood, *An Alternative To War Or Surrender* (Urbana, IL: University of Illinois Press, 1962).

26.   Walter C. Clemens, Jr., *Dynamics of International Relations: Conflict and Mutual Gain in an Era of Global Interdependence*, 2nd ed. (Lanham, MD: Rowman and Littlefield, 2004), 248–49.

27.   Matthew Bunn, "Bold Initiatives to Reduce Tensions—50 Years Ago and Today," *Belfer Center for Science and International Affairs*," June 10, 2013, http://belfercenter.ksg.harvard.edu/publication/23147/bold_initiatives_to_reduce_tensions_50_years_ago_and_today.html.

28.   Phyllis Klein, "Etzioni, Kahn Clash on Utility of War," *Barnard Bulletin*, January 14, 1963, 6, 8; Eugene B. Trainin, "Nuclear Way, Foreign Policy Debated by Etzioni and Kahn," *Columbia Daily Spectator*, January 11, 1963, 3.

29.   See J. L. Richard, *Arms Control in the Later 1980s: The Implications of the Strategic Defense Initiative* (Working Paper Series no. 3) (Canberra: Peace Research Center, Australia National University, 1986), 5.

30.   See, for instance, the discussion in James Raffel and Brian D'Agostino, "Time for an Old Blueprint," *Bulletin of the Atomic Scientists* 47:9 (November 1991), 31–33.

31.   Etzioni, *Hard Way to Peace*, 121–22.

32.   See the review of Walter C. Clemens in the *American Political Science Review* 57:3 (September 1963), 680.

33.   Robert A. Levine, "Unilateral Initiatives: A Cynic's View," *Bulletin of the Atomic Scientists* 19:1 (January 1963), 24.

34. Brian White, "The Concept of Détente," *Review of International Studies* 7:3 (July 1981), 167.

35. Levine, 24.

36. Henry Nau, *Conservative Internationalism: Armed Diplomacy under Jefferson, Polk, Truman, and Reagan* (Princeton, NJ: Princeton University Press, 2013), 30, 32.

37. Philip Green, "Alternatives to Overkill: Dream and Reality," *Bulletin of the Atomic Scientists* 19:9 (November 1963), 24–25.

38. Robert E. Osgood, *NATO: The Entangling Alliance* (Chicago: University of Chicago Press, 1962), 30.

39. See, for instance, Christoph Bertram, "The Future of Arms Control: Part II—Arms Control and Technological Change: Elements of a New Approach," *Adelphi Papers* 145 (1978), 16.

40. Thomas M. Nichols, *No Use: Nuclear Weapons and U.S. National Security* (Philadelphia: University of Pennsylvania Press, 2014), 23–24.

41. The main arguments were summarized in Robert Jervis, *Perception and Misperception in International Politics* (Princeton, NJ: Princeton University Press, 1976), 110, 111.

42. William Odom, "Transforming the Military," *Foreign Affairs* 76:4 (July–August 1997), 55; Marshal E. J. Kingston-McCloughry, "Present-Day Deterrents," *Royal United Services Institute Journal* 108:629 (1963), 47.

43. See, for instance Admiral William Crowe, Jr. with David Chanoff, *The Line of Fire: From Washington to the Gulf, the Politics and Battles of the New Military* (New York: Simon and Schuster, 1993), 98–100; Barry R. Posen, "Command of the Commons: The Military Foundation of U.S. Hegemony," *International Security* 28:1 (Summer 2003), 15–17. For a maritime perspective on the need for global presence via forward deployment written during the height of the Cold War, see Geoffrey Kemp and Harlan Ullman, *Toward a New Order of U.S. Maritime Policy* (Washington, DC: National Defense University, 1977).

44. Mary Kaldor, "Beyond the Blocs: Defending Europe the Political Way," *World Policy Journal* 1:1 (Fall 1983), 15.

45. Jervis, 110, 111.

46. Peter Wallensteen, *Understanding Conflict Resolution: War, Peace and the Global System*, 3rd ed. (London: SAGE 2007, 2009, 2012), 35.

47. "Cuban Missile Crisis Day by Day: From the Pentagon's 'Sensitive Records,'" *National Security Archive Electronic Briefing Book No. 398*, ed. William Burr, October 19, 2012, http://www2.gwu.edu/~nsarchiv/NSAEBB/NSAEBB398/, especially comments of Deputy Secretary of Defense Roswell Gilpatric on October 18, 1962.

48. Amitai Etzioni, *My Brother's Keeper: A Memoir and a Message* (Lanham, MD: Rowman and Littlefield, 2003), 73.

49. Martin Patchen, *Resolving Disputes Between Nations: Coercion Or Conciliation?* (Durham, NC: Duke University Press, 1988), 287.

50. See White, note 36, 171.

51. A copy of the speech is archived at the John F. Kennedy Presidential Library, http://www.jfklibrary.org/Asset-Viewer/BWC7I4C9QUmLG9J6I8oy8w.aspx. The speech is also extensively excerpted and discussed in Theodore Otto Windt, Jr., *Presidents and Protesters: Political Rhetoric in the 1960s* (Tuscaloosa, AL: University of Alabama Press, 1990), 64–70.

52. Amitai Etzioni, "The Kennedy Experiment," *Western Political Quarterly* 20:2–1 (June 1967), 361–80.

53. See Max Frankel writing in the *New York Times*, October 25, 1963, 6, quoted in Etzioni, "Kennedy Experiment," note 21, 367.

54. Joshua S. Goldstein and John R. Freeman, *Three Way Street: Strategic Reciprocity in World Politics* (Chicago: University of Chicago, 1990), 16.

55. Stephen G. Walker and Akan Malici, *U.S. Presidents and Foreign Policy Mistakes* (Stanford, CA: Stanford University Press, 2011), 126.

56. See, for instance, Wilhelm Agrell, "Silent Allies and Hostile Neutrals: Nonaligned States in the Cold War," *War Plans and Alliances in the Cold War: Threat Perceptions in the East and West,* eds. Vojtech Mastny, Sven S. Holtsmark, and Andreas Wenger (Abingdon, Oxon: Routledge, 2006), 147–49.

57. Cecil V. Crabb, Jr. "American Diplomatic Tactics and Neutralism," *Political Science Quarterly* 78:3 (September 1963), 419, 430.

58. Quoted in "A Bipartisan Fight for Foreign Aid," *Daytona Beach Morning Journal*, February 21, 1958, 4.

59. Kaldor, 14–15.

60. See, for instance, the National Security Council report NSC 5805, "Draft Statement of U.S. Policy Towards Yugoslavia," (February 28, 1958), archived at https://history.state.gov/historicaldocuments/frus1958-60v10p2/d120.

61. "The Laos Crisis, 1960–1963," *Milestones: 1961–1968* (Washington, DC: Office of the Historian, U.S. Department of State, 2013), https://history.state.gov/milestones/1961–1968/laos-crisis.

62. Crabb, 436.

63. Edmund F. Wehrle, "'Good, Bad Deal': John F. Kennedy, W. Averell Harriman, and the Neutralization of Laos, 1961–1962," *Pacific Historical Review* 67:3 (August 1998), 351.

64. Paul F. Langer, *The Soviet Union, China and the Pathet Lao: Analysis and Chronology* (Santa Monica, CA: RAND Corporation, 1972), v, 5–7.

65. Wehrle, 351.

66. Bruce D. Porter, *The USSR in Third World Conflicts: Soviet Arms and Diplomacy in Local Wars, 1945–1980* (Cambridge: Cambridge University Press, 1984), 86.

67. David R. Stone, *A Military History of Russia: From Ivan the Terrible to the War in Chechnya* (Westport, CT: Praeger, 2006), 230. Analyst Jeremy Azrael described it as an "all-azimuth" buildup in a variety of sectors; cf. his *The Soviet Civilian Leadership and the Military High Command, 1876–1986* (Santa Monica, CA: RAND, June 1987), 1–4.

68. Matthew J. Ouimet, *The Rise and Fall of the Brezhnev Doctrine in Soviet Foreign Policy* (Raleigh-Durham, NC: University of North Carolina Press, 2003), 66–67.

69. Richard B. Craig and J. David Gillespie, "Yugoslav Reaction to the Czechoslovak Liberalization Movement and the Invasion of 1968," *Australian Journal of Politics and History* 23:2 (August 1977), 227.

70. C.R. Mitchell, "Grit and Gradualism—25 years On," *International Interactions: Empirical and Theoretical Research in International Relations* 13:1 (1986), 59–90.

71. See Shiping Tang, *A Theory of Security Strategy for Our Time: Defensive Realism* (New York: Palgrave Macmillan, 2010), 129–130; Rachel M.

MacNair, *Psychology of Peace: An Introduction* (Santa Barbara, CA: ABC-CLIO, 2012), 180.

72. Peter Wallensteen, "The Origins of Contemporary Peace Research," in *Understanding Peace Research: Methods and Challenges*, eds. Kristine Höglund and Magnus Öberg (Abingdon, Oxon: Routledge, 2011), 21. See also Hans Günter Brauch, "Confidence Building Measures and Disarmament Strategy," *Current Research on Peace and Violence* 2:3/4 (1979), 120.

73. Etzioni, *Winning Without War*, 219.

74. Hans Günter Brauch, Czeslaw Mesjasz, and Björn Möller, "Controlling Weapons in the Quest for Peace," *The Future of the United Nations System: Potential for the Twenty-First Century*, ed. Chadwick F. Alger (Tokyo: United Nations University Press, 1998), 28.

75. John Fry, *The Helsinki Process: Negotiating Security and Cooperation in Europe* (Washington, DC: National Defense University Press, 1993), 74.

76. Cecilia Albin and Daniel Druckman, "Bargaining over Weapons: Justice and Effectiveness in Arms Control Negotiations," *International Negotiation* 19 (2014), 432.

77. Etzioni, *My Brother's Keeper*, 71.

78. Daniel Druckman, Jo L. Husbands, and Karin Johnston, "Turning Points in the INF Negotiations," *Negotiation Journal* 7:1 (January 1991), 62.

79. John Prados, "Prague Spring and SALT: Arms Limitations Setbacks in 1968," *Beyond Vietnam: The Foreign Policies of Lyndon Johnson*, ed. H.W. Brands (College Station, TX: Texas A & M Press, 1999), 19–36.

80. John Lewis Gaddis, "The Rise, Fall and Future of Détente," *Foreign Affairs* 62:2 (Winter 1983), 359.

81. Robert S. Litwak, *Détente and the Nixon Doctrine: American Foreign Policy and the Pursuit of Stability, 1969–1976* (Cambridge: Cambridge University Press, 1984), 78–79.

82. Nikolas K. Gvosdev, "The Communitarian Foreign Policy of Amitai Etzioni," *Society* 51:4 (August 2014), 376.

83. Raymond L. Garthoff, *Détente and Confrontation: American-Soviet Relations from Nixon to Reagan* (Washington, DC: The Brookings Institution, 1982), esp. 1–2; see also Gaddis, 362, noting that détente was not intended to end the arms race, but control it.

84. Litwak, 1.

85. Henry Kissinger, *Years of Upheaval* (Boston: Little Brown and Co., 1982), 600.

86. Amitai Etzioni, "Social-Psychological Aspects of International Relations," 549–50.

87. Garthoff, 35.

88. Paul H. Nitze, "Assuring Strategic Stability in an Era of Détente," *Foreign Affairs* 54:2 (January 1976), 207, 209, 210.

89. Garthoff, 2.

90. Richard Pipes, "Misinterpreting the Cold War: The Hardliners Were Right," *Foreign Affairs* 74:1 (January/February 1995), 154.

91. Itai Nartzizenfield Sneh, *The Future Almost Arrived: How Jimmy Carter Failed to Change U.S. Foreign Policy* (New York: Peter Lang Publishing, 2008), 230–34.

92. Keren Yarhi-Milo, *Knowing the Adversary: Leaders, Intelligence, and Assessment of Intentions in International Relations* (Princeton, NJ: Princeton

University Press, 2014), 149–53; John Norton, "Cyrus Vance," *American Statesmen: Secretaries of State from John Jay to Colin Powell*, ed. Edward S. Mihalkanin (Westport, CT: Greenwood Publishing, 2004), 513–17.

93. David Cortright and Raimo Väyrynen, "Chapter Four: Lessons from the End of the Cold War," *Adelphi Papers* 49:410 (2009), 72.

94. Andrei Grachev, *Gorbachev's Gamble: Soviet Foreign Policy and the End of the Cold War* (Cambridge: Polity Press, 2008), 6. Gorbachev and his team never referred to any US sources of inspiration for their "new thinking" approach. Richard A. Bitzinger, "Gorbachev and GRIT, 1985–1989: Did Arms Control Succeed Because of Unilateral Actions or in Spite of Them?" *Contemporary Security Policy* 15 (April 1994), 69.

95. A number of Western commentators have described Gorbachev's approach as approximating strategies outlined by Etzioni, Osgood, and others. Goldstein and Freeman, 154.

96. George W. Breslauer, *Gorbachev and Yeltsin as Leaders* (Cambridge: Cambridge University Press, 2002), 60.

97. See comments of Georgy Arbatov, in Robert Scheer, "He Rules Out Unilateral Concessions : Arms Freeze Possible at Summit, Soviet Aide Says," *Los Angeles Times*, September 27, 1985, http://articles.latimes.com/1985-09-27/news/mn-18089_1_soviet-union; Grachev, 56.

98. James Graham Wilson, *The Triumph of Improvisation: Gorbachev's Adaptability, Reagan's Engagement and the End of the Cold War* (Ithaca, NY: Cornell University Press, 2014), esp. 197–204.

99. Jack F. Matlock, Jr. *Reagan and Gorbachev: How the Cold War Ended* (New York: Random House, 2004), 200.

100. Alan R. Collins, "GRIT, Gorbachev and the End of the Cold War," *Review of International Studies* 24:2 (April 1998), 207.

101. Matlock, 209.

102. See, for instance, Mark Kramer, The Demise of the Soviet Bloc," *The Journal of Modern History* 83:4 (December 2011), esp. 791–95.

103. Nikolai Sokov, "Reykjavik Summit: The Legacy and a Lesson for the Future," *NTI*, December 1, 2007, http://www.nti.org/analysis/articles/reykjavik-summit-legacy/.

104. Matlock, 242.

105. Sokov, op. cit.

106. Michael Cox, "Beyond Conflict: Soviet Foreign Policy Under Gorbachev," *Beyond the Cold War: Superpowers at the Crossroads* (Lanham, MD: University Press of America, 1990), 115–16.

107. Ronald Reagan, "Remarks on Signing the Intermediate-Range Nuclear Forces Treaty," December 8, 1987, in *Public Papers of the Presidents of the United States: Ronald Reagan, 1987* (Washington, DC: Office of the Federal Register, National Archives and Records Service, Government Printing Office, 1989), 1455.

108. Breslauer, 60.

109. Memoranda prepared for and by Gorbachev in the run-up to the December 1988 speech can be found at "Reagan, Gorbachev and Bush at Governor's Island: Previously Secret Documents from Soviet and U.S. Files On the 1988 Summit in New York, 20 Years Later," eds. Svetlana Savranskaya and Thomas Blanton, *National Security Archive Electronic Briefing Book*,

261 (December 8, 2008), a http://www2.gwu.edu/~nsarchiv/NSAEBB/ NSAEBB261/.

110. Alfonso Chardy, "Truce Is A Boost To Shultz's Peace Effort, Sources Say," *Philadelphia Inquirer*, March 25, 1988, http://articles.philly.com/1988-03-25/news/26276064_1_peace-accord-sandinistas-contras.

111. Robert L. Scheina, *Latin America's Wars Volume II: The Age of the Professional Soldier, 1900–2001* (Washington, DC: Potomac Books, 2003), 1980.

112. Artemy Kalinovsky, *A Long Goodbye: The Soviet Withdrawal from Afghanistan* (Cambridge, MA: Harvard University Press, 2011), 116–19.

113. "Testimony of Robert A. Peck, Deputy Assistant Secretary of State, Before the Subcommittee on Asian and Pacific Affairs, February 25, 1988," as cited in the *Congressional Record*, Senate, February 29, 1988, 2654.

114. Leszek Buszynski, *Gorbachev and Southeast Asia* (New York: Routledge, 1992, 2013), 132–33.

115. Charles W. Freeman, "The Angola/Namibia Accords," *Foreign Affairs* 68:3 (Summer 1989), esp. 133, 134–35, 137.

116. Melvin A. Goodman, *Gorbachev's Retreat: The Third World* (New York: Praeger, 1991), 184.

117. Jacques Levesque, "The Messianic Character of 'New Thinking': Why and What For?" *The Last Decade of the Cold War: From Conflict Escalation to Conflict Transformation*, ed. Olav Njølstad (London: Frank Cass Publishers, 2004), 137.

118. Grachev, 183.

119. Andrew Kydd, "Trust, Reassurance, and Cooperation," *International Organization* 54:2 (Spring 2000), 348.

120. Stefan Lehne, *The Vienna Meeting of the Conference on Security and Cooperation in Europe, 1986–1989: A Turning Point in East-West Relations* (Boulder, CO: Westview Press, 1991), 141.

121. Collins, 211.

122. Kydd, 349.

123. Fiona Simpson, "Evolution and Innovation: Biological and Chemical Weapons," *Cooperating for Peace and Security: Evolving Institutions and Arrangements in the Context of Changing U.S. Security Policy*, eds. Bruce D. Jones, Shepard Forman, and Richard Gowan (Cambridge: Cambridge University Press, 2012), 178.

124. Cortright and Väyrynen, 72–73; see also Daryl Kimball and Tom Collina, "The Presidential Nuclear Initiatives (PNIs) on Tactical Nuclear Weapons at a Glance," *Arms Control Association*, August 2012, http://www.armscontrol.org/factsheets/pniglance.

125. A declassified copy of NSD-23 is available at http://fas.org/irp/offdocs/nsd/nsd23.pdf.

126. Ronald E. Powaski, *The Cold War: The United States and the Soviet Union, 1917–1991* (Oxford: Oxford University Press, 1998), 281–82.

127. Bitzinger, 77; Collins, 219.

128. Soviet analysts were confidently assuring Gorbachev in early 1989 that there was little danger of a complete collapse of the Soviet bloc even if greater freedom was extended to satellites; cf. "The Political Processes in the European Socialist Countries and the Proposals for Our Practical Steps Considering the Situation that Has Arisen in Them," Memorandum of the

Soviet Ministry of Foreign Affairs, February 24, 1989, quoted in Ray Takeyh and Nikolas K. Gvosdev, "Democratic Impulses versus Imperial Interests: America's New Mid-East Conundrum," *Orbis* 47:3 (Summer 2003), 418. US assessments were also not predicting any whole-scale collapse. Cf. Elaine Sciolino, "Director Admits C.I.A. Fell Short In Predicting the Soviet Collapse," *New York Times*, May 21, 1992, http://www.nytimes.com/1992/05/21/world/director-admits-cia-fell-short-in-predicting-the-soviet-collapse.html; and comments of former CIA Director Stansfield Tuner, in Milo L. Jones and Philippe Silberzahn, *Constructing Cassandra, Reframing Intelligence Failure at the CIA, 1947–2001* (Stanford, CA: Stanford University Press, 2013), 108, and larger discussion, 106–09, of American intelligence assessments of the USSR.

129. Paul Kengor, "Predicting the Soviet Collapse," *National Review Online*, July 14, 2011, http://www.nationalreview.com/articles/271828/predicting-soviet-collapse-paul-kengor.

130. NSD-23, promulgated in September 1989, still identified a powerful Soviet military establishment as a threat to the security of the United States and counseled that the United States needed to be able to deal with the USSR from a position of strength.

131. Lou Cannon, *President Reagan: The Role of a Lifetime* (New York: Public Affairs, 1991, 2000), 699–701; Norman A. Graebner, Richard Dean Burns, and Joseph M. Siracusa, *Reagan, Bush, Gorbachev: Revisiting the End of the Cold War* (Westport, CT: Praeger, 2008), 97.

132. Bitzinger, 77; see also William C. Wohlforth, "Realism and the End of the Cold War," *International Security* 19:3 (1995), 91–129.

133. Wilson, 203.

134. Kydd, 350.

135. Collins, 219.

136. Kydd, 353.

137. See, for instance, Beth A. Fischer, *The Reagan Reversal: Foreign Policy and the End of the Cold War* (Columbia, MO: University of Missouri Press, 1997).

138. Alexander L. George and Richard Smoke, *Deterrence in American Foreign Policy: Theory and Practice* (New York: Columbia University Press, 1974), 11–12.

139. This unease with the possibility of having to deal with a new superpower was reflected in the 1992 draft Defense Strategic Guidance which was leaked to the press. See Patrick E. Tyler, "U.S. Strategy Plan Calls for Ensuring No Rivals Develop," *New York Times*, March 8, 1992, http://www.nytimes.com/1992/03/08/world/us-strategy-plan-calls-for-insuring-no-rivals-develop.html?src=pm&pagewanted=1. Although official U.S. documents have never embraced this vision, one can argue that it accurately reflected views that were influential in at least some segments of the US foreign-policy community.

140. Derek Reveron, *Exporting Security: International Engagement, Security Cooperation and the Changing Face of the U.S. Military* (Washington, DC: Georgetown University Press, 2010), 2; William M. Arkin, "Military Bases Boost Capability but Fuel Anger," *Los Angeles Times*, January 6, 2002, A1.

141. Michelle Flournoy and Janine Davidson, "Obama's New Global Posture," *Foreign Affairs* 91:4 (2012), 53–54. On the bipartisan nature of this

consensus—that the U.S. must retain its forward deployments in order to manage security in different regions, see Stephen Books, G. John Ikenberry, and William Wolhlforth, "Don't Come Home, America: The Case against Retrenchment," *International Security* 37:3 (Winter 2012/13), 13.

142. Michael Mastanduno, "Preserving the Unipolar Moment: Realist Theories and U.S. Grand Strategy after the Cold War," *International Security* 21:4 (Spring 1997), 58–59.

143. Colin Powell, "U.S. Forces: Challenges Ahead," *Foreign Affairs* 71:5 (Winter 1992), 36.

144. Christopher Layne, in 1993, predicted an end to the US "unipolar moment" by 2010 and that, inevitably, other powers would rise to challenge the US position. See his "The Unipolar Illusion: Why New Great Powers Will Rise," *International Security* 17:4 (Spring 1993), 5–51.

145. G. John Ikenberry, "The Rise of China and the Future of the West: Can the Liberal System Survive?" *Foreign Affairs* 87:1 (January–February 2008), 23–37.

3

Preventing a New Cold War: US-China Relations in the Twenty-First Century

Gradualism had been an attempt to get the two superpowers of the mid-to-late twentieth century to walk back from the precipice of the Cold War that threatened to consume the world in a nuclear holocaust. During the "unipolar moment" of the 1990s and early 2000s, there was a belief that the United States would not have to face a near-peer challenger for decades to come.[1] It was thought that most states would choose to become integrated into a US-led global order—and that the danger of great-power conflict was all but over.[2] Josef Joffe urged Washington to adopt a "hub and spokes" approach to world affairs, advising that if other rising and resurgent powers were to "remain beholden to the center, they are more likely to co-balance with the United States . . . and cooperate against global threats."[3]

Gradualism thus receded from the US foreign-policy discussion during this period and was seen as having the most relevance for regional and middle powers. There was speculation that perhaps a gradualist strategy could be employed to lessen tensions between India and Pakistan, or to jump-start a peace process between Israel and its Arab neighbors.[4] Indeed, like Gorbachev, Iran's president Mohammad Khatami undertook a gradualist, reassurance approach to transforming the Islamic Republic's previously hostile relations with its neighbor, and ideological and economic rival, Saudi Arabia into a more cooperative relationship.[5] But gradualism seemed to have little relevance for how the world's sole superpower ought to conduct its relations. While Khatami's efforts to improve relations with Riyadh bore fruit, his attempts at initiating dialogue with the United States, in 1997 and again in 2001, were far less successful in inducing any sort of reciprocal response.[6]

Instead, the US approach was predicated on a twin strategy of engagement (to draw other powers into the US-led international order) and isolation (to cut off a recalcitrant "rogue state" as far as possible from the global system). During the 1990s, rogue states were an irritant but not an existential danger because "they lack the resources of a superpower, which would enable them to seriously threaten the democratic order being created around them."[7]

But the question emerged: where was a rising China to fit in? By the 1990s there were already clear indications that the People's Republic was on a trajectory not simply to be a major player in Asia but to emerge as a global great power, and even had the raw materials from which to construct superpower status at some point in the future. Many of China's neighbors began to plan for its superpower emergence at some point in the early part of the twenty-first century.[8] The United States, however, continued to assume that China's trajectory could be directed in such a way that Chinese power would not end up threatening American predominance. By the end of the decade, some observers were critical of this approach, warning that there existed a "clear potential for the People's Republic of China and the United States of America to enter a relationship of superpower contention." There were criticisms of the apparent "inability [on the part of the U.S.] to take the initiative to repair US-China relations, rather than allowing the relationship to continue to be events-driven."[9] Increasingly, there were calls for policy to not become "too dependent on exogenous and unpredictable events."[10]

The Thucydides Trap

With China posited to emerge as the next possible near-peer competitor to the United States, finding a way to avoid what seemed to be the inevitable logic of history that rising powers must seek to challenge the status quo (often popularized under the style of the "Thucydides Trap"[11]) became the defining principle for organizing US-China relations. The naïve expectation that China (assuming it did not undergo some sort of internal collapse) would not seek greater regional and global influence was not seen as a rational basis for any sort of serious planning for the future.[12] In the immediate aftermath of the 9/11 attacks, there was cautious optimism that the global war on terrorism might provide a basis for broad-based US-China cooperation. This was the hope after a series of negative incidents, including the Taiwan Straits crisis of 1995–96, the accidental bombing of the Chinese embassy in Belgrade during the 1999 Kosovo operation, and the ill will generated by Chinese commercial and technological espionage activity in the United States.[13] In September 2005, Robert B. Zoellick, then serving as the US deputy secretary of state, expressed his famous sentiment that it was the People's Republic of China becoming a "responsible stakeholder" in the US-led international system that "that has enabled its success." Beijing was invited "to shape the future international system" in partnership with Washington.[14] In particular, Zoellick noted, the United States was not interested in replicating its Cold War approach with the Soviet Union as a way to conceptualize relations with a rising China: "For fifty years, our policy was to fence in the Soviet Union while its own internal contradictions undermined it. For thirty years, our policy has been to draw out the People's Republic of China."[15] Subsequent US officials, even if eschewing the "responsible stakeholder" language, have continued to endorse the sentiment—that the United States welcomes China's emergence as a great power, does not seek to contain it or threaten its rise, and wants to pursue a positive, cooperative relationship that disproves the assumption that a rising power must of necessity confront and clash with a status quo power.[16] There is an almost palpable concern for reassuring both the Chinese and the American public that the United States does not intend to follow the twentieth-century Cold War template in structuring its approach to China in the twenty-first century.

The China engagement strategy that has been the bedrock of the US approach over the past thirty years, even as it has gone through different phases, has been seen as preferable to forcible containment (particularly of the type undertaken after World War II against the Soviet Union) or outright appeasement. However, the "responsible stakeholder" approach does have some flaws. Most notable is the assumption, as noted by John Lee, that "there is no alternative for emerging states but to compete within the existing open and liberal order. The responsible stakeholder framework does not account for the fact that rising participants – especially genuinely powerful ones – can seek to gradually dismantle and redesign the current order from within."[17] There is an assumption that the United States has the carrots to sway and impact Chinese choices toward preferred US outcomes, yet possesses sufficient sticks of deterrence (encompassing political, economic, and military instruments of power) to dissuade Beijing from trying to change the current regional and global orders.[18]

Zoellick's formulation was designed to encapsulate a bipartisan US approach to China that would avoid the fate that John Mearsheimer, writing in that same year, maintained was all but inevitable: "China cannot rise peacefully, and if it continues its dramatic economic growth over the next few decades, the United States and China are likely to engage in an intense security competition with considerable potential for war."[19] For those who share the Mearsheimer concern, the coming clash between Washington and Beijing can only be averted if China undergoes some sort of collapse that would put an end to its meteoric rise, or if the United States is no longer willing to expend the resources needed to maintain the status quo in the region.[20] (One might also envision a less binary outcome, for instance, "if China's power grows relatively slowly, if its ambitions stay constrained, and if the security dilemma is muted, the prospects for direct confrontation with the United States could remain limited."[21]) However, the second option— a substantial American disengagement from the region—is certainly not in the cards. Former Secretary of State Hillary Clinton, writing in *Foreign Policy* in 2011, bluntly committed the United States to a "pivot" (or "rebalance") to Asia:

> We need to be smart and systematic about where we invest time and energy, so that we put ourselves in the best position to sustain our leadership, secure our interests, and advance our values. One of the most important tasks of American statecraft over the next decade will therefore be to lock in a substantially increased investment— diplomatic, economic, strategic, and otherwise—in the Asia-Pacific region. The Asia-Pacific has become a key driver of global politics.[22]

Given that the United States is not prepared to depart the Asia-Pacific region and that China is not going to voluntarily halt its rise as a great power, is there a policy prescription that can avoid turning predictions of a Sino-American clash into a self-fulfilling prophecy?

Those whom Aaron Friedberg a decade ago labeled "optimists" about the course of Sino-American relations have assumed that a variety of factors will keep the relationship from spiraling out of control. These factors include US-China economic interdependence, and continuing American military superiority, and the existing network of US alliances in the region that Beijing, even with increasing defense spending, cannot hope to overcome at any point in the short run. These realities are anticipated to "act as a brake on what might otherwise be an unchecked slide toward mounting competition and increasingly open confrontation."[23] President Barack Obama would seem to be a member of this camp. He appears to believe that with careful deployment of both incentives and pressure, China can be induced to conform to US preferences, and, indeed, to adopt them as well in the long run. In August 2014, Obama acknowledged that there were going to be "tensions and conflicts" in the US-China relationship, but that "those are manageable." He went on to note: "There have to be mechanisms both to be tough with them when we think that they're breaching international norms, but also to show them the potential benefits over the long term."[24]

Some of those mechanisms have included protecting US military power into the region, continuing a number of missions (including those designed to uphold the freedom of navigation through a country's exclusive economic zone), and increasing security partnerships with both existing allies and new partners. An assessment of these efforts is that it "represents a simultaneous attempt to warn China away from using heavy-handed tactics against its neighbors and provide confidence to other Asia-Pacific countries that want to resist pressure from Beijing now and in the future."[25] This has required the United States to focus on maintaining forward presence in the Asia-Pacific region and ensuring that it would have superiority—if not outright dominance—in the air, naval, and space domains. Indeed, two of the key components of the "forward-deployed" strategy outlined by former Secretary of State Clinton are the strengthening and updating of the US network of regional alliances and "forging a broad-based military presence."[26]

In theory, it sounds very benign—US power being used to channel and safeguard "an approach [that] not only welcomes China's peaceful rise but also explicitly charts a pathway to its coveted status as a great power."[27] By setting clear limits on China's freedom of maneuver, and being prepared to enforce those lines, the United States helps to safeguard the peace and stability of the entire Asia-Pacific region upon which China's own plans for development depend. For its part, however, China has not generally recognized US intentions as benign or necessarily beneficial to Chinese interests. The American approach is not seen as an altruistic gesture on the part of Washington, but an effort to "secure Chinese cooperation in ways that benefit U.S. interests."[28] Meanwhile, Beijing looks askance at "the considerable growth in the U.S. defense budget since the end of the Cold War ... ongoing U.S. procurement of next-generation weaponry, and the significant and ongoing deployment since the mid-1990s of US power-projection capabilities on China's maritime periphery."[29] Chinese sources consistently indicate Beijing's unhappiness with US military patrols along its coastline, and unease with the network of US military bases and facilities in the region.[30] In particular, Beijing has always been suspicious of American efforts to reach out to the states, particularly the "middle powers" that ring its periphery and that, collectively and in partnership with the United States, could counterbalance China's regional advantages.[31] Consistently, China's national security establishment warns that the US objective is to use its capabilities and alliances to "encircle" China and contain its rise.[32]

In practice, therefore, the current US approach is not without its own share of risk, in particular, the possibility of a clash or confrontation—whether deliberate or accidental—between the nations. This is especially enhanced because of the measures the United States takes to guarantee that its power could be used in the event that China decides to test those limits. The Taiwan Straits Crisis of 1995–96 was the first major post-Cold War test of how far China might go to challenge—and what the United States would be prepared to do to defend—the status quo in the Asia Pacific. After Taiwan's President Lee Teng-hui visited the United States in the summer of 1995, he dropped hints that he might consider changing Taiwan's status in a way that might signal a move toward independence. The Chinese government (who consider Taiwan to be a province of a united China) then started a series of missile drills and naval maneuvers—including practice amphibious assaults—in the general vicinity of Taiwan. Ultimately there would be two broad sets of tests, in late 1995 and early 1996. As fears intensified throughout the fall and winter of 1995 that Beijing might take some sort of forceful action against Taiwan, the United States responded by orchestrating a massive move of military might, especially aircraft carrier battle groups, into the Western Pacific and into the waters adjoining Taiwan. In March 1996 then-U.-S Secretary of Defense William Perry pointedly threw down the gauntlet, stating: "Beijing should know, and this will remind them, that while they are a great military power, the premier – the strongest – military power in the Western Pacific is the United States."[33] The crisis dissipated, in part because Washington exerted a good deal of pressure on Taiwanese leaders to avoid making provocative statements, but it "underscore[d] Chinese feelings of helplessness against U.S. naval power."[34]

In April 2001, a US EP-3 surveillance plane, flying in international waters but in a position to gather intelligence on Chinese military facilities and activities, collided with a Chinese J-8 fighter. Forced to make an emergency landing on Hainan Island, the incident triggered a major diplomatic row, with Beijing refusing to release the crew until the Bush administration made sufficient gestures of apology. The collision had occurred because of more aggressive Chinese shadowing of US patrols, as a way to demonstrate China's intense displeasure at US activities off of its coastline. Just as Beijing ratcheted down the pressure after the Taiwan Straits crisis, so too, in the aftermath of the EP-3 incident, China backed off its more confrontational posture vis-à-vis US. offshore surveillance activities.[35] China appeared to search for ways, after each encounter, to decrease tensions and to reluctantly and grudgingly accept the reality of a continued US security presence in Beijing's immediate neighborhood. At the same time, after each crisis or incident, the Chinese military worked to improve its capabilities and to extend its ability to project power. In addition, it sought to bolster its arsenal of weapons and platforms designed to deny the US military the ability to operate near China's borders; at the least, it sought to significantly raise the costs of doing so.[36] Thus,

> Starting in the early 1990s, however, Chinese investments in sophisticated, but low-cost, weapons—including anti-ship missiles, short- and medium-range ballistic missiles, cruise missiles, stealth submarines, and cyber and space arms—began to challenge the military superiority of the United States, especially in China's littoral waters. These "asymmetric arms" threaten two key elements of the United States' force projection strategy: its fixed bases (such as those in Japan and Guam) and aircraft carriers. Often referred to as anti-access/anti-denial capabilities (A2/AD), these Chinese arms are viewed by some in the Pentagon as raising the human and economic cost of the United States' military role in the region to prohibitive levels.[37]

In turn, the growth in Chinese military research, spending, and acquisition could erode America's ability to shape the security environment in the Western Pacific (in the realm the Chinese refer to as the "Near Seas"), and enforce limits on Chinese activities without incurring major costs.[38] This growth pushes the United States to continue its own efforts to bolster its position in the region, positioning forces for action in the Western Pacific. In addition, it expands security cooperation with China's neighbors, as well as the potential of the United States to develop and deploy new systems that could counteract China's A2/AD capabilities.[39] Thus, the stage has been set for a destabilizing arms race in the region; as China acquires the means to push back against the US presence, the United States finds ways to maintain and improve its security position in the region, leading to redoubled Chinese efforts, and so on.

This raises the possibility that developments could spiral, raising tensions and laying the groundwork for a Cold-War style confrontation between China and the United States. These concerns have been augmented by a new series of recent Sino-American incidents in the maritime domain and airspace surrounding China. These include: (1) the October 2006 shadowing of the USS Kitty Hawk off the coast of Okinawa by a Chinese Song submarine; (2) the October 2008 detection of two Chinese subs trailing the USS George Washington off the coast of South Korea; (3) the March 2009 aggressive shadowing by Chinese planes and ships of the USNS Impeccable, an ocean surveillance vessel in the South China Sea (and a similar incident involving the USNS Victorious in the Yellow Sea in May 2009); (4) the June 2009 collision between a Chinese sub and the towed sonar array of the USS John McCain off the coast of the Philippines; (5) the November 2013 declaration by China of an air defense identification zone over large portions of the East China Sea (which the United States responded to by launching a symbolic flight of B-52 bombers without seeking any prior permission from Chinese air controllers); (6) a near collision between the USS Cowpens and a Chinese vessel in a part of the South China Sea near where China's aircraft carrier was undertaking maneuvers in December 2013; and (7) a risky interception by a Chinese SU-27 of an American P-8 surveillance plane near Hainan Island in August 2014.

Then-Secretary of Defense Chuck Hagel has noted, "China's actions raise regional tensions and increases [sic] the risk of miscalculation, confrontation, and accidents."[40] In contrast, Chinese officials—like Huang Xueping, a spokesman for the Defense Ministry—have stressed their interpretation of US activity as being illegal under international law and a violation of China's sovereign rights.[41] Retired Major General Peng Guangqian, in addressing US colleagues, bluntly noted, "It is hard to understand why American surveillance ships showed up off China's shores, thousands of miles from home. . . . If a military surveillance ship conducts military intelligence-gathering activities in another state's exclusive economic zone, it is hard to explain this as friendly behavior that is "harmless" and undertaken in "good faith." Additionally, if the US Navy does not plan to open its door for other countries' surveillance ships to conduct military intelligence-gathering operations in the sea areas off Norfolk and Newport, why does not the United States allow China the same?"[42]

After the most recent set of incidents, China and the United States traded accusations and charges. General Fan Changlong, vice chairman of China's Central Military Commission, demanded that "the United States should halt its 'close-in' aerial and naval surveillance of China." Daniel Russel countered that "the United States is justified in carrying out surveillance flights in East Asia given a lack of transparency in China's military buildup."[43] In the first term of the Obama administration, as a member of the National Security Council, Russel had helped to lay the groundwork for the American "rebalance" to Asia.

Peter Dutton sums up the current state of play as follows: "The United States and China have fundamentally different views . . . and that these views flow from strategic mistrust and from divergent conceptions of law . . ."[44] In light of that reality, Hagel did issue a useful word of advice: "[R]estraint is critically important on these issues, especially at this time."[45]

Mutually Assured Restraint

Facing the real possibility that the United States might stumble into a new Cold War with China, Etzioni reached back to his earlier work and unveiled an updated version of the gradualist approach as a way to head off an unintended and undesired clash with China. Drawing on the proactive approach of "Mutually Assured Restraint" (MAR), Etzioni has proposed that both nations: (1) pare back their military buildups and deployments; (2) place strict limits on the deployment of offensive weapons systems (either directed by China against US allies and installations or by the United States against China); (3) eschew confrontational approaches in all spheres of the global commons (including cyberspace); and (4) reduce their military deployments to "reduce the risks of unintended conflagrations."[46] Of particular importance is the proposal that "countries and territories on China's borders would be treated not as contested areas that both powers attempt to include in their military alliances, but as neutral buffer zones—similar to Austria during the Cold War."[47] In essence, MAR would guarantee to China that no state on its land frontiers would be incorporated into any US-led security alliance. This proposal would have critical implications for the current rapprochement with Vietnam, for outreach to India, for security activity in Southeast Asia, and for alliance with South Korea should the peninsula be reunified at any point in the near future. Etzioni sought to counter suggestions that MAR would, in effect, be abandoning US allies and partners in the region. He suggested that while a pullback of frontline US forces could help reduce tensions and the possibility of an accidental clash with China, U.S.

commitments to allies and partners in the region could "be supported via the remote projection of force"[48]—reviving his Cold War concept of remote deterrence. In keeping with gradualist principles, all of these arrangements that provided for restraint—whether deployment of missiles or a renunciation of cyber-warfare techniques—would be closely vetted and verified. Etzioni thus proposed a return to his earlier recommendations to establish agreements that provide for monitoring and a series of confidence building measures (CBMs) so that neither side misinterprets the actions of the other.

Further revolutions in military affairs have occurred since the 1960s, especially with regard to recent developments that enable precision targeting, as well as greater speed in transporting and supplying forces. Therefore, Etzioni maintained that the United States could afford to relax its frontline posture along China's front doors (the coastal regions), and to avoid triggering Chinese concerns about the potential for encirclement from Southern and Central Asia. The United States could still surge naval and air forces into the region on short notice if there was a security threat. Etzioni argued that a pullback would give Beijing the psychological space to, in turn, make diplomatic concessions—without significantly jeopardizing America's overall strategic position should China fail to respond to such overtures.[49]

As part of such a pullback, MAR calls for an end to surveillance missions along China's borders. Etzioni recognized that this would complicate matters for US strategic planners, but maintained that other means of technical collection would make up any of the gaps in intelligence that termination of the existing ship and air patrols would entail. In return, he expressed guarded optimism that restraint demonstrated by the United States in this area might lead the Chinese to voluntarily restrain activities that the United States would find objectionable, such as cyberespionage. Etzioni also believes that the implementation of a MAR strategy might make Beijing more willing to negotiate verifiable limits on offensive weapons systems such as antiship missiles and systems that are currently deployed against Taiwan, Japan, and other states in the region. In return for China accepting such limits, Etzioni argues for the United States to refrain from deploying its most advanced platforms in the Asia-Pacific region and to limit its overall military presence.[50]

Etzioni's contention is that creating a certain degree of space and separation between the United States and China will allow Beijing and Washington to focus more of their attention on pursuing jointly shared interests and a common agenda—by not allowing points of friction to dominate the relationship.[51] This contention parallels recommendations that have been made by Hugh White, a former senior Australian defense official who himself argues that

> Washington and Beijing [need] to agree on a new regional order that goes some way to satisfying both of them, thus providing a durable basis for peace and stability in Asia. No one can say just what such an order would look like, but realistically it must give China a bigger leadership role than it has had until now and preserve a strong U.S. role as well. In essence, China and the United States would need to find a way to share power with one another as equals.[52]

Since China is not a revolutionary power that seeks to spread its ideology throughout the world[53], there is no ideological basis for a Cold War-style rivalry between the two powers. That leaves geopolitical friction. MAR is meant to provide an escape from the "Thucydides Trap" by reducing the prospects of an incident or accident that could spark confrontations. Beyond reducing tensions, however,

> Etzioni is hopeful that MAR could lay the basis for a diplomatic settlement of the outstanding maritime territorial claims in the South and East China seas. If restraint prevails over a head-to-head approach—with the assumption being that the United States will back the claims of its allies to the hilt—Etzioni believes compromise solutions (including proposals for joint sovereignty over disputed islands or consortia to allocate resources to all claimants), which have been used to settle disputes over similarly contested territories in Europe and Eurasia, could similarly come to pass in East Asia. If the military postures now present in the area could be relaxed, it might be possible to discuss compromises, swaps, and collaborative regimes to share resources. Indeed, there is an important precedent: the seemingly-intractable border disputes between the Soviet Union and the People's Republic of China, which flared up into open conflict in 1969 and which were similarly judged to be insolvable, began to be seriously addressed after Mikhail Gorbachev took deliberate steps to reduce the Soviet military posture in the Far East. All outstanding territorial claims between Beijing and the successor states of the Soviet Union were settled during the 1990s—in part because the collapse of the USSR removed what was seen as an existential threat to the People's Republic and created the psychological space needed to conduct meaningful negotiations and to reach compromise settlements.[54]

MAR is meant to respond to former US ambassador to China J. Stapleton Roy's challenge for a "policy approach that will make a stronger and more prosperous China less threatening to U.S. interests."[55] Etzioni believes it provides a road map for the United States and China to be able to meet what many in both countries believe is the foremost challenge facing both Washington and Beijing: to build a "new relationship" that would "mitigate conflict in Asia."[56] As Etzioni himself noted, it is a strategy of accommodation and reasonable compromise that "would require China to acknowledge the legitimacy of the US presence in the Western Pacific, and the United States to allow its rival a sphere of influence that reflects regional realities."[57]

MAR might find support among some of the states of the region that are concerned about the destabilizing impacts of a Sino-American rivalry. As Singapore's Foreign Minister K. Shanmugam noted, "All ASEAN (Association of South East Asian Nations) Member States want the best possible relationship with the major powers. No ASEAN Member State wants to have to choose among the major powers."[58] In particular, a MAR approach would create a framework to allow China and the United States to be able to engage each other. The worry of many countries in the region is that a breakdown between Washington and Beijing—an inability to manage the relationship—would be "disastrous" for them, especially if they were then forced to take sides.[59]

MAR: Making the Grade?

Does MAR pass the test devised by former US National Security Advisor Stephen Hadley to identify the most critical issues any new approach to US-China relations must be able to address? Hadley argued that it must cover the following areas:

- Acceptance by the United States of the "peaceful rise" of China as a global power
- Acceptance by China of the continued U.S. role as a stabilizing presence in the Asia-Pacific region and globally
- Mutual recognition that the prosperity and success of each nation is in the best interests of the other
- Mutual recognition that each nation's success is not "zero-sum" but "win win"—that the success of one can contribute to the success of the other
- Commitment by the two countries to build their relationship by constructing patterns of cooperation based on mutual interest, mutual benefit, and mutual respect
- Acting together to manage areas of continuing difference or dispute so that they do not undermine cooperation or degenerate into confrontation or conflict[60]

A major step forward along the lines outlined by Etzioni occurred during between US President Barack Obama and Chinese President Xi

Jinping at the November 2014 summit of the APEC conclave in Beijing, China. The United States and China concluded a Military Maritime Consultative Agreement in 1998 that was meant to ensure that there would be no accidents when US and Chinese naval and air forces operated in close proximity. Further talks on putting the theory into practice had stalled for many years, and after some of the incidents where Chinese and US aircraft or vessels had had close encounters, military dialogues were even suspended or downgraded. In June 2013 at a meeting at Sunnylands in Rancho Mirage, California, President Xi Jinping restarted the process by offering drafts to President Barack Obama of two agreements on CBMs. The drafts were finalized and signed at a bilateral meeting the APEC summit. The first agreement requires timely notification by both sides of any major military maneuvers taking place in the region. The second provides for a code of conduct when the ships and planes of either state come into contact with each other—to help avoid some of the near accidents of recent years.[61] In assessing the impact of these two agreements, David Shambaugh concluded:

> The military MOUs [Memorandum of Understanding] are very important confidence building measures (CBMs) that will hopefully not only reduce the risk of military accidents and the possibility of escalation after accidents—but also will become the basis for further such CBMs in the future (mutual notification on ballistic missile launches is being discussed). Until now, the Chinese side has steadfastly rebuffed American entreaties to enter into such agreements, as Beijing argued (wrongly) that such agreements only occur between adversaries such as the United States and former Soviet Union during the Cold War. Following almost two decades (dating back to the Clinton administration) of refusing to negotiate or sign such agreements, the Chinese side has now crossed an important conceptual threshold by entering into such CBMs with the United States. The international seas and airspace adjacent to China (where U.S. military forces regularly patrol) are now safer places owing to these agreements. Taken together with intensified military-to-military exchanges over the past year, perhaps the increasingly acute "security dilemma" between the two powers is relaxing somewhat.[62]

What now remains to be seen is whether these two initial agreements will be deepened and expanded to cover additional activity. Bonnie Glaser notes that

> progressing to advance notification of major military activities and expanding the scope of military activities to include ballistic missile

and ASAT [Anti-Satellite Weapons] tests will add more substance.... As is the case with any agreement, implementation is key, and the provisions in these agreements should be mandatory rather than voluntary when both sides are ready. Periodic meetings to discuss compliance and any violations that occur will also contribute to the shared goals of reducing misunderstanding and building a sustained and substantive bilateral military relationship."[63]

Further advances in formalizing and institutionalizing additional CBMs would be an important indicator that the MAR approach has legs and could serve as a viable approach to avoiding a Sino-American Cold War.

MAR also taps into a geopolitical assessment that argues that fundamental US security interests in the Pacific are not *ipso facto* in conflict with China's efforts to ensure that its geopolitical neighborhood is friendly and responsive to its concerns. A number of strategists have argued that, despite its maritime buildup, China's primary sphere of influence remains centered in the heart of the Asian continent, whereas the American interest lies in the offshore zones of Northeast Asia and the maritime regions of Southeast Asia. Chinese predominance (although not outright domination) in the heart of Asia does not threaten US interests. This is in contrast to the situation during the Cold War where the Soviet Union and the United States were competing for influence and control in Europe, and where the two superpower blocs were overlapping and physically contiguous.[64] Thus, as Robert Ross argued, there is no need for rivalry between China and the United States, if each side is prepared to let the other enjoy a leading position in their respective zones. Moreover, the main areas where these spheres overlap—Korea, Taiwan, and the islands of the South China Sea—can be managed to prevent conflict, perhaps via some sort of mutual arrangement.[65] This follows Etzioni's own assessment that the "West could tolerate some expansion of China's regional influence" without fundamentally damaging its own security or fatally compromising the security of America's treaty allies in the Asia-Pacific region.[66]

Other members of the US national security establishment have endorsed elements of MAR or provided their own recommendations that parallel those offered by Etzioni. In 2014, James Steinberg (who had been deputy secretary of state under Hillary Clinton during Barack Obama's first term in office and who, in 2009, had proffered a framework for strategic reassurance of China[67]) and Michael O'Hanlon released their own proposals for avoiding the Thucydides Trap in the US.-China relationship. Many of them echo Etzioni's own recommendations, including: (1) limits on deployments of Chinese missiles and other offensive military systems near Taiwan in return for the scaling back by the United States of its arms sales to the Taipei regime; (2) a binding pledge that China would commit to using only peaceful means for pursuing reunification with Taiwan in return for a lasting guarantee from Washington that no Taiwanese declaration of independence would ever be recognized or supported; (3) a commitment that North Korea would remain a neutral buffer area in return for China not demanding the departure of US forces from South Korea as a precondition for eventual reunification of the peninsula; (4) pursuit of further arms-control initiatives, agreed-upon limits in defense spending, and other confidence-building measures; (5) an American cap on the number of precision strike platforms and strict limits on the deployment of any theater ballistic missile defense system (so as not to pose a challenge to the Chinese nuclear deterrent) in return for Chinese limits on the size of its nuclear force; and (6) the acceptance by the United States of strict limits on the types and numbers of surveillance and intelligence missions undertaken in close proximity to China—but with a corresponding Chinese acceptance of the right of America (and that of other countries) to navigate freely through Chinese maritime zones.[68]

Former Secretary of State Henry Kissinger has coined the term "coevolution" to describe his preferred policy approach to China.[69] Arguing that US efforts to "contain" China (or Chinese efforts to push the United States out of Asian affairs) will be counterproductive, Kissinger hopes that the creation of a "Pacific Community" would be the means by which to decrease tensions, and, just as Etzioni has also asserted, provide a framework for cooperation on common interests to be nurtured. Kissinger maintains that such an approach "means that both countries pursue their domestic imperatives, cooperating where possible, and adjust their relations to minimize conflict. Neither side endorses all the aims of the other or presumes a total identity of interests, but both sides seek to identify and develop complementary interests."[70] Indeed, one proposal derived from Kissinger's writings both on China in particular, and subsequently on the international order in the twenty-first century, closely aligns with Etzioni's advocacy of both sides taking steps taken to provide reassurance: the idea of a US-China reinsurance treaty. Such an agreement, modeled on the nineteenth-century agreements developed by Otto von Bismarck, would provide guarantees that neither country would take advantage of any conflict or trouble the other gets into with third parties. Such an arrangement is meant to reassure China that the United States would not back a coalition of local Asian states in any conflict with China (say, over competing territorial or maritime claims), while Washington would be reassured that Beijing would not take steps to solidify any sort of global-balancing coalition against the United States.[71]

Yet concerns remain: would MAR be interpreted by the Chinese national security establishment as a desire to reduce tensions, or as a sign of a lessening American commitment to Asian security? If the latter, then it runs the risk of further encouraging "Beijing in pursuing opportunities to overturn the global and particularly the regional order by reinforcing its narrative of America in decline."[72] Analysts like Joseph Bosco have argued that MAR-like proposals send the wrong signal to Beijing of American strategic ambiguity. Instead, Bosco advises, "The president should . . . draw a red line across the Asia Pacific region in response to China's threats of force in the Taiwan Strait, the South China Sea, and the East China Sea. The line would also transverse the Korean Peninsula at the 38th Parallel."[73] He thus advises, not a pullback of US forces, but a determination to patrol and enforce the frontlines in order to send a clear signal to Beijing and to other countries in the area that the United States is planning to abide by a "coherent deterrent policy covering the entire region" in an attempt to to prevent any misunderstandings.[74]

Thus, Bosco's advice directly clashes with Etzioni's call for the creation of "buffer zones" surrounding China. Etzioni's resurrection of his Cold War-era proposal for extending the Austria precedent, in its twentieth century Asia-Pacific form, would call for countries surrounding China to be formally recognized by agreement as neutral states, to belong to no military alliances, and to have neither US nor Chinese forces stationed on their territory. He envisions a North Korea (post-Kim Jong-un) and Vietnam as two such states that might be constituted as such neutral states.[75] The problem, of course, is that

> the term (and the Austria analogy) conjures up the image of a belt of surrounding states that are at worst forced to become satellites of their powerful geographic neighbor—with significant interference in both their foreign and domestic affairs; and that are at best "Finlandized," that is, expected to undertake a precarious balancing act to accommodate the wishes of the great power next door while preserving as much of its sovereignty as possible. Neither prospect

fits in well with declared U.S. policy that every state should have the full right to freely choose its policies, alliances, and commitments—particularly when those commitments reflect the will of that country's majority—without fear of coercion from any of the major powers.[76]

Indeed, Vietnam is not particularly interested in such a status, preferring to forge closer security ties with the United States precisely to help act as a counterweight to its large northern neighbor—to gain the United States as a "security warranty" against pressure exerted by Beijing.[77] In turn, this aspect of the MAR proposal contradicts current US policy, as reiterated in 2013 by Vice President Joe Biden: "We will not recognize any nation having a sphere of influence. It will remain America's view that sovereign states have the right to make their own decisions and choose their own alliances. All that remains the U.S. position; it will not change."[78]

Moreover, MAR runs up directly against the long-standing US preference for forward engagement. It flies against the current strategy of not only re-energizing long-standing bilateral security alliances, but also seeking new partnerships with states that historically were not part of the American network. The intent is a way to multi-lateralize these relationships in order to create an overarching Asian network of alliances.[79] In particular, the US security network in the region, and the access to bases it provides, is seen as providing the United States with the means to anchor its presence in the region and maintain its status as a *de facto* "resident power."[80] This latter point is critical, because Washington has consistently rejected Chinese efforts to exclude the United States from deliberations on Asian-wide issues on the grounds that the United States is a power that is extraneous to purely Asian concerns. In conceiving of itself as a *de facto* Asian power, therefore, the United States has sought to insert itself into long-standing problems between China and its neighbors, notably offering its services to broker disputes over the South China Sea.[81]

Some of the concerns about MAR-style proposals are that efforts to reassure China would weaken the US security commitment to Japan.[82] The belief of Tokyo that Washington was no longer automatically committed to its defense could lead to negative ramifications, not only for US policy but also for the overall stability of the region. The defense alliance, up to this point, has been an important reason for Japan not to remilitarize—a state of affairs that all Asian states, including China, would prefer to keep intact. In addition, the alliance remains the "linchpin" of the US position in the Asia-Pacific region, and the risk of throwing that equity away in pursuit of what could end up being the chimera of improved relations with China may not be worth the risk.[83]

Beyond that immediate issue, there is the problem of what standard of threat would be used in pursuit of a MAR-based agenda. One of the principal objections raised to Etzioni's proposals has been the axiom that China and the United States should reduce their offensive postures. This leaves open the question as to whether a Chinese capability that no longer menaces US platforms might still be viewed as a threat by a US ally. In turn, China is unlikely to give up on both systems (including its arsenal of missiles), as well as bases that might be used in an offensive manner but that Beijing views as absolutely vital in maintaining an adequate defensive deterrent. Thus, as Michael Haas observes, "It is difficult to see how China could retain a sufficient level of military capability to accomplish these goals without "threaten[ing] other nations or the international commons."[84]

Moreover, as Chinese power increases, there are concerns that the adoption of a MAR-style strategy—particularly the components dealing with arms control, pullbacks from forward positions, and limits on defense spending—would weaken U.S. deterrent capabilities . Some argue that these capabilities increasingly must rest on America's capacity to forcefully project power, not simply into the Asian theater, but directly (if necessary, against China itself), to keep open the sea lanes and to provide access to the coastline. The so-called "Air-Sea Battle" (ASB) concept, renamed in January 2015 as the "Joint Concept for Access and Maneuver in the Global Commons,"[85] is meant to provide a way to guide procurement for the US military, the development of future capabilities, and how forces would be employed in theater. It is not, in theory, directed against China specifically. Instead, Rear Admiral James G. Foggo III, the assistant deputy chief of Naval Operations for Operations, Plans and Strategy, defines it as "simply put, a set of ideas that preserves freedom of access in the global commons in the face of emerging anti-access and area denial threats. . . . The overarching objective of the Air-Sea Battle Concept is to gain and maintain freedom of action in the global commons."[86] But it is designed to persuade any potential competitor to the US strategic position in Asia (or in any other part of the world) that, in the words of Andrew Krepinevich, "he cannot achieve his objective" and that if he attempts it "he will suffer so much as a result that his anticipated costs will outweigh his gains."[87] With the possible exception of a resurgent Russia, no other major power fits the bill. As a result, others have drawn the conclusion that "Air-Sea Battle is all about convincing the Chinese that we will win this competition."[88]

The concept formerly known as ASB and MAR are not easily reconcilable, because the "Joint Concept" would require both increased spending and the maintenance of a forward-deployed military, as well as continued security engagement and cooperation with regional allies. Thus, there are concerns that the adoption of MAR might preclude the United States from meeting its obligations to its partners and allies, by inhibiting exercises, joint procurement, and deployment of American forces in theater.[89] Implicit in this argument is the assumption that creating geopolitical space for China as a gesture of reassurance creates a vacuum that Beijing will move rapidly to fill. However, other strategists have argued that the United States could implement the recommendations put forward by Etzioni without significant risk to the US strategic position or fatally compromising allied security. Etzioni himself has cited several options, among them the "War at Sea" method enunciated by Jeffrey Kline and Wayne Hughes of the Naval Postgraduate School, or the "Offshore Control Strategy" proposed by retired Colonel T. X. Hammes of the National Defense University. Both of these approaches call for using military power to contain China's efforts to extend its power from its coastal bases further out into the Pacific. These efforts would reinforce allies to guarantee their defense. Further, as necessary, the efforts would enable the creation of a maritime exclusion zone that would keep lines of communication open for US allies in the region, while putting pressure on China's ability to import or export key goods and resources.[90] In assessing these approaches, Etzioni concludes that they would indeed "allow the United States to achieve its objectives of protecting its allies and maintaining free access to sea lanes, while giving China space to back down."[91] This issue cannot be conclusively settled, however, since the determination of acceptable strategic risk remains in the eye of the beholder. This is especially true for the determination as to whether the Chinese military, even with increased spending and technological developments, does in fact pose a serious threat to US and allied security that would not be deterrable under these proposals. For instance, Bernard Cole argues that "contrary to opinions that are too widespread in the United States, Chinese military modernization during the past quarter century has been relatively moderate. . . . There is little in China's decades-old program of naval modernization that would support an offensive maritime strategy."[92] If this assessment

89

is correct, then a MAR strategy could be adopted without seriously jeopardizing American security interests for the foreseeable future.

Ultimately, however, any proposal that shifts the United States away from a strategy of forward presence and engagement in the region to remote deterrence and a more offshore approach to regional security is not likely to gain traction in the US national security establishment. For all the abstract diplomatic talk about Washington welcoming China's rise, the reality is that "China must rise in Asia before it can rise globally." Therefore, to the extent that China is required to divert attention and resources to balances other powers in Asia, it can never emerge as a true global peer competitor to the United States. This is a subtext as to why the "United States attaches high value to local Asian powers that can exert direct influence in the region."[93] In turn, the Chinese foreign-policy community is very aware of this challenge. In interpreting the conclusions reached at the December 2014 Central Work Conference on Foreign Relations, Timothy Heath concluded, "China realizes it must secure its geostrategic flanks to prepare the country's ascent into the upper echelons of global power. Chinese leaders are deeply aware of historical precedents in which aspirants to regional dominance in Asia and Europe fell victim to wars kicked off by clashes involving neighboring powers."[94]

Barring a major domestic catastrophe, however, China will continue to rise. Thus, as Hadley notes, "The United States will have to accept that as China's economy grows, its military will also expand and that its naval forces will increasingly take on a global presence and a global role."[95] The gamble, as Hadley and others recognize, is that China is also prepared to compromise with the United States and to work constructively with Washington in dealing with both regional and global issues. Yet the United States may not want to take that risk. During his tenure, there have always been concerns about the extent to which Deng Xiaoping's aphorism for guiding China's foreign policy—"hide and bide" (the *taoguangyanghui* policy)—bodes for present-day policymaking. Many have questioned whether the phrase is intended to conceal China's real intentions and to make whatever agreements on paper are needed in order to give Beijing the time to put new capabilities into the field and, at some point in the future, present its demands.[96] China remains, to American eyes, an opaque society, and the problem remains that analysts and policymakers can look at the same set of facts about China and draw very different conclusions about Beijing's true intentions.[97]

Would MAR serve Chinese strategic interests, and would the leadership in Beijing take steps of their own to validate the concept and to reassure American skeptics of its peaceful intentions? Some of its precepts might resonate with a foreign-policy establishment that sees the promotion of nonalignment on the part of middle and rising powers, especially in the Asia-Pacific region, as a way to create "global strategic space" and so weaken some of the pressures that the United States might be able to bring to bear upon China.[98] MAR might be seen as an improvement on what is generally perceived to be the default US policy status on China, described by Yuan Peng, the deputy director of the Institute of American Studies at the China Institute of Contemporary International Relations, as "containment plus engagement."[99] MAR might also be welcomed by the Chinese if it means that the United States may increase its efforts to encourage its regional allies not "to harden their bargaining positions toward Beijing" and not "to pursue their territorial claims to the extent of increasing the risk of conflict with China and escalating into larger international conflicts."[100]

Some experts believe that, as China transitions to becoming a developed country and as it relies more on the mechanisms of an information society to sustain its economy and political systems, "mutual vulnerability calls for mutual restraint in the nuclear, space, and cyber domains." The Chinese leadership might become more open to negotiating MAR-style accords because, as David Gompert and Phillip Saunders argue, "a rising sense of China's own vulnerabilities in space and cyberspace . . . should in time make Chinese leaders more receptive to mutual restraint."[101]

However, China's long-term goal does seem to be to create a concert of major and middle powers capable of establishing and maintaining a stable security order for Asian affairs, one in which China's position as the head of the hierarchy would be recognized.[102] China has also expressed a strong preference for the United States to be excluded when dealing with purely Asian regional issues.[103] It continues to view US alliances in the region as part of a strategy of encirclement and containment,[104] and will, at best, merely tolerate rather than accept, "a continuing US military and naval presence in the Asia Pacific in support of our existing alliance relationships."[105] And even if the United States were to pull back some of its forces, the reality is that "any level of forward military presence that the U.S. would define as consistent with its legitimate defensive needs, and those of its allies, is likely to be perceived as a potential threat in Beijing."[106] The prevailing view is that China's effort to "obtain regional dominance in the Asia-Pacific" has as "its primary impediment" the United States.[107] And while China would certainly be very satisfied with a United States that pulled back from security cooperation with Vietnam and recognized northern Korea (if not the entire peninsula) as a neutral buffer, would Beijing be as interested in returning the favor? If, in the next decade, Taiwan was to negotiate an arrangement on unification with China, would the Chinese government seek to reassure the United States and its allies, principally Japan, by not militarizing the island or using it as a base to project Chinese naval and air power further into the Pacific?[108]

Moreover, China, in coming years, may also question the utility of creating neutral zones around its territory as it redefines its own security needs to support its own version of forward presence. An interesting op-ed piece by Xu Yao, affiliated with the Communist Party School of the Chongqing Municipal Committee, explores ways in which China's traditional stance of noninterference in the sovereign affairs of others might be reconciled with the establishment of overseas bases.[109]

Much depends on how the Chinese, moving forward, operational-ize what Beijing has announced is its preferred model for structuring US-China relations in response to the "responsible stakeholder" para-digm: the so-called "new model of big power relations." Chinese lead-ers have put forward that this concept is based on the following three precepts: "no conflict or confrontation, mutual respect, and win–win cooperation."[110] This does not preclude adoption of a MAR-derived policy approach and in fact could be useful in framing the issues. Some analysts have argued that, in fact, this "new model" for relations "is constructive and helpful so long as it can effectively guide and encour-age a nonconfrontational foreign policy in China."[111]

It also helps that the US government has expressed its willingness to consider working under the rubric of the "new model." Statements by both President Barack Obama and his National Security Advisor Susan Rice have indicated America is committed to finding a "new model" for relations, one that would manage Sino-American competi-tion and policy differences between the two countries while anchoring cooperation in a more durable framework.[112]

Yet when it comes to matters of strategic reassurance and restraint, Beijing continues to insist that "the ball is entirely in the US's court."[113] It is not likely to take further steps as outlined by Etzioni or others who have laid out this type of agenda. At the same time, the United States may not be willing to embrace MAR-style policies because such strategies "would surely mean some acceptance, on both sides, of a transferal [sic] of power or of reduced power status and responsibility. . . . For China, its recent success may justify this way of thinking, but the United States remains preoccupied with defending its 'second to none' position (in President Barack Obama's words)." This is why some experts believe that such strategies will not be adopted as part of a new US approach for engaging China.[114]

A Need for MAR?

Some might argue that, even in the absence of strategic reassurance as part of the Sino-American relationship, simple deterrence will continue to keep the peace in Asia. However, Robert A. Manning and Barry Pavel remain concerned about the continuing lack of a strategic reassurance framework as part of the US-China relationship:

> Today, there is no effective structure of arms control, nor sufficient mechanisms for strategic consultation, crisis management, confidence building, reassurance or transparency measures with China that adequately manage risk. For nearly two decades, U.S. administrations have sought a strategic dialogue with China. But Beijing has been unwilling to engage, citing the huge discrepancy between U.S. and Chinese nuclear forces, and thus, rejecting the idea of arms control. Beijing also is uncomfortable with analogies to the USSR with the implication that China is an adversary.

> One reason for this is that China has a strategic culture in which transparency has been viewed as a weapon of the strong against the weak, and uncertainty and unpredictability are viewed as providing an advantage rather than a liability. . . . For the United States, the uncertain size and structure of China's expanding nuclear force as well as its military doctrine, its anti-space and cyber-activities along with the continued development of its Anti-Access and Area-Denial (A2/AD) conventional military capabilities are all sources of concern.[115]

Robert Merry argues that, in order to prevent conflict from erupting between the United States and China, the Obama administration (and subsequent US presidential teams) ought to "follow a carefully-calibrated policy in which America shows some empathy to legitimate Chinese security concerns while also demonstrating that it will not simply wink at bellicose actions. . . . Areas of cooperation should include proposing clearer rules of the game. A détente also needs to be encouraged between China and its neighbors."[116]

China's neighbors, even those who are U.S. allies, are also interested in a more stable, peaceful, and predictable US-China relationship:

> While none of China's neighbors want to live under China's shadow and most regional powers have been publicly or privately pleased to see the stronger US commitment to the Asia–Pacific region, very few of them can afford to antagonize a rising China. They recognize that an escalation of the geopolitical rivalry between the US and China could destroy the regional stability and prosperity.[117]

However, Japan and South Korea would be very concerned about how their existing security guarantees would be honored by the United States if forward presence was abandoned. A major unintended and undesirable consequence of carelessness in applying the MAR framework would be to incentivize both of those states to consider developing their own independent nuclear capabilities—especially given Etzioni's commitment to promoting deproliferation.

It will take conscious choices on the part of both American and Chinese leaders to bring this about. Etzioni's MAR proposals are part of the conversation as members of the extended foreign-policy communities of both countries look for ways and templates to channel the relationship away from conflict.[118] However, this "new model can be built only if China and the US demonstrate a strategic restraint and maintain a delicate balance of power to prevent their rivalry from boiling over into a new Cold War."[119]

Some of the recent signs are not positive. China has begun to strengthen its military presence in disputed maritime zones in both the South and East China Seas. Moreover, in a worrying development that runs up against the gradualist advocacy of putting distance between the forward outposts of both sides, the proposed Chinese installation at Nanji Island would put Chinese forces that much closer to US and Japanese units stationed on Okinawa.[120] Such a development would strengthen China's position to defend its claim to the Senkaku/Diaoyou islands, and enforce its air defense exclusion zone in the East China Sea. Delays in getting an agreement in place to regulate encounters between US and Chinese military aircraft are, in turn, having a negative impact on efforts to expand Chinese and American military exchanges—one of the critical ways in which to build the relationships needed to help avoid misunderstandings and reduce tensions.[121]

Nevertheless, it should be possible to anchor US-China relations in what Da Wei, the director of the American Studies Institute at the China

Institute of Contemporary International Relations has described as a "stable framework, within which the two countries' divergences can be controlled and managed so that they won't overthrow the overall situation. In the meantime, the two countries can engage in benign competition, no side can overwhelm the other. The two countries may also come into active cooperation and truly play a global leadership role together."[122] MAR may yet have a role to play in the emergence of that stable framework.

Notes

1. Stephen D. Biddle, *American Grand Strategy After 9/11: An Assessment* (Carlisle, PA: U.S. Army War College Strategic Studies Institute, 2005), 11.
2. For instance, Alexander Rahr argued that while geopolitical tensions between countries may remain, war is an impossibility in the conditions of the twenty-first century. Nadezhda Ermolova, "Zhivem v XXI veke: Voina Nevozmozhna," *Rossiiskaia Gazeta*, April 16, 2014, http://www.rg.ru/2014/04/16/rar.html.
3. Josef Joffe, "'Bismarck' or 'Britain'? Toward an American Grand Strategy after Bipolarity," *International Security* 19:4 (Spring 1995), 117.
4. Richard Haass, *The Reluctant Sheriff: the United States After the Cold War* (New York: Council on Foreign Relations, 1997), 125.
5. Ray Takeyh, *Hidden Iran: Paradox and Power in the Islamic Republic* (New York: Times Books, 2006), 68–69.
6. Ray Takeyh, *Guardians of the Revolution: Iran and the World in the Age of the Ayatollahs* (Oxford: Oxford University Press, 2009), esp. 200, 207.
7. Anthony Lake, "Confronting Backlash States," *Foreign Affairs* 73:2 (March/April 1994), 45.
8. See, for instance, Jusuf Wanandia, "ASEAN's China strategy: Towards Deeper Engagement," *Survival* 38:3 (1996), 117–128.
9. Rosita Dellios, "China-United States Relations: The New Superpower Politics," Culture Mandala: The Bulletin of the Centre for East-West Cultural and Economic Studies 3:2 (August 1, 1999), 1, 12, http://epublications.bond.edu.au/cm/vol3/iss2/1.
10. Strobe Talbott, "U.S.-China Relations in a Changing World," *U.S.-China Relations in the Twenty-First Century: Policies, Prospects and Possibilities,* eds. Christopher Marsh and June Teufel Dreyer (Lanham, MD: Lexington Books, 2003), 2.
11. Graham Allison notes, "The historian's metaphor reminds us of the dangers two parties face when a rising power rivals a ruling power." "Avoiding Thucydides's Trap," *Financial Times*, August 22, 2012, archived at http://belfercenter.ksg.harvard.edu/publication/22265/avoiding_thucydidess_trap.html.
12. Colin S. Grey, *Defense Planning for National Security: Navigation Aids for the Mystery Tour* (Carlisle, PA: Strategic Studies Institute/Army War College, 2014), 19–20.
13. This was expressed, for instance, in the 2002 US National Security Strategy. Cf. George W. Bush, *The National Security Strategy of the United States of America* (Washington, DC: White House, September 2002), 5.

14. Robert B. Zoellick, "Whither China: From Membership to Responsibility?" Remarks to National Committee on U.S.-China Relations, New York City, September 21, 2005. Archived at http://2001-2009.state.gov/s/d/former/zoellick/rem/53682.htm.

15. Ibid.

16. See, for instance, the comments made by Secretary of State Hillary Clinton and Secretary of the Treasury Tim Geithner at the conclusion of the 4th Annual Strategic and Economic Dialogue. "Remarks at the Strategic and Economic Dialogue—U.S. Press Conference," Beijing, May 4, 2012, http://m.state.gov/md189315.htm.

17. John Lee, "China Won't Be a 'Responsible Stakeholder,'" Wall Street Journal, February 1, 2010, http://www.wsj.com/articles/SB10001424052748704722 304575037931817880328.

18. Evan S. Medeiros, China's International Behavior: Activism, Opportunism, and Diversification (Santa Monica, CA: RAND Corporation, 2009), 210–11.

19. John J. Mearsheimer, "Better to Be Godzilla than Bambi," Foreign Policy 146 (January/February 2005), 47–48.

20. Nikolas K. Gvosdev, "The Ethics of Avoiding Conflict with China," Ethics and International Affairs, March 16, 2014, http://www.ethicsandinternationalaffairs.org/2014/the-ethics-of-avoiding-conflict-with-china/.

21. Aaron L. Friedberg, "The Future of U.S.-China Relations: Is Conflict Inevitable?" International Security 30:2 (Autumn 2005), 42.

22. Hillary Clinton, "America's Pacific Century," Foreign Policy, October 11, 2011, http://foreignpolicy.com/2011/10/11/americas-pacific-century/.

23. Friedberg, 43.

24. "Barack Obama talks to "The Economist: An Interview with the President," The Economist, August 2, 2014, http://www.economist.com/blogs/democracyinamerica/2014/08/barack-obama-talks-economist.

25. Mark E. Manyin, Stephen D. Saggett, Ben Dolven, Susan W. Lawrence, Michael F. Martin, Ronald O'Rourke, and Bruce Vaughn, Pivot to the Pacific? The Obama Administration's "Rebalancing" Toward Asia, Congressional Research Service report R42448 (March 28, 2012), 8.

26. Clinton, op. cit.

27. Andrew S. Erickson and Adam P. Liff, "Not-So-Empty Talk: The Danger of China's 'New Type of Great-Power Relations" Slogan,'" Foreign Affairs, October 9, 2014, http://www.foreignaffairs.com/articles/142178/andrew-s-erickson-and-adam-p-liff/not-so-empty-talk.

28. Robert S. Ross, "Towards a Stable and Constructive China Policy," NBR Analysis 16:4 (December 2005), 35. This idea that the United States is attempting to get China to help shoulder the burdens of maintaining the international system it created can also be found in Wang Jianwei, "Setting the Stakes," Beijing Review 24 (2006), 22–23. A more negative assessment, that this effort at burden sharing is an attempt to hold back China, can be found in the comments of Wang Yiwei of Fudan University's Center for American Studies, cf. his "The United States Wants to Lighten its Hegemonic Burden," Huanqiu Shibao, June 7, 2006.

29. Ross, 35.

30. "China protests U.S. spy flights near its coast," Reuters, July 27, 2011, http://www.reuters.com/article/2011/07/27/us-china-usa-spy-idUSTRE76Q3YK20110727?feedType=RSS&feedName=topNews.

31. Bruce Gilley, "China's Discovery of Middle Powers," *Middle Powers and the Rise of China*, eds. Andrew O'Neill and Bruce Gilley (Washington, DC: Georgetown University Press, 2014), 48–49.

32. See, for instance, the article penned by General Peng Guangqin, entitled "New Defense Report in Pursuit of the Super-Hegemon," in *Liaowang (Outlook)*, February 13, 2006, as an example.

33. Quoted in Steve Erlanger, "Christopher to Meet His Chinese Counterpart," *New York Times*, March 20, 1996, http://www.nytimes.com/1996/03/20/world/christopher-to-meet-his-chinese-counterpart.html.

34. Andrew S. Erickson, *Chinese Anti-Ship Ballistic Missile (ASBM) Development: Drivers, Trajectories and Strategic Implications* (Washington, DC: Jamestown Foundation, May 2013), 5.

35. Michael Ellison, "China Eases Spy Plane Surveillance," *The Guardian*, July 29, 2001, http://www.theguardian.com/world/2001/jul/30/china.usa.

36. Jing Huang, "China's International Relations and Security Perspectives," *East and South-East Asia: International Relations and Security Perspectives*, ed. Andrew T.H. Tan (Abingdon, Oxon: Routledge, 2013), 13.

37. Amitai Etzioni, "Who Authorized Preparations for War with China?" *Yale Journal of International Affairs* 8:2 (Summer 2013), 38–39.

38. Erickson, 2.

39. See, for instance, the wish list of capabilities found in Jan Van Tol (with Mark Gunziger, Andrew Krepinevich, and Jim Thomas, *AirSea Battle: A Point-of-Departure Operational Concept* (Washington, DC: Center for Strategic and Budgetary Assessments, 2010), 81–94; see also J. Randy Forbes, "America's Asia Challenges: China, Air-Sea Battle and Beyond," *National Interest*, June 9, 2014, http://nationalinterest.org/feature/americas-asia-challenges-china-air-sea-battle-beyond-10623?page=show.

40. Jon Harper, "Chinese Warship Nearly Collided With USS Cowpens," *Stars and Stripes*, December 13, 2013, http://www.stripes.com/news/pacific/chinese-warship-nearly-collided-with-uss-cowpens-1.257478.

41. Quoted in Yu Zhirong, "Jurisprudential Analysis of the U.S. Navy's Military Surveys in the Exclusive Economic Zones of Coastal Countries," *Military Activities in the EEZ: A U.S.-China Dialogue on Security and International Law in the Maritime Commons* (China Maritime Studies no. 7), ed. Peter Dutton (Newport, RI: China Maritime Studies Institute/Naval War College, December 2010), 38.

42. Peng Guangqian, "China's Maritime Rights and Interests," *Military Activities in the EEZ*, 20, 21.

43. Both quoted in Mark J. Valenica, "U.S.-China Skirmishes Beg For Guidelines on 'Spying'," *The Japan Times*, October 16, 2014, http://www.japantimes.co.jp/opinion/2014/10/16/commentary/world-commentary/u-s-china-skirmishes-beg-for-guidelines-on-spying/.

44. Peter Dutton, "Introduction," *Military Activities in the EEZ*, 11.

45. Harper, op. cit.

46. Amitai Etzioni, "MAR: A Model for US-China Relations," *The Diplomat*, September 20, 2013, http://thediplomat.com/2013/09/mar-a-model-for-us-china-relations/.

47. Amitai Etzioni, "For a New Sino-American Relationship," *Huffington Post*, September 23, 2013, http://www.huffingtonpost.com/amitai-etzioni/for-a-new-sino-american-r_b_3976743.html.

48. Amitai Etzioni, "MAR or War," The Diplomat, October 17, 2013, http://thediplomat.com/2013/10/mar-or-war/.
49. Gvosdev, "Ethics of Avoiding," op. cit.
50. Ibid.
51. Etzioni, "MAR or War," op. cit.
52. Hugh White, "Australia's Choice: Will the Land Down Under Pick the United States or China?" Foreign Affairs, September 4, 2013, http://www.foreignaffairs.com/articles/139902/hugh-white/australias-choice.
53. Friedberg, 127.
54. Gvosdev, "Ethics of Avoiding," op. cit.
55. J. Stapleton Roy, "Opportunities and Challenges for U.S.-China Relations," U.S.-China Relations in the Twenty-First Century, 109.
56. Valencia, op. cit.
57. Amitai Etzioni, "Accommodating China," Survival: Global Politics and Strategy 55:2 (2013), 45, 48.
58. K. Shanmugam, "ASEAN and its Place in the Global Architecture," Horizons 2 (Winter 2015), 123.
59. Kishore Mahbubani, "ASEAN as a Living, Breathing Modern Miracle," Horizons 2 (Winter 2015), 140.
60. Stephen J. Hadley, "US-China: A New Model of Great Power Relations" (speech delivered at the Carnegie-Tsinghua Center for Global Policy, October 10, 2013), New Atlanticist, October 11, 2013, http://www.atlanticcouncil.org/blogs/new-atlanticist/us-china-a-new-model-of-great-power-relations.
61. Bonnie Glaser, "A Step Forward in US-China Military Ties: Two CBM Agreements," Asia Maritime Transparency Initiative, November 11, 2014, http://amti.csis.org/us-china-cbms-stability-maritime-asia/.
62. David Shambaugh, "A Step Forward in US-China Ties," ChinaUSFocus, November 14, 2014, http://www.chinausfocus.com/foreign-policy/a-step-forward-in-us-china-ties/.
63. Glaser, op. cit.
64. Friedberg, 129.
65. Robert S. Ross, "The Geography of the Peace: East Asia in the Twenty-First Century," International Security 23:4 (Spring 1999), 109–111.
66. Etzioni, "Accommodating China," 46.
67. James B. Steinberg, "East Asia and the Pacific: The Administration's Version of the US-China Relationship," Keynote Speech at Center for New America Security, September 24, 2009, http://www.cnas.org/files/multimedia/documents/Deputy%20Secretary%20James%20Steinberg's%20September%2024,%202009%20Keynote%20Address%20Transcript.pdf.
68. James Steinberg and Michael E. O'Hanlon, Strategic Reassurance and Resolve: U.S.-China Relations in the Twenty-First Century (Princeton, NJ: Princeton University Press, 2014), 209–11.
69. Henry Kissinger, On China (New York: Penguin Press, 2011), 526–30; see also his interview with CCTV America, on the eve of the Obama-Xi summit, on November 7, 2014, archived at http://www.cctv-america.com/2014/11/07/henry-kissinger-talks-with-cctv-about-us-china-relations.
70. Kissinger, 526.
71. See the discussion in Niall Ferguson, "K of the Castle," Times Literary Supplement, November 26, 2014, http://www.the-tls.co.uk/tls/public/article1488107.ece.

72. Richard Burt and Dimitri K. Simes, "The Republican Mission," *National Interest*, January/February 2015, published December 17, 2014, at *National Interest online*, http://nationalinterest.org/feature/the-republican-mission-11865?page=show.

73. Joseph A. Bosco, "Draw a Big Red Line in Asia," *National Interest*, February 5, 2014, http://nationalinterest.org/commentary/draw-big-red-line-asia-9826.

74. Ibid.

75. Etzioni, "For a New Sino-American," op. cit.

76. Gvosdev, "Ethics of Avoiding," op. cit.

77. Truong-Minh Vu and Nguyen Thanh Trung, "A U.S.-Vietnam Alliance or (still) a U.S.-China-Vietnam Triangle?" *International Policy Digest*, October 3, 2014, http://www.internationalpolicydigest.org/2014/10/03/u-s-vietnam-alliance-or-u-s-china-vietnam-triangle/.

78. Remarks by Vice President Joe Biden to the Munich Security Conference. Hotel Bayerischer Hof Munich, Germany, February 2, 2013, http://www.whitehouse.gov/the-press-office/2013/02/02/remarks-vice-president-joe-biden-munich-security-conference-hotel-bayeri.

79. David A Cooper and Toshi Yoshihara, "US Responses to Middle Powers and China," in *Middle Powers and the Rise of China*, 71.

80. Patrick M. Cronin, Daniel M. Kilman, and Abraham M. Denmark, *Renewal: Revitalizing the US-Japan Alliance* (Washington, DC: Center for a New American Security, 2010), 9.

81. Mark Landler, "Offering to Aid Talks, U.S. Challenges China on Disputed Islands," *New York Times*, July 24, 2010, http://www.nytimes.com/2010/07/24/world/asia/24diplo.html.

82. Ferguson, op. cit.

83. This assessment of the US-Japan alliance is based on description provided in Paul Smith, "China-Japan Relations and the Future Geopolitics of East Asia," *Asian Affairs: An American Review* 35:4 (2009), 242.

84. Michael Haas, "A MARred Alternative: Offense, Defense and U.S.-China Relations," *The Diplomat*, October 8, 2013, http://thediplomat.com/2013/10/a-marred-alternative-offense-defense-and-u-s-china-relations.

85. The concept was renamed in part to further downplay any sense that it was being directed at China in preparation for a forthcoming war, and also to give the land forces a greater role to play. Cf. Franz-Stefan Gady, "The Pentagon Just Dropped the Air Sea Battle Name," *The* Diplomat, January 22, 2015, http://thediplomat.com/2015/01/the-pentagon-just-dropped-the-air-sea-battle-name/.

86. Harry J. Kazianis, "Air Sea Battle Defined," *National Interest*, March 13, 2014, http://nationalinterest.org/commentary/airsea-battle-defined-10045.

87. Andrew F. Krepinevich, "Strategy in a Time of Austerity," *Foreign Affairs*, 91:6 (November/December 2012), http://www.foreignaffairs.com/articles/138362/andrew-f-krepinevich-jr/strategy-in-a-time-of-austerity.

88. Greg Jaffe, "U.S. Model for a Future War Fans Tensions with China and Inside Pentagon," *Washington Post*, August 1, 2012, http://articles.washingtonpost.com/2012-08-01/world/35492126_1_china-tensions-china-threatpentagon.

89. Haas, op. cit.

90. Jeffrey Kline and Wayne Hughes, "Between Peace and Air-Sea Battle: A War at Sea Strategy," *Naval War College Review*, 65, 4 (2012), esp. 36; 23; T. X. Hammes, "Strategy for an Unthinkable Conflict," *The Diplomat*,

July 27, 2012, http://thediplomat.com/flashpoints-blog/2012/07/27/military-strategy-for-an-unthinkable-conflict/, see also T. X. Hammes, *Offshore Control: A Proposed Strategy for an Unlikely Conflict*, 258 (Washington, DC: Strategic Forum, National Defense University Institute for National and Strategic Studies, 2012).

91. Etzioni, "Who Authorized," 42.
92. Bernard Cole, *Asian Maritime Strategies: Navigating Troubled Waters* (Washington, DC: Naval Institute Press, 2013), 208.
93. Cooper and Yoshihara, 71–72.
94. Timothy Heath, "China's Big Diplomacy Shift," *The Diplomat*, December 22, 2014, http://thediplomat.com/2014/12/chinas-big-diplomacy-shift/.
95. Hadley, op. cit.
96. Steinberg and O'Hanlon, 5.
97. Drawing here from observations made by the business community. Cf. Gady Epstein, "Panda Hugger Vs. Dragon Slayer," *Forbes*, January 29, 2010, http://www.forbes.com/2010/01/29/china-google-trade-war-beijing-dispatch.html.
98. Gilley, 54.
99. Quoted in Jonathan Czin, "Dragon-Slayer or Panda-Hugger? Chinese Perspectives on 'Responsible Stakeholder' Diplomacy," *Yale Journal of International Affairs* 2:2 (Spring/Summer 2007), 105.
100. Suisheng Zhao, "A New Model of Big Power Relations? China–US Strategic Rivalry and Balance of Power in the Asia-Pacific," *Journal of Contemporary China*, posted online on October 8, 2014, and accessed at http://dx.doi.org/10.1080/10670564.2014.953808.
101. David C. Gompert and Phillip C. Saunders, "Sino-American Strategic Restraint in an Age of Vulnerability, 2, 9 (Washington, DC: Strategic Forum, National Defense University Institute for National and Strategic Studies, January 2012), 2, 9.
102. Gilley, 58.
103. For instance, Foreign Ministry spokeswoman Jiang Yu, in commenting on American offers to help mediate disputes in the South China Sea, made it clear, "We resolutely oppose any country which has no connection to the South China Sea getting involved in the dispute." Quoted in Ben Blanchard and Huang Yan, "China tells U.S. to Keep Out of South China Sea Dispute," *Reuters*, September 21, 2010, http://www.reuters.com/article/2010/09/21/us-china-seas-idUSTRE68K1DB20100921.
104. For example, see Smith, 232, for how the US-Japan alliance is viewed.
105. Hadley, op. cit.
106. Haas, op. cit.
107. Zhao, op. cit.
108. See the discussion of Japan's strategic interest in Taiwan, in Smith, 238–239.
109. Xu Yao, "Overseas Military Bases Not Alliances," *China Daily*, January 14, 2015, http://usa.chinadaily.com.cn/opinion/2015-01/14/content_19312377.htm.
110. Zhao, op. cit.
111. Cheng Li and Lucy Xu, "Chinese Enthusiasm and American Cynicism: The 'New Type of Great Power Relation,'" *China US Focus*, December 4, 2014, http://www.chinausfocus.com/foreign-policy/chinese-enthusiasm-and-

american-cynicism-over-the-new-type-of-great-power-relations/#sthash.zwQWByQj.dpuf.

112. See the "Statement by the President to the US–China Strategic and Economic Dialogue," July 8, 2014, as released by The White House Office of the Press Secretary, http://www.whitehouse.gov/the-press-office/2014/07/08/statement-president-us-china-strategic-and-economic-dialogue; and remarks by National Security Advisor Susan E. Rice, "America's Future in Asia," November 20, 2013, http://www.whitehouse.gov/the-press-office/2013/11/21/remarks-prepared-delivery-national-security-advisor-susan-e-rice.

113. Zhao, op. cit.

114. Lanxin Xiang, "True Conservatives," *Survival: Global Politics and Strategy* 53:4 (2011), 199.

115. Robert A. Manning and Barry Pavel, "How to Stop the Scary Slide in U.S.-China Ties," *National Interest*, July 14, 2014, http://nationalinterest.org/feature/how-stop-the-scary-slide-us-china-ties-10865.

116. Robert W. Merry, "Asia First," *The National Interest* 130 (March/April 2014), 8.

117. Zhao, op. cit.

118. Etzioni's MAR concept has been endorsed by dozens of leading "public intellectuals" in both the United States and China and has been briefed to government officials. See, for instance, Amitai Etzioni, "Strategic Reassurance: An Important Agenda," *The Diplomat*, May 11, 2014, http://thediplomat.com/2014/05/strategic-reassurance-an-important-agenda/.

119. Zhao, op. cit.

120. Zachary Keck, "Confirmed: China Is Building a Military Base Near Japan," *National Interest*, January 26, 2015, http://nationalinterest.org/blog/the-buzz/confirmed-china-building-military-base-near-japan-12120.

121. Joan Johnson-Freese, "U.S. Pause of Mil-to-Mil Exchanges Threatens Maritime Cooperation," *China US Focus*, February 6, 2015, http://www.chinausfocus.com/foreign-policy/u-s-pause-of-mil-to-mil-exchanges-threatens-china-u-s-maritime-cooperation/#sthash.f4LQoxBx.dpuf.

122. Da Wei, "Operationalizing A New Model of Sino-US Relations Is Possible," *China US Focus*, November 18, 2014, http://www.chinausfocus.com/foreign-policy/operationalizing-a-new-model-of-sino-us-relations-is-possible/#sthash.8bfkXXCx.dpuf.

4

Building a Global Community? The Post-9/11 Experience

In his gradualist writings of the 1960s, Amitai Etzioni not only sketched out a roadmap for de-escalating and ultimately exiting the Cold War standoff between the superpowers, but also provided a blueprint for the shape of the international order that might follow. With the prospect of nuclear annihilation receding, Soviet-American competition channeled into more peaceful pursuits around social and economic development (the "intervention for progress"), and the first steps taken toward joint projects designed to tackle global problems, Etzioni felt that the foundations would be laid for a supranational global community. The first steps would be to reform the United Nations into a more effective and activist organization, ultimately creating conditions for a world government that would be formed based on the free association of states along federal lines.[1] Etzioni's confidence in the feasibility of this outline arose not from an idealistic belief in universal human brotherhood, but from the assessment that the traditional nation-state increasingly could not solve all of a country's national security issues. Etzioni believed that "many functions that were until recently carried out quite effectively by the nation-state now require more and more international cooperation."[2] In addition, he argued that economic trends would also lead to greater integration among previously separate national economies. Such integration would occur as barriers (both regulatory and technological) that had in the past inhibited the freer flow of goods, labor, and capital between states were eroded[3]—a process that would later be designated by the term "globalization."[4]

While other parts of the gradualist program (such as linking arms reductions with verifiable inspection regimes) were seen as practical proposals that might be adopted by the US government, any talk about "world government" smacked of utopian idealism and tended to be dismissed as irrelevant and unworkable by the foreign-policy establishment of the day.[5] As some reviewers noted, Etzioni had laid out a long-term goal—with the immediate focus being on "world stability through national action, reserving world government for the distant future."[6] But the prevailing sentiment within the US foreign-policy community has been that the nation-state remains the essential—and preferred—building block of the international order.[7] Thus, discussions of moving beyond the nation-state in favor of supranational institutions did not trigger as much interest from policymakers. Yet, even if the ultimate aim of a global authority or unified planetary administration seemed far-fetched, the case was made that there was indeed value in laying out such a vision; even if it would not be realized, it might help to provide some sensible guidelines for reformers intent on strengthening international cooperation and global stability.[8]

As the Cold War was winding down, there was optimism that the post-World War II system for management of international affairs—starting with the United Nations and encompassing both functional and regional organizations—might be able to operate as originally designed.[9] Indeed, some maintained that the "end of the Cold War has opened up new possibilities for creating a new world order based on the respect for and confidence in international institutions and collective action rather than superpower alliances and balance of power."[10] Some of these themes helped to influence the writing of the section of the State of the Union address delivered by President George H.W. Bush to Congress in January 1991. In those remarks, which justified the Gulf War, he delivered his well-known invocation of "a new world order, where diverse nations are drawn together in common cause to achieve the universal aspirations of mankind—peace and security, freedom, and the rule of law."[11] Bush's National Security Advisor, Brent Scowcroft, later remarked that the phrase was meant to encapsulate the hope that "the Great Powers would really have responsibility for security around the world" and that "the Great Powers could actually act as the framers of the U.N. [he] had in mind."[12] However, the Bush administration was not prepared to undertake a massive effort to reforge the global order; instead, it focused on a more modest agenda to plant the "institutional seeds" for eventual change by promoting "regional institutional frameworks that would extend and enhance America's influence in these areas and encourage democracy and open markets."[13]

The "seeds" strategy was continued and amplified by the Clinton administration, which adopted an "enlargement" approach. Using existing alliance networks in Europe and Asia as the basis for a new international order, the expectation was that, over time, these groupings would be expanded to encompass new members and thus serve as the building blocks for a more coordinated global system.

It was an article of faith in much of the US national security establishment—both within the Bush administration as well as among those who entered the subsequent Clinton administration—that the rest of the world would sooner or later enter Western-based institutions. The thought was that the time had arrived, in the aftermath of the Cold War, to move forward on "expanding and deepening the democratic project."[14] Then-Secretary of State Warren Christopher expressed his view, which reflected a bipartisan consensus in Washington: "We must now extent to the East the benefits—and obligations—of the same liberal trading and security order that have been pillars of strength for the West."[15] Multilateral institutions were seen as mechanisms to stabilize and to integrate the new and emerging market democracies into the Western democratic world.[16] The United States was encouraged to lay out criteria for membership that would create incentives for change, and to rework the guidelines for global institutions to ensure that these transformations would be "guaranteed."[17] In turn, via the imposition of conditionality and entrance criteria for new entrants to join Western-led institutions, the United States could ensure, as a Clinton administration official put it, "to think like us and over time to act like us."[18] The expansion of Western institutions into truly global ones and the acceptance of Western-derived standards as universal were seen as inexorable. The exception comprised the few rogue states, and other recalcitrant regimes, that would have to eat their "spinach" and undertake the necessary political reforms and cultural changes to align with Western models.[19] In essence, the problem of effective global governance would be solved as most of the world's nations adapted their systems and adjusted their priorities, especially in order to conform to the criteria set out for joining Western-dominated institutions. The remaining rogue outliers could be isolated from the herd of the emerging international consensus and quarantined.[20] Indeed, during the 1990s there were explicit calls for Western countries, starting with the United States, to use their power and influence in "securing the compliance of those most resistant to and most distant from the liberal international order; these are actors located almost exclusively in non-Western societies."[21]

It was easy, in this period, to assume that the problems of global order were on the verge of being settled. Many countries seemed eager to sign treaties that pledged their commitment to act on human rights and better governance (even if many of these instruments lacked any real enforcement mechanisms). This created the impression of an emerging world community, at least on paper.[22] During this time, a weakened Russia and an inward-focused China were not primed to take active measures to block preferred Western courses of action proposed via the United Nations. Indeed, critics of American foreign policy during this period maintained that the United States and its Western allies were able to dominate the principal international organizations without much opposition, and that the United Nations, in particular, was an "obedient appendage" to Washington.[23]

The enlargement strategy, which was intended not only to expand the number of US-aligned countries but even eventually to include Russia, China, and other major non-Western powers was meant to solve the international governance problem.[24] Faith in this strategy meant that there was no particular urgency to move rapidly on the promise of a "New World Order," in part due to the lack of an overarching and existential global threat following the collapse of the Soviet Union that might have impelled such an effort.[25] Sarah Sewall has lamented the "missing of the post-Cold War moment" when new and improved global architecture might have been introduced.[26] Indeed, in retrospect there was a certain naïve optimism about the ease with which global problems might be solved in a post-Cold War atmosphere.[27] Because there was—on paper that had been initialed by many governments—the appearance of a new and stronger multilateral order, there was a tendency "to create community by fiat, to assume that treaties and transnational institutions create a rule-based international order that contains national power, and to create consensus among states as to how the 'international community' is to be governed.[28] But whether this declared new order could survive a major test was as yet undetermined. Richard Falk, writing on the fiftieth anniversary of the United Nations (1995), warned that policymakers would be forced at some point in the near future "to take into account the vulnerability of world order in its current phase."[29]

Expectations of what the new post-Cold War international order was expected to accomplish also far outstripped actual capacity. The disintegration of the Soviet Union did not automatically remove the root causes for regional and global disorder. International institutions, from the United Nations to the regional assemblages, struggled to cope with the problems generated by the Yugoslav civil wars and by the efforts to bring peace to fractured African states, as well as to oversee the reconstruction of states from Latin America to Southeast Asia. The ambitious agenda of the 1990s pushed the United Nations "far beyond its operational and conceptual reach,"[30] and exposed the limitations and weaknesses of other international and regional organizations.

There were also other problems on the horizon, including a growing backlash in a number of countries to the propositions of any sort of "new world order." Within the United States itself, there was a pronounced reaction to any apparent loss of sovereignty to the United Nations and an "inappropriate reliance on global institutions."[31] Even within Europe, where the 1992 Treaty of Maastricht had transformed a looser set of European Communities into a more binding European Union, there were concerns about the trend to transfer authority from national governments. In theory, these governments were accountable to their electorates to international organizations where "the voice of the people does not reach decision-makers in any regular or constitutional way."[32] When the George W. Bush administration took office in January 2001, it did not repudiate the enlargement strategy, but immediately signaled that it would be much less willing to make binding institutional commitments and that it "sought to reduce American exposure to global multilateral entanglements."[33]

At the same time, one of the essential assumptions of the enlargement strategy was its optimistic assessment that all countries in the world were (or, with sufficient encouragement, would soon be) on a similar path of development along Western liberal lines. However, the idea that this would produce an ideological basis for more effective international cooperation was not universally accepted.[34] It was challenged, particularly by Singapore's "Senior Minister" Lee Kuan Yew's articulation of "Asian values" in contradistinction to Western ones that were not *ipso facto* universal. The senior minister also maintained that a stable international community could not be predicated on the belief that modernization and development equated with Westernization.[35] This dovetailed with Etzioni's own concerns about the universalization of Western values and making it the sole basis of an international consensus. While recognizing the important role of Western liberalism in establishing the basis for global norms, particularly with regard to safeguarding individual autonomy, Etzioni maintained that it was important for an "east-west" dialogue to outline the contours of a middle ground that would permit a "variety of societal designs" to coexist.[36]

In addition, a view that was certainly prevalent in China (but that also resonated in other countries) was that an effective international order was based not on democracies per se but effective, strong states. If promoting democracy led to weak governments, this would be a major threat to global stability and development.[37] The starting point, therefore, ought to be the establishment of effective governance rather than adherence to liberal values.[38] Such challenges, although muted during the 1990s, called into question whether the "international community" so often invoked by American representatives had actually come into existence.[39]

The Impact of 9/11

Richard Falk's predicted shock occurred on September 11, 2001. Not simply a mass-casualty terrorist attack on American soil, "9/11 was ... a global phenomenon that rippled dramatically through the instruments of global governance."[40] It demonstrated that there were sufficient cracks in the international system to enable threats to emerge and metastasize in even the most powerful of states. The event underscored the power of a terrorist attack to destabilize the entire interconnected structure of the modern world—and raised the question as to whether effective measures to handle such problems were beyond the capacity of any one state.[41] The events of September 11th also highlighted that immediate and pressing threats like international terrorism could not wait for a generational strategy of democratic enlargement to produce more effective global governance. In order to combat the problem of transnational extremist terrorism, the United States would have to work with states that in the short term showed little inclination to adopt Western models or to uphold liberal values.

It also became clear that the 9/11 attacks were a symptom of a larger problem: the weakness of states around the world incubated dangerous instability that could then radiate outward, utilizing the pathways created by globalization to trouble the surrounding neighborhood and the world as a whole. Any effective response would have to go beyond "the destruction of a few camps or the freezing of bank accounts"[42] to focus on what was metaphorically described as "draining the swamps" that fostered terror. Such a response called for a much more resource-intensive level of intervention—one that was understood to be a "generational endeavor" that would require a coalition effort.[43]

In responding to the challenge, three different pieces of advice were provided to US policymakers, each encompassing a different perspective.[44] The first argued that the United States and whatever allies it could muster to follow Washington's direction (even outside the framework of existing alliances) must redouble their efforts to actively reshape the rest of the world along Western liberal lines; the failure during the 1990s, they argued, had been a too-passive approach. The United States could not wait for the expansion of the Western world or for other non-Western states to adopt their point of view.[45] Nor could it defer this mission to a larger coalition, which would end up being "nothing less than an invitation to paralysis."[46] American power ought to be deployed and harnessed—unilaterally, if needed— to drain the metaphorical swamps where groups like Al-Qaeda had festered, as well as eliminate other sources of threats throughout the world and then remake states and their institutions to fit within the US-led liberal order.[47] Moreover, this school of thought advised the rejection of any claim by international organizations to impose any limits on how that power could be utilized, characterizing the efforts of smaller states to "tie the United States down like Gulliver among the Lilliputians."[48]

The second piece of advice was that, even despite those concerns, the United States had to work through the existing set of multilateral organizations. Starting with the United Nations, it needed to formulate, to coordinate, and to execute a response that would be viewed as legitimate by other states and that would ensure support for any actions taken by the United States. Indeed, both the United Nations and America's leading alliance network, NATO, passed resolutions of support and pledged their aid immediately following the 9/11 attacks. Yet while the formal declarations of support were welcome, there remained the assessment that the major intergovernmental organizations were handicapped by a "consensual decision-making culture" that was seen as "too slow and cumbersome to deliver results in time."[49] The United Nations, in particular, was seen as "ineffective and unwieldy in the face of increasing global challenges and responsibilities."[50] Thus, while claiming mandates from international law and even from existing UN Security Council resolutions, in combating the new threats the United States ought not to rely on the bureaucracies created by treaty-based organizations and should utilize, as far as possible, cooperative action with other national governments.[51]

This laid the basis for a third approach, which might be characterized as "flexible multilateralism,"[52] that called for a selective approach to working with international institutions. The premise was that US options must be neither limited nor constrained by existing rules,[53] and that working to strengthen elements of global governance would indeed help to enhance American security.[54] In particular, the United States was advised to spearhead the creation of ad hoc multilateral bodies encompassing a wide variety of states that could bypass slower and more bureaucratically encumbered organizations in order to target specific problems.

In the months and years after 9/11, the Bush administration moved back and forth between these different approaches. As policy shifted between unilateralism and multilateralism, some characterized its focus as schizophrenic.[55] Richard Haass, serving at the time as the director of the policy planning staff at the State Department, coined the phrase "à la carte multilateralism" to describe how the administration planned to navigate these competing tendencies.[56] Generally, the administration was predisposed to "accept a multilateral stance when it is perceived to be in the short-term interests of the United States, but this seeming willingness is mitigated by strong countervailing instincts towards unilateral action."[57] At the same time, however, it became clear that unilateralism might not produce the desired results. There was an acknowledgment that the United States could not "resign to chaos and instability," and needed to develop and maintain a "broad, durable coalition" that would be "based on compromises and stakeholders."[58] So, in the context of the war on terror, the Bush administration sought to "draw on both the legitimacy and capacity of standing organizations as well as the agility and flexibility of ad hoc coalitions."[59] It was in the context of this debate that Etzioni returned to putting foreign policy concerns at the front of his research and writing agenda—and to reexamine the question of authority within the global community.

Etzioni's Global Authorities

After having focused primarily on domestic policy issues for two decades, and following the events of 9/11, Etzioni took a fresh look at foreign-policy issues, and especially questions of global governance. His first major work dealing exclusively with international affairs since his books on gradualism, *From Empire to Community*, was released in 2004. He reached back to his earlier writings to again take up the issue of locating the building blocks for an emerging global community. Etzioni updated and modified them for the context of the early twenty-first century—with the understanding that, over time, some of his views had become much more mainstream, even in policy circles.

For instance, the assertion that there were a set of security challenges too complex for any one state to handle has become much more generally accepted in the last two decades. Sergei Karaganov and Vladislav Inozemtsev summed up the prevailing assessment when they noted that "the individual sovereign state is no longer in a position to meet all of the economic and security challenges of the modern world."[60] In identifying those challenges, Jean-François Rischard, who served as the vice president of the World Bank from 1998 to 2005, even developed a typology of so-called "complex global issues." It identified those questions that either impact the global commons (and not just the territory of the state) or that require planetary-wide solutions—and that might thus serve as drivers for more effective cooperation among states.[61] Etzioni himself acknowledged that since he had initially focused on the question of international order in the 1960s, "problems, and the power to deal with them, have been usurped from the nation-state . . . and are now found in the never-never land of transnationality."[62]

This, of course, offers the possibility that common action in dealing with an overarching threat can help to generate a stronger transnational identity. Etzioni has posited that, in building a stronger global community, attention should be paid to the "Hobbesian agenda"—that "the first duty of the state to provide security to its people fully applies to the evolving international community."[63] If states are equally menaced by the threat of anarchic or extremist terrorist organizations deploying weapons of mass destruction, for example, and cannot guarantee their security by relying solely on their own means and resources, then there is compelling logic to find ways to cooperate. Indeed, following along the same lines as Etzioni, Alexander Wendt has argued that threat perception—whether a concrete problem such as a powerful state or terrorist actor, or a more abstract one such as climate change—provides the impetus for countries to pursue greater interdependence based on common interests and, in turn, helps to create a communal identity that legitimizes collective action.[64] The transnational, global institutions that emerge to provide security against Hobbesian threats, therefore, can lay the foundations for a gradual evolution to addressing "Lockean" concerns about guaranteeing rights.

In his discussions in his earlier works of steps that might lead to a more cohesive global community, Etzioni identified a series of collaborative projects (on development, scientific progress, space exploration, etc.) that could be undertaken by various countries as part of a reformed United Nations approach, each in and of itself a small and limited measure that could, over time, "support the evolution of an international community."[65] He did not, in this period, go into significant detail about how these transnational ventures would be structured or organized, but others also began to examine and explore the value of shared collaborative enterprises that went beyond the level of the nation-state. In 1971 Joseph Nye and Robert Keohane observed that states—even those that did not share a common ideology or worldview—could see the creation of transnational authorities as critical to their national interest if a needed function or service beyond the capacity of the individual state to deliver was provided. This could be considered either via the creation of a transnational association empowered to carry out limited and specific duties, or through the coordination of the various national bureaucracies.[66] This approach, defined by an "intensive and continuous consultation process,"[67] was focused on creating a coalition across national boundaries to address specified issues. The approach was often conducted by specific departments or agencies of a national government directly with their counterparts in other states as part of a coalition effort to tackle a specific problem or issue.[68] In turn, "recurrent international conferences and other activities . . . help to increase transgovernmental contacts and thus create opportunities for the development of transgovernmental coalitions."[69] Keohane's and Nye's assessment has been validated by the emergence of networks of officials cutting across national boundaries that are prepared to work together on issues of concern. This validation has even extended to efforts to create joint working groups among the legislators of different countries to help produce harmonized national legislation that would facilitate the work of the transnational associations.[70]

Other scholars began to build on this concept of transnationalism, particularly the emergence of cooperation between states on functional issues. In addition, they set out to explore whether those kinds of limited cooperative mechanisms (as opposed to formal treaty organizations) might emerge as the "most widespread and effective mode of international governance" because they did not necessarily depend on shared values or even common political systems in order to operate.[71] Nor did they depend upon creating new levels of bureaucracy or setting up new alliances. Instead, the networks of national agencies tasked to cooperate on dealing with a specific problem would rely on top-level political coordination or, at best, create a minimalist steering group or small-scale secretariat. Each network would be *sui generis*, and the memberships would not be coterminous; a group of states that banded together to focus on a particular health issue might not all chose to join another transnational grouping dealing with clean energy. This approach also allowed countries to compartmentalize their cooperation, in the hopes that serious disagreements with other states in one area would not necessarily preclude close and focused cooperation with those same countries in other matters. Under such an approach, states who were competitors in some arenas might be able to forge effective, limited partnerships to tackle issues of shared concern.[72] Anne-Marie Slaughter concluded that under this paradigm, "networked power flows from the ability to make the maximum number of valuable connections. The next requirement is to have the knowledge and skills to harness that power to achieve a common purpose."[73]

In his initial writings, Etzioni focused more on revamping and creating new governing structures. But his earlier optimism about international organizations appeared to be tempered by the same critique that was advanced by some within the Bush administration and that was also echoed by Rischard: "Traditional institutions are incapable of addressing the growing list of complex global issues."[74] Etzioni himself concurred by observing that the "old system," the "national governments and intergovernmental organizations . . . cannot cope with numerous rising transnational problems."[75] He also reiterated his view that there were no "magic bullet solutions," such as the instantaneous reform of the United Nations, to overcome its defects or the sudden emergence of world federalism—that both of these would occur only over a long period of evolution.[76]

One of the striking developments of the immediate post-9/11 environment was an uptick in advocacy for closer international cooperation from those who held a more "realist" perspective, and who did so based on the assessment that national security would be better served by such cooperation than it would by marshalling traditional liberal arguments for global governance.[77] Indeed, weeks after the September 11th attacks, Graham Allison, Karl Kaiser, and Sergei Karaganov proposed a "Global Alliance for Security" composed initially of the major powers (with membership ultimately expanded to other countries). The alliance recommended that constituent nations of the major powers pool their resources and capabilities in a joint effort to "prevent and fight terrorism, the proliferation of weapons of mass destruction, and the infrastructure of international criminal activities and drug traffic that feed terrorist networks."[78] These proposals, in turn, reflected changed thinking on the part of a number of governments headed by self-described realists or pragmatists, who recognized the value of stronger regional and global institutions and who acknowledged that the changed security situation required transnational coalitions that would have significant staying power and not be ephemeral or short-lived.[79] This opening to consider new forms of transnational cooperation, not only on the part of the Bush administration but visible in other governments around the world, gave Etzioni confidence that his proposals might fall on more receptive ears.

In observing the immediate post-9/11 situation, Etzioni reached a series of assessments. Without significant, long-term reform, the United Nations would not be in a position to respond effectively to the new global challenges. But he did not share the sentiment that the UN was fundamentally broken, unworkable, or not needed. Instead, Etzioni argued that the UN should retain its role as the place where global dialogues were conducted and legitimacy for different international projects bestowed, particularly on the transnational networks.[80] The value of the United Nations is that it is a "global forum—the only one of its kind that is permanent and inclusive." But, for the foreseeable future, there could be no "top-down" command from international organizations mandating policy.[81] Instead, the initiative for the formation of these new coalitions to tackle specific problems and issues would come from the nation-states whose own survival could not be guaranteed without more effective international action. Starting with terrorism—and moving to other pressing issues such as climate change and the environment, organized crime, and the proliferation of weapons of mass destruction—it would be individual countries, beginning with the United States, that would seek appropriate mandates from bodies like the UN. Countries would then assemble like-minded states to make contributions to the effort at hand. Over time, these transnational associations would develop liaisons with the emerging regional bodies and a reformed United Nations to form the new global architecture.

Thus, Etzioni wanted to focus on emerging trends that pointed the way to the promotion of a more effective global architecture, starting with the growth of transnational authorities. He took as a starting point the assessment made by Slaughter (herself building on the earlier work of Nye and Keohane) that "networks of bureaucrats responding to international crises and planning to prevent future problems are more flexible than international institutions and expand the regulatory reach of all participating nations."[82] Rather than creating a massive organizational architecture, the preferred approach of the 21st century appeared to be, as Stewart Patrick pointed out, to assemble "coalitions around specific challenges to perform discrete tasks" and for national governments to give those coalitions limited authority to act independently in pursuit of their mandate.[83] Etzioni himself recognized the utility of what he called "monofunctional transnational government networks" to develop and implement quick responses to pressing global issues, including the informal authority for members of that network to take action without having to wait for explicit home-country approval.[84] Yet, as Patrick further noted, an ad hoc approach to forming task-oriented coalitions, while it possessed the virtues of speed and flexibility, needed to be integrated into a larger strategy for sustaining global governance. Otherwise, "U.S. forays into ad hoc multilateralism could easily undermine rather than complement the formal institutions on which the United States continues to depend. The uneven experience of the Bush administration shows both the promise and pitfalls of a coalition-based approach."[85] Etzioni concurred with that judgment. The ad hoc coalitions and networks that developed, particularly to cope with the terrorist challenge after 9/11, were an important starting point to habituate countries (and particularly their bureaucracies) to working together to inculcate the habits of cooperation, as well as of developing bonds of trust among officials. Yet, over time, they would have to evolve into more formalized regional and functional associations, and ultimately to global-level authorities to which states would cede voluntarily certain sovereign responsibilities. This would be done under well-defined conditions and with limitations to more effectively deal with the types of pressing transnational issues identified by Rischard and others, closing the gap between existing needs and the responses that the existing "old system" could provide.[86]

Etzioni therefore proposed building on the momentum of the post-9/11 embrace of transnational problem-solving networks to lay the foundations for what he termed "Global Authorities." The informal understandings, ad hoc working groups, and personalized networks would, over time, be ratified and made permanent through treaties, the passage of domestic legislation, the formal allocation of budgetary resources, and the assigning of personnel with explicit mandates to take action without requiring reauthorization from the national government. The Global Authorities would thus acquire permanence and salience and would no longer be dependent on the whim of specific leaders for existence and relevance, as an ad hoc coalition might be. Moreover, these bodies would be embedded in national legislation, giving their actions legal writ and providing them with enforcement mechanisms. However, it would be important to prevent bureaucratic calcification by setting up a large organizational structure; these Global Authorities might need a small, coordinating secretariat but otherwise would retain the flexibility and agility of the existing transnational networks.[87] As political entities, Global Authorities would function on the basis of coordination rather than command.

Etzioni envisioned a first series of Global Authorities emerging to deal with a set of specific challenges that threatened the security of all states, including that of the United States. These would include authorities responsible for dealing with: (1) the challenges of transnational terrorism and extremism; (2) crime and smuggling; (3) pollution and the environment; (4) the spread of weapons of mass destruction; and (5) humanitarian relief and pacification following natural disasters or state collapse.[88]

Global Authorities would be limited in scope and focused on a particular challenge. Rather than create one overarching organization that would have multiple mandates—and run the risk that few states would agree to join or that its overall effectiveness would be diluted—Etzioni argues in favor of creating a mix of separate "elements," each focused on a specific problem area (and with no requirement that membership in one requires taking on the obligations of others).[89] In order to retain support from a wide variety of nations, the system of Global Authorities would have to be very attuned to avoiding mission creep or any broadening of its functions or mandates. A Global Authority authorized to take measures to apprehend members of transnational narcotics gangs, for instance, would not be in a position to begin engaging in election monitoring or certification of a government's popular mandate. Moreover, in matters that did not rise to the level of Rischard's complex global issues, the jurisdiction of the individual nation-state would not be usurped.[90] (States, of course, would be free to create more binding and comprehensive regional associations to serve as intermediaries between the global system of authorities and the nation-state, thus permitting a multispeed global commonwealth where states in some regions of the world might opt to cede more sovereign authority to their regional group than might others.)

To prepare the ground for the Global Authorities, Etzioni posited that two sets of dialogues would have to occur. The first, which would take place among and between societies, would deal with values—specifically, the clash between privileging the individual's right to autonomy versus the rights of the collective (a fundamental divide that impacts everything from legal systems to political structures). The goal of this dialogue would not be to "convert" anyone to either Western forms of individualism or non-Western preferences for collectivism, but seek to define the parameters of a synthesis that could help to undergird global institutions. Some, in taking up this question posed by Etzioni, have attempted to develop a new standard, that of "responsible governance." This principle would apply to a state that is committed "to improving the lives of their citizens," which then "enables them to pursue their aspirations in a manner broadly consistent with their preferences" and that does not engage in massive violations of the basic right to life.[91]

Others agree about the importance of dialogue. G. John Ikenberry, in a debate with Etzioni over these issues, argues that there might indeed be the possibility of a convergence between these differing viewpoints. Non-Western rising powers might not accept the human rights considerations that, in theory, impel Western governments to support a more expansive global community, but they may very well support stronger transnational authorities because they will see them as ways to better ensure state security. As Ikenberry puts it, a country like China "may not fully embrace the human rights vision behind the evolving norms about state sovereignty, but it will appreciate the ability of the international community to act when these dangers become overwhelming."[92]

The second set of dialogues would be about scope: what would fall under "universal governance" versus what would remain defined by local particularity? In other words, what are universal rights that must be respected and defended by all states and by the Global Authorities, and where can particularistic bonds of specific communities take precedence?[93] Those who advocate for the "responsible governance" standard would argue that global institutions would have to be responsible for dealing with the most serious threats to life—particularly those that a state government could not deal with—but that "considerable latitude" be otherwise extended to states in how they choose to define their social, political, and economic systems.[94]

Etzioni's call for an open conversation between "East" and "West" aligns with the advice provided by Thomas Nichols of the US Naval War College. Nichols argues that to avoid a breakdown of the global order, it is necessary to undertake a dialogue between the liberal, democratic, developed states of the global North and West and the rising and resurgent powers of the global South and East, both democracies and authoritarian states alike. In this dialogue, certain limits on sovereignty would be acknowledged in return for strengthened international institutions (and the view that the United States is the principal global power). Agreed-upon limits would be honored as to the scope of what can trigger any sort of intervention against or interference with the sovereign prerogatives of the individual state. In short, the bargain would be "to restrain the use of American might in exchange for the protections of a common defense."[95] As Etzioni points out, this bargain would require all sides to compromise, a step that would require the United States and other Western powers to dial back on insisting upon the universality of the whole panoply of individual rights that their systems enshrine. At the same time, it would require the neo-Westphalian powers (starting with China) to recognize even a limited set of global-level authorities over the sovereign nation-state. In response to his critics, who contend that this would represent a betrayal of Western values, particularly the stipulation that democratic regimes acceded to authoritarian systems, Etzioni maintains that we would in fact be "better off when we hold back, when [we] apply less power than we command in order to win the collaboration of others and build institutions that will serve us in the longer run, even if they entail some holding back in the shorter run."[96] An apparent backtrack on the stated US commitment to spread democracy around the world—and to accept the ability of nondemocratic states that do not share Western values to help set the global agenda—is a "painful prospect," as Nichols puts it, but necessary if these new Global Authorities are to have credible buy in from a majority of the world's state stakeholders.[97] Etzioni had been frustrated by the experience of the UN General Assembly, which could pass nonbinding resolutions that were often ignored by states and even supposedly binding resolutions passed by the UN Security Council that would then not be enforced by its members.[98]

Etzioni's proposal also draws on the realities of the major structural changes in the international system that are shifting power to the major continental powers of Asia away from the traditional locus of the trans-Atlantic basin. This development means that leading nations like China and India have ceased to be merely regional powers and now have a growing claim to be able to shape the global agenda. This will produce fundamental changes in existing alignments as well as in the structure and scope of international institutions.[99] Recognizing this, Charles Kupchan, in his recommendations for revamping the global architecture, comes to conclusions very similar to those made by Etzioni. Kupchan calls on the West

> to work with emerging powers to take advantage of the current window of opportunity to map out the rules that will govern the next world . . . The goal should be to forge a consensus . . . The West will have to be ready for compromises: the rules must be acceptable to powers that adhere to very different conceptions of what constitutes a just and acceptable order.[100]

The result would probably be more universal in scope than a number of non-Western states would like, but it would preserve a much greater degree of local particularity and exceptionalism than would suit Western nations, especially the European Union. The United States would have to accept that the resulting global architecture would leave untouched large areas where the West might wish to encourage, promote, or even mandate liberal change. For Etzioni-style Global Authorities to be able to conduct their work and carry out their mandates, countries like China would need to acquiesce to certain "gates" in the absolute wall of state sovereignty.[101] As outlined by Etzioni, one such compromise would be to make permissible, in limited and extreme circumstances, the "right to protect missions" designed to defend large numbers of civilians in imminent danger of death. However, the compromise would require the absolute foregoing of any right to use force against nondemocratic regimes whose conduct, even if reprehensible, does not rise to that standard. Comments made in 2006 by China's UN ambassador, Liu Zhenmin, seemed to suggest that this might be middle ground that China, for its part, could accept.[102] Such compromises, promoted via dialogue, would be critical for the formation of a basic consensus upon which an effective global architecture would need to rest.[103]

Once this consensus has been achieved, Etzioni takes a broadly pragmatic approach to the formulation of these new Global Authorities.

The goal is not to pressure states, particularly the more powerful actors, to join in such a fashion where they seek to avoid fulfilling obligations that they never took on in good faith, or to get signatures simply for the sake of signatures. This was one of the criticisms that had been advanced in the push to expand the numbers of states acceding to human rights treaties during the 1990s, or to sign up countries to take part in "coalitions of the willing" in the 2000s. Instead, the Global Authorities would take on functions based upon the consent of states that were pursuing their own national interests. To some extent, the growth in the authority and scope of the International Criminal Court (ICC) validates Etzioni's expectations. Given varying degrees of opposition to the breadth of a mandate for the ICC among powerful states, the Court has chosen to follow a process of "mutual accommodation" with the leading states:

> For the most part, the prosecution officials have not resisted these efforts at major-power control. They have not challenged the Security Council's restrictions on the court's freedom of action or campaigned for expanded jurisdiction. Meanwhile, the court's cautious and deferential behavior in selecting situations to investigate has continued. The historical record does not suggest that leading states have "captured" the prosecutor or other court officials. Indeed, there are notable examples of the prosecutor rejecting major-power pressure and advice. But these assertions of independence have occurred within a broadly conciliatory framework.[104]

The ICC and other international tribunals such as the International Court of Justice have demonstrated that transnational institutions with clearly defined and limited mandates are more likely to gain acceptance and to foster approval of decisions made by a body that exists above that of the nation-state. As Philip Alston of New York University observes, "The attempts that have been made so far to set up bodies that will impose meaningful constraints upon governments have been hugely resisted. Change in this whole area, even though it has been pretty dramatic by overall historical standards, is nonetheless rather slow and incremental."[105] This observation validates Etzioni's insistence on a gradualist approach; as Alston notes, standing firm on "prescribing a model which is extremely demanding and intrusive" will not be successful.[106]

Even limited authorities, however, will not be accepted unless there is a pressing need. Etzioni argues that proposed Global Authorities should meet what he calls the "triple test." First, they "should be based on a convergence of interests" among the United States, other major powers, and a majority of the world's nations. Second, they should be perceived as operating legitimately—via mandates from appropriate international bodies or national legislatures, or in accordance with treaties, for instance. Finally, they should strengthen the foundations of the emerging global community.[107] Etzioni's triple test aligns well with the criteria that Rischard laid out for judging the effectiveness of transnational networks. He offers four criteria for assessing any new regional or global architecture: it should respond to issues and crises with speed and dispatch; its actions should be perceived as legitimate; the network should reflect the views and contributions of a diverse group of members; and it should be compatible with existing institutions.[108]

Etzioni's vision of a series of Global Authorities that handle discrete functions has been echoed by other commentators. James Rosenau, for instance, endorsed the notion of disaggregated global authorities to deal with pressing issues like proliferation and the environment.[109] Inozemtsev and Karaganov acknowledged Etzioni's concept in discussing their own recommendations for eliminating threats to international peace and security.[110] American diplomat James E. Goodby (who closed out his career as the chief US negotiator for the Safe and Secure Dismantlement of Nuclear Weapons) saw in Etzioni's suggestion of Global Authorities a flexible approach to pressing international problems that was politically realizable.[111]

Etzioni argues that in the years immediately following 9/11, the seeds of several possible Global Authorities were planted based on the actions taken by the United States and others to respond to the threat posed by Al-Qaeda. The basis of their rationale was the same as that of the nation-state: providing security. We now turn to examine Etzioni's proposed "building blocks" of a new global order.

A First Test: The Fight Against Terror and the Rise of a Global Safety Authority?

Unlike earlier major acts of terrorism, the 9/11 events resonated with many governments around the world, in part because the perpetrators (the Al-Qaeda organization) had, in their pursuit of globalizing *jihad*, become involved in supporting a number of different regional groups that threatened the interests of many states. In addition, the targeting of the World Trade Center had resulted in the deaths of citizens of more than eighty countries. Ronald K. Noble, the Secretary-General of Interpol, characterized what happened as "attacks against the entire world and its citizens."[112] Finally, the attacks disrupted not just the United States but the global economy, leading to billions of dollars in direct losses and generating aftereffects that in total contributed to a 1 percent decrease in global gross domestic product.[113]

The struggle against Al-Qaeda and its affiliates provided the basis for the United States, China, Russia, India, the countries of the European Union, and other states across the Middle East, Latin America, Asia, and Africa to join together to fight a common scourge that threatened not only specific nations but the fabric of the international order altogether. It helped that Osama bin Laden, in his efforts to establish branches of his group in countries all over the world and through the support he proffered to a variety of regional insurgencies, had already established Al-Qaeda as a "true global network" with global reach that had already struck against the interests of many states.[114] A number of nations also joined the US-led fight against Al-Qaeda in the hopes of receiving support for their own more limited and focused struggles against separatists and extremists in their own territories.[115]

Even though there had been some limited cooperation among states to fight terrorism prior to September 11, 2001, especially among those countries already bound together in common security alliances, the 9/11 attacks served as a catalyst for speeding up and deepening steps to bring about much closer transnational coordination. One of the most dramatic symbols of this changed approach was the fact that Russian President Vladimir Putin was the first foreign leader to reach US President George W. Bush following the 9/11 attacks. Putin, overriding the recommendations of his senior generals and national security officials, offered Russia's assistance in intelligence sharing and promised to use Moscow's good offices to facilitate the leasing of bases in Central Asia that could be used by US and coalition forces in any military campaign against Al-Qaeda and the Taliban in Afghanistan. Both of these moves signaled significant reversals of Russia's long-standing positions of limiting American influence in its Eurasian backyard. Moreover, along with China and several of the Central Asian states, Russia had just formed in the summer of 2001 the Shanghai Cooperation Organization (SCO), a group that was formed to combat the rise of extremism and terrorism in the region but that also had an anti-American subtext. Putin's call to Bush suggested that a war on terror might lay the basis for closer cooperation between these two security organizations and provide a rationale for cooperation.[116]

Moreover, in contrast to the trends observed in the 1990s, there was now far more encouragement of the pursuit by security and intelligence agencies of different countries' of a more in-depth collaboration in combating Al-Qaeda and related terrorist and criminal organizations, "despite the fact that critical differences may exist in their respective countries' attained level of and formal commitment to constitutional democracy."[117] This included a greater willingness to share information that previously might have been withheld due to national security reasons or ideological differences.[118] One of the notable successes was a joint US-Russian sting operation that "flushed out terrorists who sought to acquire surface-to-air missiles to use against civilian airliners in US airspace."[119] This operation led to another first: Russian Federal Security Service officers testified in US courts against the terror suspects.[120]

A focus on counterterrorism also helped to bring China into the coalition. Despite ongoing concerns in the United States about China's commitment to human rights and the rule of law, the US Federal Bureau of Investigation (FBI) increased its cooperation with China after the 9/11 attacks. The FBI opened an office in Beijing, thereby facilitating the exchange of information and intelligence, and even assisted in the training of Chinese security to deal with potential threats that might arise during the 2008 Beijing Olympic Games.[121] In counterterrorism matters, the United States was no longer going to demand Chinese adherence to Western liberal standards as a precondition for assistance and cooperation between the law enforcement and intelligence agencies of both countries.

Indeed, after the crisis in US-China relations following the April 2001 EP-3 incident, which raised the specter of a Sino-American clash in the Pacific, the September 11th attacks helped to repair the damage done to the bilateral relationship.[122] In recognizing that Beijing and Washington faced a common foe, the "Chinese government welcome[d] many forms of cooperation with U.S. authorities" on a variety of counterterrorism measures including efforts to track and disrupt financing of terror groups and participation in the U.S. "Container Security Initiative" (especially in allowing inspections of cargoes bound for US ports).[123]

Throughout the 1970s, 1980s, and 1990s, a number of governments around the world blocked more robust action from being taken against terrorism in bodies like the United Nations and critical non-governmental transnational organizations like Interpol. Progress on developing a coordinated international response had lagged.[124] Much of this resistance crumbled after 9/11. In several key resolutions, the United Nations gave its blessing to the formation of a wide-ranging antiterrorism coalition. UN Security Council Resolution 1373, passed on September 28, 2001, committed all members of the UN to consider terrorism a crime in their domestic legislation, called for intelligence-sharing among states, and created a "Counter Terrorism Committee" to monitor compliance. UNSCR 1390 (January 16, 2002) imposed further sanctions on Al-Qaeda and the Taliban of Afghanistan, including the commitment to freeze all of their assets and to bar passage of their members. Interpol also become much more proactive, with the recognition that 9/11 had served as a catalyst for taking stronger coordinating action among its members to combat terrorism. This recognition brought about the creation of a Terrorism Watch List, and encouraged Interpol to reach out to conclude agreements with Europol (the European Union (EU)-level law enforcement agency) and the Arab Interior Ministers' Council to share information and coordinate databases.[125]

The demands of the war on terror also acted as a shot in the arm to other transnational associations, such as the Financial Action Task Force (FATF). Initially created by the G7 in 1989 to deal with money laundering and illicit proceeds from the drug trade, the FATF took on the additional function after 9/11 of tracking and interdicting terror financing. Demonstrating the ability of transnational networks to move much more speedily than cumbersome international organizations, FATF adopted its "special recommendations" for dealing with the specifics of terrorist financing (on top of its existing "Forty Recommendations" for combating money laundering in general) in a matter of weeks after the September 11th attacks.[126] Its membership, originally concentrated in the countries of the developed West, become more global in nature (both as a result of 9/11 and because of the ongoing shift in the world's economic center of gravity toward Asia). Today FATF encompasses representatives of nearly forty states—including all members of the Group of 20—and also coordinates the work of the regional associations (the FATF-style regional bodies, or FSRBs), which have been set up to combat money laundering and terror financing in every region of the world.[127] FATF has been described as the "global financial coalition" of the war on terror, and was designated by the G-8 and the European Union to take the lead in going after the financing of terrorist organizations, drawing also on provisions found in UNSCR 1373 to legitimate its work.[128] As a "task force" rather than a formal governmental organization, FATF has no enforcement or sanctioning power, yet wields significant influence through its ability to designate the financial institutions of a nation as noncompliant with antiterror financing directives. Its "Non-Cooperative Countries or Territories" label acted as a scarlet letter, causing banks in other countries to stop doing business with the institutions of a country so designated. Getting the description lifted required a country to demonstrate the steps it had taken to bring its banking sector into conformity. As a result, by the mid-2000s, some 130 banking jurisdictions—covering 85 percent of the world's population and up to 95 percent of the globe's economic activity—had given formal commitments to abide by FATF standards.[129] The legitimacy of the FATF designations was aided by the expert role of the national delegations in its triannual plenary sessions, the need for the organization to reach consensus in assigning its recommendations, and the fact that, beyond the formal voting members, nearly every country in the world could influence FATF via the regional associations.[130]

The ability to find consensus in bodies like FATF and to get UN Security Resolutions passed with no dissenting votes or vetoes cast reflected the extent to which most states in the world viewed Al-Qaeda as a menace. At the same time, in forging this coalition, the United States also had to be willing to set aside some of its policy preferences in order to win the support of other key powers.[131] For instance, Washington agreed to view the Chechen insurgency inside the Russian Federation more through the lens of international terrorism rather than a Russian domestic problem brought about, in part, by Kremlin policy. There was also a willingness to dial back on pressuring governments to undertake reforms if it might cause instability, based on the recognition that, in some cases, authoritarian governance might be preferable to the instability that can be created when a closed regime begins to launch reforms. This made it easier for a number of countries to pursue security and intelligence cooperation with the United States.

Writing in 2004, Etzioni looked at the vital transnational networks binding together the law enforcement and intelligence agencies of dozens of countries. He examined how this cooperation (coordinated by the United States) was achieving results in arresting key members of the Al-Qaeda network who previously would have exploited administrative and jurisdictional loopholes to avoid capture or prevent disruption of their activities.[132] Etzioni described the post-9/11 arrangements—all of the various bilateral and multilateral arrangements, both formal and informal—as the first steps toward the emergence of a "de facto Global Antiterrorism Authority" that in three years "has achieved a fair level of institutionalization . . . and routines of cooperation have been well-established and followed."[133] It was Etzioni's expectation that because it directly served the national interests of so many states, continued efforts to destroy and dismantle the Al-Qaeda network would give the antiterror coalition staying power; in his opinion, it was a "nascent authority or an institution under construction."[134] Over time, when countries saw that this emerging Global Authority was both effective in dealing with the terror threat but did not pose a threat to the fundamental sovereignty of the nation-state in other areas, they would be willing to cede more power to the authority to take action—and might be prepared to adopt this model to cope with other problems. This concept of a "Global Antiterrorism Authority" had some resonance in American political circles; in 2007, on the campaign trail for the presidential nomination, Senator Barack Obama called for the creation of a "Shared Security Partnership Program to forge an international intelligence and law enforcement infrastructure to take down terrorist networks from the remote islands of Indonesia, to the sprawling cities of Africa."[135]

In fact, Etzioni's confidence in both the enduring nature of the terror problem and the appeal of the Global Authority solution led him to predict that the ad hoc antiterror coalition was on its way to becoming a standing and permanent Global Safety Authority that would expand its mandate from combating terrorism to also dealing with the proliferation of weapons of mass destruction and the challenges of pacification in postconflict societies.[136] However, others have not shared his assessment that the emergence of the post-9/11 antiterror coalition is a net positive for efforts to set up a more global community. Consistent doubts have been raised about operations taking place "outside of the confines of legal safeguards and human rights restrictions," and thus it is not as clear that the counterterror struggle, even if it unites the security and law enforcement agencies of many nations, is contributing to the "global order of law."[137]

Finally, nearly a decade and a half after the 9/11 attacks, the initial enthusiasm that the struggle against terrorism and global anarchy might provide a workable basis for more effective international cooperation has proven to be short-lived. The US decision to pursue military action against Saddam Hussein's regime in Iraq and other political differences began to weaken the coalition.[138] After 2005, some observers began to note a drop in cooperation and a certain fraying in the global antiterror effort.[139] Significantly, the UN Security Council was never able to provide a definition of terrorism for UNSCR 1373, thus opening the door to returning to the pre-9/11 status quo where one person's terrorist was another man's freedom fighter.[140] Al-Qaeda was the only organization where there was sufficient agreement both to designate it a terrorist organization and to impose specific sanctions. Indeed, there have been some reversals in terms of seeing progress toward a more defined global antiterrorism authority. The Security Council has terminated the mandate of the independent monitoring group that was meant to check compliance with UNSCR 1390,[141] and other UN committees do not regularly update their work nor are they in a position to impose penalties against noncompliant or uncooperative states.[142]

Some of the coalition relationships also begun to fracture, damaging the close and sustained cooperation among bureaucracies that was supposed to strengthen the drive toward a Global Safety Authority. A working group convened by the US Government Accountability Office in April 2008 to discuss issues arising out of US partnerships with other countries to combat transnational terrorism identified several factors that inhibited more effective cooperation. Topping the list was the lack of trust between partners and the distrust that could be engendered by unilateral US action. In addition, other issues raised included differences in countries' foreign policy objectives, in assessment of the threat, and in the willingness to interrupt relations with states perceived to be sources for terror.[143]

The Chinese have echoed similar concerns in explaining the limits of their cooperation with the United States over counterterrorism issues. Beijing has complained that the U.S. at times conflated its own narrow national interest with the general struggle against terrorism, and was insufficiently considerate of the opinions and interests of others in the coalition. At the same time, some Chinese officials expressed worries that US-led counterterrorism efforts in the Asia-Pacific theater were also designed to check and reduce Chinese influence, and that US personnel sent to China to coordinate antiterrorist activities might also engage in espionage activities.[144] Moreover, some of the internal groups—for example, the East Turkestan Islamic Movement and the Turkestan Islamic Party—that China continues to view as terrorists because of their activities in Xinjiang are not on the US Department of State's terrorist list. This is due in some measure to ambiguity on the part of the United States over their perceived connections to Al-Qaeda and concerns about Chinese policy toward its Uighur minority.[145] Finally, there has been a noticeable shift in Chinese attitudes over the past decade—from viewing collaboration with the United States on global security issues such as terrorism as a way to forge a more equitable Sino-American partnership (with China recognized as a major stakeholder in the world order) to seeing US offers of coalition-building as a way to shift burdens and responsibilities onto Beijing.[146]

One of the biggest setbacks in transforming the antiterror coalition into a Global Safety Authority has been the deterioration of the US-Russia relationship. As the two countries disagreed on other matters (NATO expansion into Eastern Europe, independence for Kosovo, etc.), it became much harder to compartmentalize and ring-fence the cooperation on combating terrorism. In particular, as noted by Eugene Rumer, who served as the US National Intelligence Officer for Russia, there cannot be effective antiterrorist coordination if significant mistrust exists between the intelligence agencies of both countries, since "exchanges of intelligence require a closer relationship and greater mutual trust."[147] A decade after the 9/11 attacks, the poor relationship between Russian and American agencies meant that critical information obtained by the Russian security services during their stay in Russia about the persons who carried out the Boston Marathon bombing in 2013 was not passed along to U.S. officials. Having this information might have caused the FBI to place Tamerlan Tsarnaev and his brother under greater scrutiny.[148] Former U.S. Senators Sam Nunn and Richard Lugar have sounded the alarm over the breakdown of what might have been a core relationship for any emerging Global Safety Authority:

> For more than two decades, the United States and Russia partnered to secure and eliminate dangerous nuclear materials—not as a favor to one another but as a common-sense commitment, born of mutual self-interest, to prevent catastrophic nuclear terrorism. The world's two largest nuclear powers repeatedly set aside their political differences to cooperate on nuclear security to ensure that terrorists would not be able to detonate a nuclear bomb in New York, Moscow, Paris, Tel Aviv or elsewhere. Unfortunately, this common-sense cooperation has become the latest casualty of the spiraling crisis in relations among the United States, Europe and Russia.[149]

Echoing Etzioni's own arguments, both men have noted that continued, focused cooperation in this area serves the core national interests of both Russia and the United States, and does not require any catastrophic loss of sovereign authority on either side: "These steps and others could be achieved on the basis of mutual interest without major concessions from either side. This will be impossible, however, if cooperation to prevent catastrophic terrorism is regarded as a geopolitical bargaining chip."[150]

Despite the setbacks in the US-Russia counterterror efforts, cooperation has continued between Russian and European agencies, despite the Ukraine crisis.[151] And while China's cooperation with the United States on antiterrorist matters has receded in recent years, Beijing continues to pursue an active agenda with its SCO partners and with a variety of other Asian partners, including India and the Association of Southeast Asian Nations (ASEAN) states.[152] The 2014 Shanghai Cooperation Organization's antiterrorism drill (known as Oriental-2014) took place in August at the Manzhouli-Zabaykalsk border crossing between Russia and China, with personnel and observers not only from China, Russia, and the Central Asian states but also Laos, Vietnam, Afghanistan, India, Iran, and Mongolia.[153]

Terrorism is also no longer the automatic trump to geopolitics. Significantly, US efforts to enlist Chinese support in the campaign against the so-called "Islamic State" (IS) operating in parts of Syria and Iraq did not generate much support, even though the leader of the IS, Abu Bakr al-Baghdadi, placed China at the top of the list of countries that oppress Muslims. No longer expecting serious help from Washington against its own separatists in Xinjiang, and convinced that the United States is using the antiterror campaign as an excuse to accelerate efforts to remove the Syrian regime of Bashar al-Assad from power, the Chinese conveyed the message that dealing with the IS is a US problem.[154] And even though the IS is opposed by a broad coalition of states—including the United States, France, Britain, Jordan, Russia, and Iran—proposals for joint common action among the West, its Middle East allies, Russia, and Iran have foundered over major differences about the future of the region.[155]

All of this suggests that the idea of a Global Safety Authority emerging from the immediate post-9/11 coalition against Al-Qaeda is less certain today than it appeared to be a decade ago. Nevertheless, the essential building blocks remain in place.

The Proliferation Security Initiative:
An Embryonic Global Authority?

While the antiterrorist coalition never coalesced into any sort of formal arrangement, another US-led transnational association that was generated in the aftermath of the 9/11 attacks—the Proliferation Security Initiative (PSI)—has a much more credible claim to be a foundational element in any proposed Global Safety Authority. With more than 100 nations having endorsed its Statement of Principles, it has a good *prima facie* case of meeting the requirements for being considered a truly "global" undertaking.

The PSI got its start in the aftermath of the *So San* incident in September 2002, when a Spanish vessel operating as part of the Combined Task Force 150—a US-led effort to engage in maritime counterterrorism patrols in the Indian Ocean—was asked by the United States to intercept an unregistered North Korean vessel. Hidden underneath the official cargo were SCUD missile components. Because the shipment was claimed by the government of Yemen—which subsequently gave assurances that the missiles would not be transferred to third parties—the vessel was released. However, the incident exposed gaps in the existing international legal framework for dealing with the proliferation of components for weapons of mass destruction (WMD) and their delivery systems.[156]

In response, President George W. Bush tasked senior members of his administration to assess what tools were needed to prevent a future repeat of other *So San*-style incidents. That set in motion the process that was to develop, in a matter of months, the PSI.[157] Bush outlined the idea in an address he delivered in Krakow, Poland, at the close of May 2003. The United States approached a small "core group" of states to forge the PSI, foregoing, at the beginning, a broader, inclusive coalition in order to work with a much smaller group of like-minded nations possessing the necessary intelligence or maritime capabilities to lay the groundwork for the initiative. Two things were critical for success: the first was that the PSI was presented as a presidential project, and so enjoyed Bush's personal backing (and supervision); the second was that the officials sent to hammer out the PSI at a series of follow-up meetings after the Krakow address possessed "wide negotiating latitude and influence in their capitals."[158] A decision was also made not to involve international organizations like the EU and NATO in the early PSI process, in part because US officials did not want their cumbersome decision-making procedures to slow down efforts to get the PSI up and running.[159]

At the presentation of the PSI Statement of Principles in September 2003, states were invited to signify their assent. In so doing, countries pledged to take effective measures to interdict shipments of WMD materials and components, to share information with other PSI members about any such smuggling efforts, and to guarantee that they would not allow proliferation from their own territories. Signatories to the Statement of Principles were also asked to permit other PSI members to board and search aircraft and ships traveling under their flag that were suspected of proliferation violations, and to seize cargoes in their own territories before they could go onward to a final destination.[160] The initial core group was expanded to encompass additional major powers, notably Russia, which signified it would join the PSI.

The heart of the PSI is the Operational Experts Group (OEG), which serves to "translate the PSI principles into capabilities and action; planning and conducting exercises; identifying capabilities and procedures required and available for interdictions, including legal bases; intelligence sharing; and sharing lessons learned."[161] As the "political" meetings of the PSI wound down, it has been the OEG that has taken center stage for keeping the PSI up and running. It now consists of 21 key PSI states, including Germany, France, Russia, Australia, Japan, and South Korea. The OEG has been kept deliberately small so as not to impede its efficient functioning—the worry being that having all 102 PSI members represented would invite gridlock—but its members have been chosen to provide a balance of states with military and intelligence capability, influence in global shipping, and regional diversity. But the OEG is not the equivalent of the UN Security Council or the European Council, where votes are taken and decisions brought to be approved or vetoed—it serves as a clearinghouse and coordinating body.[162] It has also taken the first steps toward focusing on regional sessions that would bring together the OEG members and the rest of the PSI membership in a given area, and further develop the joint exercises that, over time, generate familiarity among the bureaucracies and militaries of partner nations.[163]

In many ways, the PSI process tracked with Etzioni's recommendations for developing new frameworks that could evolve into Global Authorities. Even though the PSI is not a UN activity, the United States and other states did propose draft resolutions for consideration by the

United Nations (UN) Security Council. UN Security Council Resolution (UNSCR) 1540, passed on April 28, 2004, bans nonstate actors from developing or acquiring WMD and calls on all states to take cooperative action to prevent illegal trafficking in nuclear, biological, or chemical weapons and their delivery systems. UNSCR 1718, passed on October 14, 2006, authorized states to intercept and inspect ships bound to and from North Korea to ensure they were carrying no WMD-related cargo. Other instruments to create a legal regime for the PSI have included the amended Convention for the Suppression of Unlawful Acts Against the Safety of Maritime Navigation (SUA) and its 2005 protocol (SUA-2005), banning the maritime transport of any WMD materials (except for some nonweapons nuclear material between signatories of the Non-Proliferation Treaty). The 2010 Beijing Convention seeks to do the same for aircraft.

Most importantly, the United States has concluded agreements with most of the countries (including Liberia, Cyprus, and Panama) under whose flags some 70 percent of the world's commercial tonnage is shipped. These treaties set out procedures by which permission can be rapidly granted to the United States (or other countries operating on behalf of the PSI) to board and search vessels in international waters, usually within two hours of the request being made.[164] In essence, by creating these blanket agreements ahead of time, the path to searching vessels traveling under these flags was streamlined.

The approach taken with the PSI therefore tracks with Etzioni's recommendations and is a real-world case of his "triple test" in action. In particular, he notes, "Because the PSI operates under international law, has been at least indirectly blessed by the UN, and has been fortified by bilateral agreements, it can defend itself against charges that it is illegitimate."[165] It certainly addresses the concerns raised by both Etzioni and Rischard about the need for a structure that can respond quickly when a problem arises. The PSI is not a traditional international organization where all members must vote in favor of carrying out an interdiction; in fact, most PSI members may be completely uninvolved in any specific incident. What the PSI sets up is a system that connects PSI members who may have information about a possible shipment with those who have the capabilities or jurisdiction to intervene; it is these "PSI participants [who] agree among themselves on the need and modalities for an interception."[166]

But the PSI has also had its setbacks. One has been the ill-defined nature of what constitutes "support." A signatory to the PSI Statement of Principles is not necessarily committed to automatically interdict vessels or aircraft at the request of the United States or other PSI participants, or to allow searches of vessels traveling under their flags, unless a bilateral agreement is already in place.[167] A number of the rising powers, starting with China, India, and Brazil, have never endorsed the initiative. In particular, Beijing, while reiterating its own commitments to nonproliferation, has raised questions "about the legitimacy and effectiveness of PSI interdictions and consequences that may arise." China has also objected to the reality that the PSI, although touted as a global initiative, was largely drawn up by the United States with the assistance of other close Western allies. (Nevertheless, while staying out of the PSI, China has made commitments to improve cooperation with the United States in terms of information-sharing about suspected cases of proliferation.)[168] There have also been complaints about the United States itself being less willing to vigorously pursue monitoring and interdiction related to shipments sent to or exported from Pakistan, India, and Israel, thereby raising questions about perceived double standards. Other states that are part of the PSI process—like Russia and Japan—are careful to avoid taking actions that might compromise their own sales of equipment.[169] The ninety-plus countries that have not signed on to the PSI weaken efforts to establish the PSI Statement of Principles "as a type of international common law against proliferation," and open gaps in which proliferators may be able to operate under less scrutiny.[170] While the PSI does claim to operate under the aegis of several UN resolutions, earlier versions of Resolutions 1540 and 1718 (which contained much stronger enforcement language) were watered down to ensure final passage, particularly in authorizing use of force if vessels refused permission to board for inspections. Explicit references to the PSI itself were also deleted.[171] While the PSI ship-boarding agreements cover a majority of the world's civilian commercial cargo fleet, the PSI is on weaker legal ground when forcibly boarding in international waters a ship registered under a country that has not consented to being searched. Finally, only a fraction of the eligible states have ratified the SUA-2005 protocol and the Beijing Convention.

Nevertheless, the PSI is credited with dozens of successful interceptions of vessels attempting to transport WMD, as well as creating deterrents for potential proliferators who are unable to access transport because of PSI measures.[172] The crown jewel of the PSI remains the interception in October 2003 of the *BBC China*, where intelligence reported that the A.Q. Khan proliferation network, having used a clandestine facility in Malaysia to manufacture components for nuclear centrifuges, was preparing to ship them to Libya via the United Arab Emirates. The vessel, the *BBC China*, was traveling under the German flag. After it had transited the Suez Canal, a joint US-UK-German-Italian operation intercepted the ship, escorted it to Italy, and confiscated the contents. Some have argued that the exposure this incident gave to Libya's clandestine WMD program helped to tip the scales in favor of Libya's decision at the end of the year to come clean on its efforts, and to renounce its WMD aspirations (a case that will be discussed in a subsequent chapter)—marking a major victory in the campaign not only to halt proliferation but to encourage deproliferation as well.[173]

A decade after its creation, the PSI is at a crossroads. Over the last five years, the number of exercises it has carried out has been halved, and meetings of the OEG have declined by two-thirds in frequency.[174] Former Pentagon official David Cooper, who was involved in helping to set up the initiative, has described the PSI as a "shark" that must "keep moving or it will die."[175] This reality highlights the concerns raised by Patrick, Etzioni, and others that ad hoc transnational arrangements remain at risk of withering on the vine if high-level political support erodes or focuses on other issues. Some observers have connected the noticeable drop-off in PSI activity after 2009 with clear signs of "initiative fatigue," as initial enthusiasm for the PSI on the part of governments waned and the threat of WMD-related terrorism seemed to recede.[176] As with the broader antiterrorism coalition, in some cases concerns about trustworthiness among partners have also limited the sharing of intelligence, with some PSI partners preferring to provide information only to others through established bilateral means rather than with the OEG as a whole.[177]

Not surprisingly, therefore, proponents of the PSI have pushed for the initiative to take the steps Etzioni recommended for the transformation of an informal coalition into a full-fledged Global Authority. This would be in keeping with promises made by President Barack Obama in 2009 to turn the PSI into a "durable international institution," and by the Obama administration in the 2010 National Security Strategy to maintain PSI as a "durable international effort."[178] These promises include (1) requiring all OEG members of the PSI to ratify the relevant SUA-2005 protocol;[179] (2) having all PSI member-states bring their domestic legislation into alignment (and augment with appropriate memoranda of understanding with other PSI participant-states so that WMD trafficking, interception, and interdiction can take place seamlessly and without any exploitation of loopholes; and (3) deepening PSI exercises and cooperative measures to involve more of a country's law enforcement and customs officers.[180] Another recommendation is having national governments explicitly set aside dedicated funding for the PSI, instead of the current practice of funding PSI work "out of hide" (e.g., from regular, nondedicated operational budgets).[181]

In his positive assessment of the PSI, Etzioni noted that it "functions continuously" and that "in a world with no central government, the PSI provides a rudimentary police force"—a building block of a future Global Safety Authority.[182] His recommendations for improvement and consolidation track with those offered by Robert Joseph, who served in senior nonproliferation positions at the National Security Council and the State Department during the George W. Bush administration and who is considered one of the godfathers of the PSI. Joseph his colleagues proposed the expansion of both the PSI legal framework and membership in order to bring in more of the rising powers of the global South and East, starting with China.[183]

The PSI also offers an example of global community-building that is not perceived as a direct challenge to national sovereignty, in contrast to the model of the EU. In recent years, complaints about the growing tendency of EU-level institutions to "steamroll" national institutions and to impose policy and mandates on member-states has raised concerns that no transnational association that aspires to have a real and lasting impact can avoid, over time, trampling on national sovereignty.[184] Instead, the PSI made it clear that it would not be "an effort in which centralized international authorities seek to override state sovereignty. Rather, the international treaty regime should share with national authorities the responsibility for addressing proliferation threats."[185]

The PSI has already influenced the development of a second transnational initiative, which also could be incorporated into a future Global Safety Authority: the Global Initiative to Combat Nuclear Terrorism (GICNT), jointly announced by Presidents George W. Bush and Vladimir Putin at the G-8 summit in St. Petersburg in July 2006. As with the PSI, a small core group of states, nominated by both the cochairs (Russia and the United States), were tasked with assembling the mandate and principles that would govern the GICNT. The PSI tilted strongly toward Western liberal democracies in its initial phase. In contrast, the GICNT, because of its Russian sponsorship, brought China (which was not a member of the PSI), as well as Kazakhstan (a major nuclear supplier), and Turkey (a major regional power for the

Middle East), into the foundational stages of the initiative. Subsequently, India and Pakistan—also both not members of the PSI—joined the GICNT. Like the PSI, the GICNT is meant to facilitate cooperation among its members to secure nuclear material, to share information on possible acts of terrorism that would involve nuclear or radiological devices, to track and monitor all shipments of such material, and to prevent individuals or groups that might seek to obtain such capacities from finding safe haven or being able to transport such material on the territories of the signatory states. One of the GICNT's strengths has been to promote joint exercises that allow the militaries, intelligence and law enforcement services, and energy ministries of the initiative countries to work together and to gain greater familiarity. Eighty-five countries have indicated their support for the principles of the initiative, and, like the PSI, the GICNT draws its legitimacy from several international treaties (the Convention for the Suppression of Acts of Nuclear Terrorism and the Convention on the Physical Protection of Nuclear Material) as well as UN Security Council 1373 and 1540.[186]

Of course, similar problems beset both the GICNT and the PSI. While many states have issued strong political statements in support of the initiative, efforts to establish a lasting and enduring financial mechanism to support the GICNT have had less success. The initiative continues to be funded in a largely ad hoc manner rather than having its own dedicated budgetary lines in the national budgets of its members.[187] There is also no provision in the GICNT for transferring funds and equipment from donor states to countries that need assistance in securing nuclear materials, and the initiative does nothing in terms of setting and enforcing common global standards for protecting nuclear sites.[188] Both the United States and Russia, as well as other nuclear powers, have also separated their military nuclear stockpiles from coverage by the GICNT. Finally, there are concerns that the deteriorating US-Russia relationship, especially because of the crisis in Ukraine, will negatively impact ongoing cooperation on nuclear terrorism issues.[189]

Nevertheless, the PSI model has value in demonstrating what the evolution to Etzioni-style Global Authorities might look like. Thus, as he concluded, "when considering a framework for the future, it would be a mistake to ignore the precedent of the PSI."[190]

A Second Test? Combating Somali Piracy

In September 2005, at the International Seapower Symposium at the Naval War College in Newport, Rhode Island, Admiral Michael

Mullen, the chief of naval operations for the US Navy, unveiled his vision of a "Global Maritime Partnership." This partnership sought to bring together the naval forces of the world to form what Mullen termed the "1000-ship Navy," which was designed to address a series of transnational challenges. Explicitly referencing the model utilized for the PSI, he saw it as a way for countries to pool resources and capabilities to form coalitions to target different transnational problems that were beyond the capacity of any one nation to solve.[191]

The eruption of well-organized pirate groups preying on international shipping—off the Horn of Africa, in the Red Sea, and in the Western Indian Ocean based in enclaves in Somalia—provided an opportunity to test the concept. After the collapse of the central Somali state in 1991, the inability of a successor government to exercise effective control over its territory not only allowed for anarchy to reign on land, but opened up the country's territorial waters, leaving them ripe for exploitation. Local fishermen who could not compete against well-organized foreign fleets poaching in their waters and who were negatively impacted by illegal dumping offshore merged with various militias and gangs to create armed seaborne bands. These bands first tried to reclaim fishing grounds for locals but then realized that piracy was a much more lucrative venture.[192]

Piracy emanating from Somalia, however, was not merely an annoyance. Half of the world's container shipments passed through the Bab el Mandab, which links the Gulf of Aden to the Red Sea, and 70% of the world's oil supply flows through the Indian Ocean. Disruption of shipping routes has a negative impact on the entire global economy and on the pocketbook interests of many nations. As Andrew Erickson and Austin M. Strange pointed out, pirate activities "pose serious threats to the economic and political stability of states throughout the world."[193]

There were already existing US-led naval task forces in the area charged with carrying out counterterrorism missions and ensuring that the Straits of Hormuz—through which some 40 percent of the world's oil supply transits—remained open. The overarching "Coalition Maritime Forces" (CMF) construct for coordinating patrols in this region, headquartered at the US Navy Central Command and Fifth Fleet Headquarters in Bahrain, is a US-created coalition that comprises ships and personnel from thirty nations and that is under the overall command of a US admiral. CMF stood up a distinct Combined Task Force (CTF-151) in January 2009 to specifically deal with

Somali piracy. Other countries and organizations also decided to send vessels into the region.

UN Security Council Resolution 1816passed on June 2, 2008, was the first in a series of resolutions (followed by 1838, 1846, 1851, and 1897) that authorized nations to deploy their naval forces inside Somalia's territorial waters and in the area of the Gulf of Aden and the Western Indian Ocean to carry out antipiracy operations; UN member-states were encouraged to pool their efforts. These UN resolutions extended legitimacy to the different efforts undertaken by individual nations, coalitions, and regional alliances to combat the scourge of piracy off the coasts of Somalia.

Distinct from CMF, NATO also set up a series of task forces to patrol the regionthat operated under alliance command and that reported through the chain to headquarters in Brussels, rather than through the US Central Command; this format appealed to states who wanted to take part in the mission but who did not want to be a contributor to a specifically US-led effort. The EU, anxious to further demonstrate the utility of its own fledgling security efforts, set up its own antipiracy mission (Operation Atalanta). In addition, a number of nations sent naval forces that were not subordinated to any of these three task forces (CTF-151, NATO or the EU) but that remained under separate jurisdiction; these included detachments from Russia, Japan, Korea, Malaysia, India, and China. Countries like India, Russia, and China had a clear desire to take part in the mission, but did not want to subordinate their forces to the command of a US, NATO, or EU authority.

This reality, however, did not produce anarchy. An "internationally recognized transit corridor" was created for ships to traverse through the areas most affected by pirate attacks. More importantly, a coordinating structure—the "Shared Awareness and Deconfliction" forum (SHADE)—was created that meets at the US Naval headquarters in Bahrain. All navies taking part in the antipiracy operation are affiliates of SHADE, which is "not an organization but a facilitating venue."[194] SHADE is not a command structure; its chairmanship, which rotates among the three coalition task forces, convenes meetings but is not vested as any sort of supreme commander. SHADE cannot impose directives on any of the individual nation's ships or on the three separate task forces, but it sets up schedules, keeps lines of communication open, and coordinates activities. What it helps to ensure, as Lt. Colonel Chen Peiling, a Chinese officer who worked at SHADE noted, is that gaps between the different piracy task forces are filled in to increase comprehensive coverage.[195] Each of the three task forces coordinates the efforts of its constituent parts; the Convoy Coordination Working Group sets patrol schedules for the "independents" and meets as a body prior to the overall SHADE session.[196]

SHADE takes a series of separate flotillas and helps to wield them into a more effective antipiracy patrol, but through voluntary coordination rather than command. Observers have been struck by the high level of collaboration among the various task forces and by how the different naval units were able to coordinate. For instance, in April 2009 a chemical tanker that had been captured by pirate groups (and released after the owners paid a ransom) broke down as it was leaving Somali waters. Fearful of being captured by a different gang, the captain of the Stolt Strength radioed for assistance. As J. Peter Pham, a piracy expert who spoke with Captain Abelardo Pacheco, related:

> A German warship participating in the European Union Naval Force (EU NAVFOR) anti-piracy Operation Atalanta stopped by to give the stranded boat's crew emergency water, food, and medical treatment before moving on to another mission. . . . [A] U.S. Navy vessel came alongside and delivered bunkered fuel. . . . [T]he Chinese People's Liberation Army Navy *Type 054A Jiangkai II*-class frigate *Huangshan* began escorting the *Stolt Strength* to the Omani port of Salalah . . .[197]

The SHADE experience offers the first real "glimpse" into how a possible Global Safety Authority might actually function. A Royal Navy officer who was present at SHADE noted the incredible nature of the scene; on an American naval base he would be seated between a Russian admiral and a Chinese brigadier general, with officers present from nations ranging from Pakistan and Turkey to Japan, Greece, and Spain, all working together to combat a common problem.[198] Indeed, there were proposals, some explicitly linking back to Etzioni's own concept of the Global Safety Authority, to use SHADE as a model to develop other such coordinating bodies to deal with other security issues.[199]

Ironically, however, the antipiracy mission has become a victim of its own success. With attacks emanating from Somalia now virtually nil, the sense of urgency to forge a closer partnership has receded. Moreover, the piracy issue, which several years ago commanded headlines and considerable attention from governments, has faded from view; this mission is no longer high profile or critical. Nevertheless, the SHADE experience does provide lessons that would be critical in taking any moves toward making the Global Safety Authority more of a reality.

Testing the Concept Regionally: The ASEAN Experience

Can Global Authorities of the type Etzioni proposes really function and be effective if the state stakeholders are defined by different forms of government and clashing political values? One challenge to Etzioni's proposal is that there can be no lasting and detailed cooperation between authoritarian and liberal democratic states, and that this chasm will impede the effective functioning of any proposed Global Authority. In other words, the lack of agreement on core political questions will make any transnational association unworkable and unsustainable. This argument parallels the experience of the EU, where fundamental agreement on social, political, and economic issues was a necessary precondition to forging a closer regional association.

At a regional level, however, we have an interesting test case of the Etzioni thesis: the ability of the nations that comprise ASEAN to produce functional transnational authorities that help to inculcate a sense of community. Initially set up in 1967, and further established by a Treaty of Amity and Cooperation concluded in 1976, ASEAN is a regional organization that is in the process of transitioning into a community of nations made up of democracies, authoritarian regimes, and variations in between.[200] Yet, as Rodolfo Severino, Secretary-General of ASEAN from 1998 to 2002, has observed, the organization applies no criteria for membership on the part of any applicant state related to the character of its political regime or its ideological orientation.[201] ASEAN commits itself to strict noninterference in the domestic affairs of its member-states.[202] This makes ASEAN more of an analog to the diversity in state systems and practice found throughout the world, in contrast to the EU, which, via its Copenhagen Criteria, imposes a liberal democratic template that must be acted upon by its aspirant members.[203]

K. Shanmugam, the foreign minister of Singapore, has noted that ASEAN was created not on the basis of any sort of idealistic belief in regional cooperation but out of very realist concerns about the fragile security situation in the region, sometimes described as the "Balkans of Asia."

The goad for bringing together the states into this association was: (1) preventing strife within member-states from spilling out to negatively impact the area as a whole; (2) averting regional interstate conflict; and

(3) mitigating the competition among the Great Powers, each of which was searching for influence in the region.[204] Subsequent decisions to strengthen the organization have come about in response to other crises that negatively impacted the ability of individual states to be able to cope.[205]

ASEAN utilizes two core concepts as represented by the Indonesian terms *musjmawarah* (consultation) and *mufukat* (consensus) to conduct decision making within the organization, which focuses on conflict avoidance and the promotion of mutual security.[206] (These values are akin to Etzioni's own call for dialogue to serve as the basis for establishing the parameters of the proposed Global Authorities.) Decisions are thus not based on confrontational or adversarial voting but must be harmonized in a way that is "agreeable to all parties before it is adopted." (This approach also allows individual members to reach bilateral arrangements with each other if a pan-ASEAN solution is not immediately forthcoming.)[207] ASEAN thus differs from the model of the EU, especially in its more informal approach to transnational cooperation and its more limited reliance on legalistic mechanisms to enforce mandates.[208] However, it has gradually moved to develop some permanent institutions (secretariats and coordinating centers) and assembles not only annual summits of leaders, but also regularly scheduled consultations among specific ministries (defense, interior, finance, etc.). These allow the heads and staffs of the functional executive departments of each member-state to become habituated to meeting, planning, and working together. Even if a sense of a common ASEAN identity is more or less nonexistent among average citizens of the region, there has been some development of a regional identity among elites and government officials precisely because of this increased interaction.[209]

In the pre-9/11 period, as Jonathan Chow has noted, the ASEAN insistence on protecting sovereignty and an iron-clad commitment to noninterference in the domestic affairs of its members meant that "[S] substantive security cooperation within ASEAN historically has been difficult to achieve. Member states vigilantly guard their sovereignty and are wary of potential encroachments on their domestic policies. It has not been uncommon for national interests to derail regional initiatives."[210] There were exceptions; given the scourge of narcotics production and trafficking from the region, there were efforts to set up a regionwide plan, to be coordinated by ASEAN, to reach the goal of a "drug-free" Southeast Asia by 2015, anchored first by a meeting of Senior Officials on Drugs Matters and then reviewed by a biannual Ministerial Meeting on Transnational Crime.[211]

But beyond fledgling and limited cooperation on narcotics, there was little enthusiasm for pursuing a more unified effort to combat terrorism, in part from fears that this might open the door to more substantive interference in the domestic political affairs of the members. Terrorist groups had learned to take advantage of this reluctance to act in a more unified, regional fashion by the ASEAN member states. As Chow further observed: "The organizational sophistication of terrorist groups such as al-Qaeda and Jemaah Islamiyah (Islamic Organization, JI) and their ability to shift smoothly across borders contrasted starkly with major inconsistencies in the domestic legal systems, law enforcement mechanisms and security priorities of the ASEAN states."[212]

In the immediate aftermath of 9/11, ASEAN states were divided over whether to support US military action in against the Taliban in Afghanistan, and the degree to which they should offer support to Washington. ASEAN member-states signed a "Declaration on Joint Action to Counter Terrorism" on November 5, 2001, signaling a general intent to combat terrorism but failing to settle some of the critical operational questions about "the methods for combating terrorism through multilateral cooperation."[213] Individual ASEAN countries went ahead to accept American aid, and the Philippines even conducted joint operations against local groups alleged to have Al-Qaeda links with US forces. The ASEAN approach allows groups of ASEAN members to create linkages when the full consensus of the organization is not possible. In keeping with this approach, in May 2002 several states set up an exchange to share airline passenger lists, blacklists, and fingerprint databases while also hosting joint training exercises and working to improve border security.[214]

This ad hoc approach changed in the aftermath of the Bali bombings in October 2002. With a major terrorist attack now having taken place in the region that targeted an ASEAN member (Indonesia), governments were now more prepared to act to develop a more concrete, formalized, and structured institutional response.[215] This was reflected in a series of ASEAN meetings of the relevant ministers, as well as of diplomats and experts, to plot out the course of how more effective transnational cooperation against terrorism would take place. This included increased intelligence-sharing, which led to a dramatic series of arrests that helped to cripple the JI network in 2003. It also led, in July of that year, to the establishment of the Southeast Asian Counterterrorism Center. The creation of this center demonstrated a renewed effort to try and harmonize national laws dealing with terrorism, such as the decision by Thailand, Cambodia, and Brunei to join the database exchange and border training program set up by the Philippines, Malaysia, and Indonesia the previous year.[216] In addition, in November 2004, eight ASEAN states concluded a Mutual Legal Assistance Treaty, allowing for the signatories to share evidence, to serve legal documents in their respective national jurisdictions, and to recover proceeds; it also identified nearly 200 criminal offensives (and not simply terrorism) where the treaty's provisions would apply.[217] In addition, the ASEAN Regional Forum—the mechanism by which ASEAN dialogues with its partners (the European Union, the United States, Russia, China, Japan, and Australia)—convened the first "Intersessional Meeting on Counterterrorism and Transnational Crime" in March 2003, giving the ASEAN states the opportunity to request assistance on specific topics (such as improving identification systems) from countries outside the region. Subsequent joint declarations were concluded with many of these partners, as well as with the "plus Three" (Japan, South Korea, and China) in the months that followed. Further steps toward institutionalizing cooperation on counterterrorism and other transnational criminal matters among the national police forces of the ASEAN states (and enhancing their cooperation with ASEAN's dialogue partners) came with the decision in 2009 to set up a permanent secretariat and coordinating center for ASEANPOL—the assemblage of the organization's national police chiefs.[218]

Part of the way ASEAN navigated what might have been a difficult question—determining who is a "terrorist"—was to "depoliticize" the question by focusing not on the religious, ethnic, or political identity of groups or their demands but instead on the methods they used. This was an attempt to focus on terrorism as a criminal act that threatened the security of the state.[219] Building on preexisting efforts to combat drugs, closer cooperation in fighting terrorism has, in turn, helped to facilitate calls for joint action on other security threats—including other transnational crimes such as trafficking, proliferation, and environmental considerations.[220] Indeed, the ASEAN approach of networking and relying on informal transnational associations now means that, under its aegis, some 1,000 meetings are held each year "to discuss topics ranging from climate change to cultural exchange.

Consequently, thousands of invisible informal networks have evolved in the region."[221]

The severe acute respiratory syndrome (SARS) that occurred in 2003 and the tsunami that took place in December 2004, unlike the Bali bombings, also helped to prod efforts to promote closer collaboration via transnational networks. In the aftermath of SARS and the "bird flu" epidemic the following year, ASEAN itself and the ASEAN "plus Three" framework (APT) set up a series of institutions to prepare the region for another pandemic.[222] These included the APT Regional Disease Surveillance Network, which administers the protocols for sharing information on any potentially hazardous emerging infectious disease. In 2004, to deal with "bird flu," the APT set up a task force which evolved into the Regional Multi-Sectoral Pandemic Preparedness Strategic Framework, and maintains a network for training field teams to deal with outbreaks. ASEAN can also utilize its Risk Communications Resource Center to help with response coordination. All of this had led the World Health Organization to note that East Asia "is more prepared than any other region to respond to a possible pandemic with its existing mechanisms of surveillance and transparency."[223]

Space does not permit an extensive look at ASEAN structures that have emerged over the past decade. Yet, the threats that have beset the region have definitely aided the community-building process. As ASEAN now prepares for the next level of integration—to create political, economic, and cultural communities—it has to face the possibility that the "low-hanging fruit" may have already been harvested in terms of the tasks on which it is possible to gain consensus for creating stronger transnational authorities.[224] Moreover, there are some weaknesses in the current ASEAN approach. ASEAN as a whole still relies on trust that the member states will carry out the tasks that the coordinating institutions request of them; there is no mechanism for monitoring and enforcing what, after all, remain voluntary commitments made by the states.[225] Of particular concern is that, as a regional organization, ASEAN does not have the power to interpret its own statutes and documents—especially the ASEAN Convention on Counter Terrorism, which is left up to the discretion of the members—nor any authority to adjudicate if different ASEAN countries come up with different interpretations of their requirements.[226] The Mutual Legal Assistance Treaty does not provide for extradition of suspects, and domestic laws still trump the treaty if there is any particular conflict.[227] ASEAN-level capabilities are still weak and undeveloped; much of the operational side, particularly in security matters, is carried out by specific bilateral or trilateral arrangements between specific ASEAN states (such as the antipiracy patrols in the Straits of Malacca.)[228] ASEAN members with particular capabilities or resources (such as intelligence) are not always willing to share fully with other ASEAN states if they are perceived as less reliable, thus hampering some cooperation.[229] More needs to be done, particularly in having ASEAN states work more closely together to monitor religious extremists, to stem the flow of recruits from the region to organizations such as the Islamic State of Iraq and Syria, and to continue to implement agreements. In particular (1) not all the mandates in the "Master Plan on ASEAN Connectivity," meant to facilitate the free movement of goods and people throughout the region, have been enacted; (2) some ASEAN states have not signed all the agreements to put into place the ASEAN "Open Skies" policy; and (3) the ASEAN "Single Window" project designed to expedite cargo clearances is not fully operational because national governments have not taken all the steps needed to set up the national "Single Windows."[230] Finally, even given the closer cooperation among ASEAN members, those transnational institutions that have been set up to combat specific threats have not engendered a strong sense of ASEAN "community" among the member-states.

Despite all of the difficulties and limitations of the ASEAN institutions, some observers believe that the "ASEAN way" provides a middle path between Western and non-Western approaches to transnational governance.[231] It offers an example of how states that have not come to accept common standards or values can pool their resources, "thus enabling its members to co-operate on a legal-technical rather than political basis"[232] to deal with critical issues. As such, the ASEAN way demonstrates that the model of Global Authorities as proposed by Etzioni is not outside the realm of realistic possibilities for restructuring the international system in the twenty-first century. Indeed, as Kishore Mahbubani has noted:

> With the emergence of new non-Western powers, the world at large is moving from a mono-civilizational world to a world where many successful civilizations will share economic and political space with each other. Creating a peaceful and cooperative multi-civilizational world will not be easy. Hence, the world will be looking for examples of successful multi-civilizational cooperation. Here the EU has no lessons for the world, but ASEAN certainly does.[233]

Concluding Thoughts

The ASEAN experience with transnational authorities does seem to validate a key proposition of Etzioni's vision: that it is possible to create functional, transnational authorities that encompass states that embrace a wide variety of political systems. It stands against the argument sometimes proffered in Washington that detailed, focused cooperation is not possible on critical global issues if countries have diverging values and domestic political systems, or do not share the same overall foreign-policy vision and objectives.[234]

None of the nascent Global Authorities Etzioni identifies, however, has achieved critical mass, and there are no guarantees (as with the PSI) that they will endure and set down lasting institutional roots. Some have argued, in fact, that the proposed Global Security Authority, "let alone global authorities in the other fields Etzioni distinguishes, may become a lasting element of a new global architecture is then highly doubtful."[235] Despite signs of informal cooperation and coordination, proposals to institutionalize linkages among key countries—say, under the aegis of the Group of Twenty (G-20)—by creating a permanent Security Forum alongside meetings of the finance ministers and heads of state have gone nowhere.[236] Thus, the key next step in building effective Global Authorities—what Etzioni described as "crowning," the tying together of these various separate transnational projects under the same institutional umbrella—has not been taken.[237] The PSI, SHADE, GICNT, and other transnational groupings that have emerged since 9/11 to cope with different aspects of global disorder have not been tied together into a common endeavor, making it harder for this patchwork to become a seamless garment that would become a Global Safety Authority.

In addition, there is another emerging trend at work in international politics that complicates matters—the increased preference of some rising non-Western powers to bypass existing Western-created institutions, route around the United States, and set up alternative structures.[238] This complicates matters because Etzioni's original vision for Global Authorities was to build on the trend of harnessing the overwhelming military and economic power of the United States with the consent, consultation, and contributions of other nations to produce unified action. (This is also the vision presented in the 2015 *National Security Strategy* released by the Obama administration.[239]) We now face a situation where, over the next several years, we may see a series of competing embryonic Global Authorities being set up by different major powers, each promoting different goals and norms, and competing for the allegiance and support of undecided nations all over the world.[240] China's president Xi Jinping is now proposing to create so-called "destiny communities" (*mingyun gongtongti*), which would leverage China's existing ties with other countries toward the development of "security and political communities"[241] and would explicitly exclude the United States from participation. The 2014 G-20 summit in Brisbane, Australia, demonstrated some of the cleavages between the countries of the developed West and those of the rising South and East, and highlighted some of the difficulties in forging a workable consensus.[242]

Recommendations for compromise and dialogue among the major powers, along the lines that Etzioni, Ikenberry, Kupchan, and others have proposed, may provide a way forward. But there must also be an impetus to act. For a brief moment, 9/11 scared the governments of the world badly enough that they began to envision what the future might be like if there was a string of successful follow-up attacks around the world. That fear helped to motivate the political breakthroughs that led to the formation of the ad hoc antiterror coalition and more organized efforts like the PSI. As that concern has receded, however, the push for more effective Global Authorities has stalled. As occurred in the aftermath of the Cuban Missile Crisis, the fear that had spurred governments to act following 9/11 dissipated in the years that followed and ended the early momentum surrounding the establishment of the Global Authorities. Subsequent events—smaller-scale terrorist attacks, the SARS and Ebola health crises, and even the financial crisis of 2008–09—have not served to keep up the momentum to goad governments into moving on the agenda of setting up Global Authorities. Nevertheless, a foundation has been laid that can be built upon in the future if and when there is another critical shock to the global order.

Notes

1. See Amitai Etzioni, *The Hard Way to Peace: A New Strategy* (New York: Crowell-Collier Press, 1962), 173–201; Amitai Etzioni, *Winning Without War* (Garden City, NY: Doubleday and Company, Inc., 1964), 215–58.
2. Etzioni, *Hard Way*, 182.
3. *Etzioni, Winning Without War*, 228.
4. The term "globalization," as understood in this meaning, was popularized in a famed 1983 *Harvard Business Review* article by the economist Theodore Levitt (who would be a colleague of Etzioni's during the latter's residence

at the Harvard Business School). Cf. Theodore Levitt, "The Globalization of Markets," *Harvard Business Review*, May 1983, https://hbr.org/1983/05/the-globalization-of-markets.

5.   Dennis Hale, "Communitarianism: The Highest State of Progressivism—The Active Society Revisited," *The Active Society Revisited*, ed. Wilson Carey McWilliams (Lanham, MD: Rowman and Littlefield, 2006), 125, 126.

6.   Owen Chamberlain, "Gradualism," *Bulletin of the Atomic Scientists* 18:8 (October 1962), 31.

7.   John Yoo, *Point of Attack: Preventive War, International Law and Global Welfare* (Oxford: Oxford University Press, 2014), 160; Robert I. Rotberg, "The Failure and Collapse of Nation-States: Breakdown, Prevention and Repair," *When States Fail: Causes and Consequences*, ed. Robert I. Rotberg (Princeton, NJ: Princeton University Press, 2004), 1.

8.   See, for instance, William E. Scheuerman, *The Realist Case for Global Reform* (Cambridge: Polity Press, 2011).

9.   Teresa Whitfield, *Friends Indeed?: The United Nations, Groups of Friends, and the Resolution of Conflict* (Washington, DC: United States Institute of Peace, 2007), 19.

10. Signe Burgstaller, *U.N. Conflict Management: An Institutionalist Perspective* (Stockholm: Swedish Defense Research Establishment, 1994), 1.

11. "Address Before a Joint Session of the Congress on the State of the Union," January 29, 1991, http://www.presidency.ucsb.edu/ws/?pid=19253.

12. "Interview with Brent Scowcroft," part of the George H. W. Bush Oral History project of the Miller Center of the University of Virginia. Transcript available at http://millercenter.org/president/bush/oralhistory/brent-scowcroft.

13. G. John Ikenberry, "State Power and International Institutions: America and the Logic of Economic and Security Multilateralism," Multilateralism and Security Institutions in an Era of Globalization, eds. Dimitris Bourantonis, Kostas Ifantis, and Panayotis Tsaknoas (Abingdon, Oxon: Routledge, 2008), 36.

14. Comments of Adrian Karatnycky, then the head of Freedom House, quoted in Nikolas K. Gvosdev, "Achieving a Global Community, Realistically," *The Good Society* 14:3 (2005), 10.

15. Warren Christopher, *In the Stream of History: Shaping Foreign Policy for a New Era* (Stanford, CA: Stanford University Press, 1998), 166.

16. Ikenberry, 36.

17. See Morton H. Halperin, "Guaranteeing Democracy," *Foreign Policy* 91 (Summer 1993), 112–115.

18. Quoted in Ikenberry, 37.

19. For the use of the "spinach" metaphor, see Strobe Talbott, *The Russia Hand: A Memoir of Presidential Diplomacy* (New York: Random House, 2002, 2003), 76.

20. For instance, the so-called "Copenhagen Criteria" for prospective applicants to join the European Union require political and economic reforms designed to help inculcate a "European" attitude toward both domestic and international issues. See, for instance, Tanja Marktler, "The Power of the Copenhagen Criteria," *Croatian Yearbook of European Law and Policy* 2 (2006), esp. 344–48.

21. Michael N. Barnett, "Bringing in the New World Order: Liberalism, Legitimacy and the United Nations," *World Politics* 49 (July 1997), 545.

22. Brian Greenhill and Michael Strausz have discussed this trend with regard to the Genocide Treaty. "Explaining Nonratification of the Genocide Convention: A Nested Analysis" *Foreign Policy Analysis* 10:4 (October 2014), 371, 379.

23. See, for instance, Raju G.G. Thomas, "The South Asian Security Balance in a Western Dominant World," *Balance of Power*, eds. T.V. Paul, James J. Wirtz, and Michel Fortmann (Stanford, CA: Stanford University Press, 2004), 316–17.

24. See, for instance, the justifications for permitting normal trading relations between the United States and China and for ratifying China's entry into the World Trade Organization—that bringing Beijing into a major Western-derived rules-based organization would lead, over time, to fundamental change in China itself and its evolution along Western lines. Kathleen Michels et al., "China and the World Trade Organization," *China in Transition*, ed. K.S. Sim (Hauppauge, NY: Nova Science Publishers, 2003), 70–72.

25. Etzioni himself observed in 1995 that the United States was playing a lower key role in the world and that this was "compatible with the need to focus on neglected domestic matters such as deficit reduction and welfare reform." This was in the context of urging Washington to shift from a peace-imposing to a mediation role in solving pressing regional conflicts. See Amitai Etzioni, "Rethinking Peacekeeping, Beyond Intervention to Mediation," *The Washington Quarterly* 18:3 (Summer 1995), 75–87.

26. Sarah B. Sewall, "U.S. Policy and Practice Regarding Multilateral Peace Operations," Carr Center for Human Rights Policy Working Paper 01-3 (February 1, 2001), 33.

27. Leonie Murray, *Clinton, Peacekeeping and Humanitarian Interventionism: Rise and Fall of a Policy* (Abingdon, Oxon: Routledge, 2008), 53.

28. Nikolas K. Gvosdev, "Communitarian Realism," *American Behavioral Scientist* 48:12 (August 2005), 1595.

29. Falk, 101.

30. Seawall, 2.

31. Richard Falk, "Explaining the UN's Unhappy 50th Anniversary: Towards Reclaiming the Next Half-Century," *A United Nations for the Twenty-First Century: Peace, Security, and Development*, eds. Dimitris Bourantonis and Marios L. Evriviades (The Hague: Kluwer Law International, 1996), 90.

32. Ralf Dahrendorf, "Can European Democracy Survive Globalization?" *The National Interest* 65 (Fall 2001), 21.

33. Ikenberry, 38.

34. Barrett L. McCormick lays out the arguments—and their implications—of both the "end of history" thesis (that ideological questions have been solved in Western liberalism) and the "democratic peace" theorem (that democracies share values and will converge in their perspectives on international order), in his "Introduction," in *What If China Doesn't Democratize: Implications for War and Peace* (Armonk, NY: M.E. Sharpe, 2000), esp. 5–7.

35. See Lee Kwan Yew's interview with Fareed Zakaria, "A Conversation with Lee Kuan Yew," *Foreign Affairs* 73:2 (March/April 1994), 109–126,

http://www.foreignaffairs.com/articles/49691/fareed-zakaria/a-conversation-with-lee-kuan-yew.

36. Etzioni, *From Empire to Community*, 50.
37. Barrett L. McCormick, "U.S.-PRC Relations and the 'Democratic Peace,'" in *What If China Doesn't Democratize*, 314–315.
38. See, for instance, Robert B. Albritton and Thawilwadee Bureekul, "Are Democracy and 'Good Governance' Always Compatible? Competing Values in the Thai Political Arena," *Democracy, Governance and Development Working Paper Series* 47 (2009).
39. Pang Zhongying, "Some Points on Understanding China's International Environment," *National Interest*, October 23, 2002, http://nationalinterest.org/article/some-points-on-understanding-chinas-international-environment-2150.
40. Steven E. Miller, "The War on Terror and International Order: Strategic Choice and Global Governance," *Rising States, Rising Institutions: Challenges for Global Governance*, eds. Alan S. Alexandroff and Andrew Fenton Cooper (Washington, DC: Brookings Institution, 2010), 266.
41. Derek S. Reveron, *Exporting Security: International Engagement, Security Cooperation, and the Changing Face of the U.S. Military* (Washington, DC: Georgetown University Press, 2010), 21, 39.
42. Ray Takeyh and Nikolas K. Gvosdev, "Do Terrorist Networks Need a Home?" *Washington Quarterly* 25:3 (Summer 2002), 106.
43. David L. Phillips, "Draining the swamp of support for terrorism," *CNBC*, January 9, 2015, http://www.cnbc.com/id/102325911#.
44. William Crotty, "Conclusion: Terrorism, Security and the American State," *The Politics of Terror: The U.S. Response to 9/11*, ed. William Crotty (Boston: Northeastern University Press, 2004), 290.
45. Nikolas K. Gvosdev and Ray Takeyh, "Triumph of the New Wilsonism," *The National Interest* 117 (January/February 2012), 12.
46. Paul Dibb, "The Future of International Coalitions: How Useful? How Manageable?," *The Battle for Hearts and Minds: Using Soft Power to Undermine Terrorist Networks*, ed. Alexander T. J. Lennon (Washington, DC: Center for Strategic and International Studies, 2003), 35.
47. See, for instance, G. John Ikenberry. "Is American Multilateralism in Decline?" *Perspectives on Politics* 1:3 (September 2003), 533–49.
48. Joseph Nye, "Seven Tests: Between Concert and Unilateralism," *The National Interest* 66 (Winter 2001/02), 9. See also the comments made by Richard Perle about why seeking mandates from the United Nations or NATO in the aftermath of 9/11 would set a bad precedent for the United States, in "After September 11: A Conversation," *The National Interest* 65–S (Thanksgiving 2001), 13.
49. Michael Rühle, "NATO After Prague: Learning the Lessons of 9/11," *Parameters* 23:2 (Summer 2003), 91.
50. Luisa Blanchfield, *United Nations Reform: U.S. Policy and International Perspectives*, Congressional Research Service report RL33848 (December 21, 2011), 1.
51. Jofi Joseph, "The Exercise of National Sovereignty: The Bush Administration's Approach to Combating Weapons of Mass Destruction Proliferation," *The Nonproliferation Review* 12:2 (July 2005), 379.

52. The term comes from Chinese discussions about the extent to which Beijing should take part in multilateral activities in East Asia, and the assessment that China ought to tailor its involvement based on geopolitical and geo-economic factors. See Jianwei Wang, "China's Multilateral Diplomacy in the New Millennium," *China Rising: Power and Motivation in Chinese Foreign Policy*, eds. Yong Deng and Fei-Ling Wang (Lanham, MD: Rowman and Littlefield, 2005), 167. The idea was developed much more fully in Pang Zhongying's article ("China's Asia Strategy: Flexible Multilateralism") that appeared in the Chinese journal *World Economics and Politics* 10 (2001), 30–36.

53. All factions within the George W. Bush administration shared this concern. Both Secretary of State Colin Powell and Secretary of Defense Donald Rumsfeld agreed that the requirements of any alliance or coalition should not constrain the ability of the US government to defend its territory and citizens. See Colin Powell's testimony, "The Campaign Against Terrorism," before the Senate Foreign Relations Committee (October 25, 2001) and Rumsfeld's interview with Larry King, CNN, December 5, 2001, http://www.defense.gov/transcripts/transcript.aspx?transcriptid=2603.

54. Stewart Patrick, "Prix Fixe and à la Carte: Avoiding False Multilateral Choices," *The Washington Quarterly* 32:4 (October 2009), 83.

55. Jeffrey W. Knopf, "Wrestling with Deterrence: Bush Administration Strategy after 9/11," *Contemporary Security Policy* 29:2 (August 2008), 240.

56. Thom Shanker, "White House Says the U.S. Is Not a Loner, Just Choosy," *New York Times*, July 31, 2001, http://www.nytimes.com/2001/07/31/world/white-house-says-the-us-is-not-a-loner-just-choosy.html.

57. J. Richard Powell, "The Presidency Responds: The Implications of 9/11 for the Bush Administration's Policy Agenda," *The Politics of Terror*, 274.

58. Fareed Zakaria, *The Post-American World: Release 2.0* (New York: W.W. Norton and Co., 2008, 2011), 56.

59. Patrick, 83.

60. Vladislav Inozemtsev and Sergei Karaganov, "Imperialism of the Fittest," *The National Interest* 80 (Summer 2005), 74.

61. Jean-François Rischard, "Global Issues Networks: Desperate Times Deserve Innovative Measures," *The Washington Quarterly* 26:1 (Winter 2002/03), esp. 17–20.

62. Etzioni, *From Empire to Community*, 9.

63. Etzioni, *From Empire to Community*, 117.

64. See Alexander Wendt, "Collective Identity Formation and the International State," *American Political Science Review* 88:2 (June 1994), 389.

65. Etzioni, *Winning Without War*, 236.

66. Joseph S. Nye, Jr. and Robert O. Keohane, "Transnational Relations and World Politics: An Introduction," *International Organization* 25:3 (Summer 1971), 339. Transnational authorities regulating finance and transportation are two of the examples they provide.

67. Robert O. Keohane and Joseph S. Nye, *Power and Interdependence: World Politics in Transition* (Boston, MA: Addison Wesley, 1977), 25.

68. Robert M. Cutler, "The OSCE's Parliamentary Diplomacy in Central Asia and the South Caucasus in Comparative Perspective," *Studia Diplomatica* 59:2 (2006), 79–80.

69. Robert O. Keohane and Joseph S. Nye, "Transgovernmental Relations and International Organizations," *World Politics* 47 (October 1974), 50.

70. See Michael Lipson's discussion of this evolution among export-control officials, in "Transgovernmental Networks and Nonproliferation: International Security and the Future of Global Governance," *International Journal* 61:1 (Winter 2005/2006), 190.

71. See, for instance, Anne-Marie Slaughter, "The Real New World Order," *Foreign Affairs* 76:5 (September–October 1997), 185.

72. See, for instance, Richard Haass, "The Palmerstonian Moment," *The National Interest* 93 (January/February 2008), 10.

73. Anne-Marie Slaughter, "America's Edge: Power in the Networked Century," *Foreign Affairs* 88:1 (January/February 2009), 100.

74. Rischard, 17.

75. Etzioni, *From Empire to Community*, 144.

76. Etzioni, *From Empire to Community*, 161.

77. One interesting sign of this has been the embrace of the climate-change issue as a pressing national security concern—as well as calls for more extensive intergovernmental action to meet this threat—by national militaries and their civilian security counterparts. See the essay penned by Des Browne, the former UK Secretary of State for Defense, and Michael Shank, "A Clear and Present Danger to Planet Earth: Climate Change," *The National Interest*, January 26, 2015, http://nationalinterest.org/feature/clear-present-danger-planet-earth-climate-change-12107.

78. Graham Allison, Karl Kaiser, and Sergei Karaganov, "The World Needs a Global Alliance for Security," *International Herald Tribune*, November 21, 2001, http://www.nytimes.com/2001/11/21/opinion/21iht-edgraham_ed3_.html.

79. Dibb, 33.

80. "Amitai Etzioni—Inteview," *Federalist Debate* 20:3 (November 2007), http://www.federalist-debate.org/index.php/current/item/291-amitai-etzioni.

81. Etzioni, *From Empire to Community*, 206.

82. Slaughter, "The Real New World," 185.

83. Patrick, 83.

84. Etzioni, *From Empire to Community*, 162.

85. Patrick, 83.

86. Etzioni, *From Empire to Community*, 160, 162–63.

87. Etzioni has expressed concerns that new global institutions not duplicate the "cumbersome" setup of the organizations created under the "old system." Cf. "Amitai Etzioni—Interview," op. cit.

88. See, for instance, "Amitai Etzioni—Interview," op. cit.

89. See, for instance, his comments in "Tomorrow's Institution Today," *Foreign Affairs* 88:3 (May/June 2009), 7, 11.

90. This is in keeping with what is for Etzioni a key communitarian principle of subsidiarity: the lowest level of authority capable of dealing with a problem should have jurisdiction. In his discussion of the global architecture, he draws a clear distinction between missions that would come under the aegis of the central/global authority versus others that would remain clearly in the zone of local/national jurisdiction. "Amitai Etzioni—Interview," op. cit.

91. See, for instance, Charles A. Kupchan, *No One's World: The West, the Rising Rest and the Coming Global Turn* (New York: Oxford University Press, 2012), 189.
92. Amitai Etzioni and G. John Ikenberry, "Point of Order: Is China More Westphalian than the West?" *Foreign Affairs* 90:6 (November/December 2011), http://www.foreignaffairs.com/articles/136548/amitai-etzioni-g-john-ikenberry/point-of-order.
93. Etzioni, *From Empire to Community*, 39–40, 44, 45.
94. Kupchan, 189–90.
95. Thomas M. Nichols, *Eve of Destruction: The Coming Age of Preventive War* (Philadelphia,: University of Pennsylvania Press, 2008), 147.
96. Etzioni, *From Empire to Community*, 59.
97. Nichols, 147.
98. Etzioni, *From Empire to Community*, 204–05.
99. See, for instance, David B. H. Denoon, *The Economic and Strategic Rise of China and India* (New York: Palgrave Macmillan, 2007).
100. Kupchan, 186–87.
101. Nichols, 146–48.
102. Etzioni and Ikenberry, op. cit.
103. On the importance of a basic consensus, see Amitai Etzioni, "Affective Bonds and Moral Norms: A Communitarian Approach to the Emerging Global Society," *Internationale Politik und Gesellschaft* 3 (2005), 133, drawing in turn on observations made by Talcott Parsons about the importance of this consensus for the successful functioning of any political body, in *Toward a General Theory of Action* (Cambridge, MA: Harvard University Press, 1951).
104. David Bosco, *Rough Justice: The International Criminal Court in a World of Power Politics* (New York: Oxford University Press, 2014), 22.
105. Philip Alston and John Tessitore, "EIA Interview with Philip Alston on a World Court for Human Rights," *Ethics and International Affairs*, November 10, 2014, http://www.ethicsandinternationalaffairs.org/2014/eia-interview-with-philip-alston-on-a-world-court-for-human-rights/.
106. Alston and Tessitore, op. cit.
107. Etzioni, *From Empire to Community*, 116.
108. Rischard, 29–31.
109. James Rosenau, "Conclusions. Governing the Ungovernable. The Challenge of a Global Disaggregation of Authority," *Contemporary Global Governance: Multipolarity Versus New Discourses on Global Governance*, eds. Dries Lesage and Pierre Vercauteren (Brussels: Peter Lang, 2009), 261–62.
110. Inozemtsev and Karaganov, 74.
111. One example where he believes Etzioni's Global Authority approach might be useful is the creation of an authority that would manage the atomic fuel cycle for more states that want nuclear power but would reduce risk of weapons proliferation. See James E. Goodby, "Internationalizing the Fuel Cycle," *Reykjavik Revisited: Steps Toward a World Free of Nuclear Weapons*, ed. George P. Schultz (Stanford, CA: Hoover Institution Press, 2008), 347.
112. Ronald K. Noble, "September 11, 2001 : Attack on America," 70th Interpol General Assembly Speech, Budapest, Hungary, September 26, 2001, archived at http://avalon.law.yale.edu/sept11/interpol_006.asp.

113. See Dick K. Nanto, *9/11 Terrorism: Global Economic Costs*, Congressional Research Service report RS21937 (October 5, 2004).

114. Victor D. Comras, *Flawed Diplomacy: The United Nations and the War on Terrorism* (Washington, DC: Potomac Books, 2008), 42.

115. Nichols, 97.

116. Nikolas K. Gvosdev and Christopher Marsh, *Russian Foreign Policy: Interests, Vectors and Sectors* (Los Angeles, : Sage, 2013), 85–86; Chris Dalby, "NATO-SCO: Partners, if not Allies," *World Post*, December 1, 2010, http://www.huffingtonpost.com/chris-dalby/nato-sco-partners-if-not_b_790232.html.

117. Mathieu Deflem, "Global Rule of Law or Global Rule of Law Enforcement? International Police Cooperation and Counterterrorism," *Annals of the American Academy of Political and Social Science* 603 (January 2006), 241.

118. For instance, a US-Russia working group was set up to facilitate information exchange. Cf. Aglaya Snetkov, "When the Internal and External Collide: A Social Constructivist Reading of Russian Security Policy," *Russia and the World: The Internal-External Nexus*, eds. Natasha Kurht (Abingdon, Oxon: Routledge, 2013), 137.

119. Nikolas K. Gvosdev and Dimitri K. Simes, "Rejecting Russia?" *The National Interest* 80 (Summer 2005), 5, at http://nationalinterest.org/article/rejecting-russia-1083.

120. Details of the case are available at the FBI website, http://www.fbi.gov/news/stories/2005/december/missile_sting121905.

121. Paul Close, David Askew, and Xu Xin, *The Beijing Olympiad: The Political Economy of a Sporting Mega-Event* (Abingdon, Oxon: Routledge, 2007), lxxix.

122. Shannon Tiezzi, "Can the U.S. and China Cooperate to Fight Terrorism?" *The Diplomat*, May 3, 2014, http://thediplomat.com/2014/05/can-the-u-s-and-china-cooperate-to-fight-terrorism/.

123. Denny Roy, *Lukewarm Partner: Chinese Support for U.S. Counter-Terrorism in Southeast Asia* (Honolulu,: Asia-Pacific Center for Security Studies, 2006), 2.

124. Deflem, 244; see also the narrative in Comras.

125. Deflem, 244–48.

126. Alain Damais, "The Financial Action Task Force," *Anti-Money Laundering: International Law and Practice*, eds. Wouter H. Muller, Christian H. Kalin, and John G. Goldsworth (London: John Wiley and Sons, 2007), 73.

127. See, for instance, Thomas J. Biersteker, Sue E. Eckert, and Peter Romaniuk, "International Initiatives to Counter The Financing of Terrorism," *Countering the Financing of Terrorism*, eds. Thomas J. Biersteker and Sue E. Eckert (Abingdon, Oxon: Routledge, 2008), 240, 242, 243.

128. Yee Kuang Heng and Ken McDonagh, "The Other War on Terror Revealed: Global Governability and the Financial Action Task Force's Campaign Against Terrorist Financing," *Review of International Studies* 34 (2008), 555, 570.

129. Yee and McDonagh, 565–66.

130. Damais, 72.

131. Dibb, 33–34.

132. Etzioni, *From Empire to Community*, 104–07.

133. Etzioni, *From Empire to Community*, 106.
134. Etzioni, *From Empire to Community*, 107.
135. "Obama's Speech at Woodrow Wilson Center," *Council on Foreign Relations*, August 1, 2007, http://www.cfr.org/elections/obamas-speech-woodrow-wilson-center/p13974.
136. Etzioni, *From Empire to Community*, 163.
137. Deflem, 241.
138. As early as December 2001 there were warnings about how the pursuit of US military action against Iraq might fracture the antiterror coalition. See Ivo Daalder and James M. Lindsay, "Nasty, Brutish and Long: America's War on Terrorism," *Brookings Issue Brief*, December 2001, http://www.brookings.edu/research/articles/2001/12/terrorism-daalder.
139. See, for instance, Tiezzi, op. cit.
140. Mirko Sossai, "'UNSC Res.1373 (2001) and International Law-Making: A Transformation in Nature of the Legal Obligations for the Fight Against Terrorism?" Paper presented at the Agora on Terrorism and International Law, Inaugural Conference of the European Society of International Law, Florence, May 14, 2004, 7, http://www.esil-sedi.eu/sites/default/files/Sossai_0.PDF .
141. Comras, xv.
142. "The Global Regime for Terrorism," Council on Foreign Relations issue brief, June 19, 2013, http://www.cfr.org/terrorism/global-regime-terrorism/p25729.
143. *Highlights of a Forum: Enhancing U.S. Partnerships In Countering Transnational Terrorism*, GAO report no. GAO-08-887SP, July 31, 2008.
144. Roy, 2.
145. Tiezzi, op. cit.
146. Yong Deng, "China: The Post-Responsible Power," *The Washington Quarterly* 37:4 (Winter 2015), http://twq.elliott.gwu.edu/china-post-responsible-power.
147. Linda Kintsler, "A Year After the Boston Bombing, U.S.-Russia Counterterrorism Cooperation Is Only Getting Worse," *The New Republic*, April 16, 2014, http://www.newrepublic.com/article/117396/us-russia-counterterrorism-cooperation-has-only-gotten-worse.
148. Michael S. Schmidt and Eric Schmitt, "Russia Didn't Share All Details on Boston Bombing Suspect, Report Says," *New York Times*, April 9, 2014, http://www.nytimes.com/2014/04/10/us/russia-failed-to-share-details-on-boston-marathon-bombing-suspect.html?_r=0.
149. Sam Nunn and Richard Lugar, "The United States and Russia Must Repair Their Partnership on Nuclear Security," *The Washington Post*, January 23, 2015, http://www.washingtonpost.com/opinions/the-united-states-and-russia-must-repair-their-partnership-on-nuclear-security/2015/01/23/555b9a60-a271-11e4-903f-9f2faf7cd9fe_story.html.
150. Nunn and Lugar, op. cit.
151. Vladimir Isachenkov, "Russian FM Pledges Cooperation With West to Combat Terror," *ABC News*, January 21, 2015, http://abcnews.go.com/International/wireStory/russian-fm-pledges-cooperation-west-combat-terror-28367237.

152. Austin Ramsey, "China Criticizes U.S. Terrorism Report," *New York Times*, May 2, 2014, http://sinosphere.blogs.nytimes.com/2014/05/02/china-criticizes-u-s-terrorism-report/?_r=1.

153. Guo Renjie, "China, Russia hold 'Oriental - 2014' Joint Anti-Terrorism Drill," *China Military Online*, August 27, 2014, http://eng.chinamil.com.cn/news-channels/china-military-news/2014-08/27/content_6114137.htm.

154. Yo-Jung Chen, "Zhou Yongkang, Islamic State and China's Pivot West," *The Diplomat*, September 9, 2014, http://thediplomat.com/2014/09/zhou-yongkang-islamic-state-and-chinas-pivot-west/; Shannon Tiezzi, "Will China Join the Fight Against Islamic State?" *The Diplomat*, September 12, 2014, http://thediplomat.com/2014/09/will-china-join-the-fight-against-islamic-state/.

155. See, for instance, the analysis presented by Anna Borshchevskaya, "Why Russia Will Be the Big Winner in The Next Round of Syria Peace Talks," *Business Insider*, January 27, 2015, http://www.businessinsider.com/anna-borshchevskaya-russia-winner-in-next-round-of-syria-peace-talks-2015-1.

156. Etzioni, "Tomorrow's Institution Today," 7.

157. Susan J. Koch, *Proliferation Security Initiative: Origins and Evolution*, Center for the Study of the Weapons of Mass Destruction Occasional Paper 9. (Washington, DC: National Defense University Press, 2012), 4–7.

158. Koch, 9, 10, 11.

159. Koch, 11.

160. Koch, 17.

161. *The Proliferation Security Initiative: A Model for Future International Collaboration*, ed. Robert Joseph (Fairfax, VA: National Institute Press, 2009), 25.

162. Etzioni himself notes: "The PSI has no council in which one member can exercise veto power. It has no multistate committees that must unanimously approve each target, as was the case for a while for NATO during its bombing operations in Kosovo in 1999. And it has no bureaucracy that must be paid for and monitored and that may hinder action with red tape, turf wars, or office politics." Etzioni, "Tomorrow's Institution Today," 8.

163. Koch, 21.

164. Charles Wolf, Brian G. Chow, and Gregory S. Jones, *U.S. Combat Commands' Participation in the Proliferation Security Initiative: A Training Manual* (Santa Monica, CA: RAND Corporation, 2009), 10.

165. Etzioni, "Tomorrow's Institution Today," 9.

166. *Proliferation Security Initiative*, 30.

167. Mark J. Valencia, "The Proliferation Security Initiative: A Glass Half-Full," *Arms Control Today*, June 2, 2007, http://www.armscontrol.org/act/2007_06/Valencia.

168. Ye Ru'an and Zhao Qinghai, "The PSI: Chinese Thinking and Concerns," *The Monitor* (Center for International Trade and Security), 10:1 (Spring 2004), 23, 24.

169. Valencia, op. cit.

170. *Proliferation Security Initiative*, 23.

171. Valencia, op. cit.

172. Etzioni, "Tomorrow's Institution Today," 10; *Proliferation Security Initiative*, 29.

173. Robert Joseph, who served as the senior director for proliferation matters for the National Security Council during the first term of the George W. Bush administration, and who spearheaded the talks with Libya that led to the agreement to give up WMD, has described the incident in his *Countering WMD: The Libyan Experience* (Fairfax, VA: National Institute Press, 2009), 40–41; see also *Proliferation Security Initiative*, 30–31.

174. Ian Williams, "Proliferation Security Initiative: Ten Years On," Arms Control NOW, May 28, 2013, http://armscontrolnow.org/2013/05/28/proliferation-security-initiative-ten-years-on/.

175. Quoted in Koch, 30.

176. Koch, 23.

177. Koch, 14.

178. Quoted in Mary Beth Nikitin, *The Proliferation Security Initiative*, Congressional Service Research report RL34237 (June 15, 2012), i.

179. Ironically, American ratification has been held up by US domestic politics in terms of scheduling votes in the Senate.

180. See, for instance, Aaron Dunne, *The Proliferation Security Initiative: Legal Considerations and Operational Realities*, SIPRI Policy Paper 36 (Stockholm: SIPRI, May 2013).

181. *Proliferation Security Initiative*, 42.

182. Etzioni, "Tomorrow's Institution Today," 9.

183. *Proliferation Security Initiative*, 38–40; Etzioni, "Tomorrow's Institution Today," 10–11.

184. "Another EU Threat to National Sovereignty," *The Telegraph*, April 14, 2014, http://www.telegraph.co.uk/news/worldnews/europe/eu/10765509/Another-EU-threat-to-national-sovereignty.html.

185. Quoting Baker Spring of the Heritage Foundation, in Jofi Joseph, "The Exercise of National Sovereignty: The Bush Administration's Approach to Combating Weapons of Mass Destruction," *The Nonproliferation Review* 12:2 (July 2005), 379.

186. For more details, see the fact sheet and chronology of GICNT activities provided by the Nuclear Threat Initiative, http://www.nti.org/treaties-and-regimes/global-initiative-combat-nuclear-terrorism-gicnt/; *Proliferation Security Initiative*, 49–52.

187. Alan Heyes, Wyn Q. Bowen, and Hugh Chalmers, *The Global Partnership Against WMD: Success and Shortcomings of G8 Threat Reduction Since 9/11* (London: RUSI, 2011), 29–30.

188. "The Global Initiative to Combat Nuclear Terrorism," *Stimson Center*, May 30, 2007, http://www.stimson.org/the-global-initiative-to-combat-nuclear-terrorism-/.

189. Dennis Lynch, "Russia Ends Nuke Cooperation With US, Endangers Global Terrorism Fight," *International Business Times*, January 21, 2015, http://www.ibtimes.com/russia-ends-nuke-cooperation-us-endangers-global-terrorism-fight-1789400.

190. Etzioni, "Tomorrow's Institution Today," 11.

191. Admiral Michael G. Mullen, "Keynote Address: A Global Network of Nations for a Free and Secure Maritime Commons," in *Seventeenth International Seapower Symposium: Report of the Proceedings, 19-23 September 2005*, ed. John B. Hattendorf (Newport, RI: U.S. Naval War College, 2006), 6.

192. Tristan McConnell, "Somali Pirates' Rise Linked to Illegal Fishing and Toxic Dumping," *Global Post*, March 16, 2012, http://www.globalpost.com/dispatch/news/regions/africa/120306/pirates-Somalia-how-it-started%20.

193. Andrew S. Erickson and Austin M. Strange, *No Substitute for Experience: Chinese Antipiracy Operations in the Gulf of Aden*, China Maritime Study 10 (Newport, RI: China Maritime Studies Institute-Naval War College, 2013), 11.

194. Erickson and Strange, 59.

195. Quoted in Erickson and Strange, 62.

196. Erickson and Strange, 63.

197. J. Peter Pham, "Countering Somali Piracy by Involving the Private Sector," *World Defense Review*, April 30, 2009, at http://worlddefensereview.com/pham043009.shtml.

198. Erickson and Strange, 62–63.

199. See, for instance, Nikolas Gvosdev, "Making the G-20 a True Global Security Forum," *World Politics Review*, January 11, 2011, http://www.worldpolitics-review.com/articles/7531/making-the-g-20-a-true-global-security-forum.

200. See the comments of former Indonesian Foreign Minister N. Hassan Wirajuda, "ASEAN's Community-Building Process," *Horizons* 2 (Winter 2015), 128–29.

201. Rodolfo C. Severino, *Southeast Asia in Search of an ASEAN Community: Insights from the Former Secretary General* (Singapore: Institute of Southeast Asian Studies, 2006), 80.

202. A more detailed discussion of the "ASEAN Way," designed to prevent conflict between members and to eliminate the possibility of internal subversion of the member-states by outside forces, can be found in Amitav Acharya, *Constructing a Security Community in Southeast Asia: ASEAN and the Problem of Regional Order* (Abingdon, Oxon: Routledge, 2001), 47–49.

203. See the comments of Termsak Chalermpalanupap, a special assistant to the ASEAN Secretary General, in "ASEAN-10: Meeting the Challenges," *ASEAN*, June 1, 1999, http://www.asean.org/resources/item/asean-10-meeting-the-challenges-by-termsak-chalermpalanupap.

204. K. Shanmugam, "ASEAN and its Place in the Global Architecture," *Horizons* 2 (Winter 2015), 117–19.

205. Wirajuda, 126.

206. Donald E. Weatherbee, *International Relations in Southeast Asia: The Struggle for Autonomy* (Lanham, MD: Rowman and Littlefield, 2009), 128.

207. Jonathan T. Chow, "ASEAN Counterterrorism Cooperation Since 9/11," *Asian Survey* 45:2 (March/April 2005), 303–04.

208. See Amit Acharaya, "Security Challenges in the ASEAN Region," (presentation to the Securing Asia Conference, London, June 25–26, 2012), http://amitavacharya.com/sites/default/files/ASEAN-Securing%20Asia%20-London%20Presentation.pdf.

209. Rizal Sukma, "The ASEAN Charter: Neither Bold Nor Visionary," *The Road to Ratification and Implementation of the ASEAN Charter*, ed. Pavin Chachavalpongpun (Singapore: Institute of Southeast Asia Studies Press, 2009), 47.

210. Chow, 304.

211. Riddhi Shah, "An 'ASEAN Way' of Combatting National Crime," *SSPC Issue Brief* 7 (February 2013), 4.
212. Chow, 305.
213. Chow, 308–09.
214. Chow, 312–13.
215. Alfred Gertsl, "The Depoliticisation and 'ASEANisation' of Counter-Terrorism Policies in South-East Asia: A Weak Trigger for a Fragmented Version of Human Security," *Austrian Journal of South-East Asian Studies* 3:1 (2010), 64.
216. Chow, 317; Gertsl, 64.
217. Chow, 319.
218. Shah, 4; Gertsl, 64; "ASEAN to Set Up Security Agency on Lines of Interpol," *Zee News*, May 14, 2009, http://zeenews.india.com/news/world/asean-to-set-up-security-agency-on-lines-of-interpol_531823.html.
219. Gerstl, 66.
220. Shah, 4.
221. Kishore Mahbubani, "ASEAN as a Living, Breathing Modern Miracle," *Horizons* 2 (Winter 2015), 147.
222. "Thailand: Learning the Lessons from SARS and Bird Flu," *IRIN*, April 29, 2009, http://www.irinnews.org/report/84158/thailand-learning-the-lessons-from-sars-and-bird-flu.
223. Mely Caballero-Anthony and Gianna Gayle Herrera Amul, "Did SARS Prepare East Asia for Ebola?" *The Diplomat* (October 18, 2014), http://thediplomat.com/2014/10/did-sars-prepare-east-asia-for-ebola/.
224. Tang Siew Mun, "Keeping the Momentum of Asean's Community Building," *The Straits Times*, January 31, 2015, http://news.asiaone.com/news/asian-opinions/keeping-momentum-aseans-community-building.
225. Shah, 6.
226. Gerstl, 66.
227. Chow, 319.
228. Acharaya, "Security Challenges," op. cit.
229. Gerstl, 64.
230. Mahbubani, 142–143.
231. Shah, 8.
232. Gerstl, 67.
233. Mahbubani, 145–146.
234. See, for instance, the discussion about whether the United States and Russia can work together given major divergences in values and political systems, in *Russia and U.S. National Interests: Why Should Americans Care?*, A report of the Task Force on Russia and U.S. National Interests (Washington, DC: Belfer Center and the Center for the National Interest, October 2011), 10–11, http://www.cftni.org/Russia-and-US-NI_final-web.pdf.
235. Menno R. Kamminga,"Etzioni's Communitarian Realism as a Guide to Foreign Politics?" *PHILICA.COM* 158 (April 20, 2009), http://philica.com/display_article.php?article_id=158. .
236. Gvosdev, "Making the G-20," op. cit.
237. Etzioni, *From Empire to Communty*, 173.

238. This trend was identified by Nazneen Barma, Ely Ratner, and Steven Weber, "A World Without the West," *The National Interest* 90 (July/August 2007), 23–30.

239. The strategy expresses the sentiment that "no global problems . . . can be solved without the United States" but also recognizes that "few . . . can be solved by the United States alone." *National Security Strategy, February 2015* (Washington, DC: The White House, 2015), 2, 3.

240. I use here the typology put forward by Harry Harding, that there are two principal "political parties" (the developed West versus a looser Russia-China and other rising-powers coalition) each vying to set the parameters for how the international community will operate. See his comments at "The Rise of the Rest: How the Ascent of China and Russia Affects Global Business and Security" (event held at the Carnegie Council for Ethics and International Affairs, New York, July 14, 2008), http://www.policyinnovations.org/ideas/briefings/data/000066.

241. Deng, op. cit.

242. Nikolas Gvosdev, "Challenge from the East," *Ethics and International Affairs*, November 12 (2014), http://www.ethicsandinternationalaffairs.org/2014/challenge-from-the-east/.

5

The Security First Paradigm

The foreign policy approach that Etzioni developed throughout his career defies easy categorization. The gradualism he propounded in the 1960s, and updated following the 9/11 attacks, foresaw the emergence of a new global system. This system is defined by an end to superpower conflict, and by an eventual convergence of interests that lead to more effective supranational institutions augmenting and supplementing the national state—an end state that many might characterize as liberal and utopian. Yet, in the process of reaching this goal, he appealed to national interests—the foremost being state security—not idealism about the unity of the human family, and led a series of compromises and dialogues in which many traditional liberal issues (such as promoting civil and political rights) played a less important role in how policy was to be crafted. Etzioni's call for new Global Authorities was based on his assessment that it was the optimal way to ensure the peace, security, and prosperity of the United States (and by extension, of other countries) in the post-Cold War world of the twentieth century. Etzioni foresaw a gradual formation of regional associations and, ultimately, a global community where certain sovereign responsibilities are voluntarily transferred by states under well-defined conditions to larger associations. This transfer would occur because states would voluntarily recognize that this was the most effective method to deal with pressing transnational threats (from the spread of weapons of mass destruction to the effects of climate change) that no one single country could unilaterally address. This scenario is based on the recognition that the individual nation-state is "no longer equipped to do the job it was created for"—to provide security for its citizens.[1] In other words, transnational institutions with effective power would grow and develop from the free choice of sovereign states, rather than from force and compulsion exerted in the name of idealism. In assessing Etzioni's positon, Hebrew University political scientist (and Israeli diplomat) Shlomo Avineri characterizes Etzioni as a "liberal realist" because "his normative goals are liberal, but he realizes that in order to implement them, both on the national and international level, one has to possess a sober assessment of reality and know how to build the social and political alliances necessary for their realization."[2] Part of the way to ensure an effective buy-in to this new global architecture would be to guarantee that a wide degree of social and political variation among its constituent member-states would be preserved, what Etzioni termed as "particularism within universalism."[3]

A related corollary is that the United States and other countries, in pursuit of a more secure and peaceful international order, should concentrate their efforts in ensuring that states are effective purveyors of internal stability and order and are not exporters of strife and tension. In keeping with a gradualist approach, they should concentrate on setting conditions for effective (albeit nontyrannical) governance first. Such an approach would create room for an eventual evolution in a more liberal direction, within the context of a "moral dialogue" between Western and non-Western societies carried out by civil society and representatives of communities (religious, cultural, etc.) rather than governments.[4]

Thus, the deployment of pressure (and even the possibility of force) against a country should be reserved for transgressions that threaten the security of other states or the global order or that violate the most basic of human rights, starting with the primacy of the right to life itself. Pressure and force should not be dissipated because of the dislike of a country's social, economic, and cultural choices, which may deviate significantly from Western norms. In keeping with Avineri's observation, which fits in with Etzioni's concept of "realism"—the recognition that there is a finite amount of will and resource to engage in any major intervention—and so any intervention ought to be selected with care.[5]

However, a more gradual, sequenced approach, both to building more effective institutions of international governance and to promoting reform in states around the world—as well as accepting the very idea of a dialogue on human rights and democracy—runs up against what has been the dominant attitude in many US foreign-policy circles since the end of the Cold War. This attitude is epitomized by the view that it is possible to use "America's unrivaled military, economic, and political power to fashion an international environment conducive to its interests and values"[6] and to impose a ready-made template for societal reform. Why should this approach—the utilization of power to bring about change that aligns societies and the global order more in line with American (or Western) values and preferences—not be adopted as the guiding national strategy for the United States? Why does Etzioni adopt the tools of *realpolitik* rather than embrace the apparatus of *idealpolitik*[7] (or *moralpolitik*) to deliver on security and evolution toward a more stable and lasting global community?[8]

Promoting Democracy, Promoting Security?

Current American assessments of international politics start with the presupposition that "the character of a regime has an impact on its foreign policies; thus, the effort to create a more stable and secure community of nations rests on the extent to which countries share common political values."[9] As a result, a democratic form of governance is viewed as a necessary prerequisite both for internal and external security.[10] It is also a necessary precondition for building any effective transnational association. As a senior US government official notes, "If you have a band of democratically-minded countries that accept rule of law, then they will look towards other means to resolve disputes, not undertaking aggressive behavior."[11] Thus, the so-called "democratic peace theory" holds that "durable stability . . . flows from a domestic politics built on consensus and peaceful competition, which more often than not promotes similar international conduct for governments."[12] Moreover, some believe that it is possible to simultaneously promote stability, reconstruction, and democratization—assuming there is sufficient commitment of resources and effort.[13]

Following this line of thinking, the reconstruction of societies along democratic lines is not simply a moral or humanitarian issue, but a security one.[14] This remains the default setting for US foreign policy; the *2015 National Security Strategy* explicitly declares that "defending democracy and human rights is related to every enduring national interest."[15] Construction of a democratic regime (on the Western liberal model) would ensure conflict resolution, and, particularly in divided or fractious societies, provide a process for peaceful reconciliation that would stabilize governments and contribute to regional security.[16] In turn, the successful democratization of one state is expected to "spill over and create pressures and incentives for democratization in neighboring states."[17] Indeed, a major justification for the decision not simply to use force to compel deproliferation in Iraq in 2003 but to overthrow the regime and institute an occupation designed to remake Iraq into a liberal democratic state was done under the assumption that altering the authoritarian status quo in the Middle East would bring about far-reaching security benefits for the United States as well as uphold American values.[18] Moreover, as the number of pro-American democracies grew in the world, they would become the majority in international organizations, allowing for a Western vision to become the global norm. Charles Krauthammer summed up the prevailing sentiment by arguing that the "promotion of democracy multiplies the number of nations likely to be friendly to the United States."[19] In turn, this process

> would knit the nations of the world together into a global community espousing common values and shared interests, backed up by a rising tide that would "lift the boats" of all nations and eliminate the need for zero-sum perspectives in world affairs. . . . [T]his process [would] be accompanied by an alignment of other nations with US values and interests . . .[20]

Indeed, the promotion of democracy might even solve many of the pressing international security problems that beset the United States today. For instance, a strategy of encouraging democratic change was seen as the most effective way to deal with Iran's pursuit of a nuclear capability, since a future democratic Iran that would be "pro-American and pro-democracy" would "have much less need for nuclear weapons [and] would become an American strategic partner in the region.[21]

For many in the US government, the experience of East-Central Europe in the years immediately following the opening of the Berlin Wall, the collapse of the Soviet bloc, and the disintegration of the USSR itself seemed to validate this approach. A democratic opening in one state (Poland) helped to spur other, largely peaceful, revolutions across the region. Focused assistance provided by the United States and the countries of Western Europe helped to start and buttress a process of democratization. The post-Communist governments which came to power pursued liberal democratic and free-market reforms and also shifted their geopolitical alignments to move closer to the United States in security matters.[22] Responding to American concerns about the proliferation of nuclear weapons, post-Soviet successor states gave up their independent capabilities. Particularly in the so-called "northern tier," the four countries that formed the Visegrad Group (Poland, Hungary, the Czech Republic, and Slovakia) agreed to work together and support each other's aspirations for membership in Euro-Atlantic institutions (the European Union and the North Atlantic Treaty Organization [NATO]).[23] Indeed, these countries were soon viewed as more reliable

American security partners than the long-established European treaty allies, forming a group labeled in 2003 by then- Secretary of Defense Donald Rumsfeld the "New Europe" and often described as forming a promising new bloc of US partners.[24] The Eastern European experience was thus assumed to be a template that could be replicated successfully in other parts of the world, and that would lead to similar results by producing stable liberal democratic governments that would become close partners in maintaining the security of the United States.[25] This is a critical point, because, as John Owen IV notes, "the argument that democracies do not fight one another does not have any practical implications for the foreign policymaker. It needs an additional or minor premise, such as 'the United States can make Iraq into a democracy at an acceptable cost.'"[26]

Certainly, a vision of a world of peaceful (and pro-American, to boot) democracies—and an apparent pathway to support rapid and easy democratic change in formerly authoritarian or failed states—is compelling for US policymakers. Yet it may not entirely reflect reality. Some US officials concede that the world envisioned by the democratic peace theory is a long-term outcome, and that the process of democratization can be "unclear and uncertain" and have a "destabilizing impact."[27] This raises the question as to whether it should serve as the basis for immediate policy.

Beyond that, there have been criticisms of the democratic peace theory as a whole. How one defines what constitutes a "democracy" (or a "liberal regime"), and how one applies those definitions, can allow for a certain massaging of the data to maintain the assertion that no democracy has ever fought another.[28] If one uses the standard of a fully developed democratic regime, then, historically, there have been relatively few democracies and those have had little reason to fight.[29] Finally, there is the question of causality: Do the democracies that are used as the basis for democratic peace theory not have security problems with each other because they are democracies, or did the states resolve their pressing security issues and settle questions of regional primacy and territorial claims (which often are the basis for wars) prior to democracy taking root?[30] If the latter is true, then it represents a dramatic shift in policy imperatives—toward focusing efforts on altering the external conditions between states rather than concentrating attention on the internal forms of government. This can become especially important if, as some evidence suggests, democratizing states that have not yet become fully consolidated may be more, rather than less, prone to internal violence and external conflict, as the work of Edward Mansfield and Jack Snyder has demonstrated.[31] Even those identified as "liberal internationalists," who believe in the long-term applicability of the democratic peace theory, acknowledge this reality. Anne-Marie Slaughter, who headed the policy planning staff at the State Department for Secretary Hillary Clinton during the first term of the Obama administration, has observed that "a transitional democracy, a weak democracy, a democratizing country, those countries are often very unstable and often more warlike. . . . Long term, it is in our interests [to see democracies emerge], but short term – and certainly trying to topple a regime to establish a democracy – that's not going to help our security."[32] Similarly, if, as some have argued, what appears to be validation of the democratic peace theory—the long interval of peaceful integration that has marked the Euro-Atlantic basin—is in fact the result not of shared political systems but common security considerations,[33] then one draws very different policy conclusions. Namely, that it is the creation of a security community, not the spread of democracy, that is the critical driving factor—an observation that features prominently in Etzioni's own recommendations.

Much also depends on whether post-Soviet East-Central Europe turns out to have been a very special case where a rapid transition could occur with some degree of Western assistance. As Tom Carothers notes, the preferred American "model of transition featuring a decisive breakthrough in which the old regime collapses and the country moves very quickly to open national elections, followed by longer-term processes of state reform and civil society strengthening" is not going to characterize most countries. As he continues, "Only a minority of countries in the past several decades have closely adhered to this model, however, and they have been (as in Central Europe) generally well positioned in terms of facilitative factors."[34]

In the overall assessment, the expert consensus is that, in general, "democratization is not a guarantee of improved security."[35] There is also the reality that with few exceptions there is always the risk of democratic reversals or breakdowns; the transition is rarely smooth and linear.[36] Even in Eastern Europe—if defined to include the Balkans and the former Soviet space—there were a series of conflicts, most notably the "wars of succession," that broke out in the former Yugoslavia. Ultimately, the template used in Eastern Europe can only succeed in other areas if certain preconditions are in place that depend on the legacy left by the previous administration and the nature of that society—and assuming that substantial reform is not possible in states that are at war, that are undergoing significant conflict, or that have failed.[37] This fits in with an observation made both by Etzioni and by G. John Ikenberry, namely, that the problems of Hobbes must be solved before the promise of Locke can be realized.[38] In other words, the creation of a functioning and orderly government that can ensure security must precede efforts to open and liberalize the regime—and creating a secure region and world must be the first priority of any emerging Global Authorities.

A second problem is one termed in this book as "the countdown of the competing clocks": the notion that regimes may not fall or be democratized before they have crossed important and significant milestones. For instance, a state might obtain mastery of the technology needed to produce nuclear weapons and their delivery systems before democratization may have had a chance to reach critical mass. (This assumes that a democracy would either give up such programs or could be trusted with the technology. But the first scenario is not operative if a democratic state facing the same security threat as its authoritarian predecessor decides not to give up such a deterrent. The second is based on the belief that a democracy could be better trusted with such weaponry—but the damage to the world's deproliferation effort would still be done.)

Another variant is that a regime may outlast economic sanctions imposed against it for its internal transgressions or external behavior because it possesses a commodity or service that is critical to the global economy. In keeping with the observation that democratization may end up being a long-term process, a country may not have the luxury of waiting until an odious regime becomes more acceptable before deciding to engage it diplomatically.[39] It is not an option, with the exception of a few minor countries that are located neither in critical regions of the world nor who possess needed capabilities or resources, for the United States to take the position, "We're not going to deal with you if you're not a democracy."[40]

If that is the case, then the United States is presented with several dilemmas. The first is grappling with what Ian Bremmer has labeled the "J-curve" problem: that stable but closed and authoritarian states that begin to open up and liberalize must pass through "a transitional period of dangerous instability," and may, in fact, not continue to pursue reforms.[41] This imposes on policymakers the need "to measure the pros and cons [of] whether the security of stability or the insecurity of democracy is better," given that the political turmoil that can be unleashed in efforts to promote radical and sudden political change, that "decreases the ability of the new regimes to maintain security domestically and consequently the stability of the region."[42] The second dilemma is the recognition that sometimes illiberal, authoritarian regimes have been more inclined to support the US security agenda and to offer tangible assistance in furthering American goals than more liberal, democratic regimes. Indeed, as we have seen even in the recent past,

> Shared democracy is no guarantee of common action. After all, the famed 'coalition of the willing' assembled to topple Saddam Hussein included authoritarian dictatorships such as Azerbaijan, Eritrea, and Uzbekistan as well as established democracies such as the United Kingdom and Australia. At the same time, many of the world's leading democracies, such as France, Germany, New Zealand, and India–not to mention emerging democracies in America's own backyard such as Mexico and Chile–opposed U.S. actions. Whether a country was democratic had no bearing on its decision whether to join forces with the United States against Saddam Hussein.[43]

So the debate continues over the relevance of a regime's internal governance and values to its ability to be a useful and beneficial ally of the United States.

The Moral Dilemma

Americans have never been comfortable with a pure *realpolitik* approach to foreign affairs.[44] The so-called "American missionary impulse"—the desire to intervene in the affairs of others in an effort to improve their quality of life, to "fix the world" (and, in the process, win new friends and partners)—is a driver for US foreign policy that cannot be ignored.[45] As Donald Emmerson, describing a contrasting *moralpolitik*, notes:

> As long as outrages are committed, outrage will be felt. Democracy necessarily includes and preserves the chance to translate anger into policy - moral revulsion into humanitarian intervention. . . . In a globalized world, moral indignation may be instantly ignited by media coverage of crimes that, in earlier times, might have remained obscure. Democratization has made governments more subject to pressure from activists not to stand idly by in the face of evil.[46]

The end of the Cold War and the collapse of the bipolar world helped to liberate these tendencies in the United States and in other Western states, to emphasize the moral dimension, and to engage in "ethical foreign-policy activism" designed to support human rights.[47] Indeed, the 1999 NATO intervention undertaken in opposition to Serbia and in support of Kosovo is often seen as the humanitarian intervention *par excellence*. In commenting on the decision to use force against Slobodan Milosevic's government, former Czech president Vaclav Havel set the tone for how this and other interventions would be characterized. He observed that NATO "is fighting out of a concern for the fate of others. It is fighting because no decent person can stand by and watch the systematic, state-directed murder of other people. It cannot tolerate such a thing. It cannot fail to provide assistance if it is within its power to do so."[48] Moreover, there has been a clear trend over the last twenty years for the United States and other Western countries to increasingly narrow the permissible deviations in the understanding, definition, prioritization, and application of human rights.

Interventionists routinely attach the caveat, as Samantha Power noted in her 2013 confirmation hearings to become the US Ambassador of the United Nations, "that America cannot—indeed, I know that America should not—police every crisis or shelter every refugee. While our goodwill knows no bounds, our resources are of course finite, strained by pressing needs at home. And we are not the world's policeman. We must make choices based on the best interests of the American people."[49] Nevertheless, the argument is made—in both conservative and liberal circles—that

> American foreign policy should be informed with a clear moral purpose, based on the understanding that its moral goals and its fundamental national interests are almost always in harmony. The United States achieved its present position of strength not by practicing a foreign policy of live and let live, nor by passively waiting for threats to arise, but by actively promoting American principles of governance abroad: democracy, free markets, respect for liberty.[50]

These sentiments find their way into the key strategy documents of the US government: the *2015 National Security Strategy* links the pursuit of American national interests with respect for "universal values" that are later identified with America's own "founding values."[51]

Those inclined to support this view—of tying American power to the promotion of its values—do acknowledge, "This is not a plea for foreign policy as 'social work,' a struggle against distress everywhere in the world." However, Stanley Hoffmann argues that it serves as

> a reminder that certain levels and kinds of distress are morally unacceptable and certain political, economic, and social breakdowns too dangerous to world order to be ignored. . . . For we live in a world in which apathy about what happens in "far away countries of which we know nothing" can all too easily lead–through contagion, through the message such moral passivity sends to troublemakers, would be tyrants, and ethnic cleansers elsewhere–not to the kind of Armageddon we feared during the Cold War but to a creeping escalation of disorder and beastliness that will, sooner or later, reach the shores of the complacent, the rich, and the indifferent.[52]

Consistently, American political leaders emphasize that US action in the world ought to be informed by and reflect "our values" and be consistent with core moral principles.[53] We stand for principles not "just because we think it's going to advance our interests" but "because that's who we are."[54]

But any desire to harness foreign policy in the service of moral ends must also address a related question: the balance between a "morality of intentions" and a "morality of results." Certainly, there is a compelling argument that, no matter the motive, "interveners do bear some moral responsibility for what happens in an area after they have undertaken action that removes the existing government," and that if an intervention worsens the situation it was meant to improve, it might then not be seen as the most ethical choice.[55] Anatol Lieven and John Hulsman have argued that the responsible policymaker who seeks to be moral in decision making must focus his or her "concentration on achievable results rather than good intentions." Thus, "under an ethic of responsibility, having good intentions is not remotely adequate. One must weigh the likely consequences and, perhaps most important, judge which actions are necessary to achieve essential goals. An ethic of conviction, although superficially moral, has a tendency to be indifferent to the consequences of actions in the real world."[56]

This also brings up the question of defining success. As C.A.J. Cody notes, writing about what defines "success" in terms of an armed intervention:

> There is a conflict here between different understandings of success. Should we think of success in a short-term way as saving these lives

now, or restoring these people to their homes, or should the criterion of success embrace longer-term objectives such as ensuring political stability and enduring safety for any in the area threatened with the same kind of persecution? Clearly, both accounts of success have their attractions, but equally clearly they are in tension in that they dictate different policies and forms of intervention.[57]

So, there can be a two-part test to assess the morality of a foreign-policy action. The first part is whether the action conforms to, or is in support of, a particular moral or ethical imperative. The second part is whether the pursuit of a moral objective should be undertaken even if there is no guarantee of success and if a failure might worsen conditions. We can categorize them as the "two responsibilities": a responsibility to our values and a responsibility to be responsible. This sentiment was expressed in President Barack Obama's introduction to the *2015 National Security Strategy*. He counseled that "hard choices" will have to be made from "among competing priorities"—some based on values, others based on interests—keeping in mind the prospects for success while avoiding over-stretch.

Applying Theory to Action

These discussions make for great debates in common rooms, but they are more than just academic exercises: how the relevant questions are answered has a direct impact on what policies are chosen.[58] These debates—over whether spreading American/Western/liberal values enhances American security and leads to a more secure global order and whether intent or outcome ought to be the guiding metric for assessing policy choices—became especially salient in the immediate run-up to and in the aftermath of the 2003 invasion of Iraq.

This is not a place to re-litigate the question of the reliability of the intelligence about Saddam Hussein's Iraq, particularly claims about his possession of working weapons of mass destruction (WMDs), as opposed to programs that may or may not have been in abeyance. Accepting all of the standing assumptions—that Hussein possessed a WMD stockpile or at least all the component parts, that he was engaged in actions to subvert the regional order and even to create problems at the global level, and that he was not prepared to cooperate with the United States and other Western powers in resolving the existing standoff over inspections of his capabilities—did not lead to one single policy outcome for resolving the problem. Agreeing that Saddam Hussein posed a threat to US interests, and that his regime had committed vile and odious violations of human rights, two very different options were discussed and debated about what the proper American response ought to be.

The first argued that Saddam Hussein could not be trusted to remain in power and needed to be removed, but that US national security interests needed to do more than simply decapitate the old regime. The creation of an Iraqi democracy—even an imperfect one—would reorient the geopolitics of the region. It would also align US security interests with its own values, since a post-Saddam state was expected to become a security partner of the United States, an ally in the fight against Al-Qaeda and Iran, and even perhaps the third Arab state to recognize Israel. Moreover, an Iraqi democracy would pay a moral debt to the Iraqi people for the "realist" decision, twelve years earlier, to abandon the effort to march on Baghdad to depose Hussein—even after the crimes he had committed against his own people. This could occur with relative ease and at low cost, and on a quick timetable. Iraqis would work with US forces to undertake this transformation, and to accept American tutelage and guidance in the process.[59]

The second approach made the case for very strict containment of Iraq and extremely intrusive inspections of the country's military and industrial facilities to verify that there were no foundations for the maintenance or manufacture of WMDs. In this scenario, this was the immediate and pressing security challenge. The emphasis was on a prophylactic solution that would strengthen the "box" holding Saddam in place, thereby mitigating the threat he might pose and using military force to achieve only very specific tasks and objectives (e.g., the destruction of any confirmed WMD facility). Those arguing for a more containment-style approach also maintained this policy would have much greater international support (and would help to guarantee a more coherent coalition should force have to be used later on). A focus on regime change and reconstruction, it was argued, would take attention and resources away from other pressing concerns, beginning with the war on terror, and could complicate the international relationships necessary for that war's successful prosecution. Premature removal of the regime—where conditions did not exist for a stable, rapid, and smooth transfer of power—would not lead to a better situation on the ground, either for Iraqis or for US security interests. At the same time, it would be prudent to prepare for that eventuality and for it to occur under better conditions than presented themselves in the spring of 2003. In any event, the United States would have to prepare for the opening of a Pandora's box of ethnic, religious, and sectarian strife that would complicate any reconstruction effort and that might even worsen conditions for the civil populace and allow forces hostile to the United States to take root.[60]

More than a decade after the invasion, the balance sheet continues to be tallied. Proponents and opponents of the war point to different items to justify their position. Supporters can argue that the invasion: (1) removed from power a brutal regime that was continuing to destabilize the entire Middle East; (2) conclusively verified that Iraq did not possess WMDs and that its programs could never be revived; and (3) played a crucial role in convincing another "rogue," Muammar Gadhafi of Libya, to come in from the cold. Supporter of the invasion also assert that the postinvasion and postoccupation elections offered not only Iraqis, but others in the region, a glimpse at possible liberal democratic alternatives for governance—what former Vice President Dick Cheney has referred to as a "ripple effect." Opponents cite the postinvasion chaos in Iraq, including the low-level sectarian civil war, that led to large numbers of casualties and refugees and that contributed to a much worse level of public services than existed at the height of the Ba'athist regime. The United States carried out the war and subsequent reconstruction efforts at a price tag of nearly $1 trillion and thousands of US lives lost or wounded. More Iraqis ended up being killed or displaced as a result of the war and subsequent occupation than had suffered under the tyranny of the Ba'athist regime. The destruction of the Iraqi state removed an important bulwark holding Iranian influence in check, and gave transnational terrorist groups an important new base of operations within the parts of Iraq that were no longer effectively controlled by the central government. Meanwhile, the focus on nonexistent Iraqi WMDs allowed North Korea to cross the nuclear finish line. Some have also argued that the Iraq operation proved to be a critical distraction that allowed China to make gains in consolidating its position in the Asia-Pacific region and in other parts of the world. Concerns have also been raised that the United States, by pushing to go to war in Iraq without an explicit United Nations (UN) Security Council resolution, damaged prospects for cooperation with other states, weakened the UN system, and squandered a great deal of America's "soft power" in attracting allies and partners to its causes.[61] In assessing the debate over the Iraq War, Joseph Nye concludes that, at present, when most Americans look at the balance sheet, a majority will conclude that those who were skeptical of this endeavor have been proven correct.[62] The outcome of events in Iraq has also reignited the debate over the proper role and use of moral considerations: should the Iraq campaign be assessed against the stated objectives or the actual results?[63]

The size and scale of the Iraq operation—both the military campaign and the subsequent occupation—is, as Steve Simon characterizes it, "a supremely serious American initiative whose outcome will have equally serious implications for the ability of the United States to act in the world and influence events in the world in the coming years."[64] The transformation of American foreign policy that has resulted has led to a diminished willingness to intervene or, when action is deemed to be unavoidable, to limit the scope of US involvement to the bare necessities.[65] There has been a definitive rise in what might be termed "neo-isolationist" sentiments. At the same time, however, there has remained a constant search for a workable paradigm for American foreign policy that answers moral considerations and that provides a rationale for American intervention and engagement, yet can provide a template for avoiding perceived disasters like the Iraq War. "Smart power" and "pragmatic realism" have been some of the offerings presented and the "tag lines" embraced by US government officials to describe a post-Iraq approach.[66]

Etzioni supported the initial military actions taken in the aftermath of 9/11, including the decision to undertake a campaign in Afghanistan against the Taliban and Al-Qaeda, but he declined to join a second group that endorsed the Bush administration's decision to go to war in Iraq in 2003. He was not opposed, in theory, to using military force as a way to guarantee deproliferation of a dangerous regime. But Etzioni did not feel that the proposed action against Iraq—and the wide-ranging reconstruction plans beyond the more limited deproliferation aims—could be justified. He did not believe that Saddam Hussein's regime posed an immediate and imminent threat that could only be responded to by war, particularly when other options, including a series of intrusive inspections, had not been fully exhausted. There was no compelling convergence of interests among the major powers that led to a decision for war. He did not believe Iraq possessed the necessary preconditions for making any sort of rapid jump to democracy. Finally, Etzioni was concerned about the damage to American credibility if the United States was unable to deliver on its ambitious agenda for Iraq.[67] In particular, by early 2004, he was concerned about what he termed the "Vietnamesque effect" of Iraq on US policy. As the Vietnam War dragged on, draining US resources and damaging America's ability to project power and sustain coalitions. Similarly, the chosen policy for Iraq would suck the United States into a guerilla conflict or insurgency that would sap its military potential and contribute to the further erosion of US credibility. In addition, it would lead to increased opposition at home that would divide the country as well as cause further rifts between the United States and the key partners it needed to undertake other critical global initiatives. Finally, the strategy would prove to be unsustainable and the United States would look ineffective.[68]

Of particular concern to Etzioni was the rapid decline in US power and influence as a result of missteps like the Iraq War, and the expenditure of American resources to doggedly pursue unrealistic goals. Rosy predictions that the campaign would be wrapped up in a matter of months, and that US expenditures would be largely recouped by Iraqi oil revenues, had panned out. By 2008, the United States had once again run up significant budget deficits (in contrast to the surpluses achieved by the end of the 1990s). Its "soft power" had been damaged by negative publicity resulting from abuses committed by American troops in Iraq and by its apparent failure to bring stability to the region. Rifts were opening up with traditional allies, while challengers who, at the beginning of the decade, were looking for ways to reach accommodation with the United States (witness Vladimir Putin's and Hu Jintao's early overtures to Washington), were now exploiting the sense of American distraction and weakness.[69] In observing these developments, Antonio de Aguiar Patriota, a former Brazilian Minister of External Affairs, noted that the United States was no longer "in a position to single-handedly determine international outcomes."[70]

Etzioni was not satisfied with simply being a critic of the policies adopted by the Bush administration. He wanted to provide a road map that could help the United States to navigate out of the Iraq quagmire, to avoid repeating similar mistakes in the Afghan mission, and to provide guidance for how the United States could pursue a principled but pragmatic foreign policy.[71] This task helped him to crystalize the gradualism and communitarian strains of his earlier writing into a new paradigm which he labeled "Security First."

The Security First Paradigm

Etzioni's Security First approach is based on the starting observation that "the world is a harsh place and that it is difficult to change, and hence we should carefully select where we employ the scarce resources we actually command."[72] Thus, it focuses on a morality of achievability and sustainability rather than on intention and a grand vision.

The approach places a premium on avoiding disorder whenever possible—even that caused in the apparent service of a good cause. For Etzioni, chaos is the biggest violator of human rights, starting with the core right to life and the right to enjoy basic security of both the person and of property. The better that life is protected, the greater chance there is for the extension and furtherance of other rights. Thus,

> basic security is more urgent than other rights in dealing with fail-ing states, rogue nations and genocide. In addition, the chaotic and violent international system sometimes produces conditions even more brutal than the internal conditions of most states. Therefore, this dictum applies with special force to attempts to form a stable global order. So moral arguments and empirical evidence support the same proposition: In circumstances where political right and security come into conflict - a common condition - the right to basic security must prevail.[73]

Security First calls for a sober assessment of the world's problems, with prioritization given to tackling threats that are the most egregious and universally applicable. It counsels a willingness to trade or overlook lesser faults if it secures effective action against the most dangerous and endemic challenges.

The foreign policy decision maker must be guided by the ethics of a battlefield surgeon engaged in triage, not those of a family practitioner operating in a peaceful suburban neighborhood. Torpedoing the pos-sibility of cooperation with states whose help and capabilities might be absolutely essential in solving issues of grave concern like nuclear ter-rorism or environmental catastrophe because of disagreements—even sincere and well-founded ones—over a state's restrictions of freedom of speech, religion, or expression seems to Etzioni to be the height of folly.

Because the use of military force—essentially the employment of the tools of chaos by a state—is so fraught with peril, it must be used only when all other options have been exhausted. Etzioni would point to the reality that, in recent times, very few societies have been shown to enjoy a higher quality of life or greater social peace as a result of war or armed intervention. This assessment, part of what he terms the "mul-tiple realism deficiency disorder" that afflicts US foreign policy decision making,[74] is meant as a warning for those who have seen military action as a tool for social improvement. Another part of the disorder is the inconsistent overestimation of US capabilities and the consequential underestimating of the actual amount of time and resources an operation might need. Destruction might have to be wrought to prevent a worse evil from occurring (say, to stop a genocide or to prevent a regime from acquiring WMDs when all other means have failed). But Etzioni rejects the idea that war clears away the wreckage of the old regime swiftly and cleanly, allowing for an unencumbered fresh start.

Etzioni's Security First paradigm is comprised of the following general principles:

(1) There are an insufficient number of advanced, developed democracies that can solve critical world and regional problems by relying solely on their own resources and capabilities.

(2) Nondemocratic, nonliberal states and societies must be solicited as partners, but they will not accept any such invitation if they believe cooperation with the United States and its allies will be followed by attempts to bring about forcible regime change.

(3) To forge effective cooperation with such states, a bargain to cooperate on the "big issues" must include the right to be "left alone" on lesser issues where their practices conflict with the preferences of a liberal democracy. Etzioni would argue for an accord that would gain universal commitment to a series of basic "right to life" protections. However, as he maintains, a regime that possesses good governance and that guarantees basic security is sufficient for the time being and should be able to partner with the United States and enjoy regime security. There is no need to demand immediate steps toward achieving a constitutional or democratic regime.

Evaluation of the call for conditional sovereignty should be based on the obligations of states to both protect and prevent gross violations of the basic rights of their citizens, and to address threats that could imperil the safety of their own people (as well as others). Etzioni stresses the importance of not setting the bar too low for what would constitute a violation of those commitments. Otherwise, "numerous grounds could then be used to legitimate intervention, such as election fraud, or violations of the freedom of the press. This could easily lead to rising numbers of armed international conflicts, as any nation seeking to intervene in another for its own benefit—for instance, to gain control of oil or access to ports—could find some justifiable reason."[75]

(4) Moderation in behavior rather than conformity in belief is the driving goal—the notion that "bad regimes can improve their behavior."[76] Getting an illiberal state or political movement to moderate and temper its internal and external actions (for example, eschewing violence) is better than gambling on regime change that could either destabilize a country (if it succeeds), or alienate a government and cause it to withdraw from any cooperative efforts (if it fails).

(5) Regimes that enjoy a greater degree of security will be more inclined to take part in cooperative efforts designed to safeguard all states—democracies and nondemocracies—from common threats. This security includes pledges that US power will not be directed at a country because of how it conducts internal, domestic matters that do not violate the basic rights of its citizens. Countries that enjoy this security will be more likely to support more vigorous action, including US efforts to combat common problems. Etzioni is willing to set down the following broad rule: "Military interventions should for now be limited to preventing genocide and ethnic cleansing as well as the acquisition of nuclear arms by states that actively threaten others. Other remedies—for instance, economic sanctions or incentives—can be applied much more liberally, both to avoid humanitarian catastrophes and to foster deproliferation."[77]

In turn, the types of *causus belli* that might trigger an armed intervention are thereby reduced, as it were, to two types of actions. The first is behavior that threatens the very nature of the global order (proliferation of WMDs among terrorists, for instance); the second, egregious actions that undermine the very basic right to survival. Etzioni maintains that the United States and other countries must absolutely be prepared to intervene and to use overwhelming force in a focused and decisive manner. For Security First to have any credibility, it is absolutely critical to demonstrate that red lines—particularly when dealing with questions such as nuclear proliferation—will be enforced. However, the use of force must be very targeted to deal with the specific violation, say, to protect a designated civilian population from attack, and to avoid the temptation of mission creep (wholescale regime change and reform). The goal must be to do what is needed to terminate the offending behavior.

This recommendation to use force less more effectively is an outgrowth of an observation that the United States, in particular, has engaged in a series of interventions on a regular basis, but has done so in a haphazard and unfocused way.[78] In many cases, when the United States has resorted to force, it has been neither fully committed nor prepared to employ the action in a way that would guarantee success. This leads other countries to be concerned about becoming the targets of a US-led intervention, and to lose respect for the effectiveness of US power. This occurs precisely because of the lack of American follow-through and commitment. Security First would attempt to make the exercise of US. power predictable and to reduce uncertainty about when, where, and under what circumstances Washington would be prepared to undertake military action.

The Security First paradigm rejects the idea of using external military pressure to bring about change in other societies. In essence, it asks those who are dissatisfied with the level of civil, political, or social freedom in their countries to forego asking for American or Western forcible intervention to bring about immediate relief in the short run. This is seen as the price to be paid for maintaining a series of cooperative relationships and security bargains that will enhance regional and global security.

Etzioni's gamble is that a Security First approach could create conditions for long-term, sustainable evolutionary change in a more liberal direction that would end up being more effective than the track record of the interventionists. Moreover, his Security First approach envisions that extensive civil society efforts (that is, efforts that are not government-sponsored or controlled) to educate and persuade other societies to undertake reform would remain intact, so that "preaching" about rather than "promotion" of liberal democracy would continue. Etzioni's confidence in this outcome is buttressed by the assessment that such long-term change did occur in East Asia over several decades: as regimes enjoyed a greater degree of internal and external security—and the rising prosperity these conditions generated—there was a greater willingness to explore reform, to push for greater openness and pluralism, and to anchor governance in adherence to the rule of law.[79] Indeed, some researchers have explicitly cited developments in Southeast Asia over the past several decades as validation of the Security First approach, noting that the creation of benign security conditions allowed for more stable governments and thus a greater chance to sustain democratic openings.[80] In turn, the resources of the community that promotes American democracy can be better utilized to take advantage of these internal shifts, and to assist a domestic process in favor of change when it is sustainable and supported by the proper preconditions.[81]

Etzioni is comfortable (in a moral sense) asking for this trade-off because there is also some empirical evidence that suggests that pushing democratization, particularly in societies that are ill-prepared to make such a transition, does not enhance security and can lead to worse outcomes in terms of human rights.[82] This is because the "right to security takes precedence over all others [since] . . . all the others are contingent on the protection of life." Therefore, "the Security First principle does not favor curtailing well-established freedoms for marginal gains in security in London, Paris or New York. But it does command first priority of place where people cannot walk the streets, work, study or worship without fear of being bombed or kidnapped, tortured or maimed."[83]

This is why Etzioni remains leery of the idea of creative destruction—the notion that destroying tyrannical old regimes would unleash creative and positive forces to remake societies in more liberal images.[84] The proposition that the absence of government is preferable to the existence of an authoritarian regime, while it might sound appealing in theory, rarely leads to good outcomes. This recognition is even built into the U.S. Declaration of Independence, where Thomas Jefferson recognized that "governments long established should not be changed for light and transient causes." Kanan Makiya, an ardent advocate for the overthrow of Saddam Hussein, reached similar conclusions after observing the chaos and disorder that gripped post-Saddam Iraq. He noted that "our species, at least in its modern garb, needs states, even imperfect ones. States are still the cornerstones of our security as individuals, and provide at least the possibility of a civilized way of life."[85] In essence, Etzioni takes the position that most states have the opportunity, over time, to be rehabilitated rather than wrecked—even if the process is generational rather than instantaneous.[86] He also notes that "autocracy wreckers . . . are not necessarily democracy builders"—that opponents of existing authoritarian regimes may not be able to or are not interested in pursuing reform and change, and thus should not be cast into that role.[87] Therefore, in evaluating the Etzioni position, James Steinberg concludes that "the best way to be a democracy advocate is to put security first."[88]

The focus of Etzioni on what he terms "de-tyrannization" (as opposed to democratization) arises out of his conclusion that, despite predictions about the "end of history," there remains significant resistance in many parts of the world to the precepts of liberal democracy. In addition, a number of countries lack the necessary preconditions for moving ahead with any program of democratization. For the latter, those who support a sequentialist approach to change argue that

> certain preconditions, above all, the rule of law and a well-functioning state, should be in place before a society democratizes. . . .
> In some countries, staying with an existing autocratic regime is

a better alternative. Where outside actors do want to promote positive political change in a nondemocratic society, they should concentrate first on helping it to achieve the rule of law and a well-functioning state.[89]

In all cases, if liberal democracy is not a realistic possibility, there can exist other types of regimes—from illiberal democracy to soft authoritarianism—that may work to cooperate on vital issues, to reject terrorism and extremism, and to create conditions for eventual evolution along more liberal lines.[90] These governments may also enjoy some degree of legitimacy even if they are not empowered by the ballot box.[91] By rejecting the binary division of the world espoused by some thinkers, such as Robert Kagan, into democratic allies and authoritarian opponents,[92] Etzioni's concept of the "illiberal moderate" reframes the picture. The assumption that only those who share a commitment to liberal values can be effective partners consigns all nonliberal forces beyond the pale, and draws no real distinctions between the minority who actively seek to damage Western interests and the vast majority with no such aims. Etzioni argues instead that illiberal moderates share common ground in seeking stability and peace, accepting basic rights, and having a willingness to cooperate to achieve certain global aims. They do not, however, accept the full range of social, political, and individual rights that Western liberalism defines as universal human rights. Rather, they maintain that some individual lifestyle choices must be subordinate to the standards set down by the larger community or collective. Faced with the prospects of forcible Westernization and liberalization, illiberal moderates who would cooperate on a security agenda would turn to resistance if faced with cultural and social engineering. Particularly in the Islamic world, Etzioni saw illiberal moderates as the crucial "global swing vote" whose alienation from the West would be highly problematic for success in matters like the war on terror.[93] (At the same time, it should be noted that, based on interpretations of Etzioni's domestic communitarian writings, he would support liberal democracies that give asylum and refuge to those advocates of Western liberalism who would chafe under the administration of illiberal moderates.[94])

There is also a second trade-off that Etzioni asks for: that citizens of some states (and their governments) voluntarily forego some of their theoretical rights under international law to freely choose their international relationships in order to help guarantee stability. Arising out of his initial gradualist proposals and his subsequent development of Mutually Assured Restraint, Etzioni argues for those states that lie between the great powers and major blocs to accept some form of neutral status as a way to decrease tensions and to facilitate cooperation among the key power centers on key global issues that he feels are essential for overall global security.[95] In return for foregoing the option of joining specific military alliances or blocs, neutral buffer states would have to be guaranteed the ability to determine their own domestic institutions and to pursue their economic interests.[96] Thus, the United States would pledge not to expand its system of alliances to encompass nations on the Chinese or Russian frontiers in return for firm, actionable commitments by both Moscow and Beijing to cooperate on critical issues. One such issue is accepting the necessity for interventions when diplomacy has failed in order to deproliferate regimes of concern or to stop massive violations of the right to life). In turn, these countries would refrain from interference in the affairs of states lying on their borders as long as a set of minimal security conditions were being respected.[97]

The implications of a Security First paradigm will be explored in subsequent chapters that deal specifically with questions like deproliferation, state-building, and other transnational challenges of the twenty-first century. Etzioni's general advice to the policymaker, however, can be summed up in these three points of guidance:

(1) Before undertaking attempts at liberalization, focus on bringing about order in states, including the acceptance of illiberal and authoritarian outcomes if they secure the right to life and the possibility of evolution.

(2) Focus on what states do to enhance regional and global security versus their conformity with liberal values.

(3) Create transnational institutions that enhance the security of their members and that create patterns of cooperation.

This approach does not nest easily within any of the four dominant US foreign policy perspectives identified by Colin Dueck.[98] The first of these is strategic disengagement (a US withdrawal from political and military commitments made during the Cold War). The second is balance-of power realism (focusing on preserving stability in the international system even at the expense of promoting US values). The third perspective is primacy (aggressively maintaining American political and military predominance in the world and preempting challenges to a US-led international order). Finally, the fourth perspective is liberal internationalism (with an emphasis on promoting democracy and human rights throughout the world and harnessing US power to achieve these ends). Instead, as Dan Drezner has observed, Etzioni mixes elements drawn from each of these approaches.[99] I myself have characterized Etzioni's approach as "communitarian realism," based on his assessment that closer international cooperation and the emergence of a more effective global community will come about because of traditional realist concerns about security rather than idealistic beliefs in universal principles.[100]

Situating the "Security First" Approach

In the type of world order Etzioni hopes will emerge in the coming centuries—one defined by a strong global community—his vision is quintessentially liberal. However, as Etzioni himself has noted, his paradigm for foreign affairs "views the faith that many liberals have in international institutions, laws and networks, the United Nations included [,] as an essential but insufficient foundation for a sound new global architecture."[101] Instead, as he noted, "a major advance in the efficiency of international institutions may follow, not because of some sudden drastic change in human nature, or the long-awaited elimination of power politics, but because the strengthening of global institutions will serve the deepest national interests of the . . . superpowers and of many smaller ones."[102] To this extent, Etzioni shares with the realists an emphasis on the importance of national interests rather than imperatives of an as-of-yet unformed and inchoate international system as the key driver for international relations, starting with the search for national security. A successful foreign policy, in Etzioni's view, must not only satisfy concerns about legitimacy—the starting point of the liberal internationalists—but must also ensure "a convergence of interests for the various actors involved."[103]

Etzioni shares with the strategic-disengagement advocates similar concerns about the efficacy of most US military interventions—as well as American overreliance on the military instrument—and about the advisability of large-scale deployments of US force overseas. (Etzioni's concept of "remote deterrence" that was explored in earlier chapters shares considerable overlap with a strategy of offshore balancing). But he parts company with the isolationist tendencies inherent in this approach, which he believes would work against US. efforts to take part in transnational community-building efforts. Communitarians also do not subscribe to the primacist assertion that it is "America's destiny to police the world" or "to impose a Pax Americana"[104], sharing with the realists the belief that the application of U.S. might around the world leads to an inevitable backlash—but hold out the hope that the U.S. exercise of power can be channeled into creating a "legitimate new global architecture" that would achieve buy-in from other countries.[105] In turn, primacists are leery of tying the United States to any international system that would appear to inhibit American freedom of action on the world stage.

Whereas traditional realists focus on creating a stable balance within the global system, Etzioni does not divorce moral considerations from his foreign-policy approach; the communitarian paradigm "considers normative elements an important factor in international relations."[106] No global system will be stable over the long term if its legitimacy is questioned by large numbers of people, and if such support "is attained by providing not simply protection against hypothetical and abstract dangers, but the positive and concrete sense of care that attends the promotion of social welfare and human dignity."[107]

Etzioni's blending of varying liberal and realist precepts in foreign policy,[108] and the difficulty in precisely pigeonholing his approach into a defined place on the US political spectrum,[109] is frustrating to those commentators who are eager to fit his views into the proper box. As discussed earlier in this chapter, the Security First approach propounds that societies must enjoy a modicum of good order, even if the politics are initially illiberal or authoritarian, before even considering a transition to a more open society. This approach contrasts with the preference of most American decision makers to support rapid liberalization even at the expense of social stability. So when Etzioni places a greater emphasis on Security First, he aligns his view with the realist and strategic disengagement critiques of US interventionism. Yet, Etzioni's approach shares with the primacists and the liberal internationalists an appreciation for the importance of values in foreign policy. But whereas the latter two assume that the United States (or the larger Western world) offers a ready-made template that the rest of the world need merely implement, Etzioni argues that the "advance of democracy, human rights and the free market [is] merely half of the global normative trend and needed normative basis for a sound global order."[110] Furthermore, based on the track record of the initiation by the United States of successful political transformations to sustainable liberal forms of governance in other countries, he advises U.S. policy-makers to forego efforts at regime change "and largely let internal forces lead domestic political progress."[111] Moreover, while Etzioni's paradigm places a high priority on seeking peaceful resolutions to disputes—a central tenet of the liberal view—he has notbeen reflexively "anti-war" in his approach to world affairs. The rules and norms of the international community must be backed up, by force if necessary, if the safety and security of its members are to be ensured. As Etzioni concludes, "Soft power is preferable in general, but in several critical circumstances the application of hard power regrettably cannot be avoided."[112] Etzioni's work indicates that he is willing to accept the use of military force, even as a last resort, as part of the strategy of ensuring security. This is one of the characteristics that distinguishes his approach from some of his liberal colleagues, who have been far less comfortable with the employment of the military instrument of power. He thus advocates a "mixture" of both "hard" and "soft" power resources that ought to be deployed to ensure the security of the international order.[113]

American policymakers are on the lookout for an approach to world affairs that retains US involvement and leadership in the international system but that avoids overstretch; that is, an approach that is true to a moral compass but not draining of American resources and energy.[114] Security First was a direct response to what has been labeled the "Iraqistan syndrome"—the "popular aversion towards prolonged stabilization missions" that have defined US foreign policy for much of the post-Cold War era.[115] The Iraqistan syndrome builds on the observable track record that countries like the United States have overestimated their abilities to initiate and sustain broad-based transformations in other societies while mitigating the security risks.[116] At the same time, as former Australian Prime Minister Kenneth Rudd has observed, the challenge now facing policymakers is not to transform the world but to "quarantine and manage" critical problems.[117] Can the Security First approach fit the bill?

It is interesting to note the extent to which governments have already started to act on some of Etzioni's recommendations. This began with a more deliberate shift to a Security First approach, as the initial post-Cold War optimism about the ease and speed at which liberal transformations could be successfully undertaken dissipated.[118] Several observers detect the influence of the Security First approach—or at least adoption of some of its precepts—in changes to the US approach toward Southeast Asia and in the European Union approach toward the Balkans after the mid-2000s. After pouring in large amounts of resources in an attempt to reconstruct Bosnia as a liberal multi-ethnic democracy, with middling results, the EU in the mid-2000s shifted its approach toward aiding governments in their efforts to establish security and order before pushing on to liberalizing reforms.[119] In Southeast Asia, an approach similar to Security First has generally defined US outreach to the nations of the region, emphasizing the forging of security cooperation while creating conditions for evolutionary change without exerting pressure for immediate reforms.[120] Indeed, this has been most notable in the about-face in US relations with Myanmar. This has been evidenced in the moving away from US efforts to isolate the regime for its authoritarian practices in favor of fostering engagement, with an eye to bolstering regional security and balance against a rising China. There has been a simultaneous shift to the encouragement of evolutionary reform rather than holding out for regime change.[121] The general failure of the Arab Spring to bring about a wave of liberalization in the Middle East—dubbed the "Arab Winter"—has also helped to reinforce tendencies to adopt a Security First-style approach.[122]

The shift implicit in Security First—from promoting democracy to encouraging liberal evolution by creating conditions of stability both within states and in the larger regional and global order—has the possibility of addressing a critical problem in US foreign policy: the credibility gap. The American willingness to tolerate and even work with dictatorial and authoritarian regimes that cooperate on critical issues of concern to the United States, even in light of solemn pronouncements about the obligation to end tyranny and spread democracy, has, as Anne-Marie Slaughter observes, set the United States to "look like complete hypocrites in the eyes of the world."[123] Joseph Nye concurs, noting that "when rhetoric greatly outstrips reality, it is seen as hypocrisy in the eyes of others."[124] This is why he believes that the Security First approach might have potential, by openly seeking a balance between pragmatic considerations and idealism. The approach may make possible a "stable synthesis" that would allow the United States to continue to articulate its values but without undermining them or the possibility of effective cooperation with nondemocratic regimes.[125] The Security First paradigm tracks with the advice given by Robert W. McElroy in his groundbreaking 1992 work *Morality and American Foreign Policy*: that governments can allow their actions to be guided by moral considerations if no vital security interest is at risk, or if the negative impacts of an action do not outweigh its direct moral value.[126] The Etzioni approach can thus be grouped within the context of an "indirect pursuit of human rights—human rights as the by-product of public policy and international diplomacy."[127]

Criticisms of the Security First Approach

Very few would contest Etzioni's contention that an effective foreign policy requires prioritization and hard choices. Yet some of the assumptions that buttress the Security First paradigm have come under criticism. Glyn Morgan outlines the various objections to Etzioni's Security First paradigm:

> Classical realists will reject his appeals to morality and his focus on the basic security of all. Democratic globalists and Western imperialists will oppose his toleration of nondemocratic states. And proponents of global justice and cosmopolitan democracy will find his conception of basic security too minimalist and his institutional proposals, which accept the basic features of the current international state system, insufficiently radical or revolutionary.[128]

One of the consistent complaints about any sort of a Security First approach is that it might be quite easy for the things that ought to follow in the second, third, and fourth positions to fall by the wayside. Does the paradigm, as presented by Etzioni, address the concern Slaughter and others have raised, that, in the end, using security as the first organizing principle of foreign policy leads to turning a blind eye to human rights considerations?[129] Does it, in essence, allow "putting off for decades or indefinitely" any efforts to encourage reform, greater openness, and moves toward democracy?[130] The fear expressed by some within the democracy-promotion community is that a Security First-style approach could very easily lead to the rationalization of ending the pressure for reform on the dictatorships and authoritarian regimes, whose cooperation is needed for short-term security cooperation. Moreover, there is considerable skepticism about Etzioni's call to rely on civil society and the nongovernmental sector to take the lead to encourage change (relying on "preachers" rather than "warriors").[131] Under this approach, which is seen as insufficient, democracy promotion is credible and effective only when it has the full power of the US government behind it.[132]

Beyond that, a key criticism of the Security First paradigm is that it may not prove to be workable. Morgan believes that "it is simply not possible for the United States and its allies to act in the way that Etzioni recommends. The impossibility here arises out of the conjunction of two different problems . . . first, the multiple different threats to security, and second, the requirement of nonselectivity." As he sees it, the challenge of guaranteeing a basic level of security would outstrip the capacity of the United States and its allies In order to cope with this problem, the United States would be forced to ignore security challenges that would not pose a direct threat to US interests—and in so doing, undermine the effort to create a new global architecture.[133] Finally, Morgan maintains that the Security First paradigm does not offer clear and effective answers to two critical questions: "What threats warrant military intervention? and When is a response to these threats legitimate?"[134]

Others echo this complaint about the lack of clarity in Etzioni's proposal. It is, in the words of Jean Behtke Elshtain, too "loosey-goosey." She highlighted two particular problems. The first is the perceived reliance on any sort of transnational consensus for defining global security problems. Elshtain doubts whether nondemocratic states would really develop a convergence of interests with the United States and its allies that could permit effective joint action. The second problem is the nature and limits of the proposed bargain of foregoing coercive regime change in return for security cooperation. Would this mean foregoing any and all support for movements that seek liberal change in those societies, and would such a pledge "dishearten many domestic opponents of dictatorial regimes?"[135] The implication is not simply that these opponents deserve moral support but that, if they were to come to power, they would be more likely to cooperate with the United States on security matters.[136] Stanley Renshon picks up on this point to charge that the Security First paradigm would dishearten those struggling for democratic change around the world, and argues that Etzioni "neglects the many ways in which pushing for democracy and helping internal regime opponents can help bring about desired ends."[137]

Some have argued that any approach that privileges security issues at the expense of democracy promotion will, in the end, achieve neither. To the extent that the United States has already adopted elements of this approach, critics have maintained that major global efforts to tackle pressing concerns have not materialized while the advance of democracy has not only stalled but started to give ground.[138] Any shift toward putting security concerns first signals to governments around the world that the "pressure is now off" to enact reforms, and that aid and cooperation with continue; meanwhile, the influence that the United States and European states might bring to bear to push for liberalization is lessened.[139] Yet, there is little evidence to suggest that, in return for easing off on democratization, authoritarian regimes have been willing to increase their cooperation with the West on security matters. Thus, critics of Security First maintain that the search for security and the push for democracy must occur in tandem.[140]

While Etzioni's support for a sequenced, evolutionary approach makes sense in theory, there are some problems in practice. Most importantly, as the work of Joel Migdal and others notes, the first stage of establishing security often does not lead to the second stage of creating conditions for reform and modernization, especially the development of "an effective state bureaucracy that can carry out the many functions demanded of a modern state."[141] Just as the Central European experience might be misapplied by democracy promoters, critics of a Security First approach also point out that the pattern of transitions toward more open political and economic systems observed in East Asia may also be *sui generis*, or at least a distinctive process based on the desire of Asian leaders to pursue economic development that may not be replicable in other parts of the world.[142] In general, critics argue, an emphasis on stability does not create incentives for reform. Instead, "for every effective state-building strongman of the past century, there have been dozens more autocrats whose self-serving, erratic leadership has resulted in tremendously debilitated states rife with patronage, corruption, and incompetence."[143] In particular, critics can point to the example of Azerbaijan, where an emphasis on joint security cooperation against threats posed by Russia, Iran, and Islamic extremists, along with gentle encouragement to pursue liberalization, have not borne fruit.[144] The decision to promote an evolutionary transition of power in Yemen—with an eye to preserving vital counterterrorism cooperation with the Yemeni government—has also come under intense criticism since its collapse in January 2015 due to internal rebellions. Trying to focus on security cooperation while hoping to encourage a dysfunctional government to reform is an approach that did not work in the Yemen case.[145]

These objections contribute to the unease that policymakers have in embracing fully the Security First paradigm. As noted by James Steinberg, who was to serve as Deputy Secretary of State in the first term of the Obama administration, Etzioni's recommendations to overlook the sins of "illiberal moderates" and to ask people to put their faith in long-term evolutionary transitions "doesn't ease the dilemma of policy makers in the here and now who are criticized for bunking with very uncomfortable bedfellows."[146] US officials believe that they cannot be seen as abandoning full-fledged support for immediate progress on democratization and human rights, and that even if such commitments are purely rhetorical, they can still complicate the effort to use the Security First approach as the organizing principle for relations with other countries.[147]

Even President Barack Obama, whose initial foreign-policy outlook was described in terms similar to those used to characterize Etzioni,[148] has not been entirely comfortable with the recommendations sketched out by Etzioni. At the beginning of his term, the president seemed to endorse a Security First style approach. He noted that effective negotiations could not be carried out with states of concern to change their behavior or to get them to cooperate with the United States if forcible regime change remained on the agenda. He also expressed concerns that revolutionary decapitations of dictatorships often led to instability and often did not produce a stable democracy.[149] However, this perspective was understood to be driven by pragmatism, not conviction, with some observers suggesting that if conditions warranted, Obama might adopt a more idealistic approach.[150]

Indeed, the 2015 Summit on "Countering Violent Extremism" convened by the president in Washington showed the limits of the extent to which Obama has been willing to accept the type of proposals advanced by Etzioni. Obama's call for greater dialogue echoes Etzioni's own advice, yet the president is far less comfortable with the idea of embracing illiberal moderates. For Obama, dialogue is meant to lay the groundwork for a transition to liberal democracy and the adoption of the more expansive view of individual social and political rights that characterizes Western societies. (The summit also opened up some ground between those who, like the president, argue that democracy is the solution to terrorism and those who make the case for "good governance" that could deliver prosperity and stability.)[151]

An Inability to Resist the Siren Song? Libya and Egypt after 2011

As rational and pragmatic as the Security First approach may appear, how effective is it as an antidote to the "siren song" that it is possible and feasible to "reshape the world" in the American image,[152] to use American power as a force for transformation?

In August 2010, President Obama crafted Presidential Study Directive 11, "Political Reform in the Middle East and North Africa," which was meant to review US policy. This document appeared to take a Security First-style approach to the question of political unrest in the region. It tasked the US government to examine ways to work with existing allied regimes to remain on an evolutionary path for change, and to minimize the potential risks to American interests—while also recognizing that massive violations of the right to life on the part of governments seeking to put down protests would complicate matters.[153]

The start of the Arab Spring in Tunisia in December 2010, and the spread of demonstrations and protests across the entire region calling for political change, created the impression that this could be Obama's equivalent of 1989. It signaled the possibility that a wave of authoritarian regimes would collapse, as occurred in Eastern Europe two decades before, to be replaced by liberalizing, democratizing governments whose leaders would partner with Washington to bring about change.[154]

As protests continued in Egypt throughout January, the initial focus remained a Security First approach: crafting a stable transition that would allow Hosni Mubarak to turn over power in an orderly fashion without jeopardizing the important areas of cooperation between the United States and Egypt, including maintenance of the Egypt-Israel peace treaty and cooperation against terrorist movements. At the end of January, special envoy to Egypt Frank Wisner laid out a plan that followed a time-tested pattern for evolutionary political change that had been successfully utilized in East Asia: Mubarak would not run for reelection, but would serve out his term of office, start the reform process, and lay the groundwork for elections.[155] This outcome was unacceptable to the protestors in Tahrir Square, and also proved to be unacceptable to the idealists within the Obama administration, who convinced the president that support for Mubarak's immediate ouster would neither jeopardize US interests nor prevent rapid progress for liberalization.[156] Obama himself declared, "America's interests are not hostile to peoples' hopes; they're essential to them."[157] Mubarak's subsequent fall created conditions for the Muslim Brotherhood to win parliamentary and presidential elections; that government, in turn, was overthrown by the military in 2013, thereby bringing Egypt full circle. The military regime has effectively ended any efforts to push liberal economic and political reform, and has also created some distance in its security cooperation relationship with Washington. Thus, in coping with the reality of Abdel Fatah al-Sissi's regime, some commentators are now calling for a US policy that tracks with the Security First propositions. This would call for a focus on restoring a US-Egypt security collaboration, the goals of which would be to get the Egyptian economy to return to Mubarak-era levels of productivity, and to create an environment where the regime can feel secure enough to take some steps toward limited political and economic reform. Even if these levels were not particularly prosperous, they would represent a major improvement over the current economic stagnation. The alternative is to risk alienating a country upon which the stability of the entire region rests.[158]

It was, however, the decision by the Obama administration to begin an air campaign against the Libyan regime of Muammar Gadhafi in March 2011 that represented a complete rejection of the precepts of Security First. Etzioni had seen Libya as the test case for the feasibility of the Security First approach. In addition to the deproliferation question, which will be addressed in greater detail in the subsequent chapter, the normalization of relations between Libya and the West— and the effective guarantees given to the Gadhafi regime of US efforts to promote forcible regime change—had led to Libyan cooperation with a good deal of the Western agenda. In June 2010 US ambassador Gene Cretz spoke on the progress made in US-Libya relations, and, in so doing, touched on a number of points that defined the Security First paradigm:

> We have core equities at stake in Libya, in the areas of nonproliferation, counterterrorism, military, economic, political, and public diplomacy cooperation, and we consider Libya a strategic ally in the region.
>
> Libya continues to serve as a model for global nuclear nonproliferation efforts. In working with the Libyans to fulfill their commitments to dismantle weapons of mass destruction programs, we are jointly advancing the principles of a nuclear and weapons of mass destruction–free world advocated by the President during his Nuclear Security Summit and the recent Nuclear Nonproliferation Treaty Conference in New York. The Libyan leader has shared these calls for a nuclear free world in his recent speeches. . . .
>
> Today, Libya remains a strong ally in countering terrorism in a volatile region. It has fought the expansion of Al Qaeda in the Islamic Maghreb, has condemned kidnappings, and has taken a position against the paying of ransom to kidnappers. Libya also has taken the lead in developing new approaches to counterterrorism, undertaking serious rehabilitation efforts with Libyan Islamic Fighting Group members and other former extremists. This initiative has arguably influenced the Libyan Islamic Fighting Group's decision to break ties with the Al Qaeda in the Islamic Maghreb network.
>
> Libya's efforts in this regard, led by [Seif al-Islam Gadhafi], are under careful review by international counterterrorism experts and are

worthy of further attention. They may serve as a model to apply to other extremist groups across the globe.

> Our counterterrorism cooperation with Libya provides new venues for public security training and reform, initiatives that could, over time, help address many of our longstanding human rights concerns.[159]

There was guarded optimism that Libya might follow the Taiwan precedent where a more liberalizing son (in this case, Seif-al-Islam) would take power after the death of the father and initiate the transition to democracy.[160]

Yet once the uprising against Gadhafi began in February 2011—and the Libyan leader responded with force to put down any challenge to his regime—Gadhafi's image, and the image of his family, changed. No longer was he a strategic partner who might lay the basis for eventual reform; he was a bloodthirsty tyrant. The United States could not stand idly by and allow him to crush the rebellion in blood, especially when the opposition proclaimed its fealty to democratic principles.[161] Once assurances had been received from anti-Gadhafi forces of their commitment to democracy, a United Nations resolution authorizing the use of military force to protect civilians had been passed, and the president was told that the operation could go forward without requiring a US ground force, the decision to move ahead with Operation Odyssey Dawn was made.[162] If, as Secretary of State Clinton and other advocates of intervention noted, it was not possible for the United States to intervene everywhere to stop evil, it could be done in Libya without great risk to American interests.

Obama himself was quoted by a senior administration official as saying that the Libya operation "is the greatest opportunity to realign our interests and our values."[163] Initially, in the immediate aftermath of Gadhafi's fall and the formation of a provisional government, the intervention was hailed as a great success, proof "that use of limited force—precisely applied—can affect [sic] real, positive political change."[164] It was seen as a possible template for how US power could be harnessed in the service of American ideals in other parts of the world.[165] Immediately after the intervention concluded, Etzioni himself acknowledged that it had been a military success. He validated the "light footprint" concept in particular. At the same time, he expressed concern that mission creep (expanding the scope of the operation from protecting civilians, which did not require Gadhafi's overthrow) to forcible regime change—and the impact of the sudden destruction of the old government without a clear replacement—might lead to problems.[166]

Etzioni's concerns were validated by events. The initial sense of optimism that Libya represented a better way to intervene has been replaced by disillusionment as post-Gadhafi Libya has unraveled. Indeed, there has been no transition to democracy—an impossibility when there are competing factions each claiming to be the legitimate government. Moreover, "Libya has turned into the kind of place U.S. officials most fear: a lawless land that attracts terrorists, pumps out illegal arms and drugs and destabilizes its neighbors."[167] The collapse of the Libyan government, in turn, unleashed waves of instability that destroyed another fragile democracy in North Africa—Mali.[168] All of these setbacks, in turn, led to policy deadlock in Washington as the question of what to do to halt the violence in Syria came up on the agenda. Added to the perception that the Libya intervention had not worked out were concerns that the strongest elements in the anti-Assad coalition were anti-American Islamist extremists.[169]

Today, there is a growing assessment that the Obama administration should not have given in to the siren song of "low-cost, no-consequence" intervention.[170] Former Senator Richard Lugar, who headed the Foreign Relations Committee at the time of the Libya operation, could have taken a page directly from the Security First paradigm when he observed, "There wasn't enough thought given to how we were going to make sure these people had the security and freedom we wanted them to have."[171] There has also been a reassessment of the assumption that the best way to promote democracy in Libya was to support the violent overthrow of the regime. As Alan Kuperman notes, "Libya has not only failed to evolve into a democracy, it has devolved into a failed state. Violent deaths and other human rights abuses have increased sevenfold."[172] Under such conditions, as Etzioni had noted, no transition or reform would be possible. At the same time, keeping in mind the guiding principle of Security First that proposed action should not worsen the global security situation, "the Libya intervention has harmed other U.S. interests as well: undermining nuclear non-proliferation, chilling Russian cooperation at the UN, and fueling Syria's civil war," as well as turning Libya into a safe haven for terrorists and criminal networks.[173]

Kuperman argues that Libya took the first steps toward an evolutionary path for change when, in late 2010, Gadhafi seemed to permit his son Saif to begin overseeing modest reforms. Kuperman's conclusion is that, while Saif "was not going to turn Libya into a Jeffersonian democracy overnight, he did appear intent on eliminating the most egregious inefficiencies and inequities of his father's regime." As Kuperman points out, many of the senior officials who formed the first, abortive transitional administration had been brought into the government by Saif. If these assessments are correct, they would buttress Etzioni's preference for imperfect and slow evolution rather than gambling on sudden regime change—a gamble which, as Kuperman notes, often only ends up fueling civil war, "destabilizing the country, endangering civilians, and paving the way for extremists."[174]

Another question is whether the Libya operation qualified, under Etzioni's stricter "primacy of life" standard for intervention? The Amnesty International report issued in the summer of 2011 maintains that Gadhafi's forces responded to peaceful protests with armed force, but defections from the security services and the seizure of police headquarters and military depots enabled revolutionary forces to become an armed opposition.[175] Etzioni's Security First approach might have supported the strict interpretation of UN Security Council Resolution 1973, which permits the creation of safe havens for civilians to find refuge from battles between government forces and the rebels (similar to the ones created for the Kurds in 1991 following the Gulf War). But in keeping with that interpretation, the Security First approach would not have supported the authorization of an armed attack against the Gadhafi regime. In addition, undertaking a far more limited mission geared for civilian relief might have prevented the subsequent rupture with Russia and China. Both countries have become much more suspicious of US-proposed resolutions calling for intervention in other parts of the world, based on the claim that they were "deceived" by the West over the true intent of the Libya operation.[176] Moreover, diplomatic options for mediating the crisis had not been fully exhausted. The African Union's proposed road map for defusing the situation—and providing a staged, sequential process for an orderly transition of power—was not given sufficient consideration by the United States, France, or Britain as a viable alternative to forcible regime change.[177] An administration guided by the precepts of a Security First approach might have been more willing to explore this option, mindful of the negative consequences of the collapse of Libya for the human-rights situation as well as for regional and global security. Instead, the fallout from Libya has made it less likely that a strong international consensus about the desirability and necessity for future interventions can be found.

Might these setbacks in places like Egypt and Libya, on top of earlier failures such as Iraq, create a renewed opening for a reconsideration of the Security First approach?[178] The Arab Spring created a "highly versatile geopolitical situation" where the prospects for quick and stable transitions to democracy are now highly unlikely, while the region has been plunged into turmoil.[179] At the same time, conditions of growing budget austerity in the United States make it clear that Washington cannot launch new "Marshall Plans" fueled by generous amounts of American resources and attention as a way to reshape states into liberal democratic allies.[180] Given that reality, a second look at the Security First paradigm—concentrating efforts on producing regimes and partners capable of providing security both at home and beyond their borders, and leaving open the possibility of a longer-term transition to more liberal forms of governance—may be justified.

Notes

1   Amitai Etzioni, *The Hard Way to Peace: A New Strategy* (New York: Crowell-Collier Press, 1962), 182.

2.   Correspondence of Professor Avineri with the author, January 9, 2015.

3.   Amitai Etzioni, *From Empire to Community: A New Approach to International Relations* (New York: Palgrave Macmillan, 2004), 43.

4.   These arguments were laid out in depth in Amitai Etzioni, *Security First: For a Muscular, Moral Foreign Policy* (New Haven, CT: Yale University Press, 2007).

5.   See the Preface to Etzioni, *Security First*, esp. ix–xi.

6.   Ivo H. Daalder and James M. Lindsay, "The Globalization of Politics." *Brookings Review* 21 (Winter 2003), 12.

7.   See, for instance, Strobe Talbott, "Democracy and the National Interest," *Foreign Affairs* 75:6 (November/December 1996). "*Idealpolitik*" is defined on p. 47.

8.   For instance, there was confidence expressed by some that democracy promotion could lead to security and, in the few cases where it might not, policies could be adopted to minimize any risks. See Sean M. Lynn-Jones, "Why the United States Should Spread Democracy," Discussion Paper 98–07, Center for Science and International Affairs, Harvard University, March 1998, http://belfercenter.ksg.harvard.edu/publication/2830/why_the_united_states_should_spread_democracy.html.

9.   Derek S. Reveron, Nikolas K. Gvosdev, and Thomas Mackubin Owens, *US Foreign Policy and Defense Strategy: The Evolution of an Incidental Superpower* (Washington, DC: Georgetown University Press, 2015), 119.

10. See, for instance, the discussion about the application of this approach to the Middle East, in Brieg T. Powel, "The Stability Syndrome: US and EU Democracy Promotion in Tunisia," *The Foreign Policies of the European Union and the United States in North Africa: Diverging or Converging Dynamics?* eds. Francesco Cavatorta and Vincent Durac (Abindon, Oxon: Routledge, 2010), 58.

11. Quoted in Alexander T.J. Lennon, "Views on Democracy Promotion From the Strategic Community," *Democracy in U.S. Security Strategy: From Promotion to Support* (Washington, DC: CSIS Press, 2009), 11.

12. Mark P. Lagon, "Promoting Democracy: The Whys and Hows for the United States and the International Community," *Markets and Democracy Brief* (Council on Foreign Relations), February 2011, http://www.cfr.org/democracy-promotion/promoting-democracy-whys-hows-united-states-international-community/p24090.

13. See, for instances, the points in Larry Diamond, "Promoting Democracy in Post-Conflict and Failed States: Lessons and Challenges" (paper presented at the National Policy Forum on Terrorism, Security, and America's Purpose, New America Foundation, Washington, DC, September 6–7, 2005), https://web.stanford.edu/~ldiamond/papers/PromotingDemocracy0905.htm.

14. See, for instance, the arguments laid out by Robert Kagan and Ronald D. Asmus, "Commit for the Long Run," *Washington Post*, January 29, 2002, archived at http://www.cfr.org/world/commit-long-run/p4310.

15. *National Security Strategy, February 2015* (Washington, DC: The White House, 2015), 19.

16. Oisin Tansey, *Democratization and International Administration* (Oxford: Oxford University Press, 2010), 23.

17. Daniel Lieberfeld, "Theories of Conflict and the Iraq War," *International Journal of Peace Studies* 10:2 (Autumn/Winter 2005), 11.

18. John M. Owen IV, "Iraq and the Democratic Peace," *Foreign Affairs* 84:6 (November/December 2005), http://www.foreignaffairs.com/articles/61206/john-m-owen-iv/iraq-and-the-democratic-peace.

19. Charles Krauthammer, "The Unipolar Moment Revisited," *The National Interest* 70 (Winter 2002/03), 15.

20. Reveron, Gvosdev, and Owens, 244.

21. Abbas Milani, Michael McFaul, and Larry Diamond, *Beyond Incrementalism: A New Strategy for Dealing with Iran* (Stanford, CA: Hoover Institution, 2005), 5. It should be noted, however, that the specific strategy that these three authors called for was not forcible democratization and deproliferation via military force, but negotiating a freeze with the current regime, restoration of ties, and then democracy promotion by peaceful means. In some ways, it parallels some of the policy recommendations made by Etzioni. What is important here, however, is to note the idea that democratization would be the ultimate solution to the problem.

22. "Push to Export Democracy Produces Surprises," *All Things Considered (National Public Radio)*, January 28, 2006, http://www.npr.org/templates/story/story.php?storyId=5176545 .

23. Paul Latawski, *The Security Road to Europe: The Visegrad Four* (London: Royal United Services Institute for Defence Studies, 1994), 15.

24. Justin Paulette, "America's Future in New Europe." (Ashland, OH: Ashbrook Center, June 2011), http://ashbrook.org/publications/oped-paulette-11-new-europe/.

25. See the comments of Nikolas K. Gvosdev in the first panel, "Revisiting the Case for Democracy Assistance," at the *Does Democracy Matter* conference cosponsored by the Foreign Policy Research Institute and the Woodrow

Wilson Center, Washington, DC, October 20, 2014, http://www.wilsoncenter. org/event/does-democracy-matter.

26. Owen, op. cit.

27. Lennon, 11.

28. David E. Spiro, "The Insignificance of the Liberal Peace," *International Security* 19:2 (Autumn, 1994), 55–62.

29. John Mearsheimer, "Back to the Future: Instability in Europe After the Cold War," *International Security* 15:1 (Summer 1990), 50–51.

30. See, for instance, William R. Thompson, "Democracy and Peace: Putting the Cart Before the Horse?" *International Organization* 50:1 (Winter 1996), 141–74.

31. See, for instance, Edward D. Mansfield and Jack Snyder, *Electing to Fight: Why Emerging Democracies Go to War* (Cambridge, MA: Belfer Center for Science and International Affairs, 2005).

32. "Experts Discuss Global Democracy," *PBS Newshour*, July 4, 2007, http:// www.pbs.org/newshour/bb/politics-july-dec07-democracy_07-04/.

33. Joanne Gowa, *Ballots and Bullets* (Princeton: Princeton University Press, 1999), 113.

34. Thomas Carothers, "The 'Sequencing' Fallacy," *Journal of Democracy* 18:1 (January 2007), 25.

35. Herbert Wulf, "Security Sector Reform in Developing and Transitional Countries," *Berghof Research Center for Constructive Conflict Management* (July 2014), 2.

36. Gerardo L. Munck, "Democracy Studies: Agenda, Findings, Challenges," *Democratization: The State of the Art*, ed. Dirk Berg-Schlosser (Opladen, Germany: Barbara Budrich Publishers, 2007), 59.

37. Wulf, 6–7.

38. Amitai Etzioni and G. John Ikenberry, "Point of Order: Is China More Westphalian than the West?" *Foreign Affairs* 90:6 (November/December 2011), http://www.foreignaffairs.com/articles/136548/amitai-etzioni-g-john-ikenberry/point-of-order.

39. For a discussion of these factors, see Nikolas K. Gvosdev, "The Other Iran Timetable," *National Interest*, April 26, 2007, http://nationalinterest.org/commentary/the-other-iran-timetable-1567; and Nikolas K. Gvosdev, "Playing the Clock on Iran's Regime," *World Politics Review*, January 29, 2010, http://www.worldpoliticsreview.com/articles/5018/the-realist-prism-playing-the-clock-on-irans-regime.

40. Slaughter, in "Experts Discuss Global Democracy," op. cit.

41. Ian Bremmer, *The J-Curve: A New Way to Understand Why Nations Rise and Fall* (New York: Simon and Schuster, 2006), 4.

42. Peter Rada, "Rethinking the "Democratic Peace Theory: Turbulent Democratization in North Africa and the Middle East and the External Dimnension," *Panorama of Global Security Environment 2012*, eds. M. Majer, R. Ondrejcsák, and V. Tarasovič (Bratislava, Slovakia: CENAA, 2012), 427.

43. Nikolas Gvosdev, "War Was a Catalyst, but For What?" *Washington Monthly* 37:5 (May 2005), 26, http://www.washingtonmonthly.com/features/2005/0505.gvosdev.html.

44. Reveron, Gvosdev, and Owens, 119.

45. Bill Keller, "The Return of America's Missionary Impulse," *New York Times Magazine*, April 15, 2011, http://www.nytimes.com/2011/04/17/magazine/

mag-17Lede-t.html?_r=0; see also the observation of an "Ascendant United States" believing it ought to "shape the world in its own image." Dominic Tierney, "The Rise of Alien Warfare," *The National Interest* 136 (March/April 2015), 21.

46. Donald K. Emmerson, "Moralpolitik: The Timor Test," *The National Interest* 58 (Winter 1999/2000), 64, 68.

47. David Chandler, "Rhetoric Without Responsibility: The Attraction of 'Ethical' Foreign Policy," *British Journal of Politics and International Relations* 5:3 (August 2003), 310.

48. Richard Falk,"Kosovo, World Order, and the Future of International Law," *American Journal of International Law* 93:4 (1999), 848.

49. Hearing of the Senate Foreign Relations Committee, Chaired by Senator Robert Menendez (D-NJ). Witness: Samantha Power, Nominee to be Representative of the United States to the United Nations, Representative of the United States in the Security Council of the United Nations, and Representative of the United States to the Sessions of the General Assembly of the United Nations, United States Senate, July 17, 2013, archived at http://blog.unwatch.org/index.php/2013/07/19/samantha-powers-nomination-hearing-video-transcript/.

50. William Kristol and Robert Kagan, "Toward a Neo-Reaganite Foreign Policy," *Foreign Affairs* 75:4 (July/August 1996), 27.

51. *National Security Strategy*, 2, 3.

52. Stanley Hoffmann, "In Defense of Mother Teresa: Morality in Foreign Policy," *Foreign Affairs* 75:2 (March–April 1996), 175.

53. As an example, see President Barack Obama's address to the graduating class at West Point, May 28, 2014, where he notes, "The values of our founding inspire leaders in parliaments and new movements in public squares around the globe." Later, he reiterates that in taking action around the world, "we must uphold standards that reflect our values." A transcript and video of the speech was made available by Catherine Traywick of *Foreign Policy*, http://foreignpolicy.com/2014/05/28/president-obama-at-west-point-watch-the-speech-read-the-transcript/.

54. Slaughter, quoted in "Experts Discuss Global Democracy," op. cit.

55. Nikolas K. Gvosdev, "What Metrics for Assessing the Ethics of Intervention?" *Ethics and International Affairs*, June 24, 2014, http://www.ethicsandinternationalaffairs.org/2014/what-metrics-for-assessing-the-ethics-of-intervention/.

56. Anatol Lieven and John Hulsman, "Ethical Realism and Contemporary Challenges," *American Foreign Policy Interests* 28:6 (2006), 417, 418.

57. C.A.J. Cody, *The Ethics of Armed Humanitarian Intervention*, Peaceworks 45 (Washington, DC: United States Institute of Peace, 2002), 30.

58. A point raised by Senator Richard Lugar, chairman of the Senate Foreign Relations Committee, in discussing policy choices on Iraq. "Iraq Transition," hearing before the Senate Foreign Relations Committee, April 22, 2004, with transcript archived at http://www.iraqwatch.org/government/US/HearingsPreparedstatements/us-sfrc-transcript-042204.htm.

59. A leading example of this view is the statement issued by Senator John McCain, "A Fight for Freedom," *Washington Post*, March 23, 2003, archived at http://www.iraqwatch.org/government/US/Letters,%20reports%20and%20statements/mccain-032303.htm.

See also, for instance, testimony provided during the "Department of Defense Budget Priorities for Fiscal Year 2004," Hearing before the House Committee on the Budget, 108th Congress/Session1, February 27, 2003, http://www.gpo.gov/fdsys/pkg/CHRG-108hhrg85421/pdf/CHRG-108hhrg85421.pdf; "The Reconstruction of Iraq," Hearing Before the House International Relations Committee, 108th Congress/Session 1, May 15, 2003, http://www.iraqwatch.org/government/US/Hearings-Preparedstatements/hirc-iraqfuturetranscript-051503.html#FT; Paul Wolfowitz (Deputy Secretary of Defense), "Eliminating the Threat to World Security Posed by the Iraqi Regime and Halting the Torture, Imprisonment and Execution of Innocents," Foreign Press Center Briefing, Washington, DC, March 28, 2003, http://2002–2009-fpc.state.gov/19202.htm; Marc Grossman (Under Secretary of State for Political Affairs), "Assisting Iraqis with Their Future: Planning for Democracy," Foreign Press Center Briefing, Washington, DC, March 19, 2003, http://2002–2009-fpc.state.gov/18836.htm.

60. One of the most famous public statements of many of these concerns was presented by former National Security Advisor Brent Scowcroft, in "Don't Attack Saddam," *Wall Street Journal*, August 15, 2002, http://www.wsj.com/articles/SB1029371773228069195; concerns were also expressed in two Intelligence Community Assessments distributed by the National Intelligence Council in January 2003, *Regional Consequences of Regime Change in Iraq* and *Principal Challenges in Post-Saddam Iraq*. The declassified portions of those reports are included as part of the report, "Prewar Intelligence Assessments About Postwar Iraq," Senate Select Committee on Intelligence, 110th Congress/Session 1, May 25, 2007, archived at http://fas.org/irp/congress/2007_rpt/prewar.pdf.

61. A number of symposia were convened and retrospective articles written to assess the impact of the Iraq War ten years after its start. These include Nadim Shehadi, "One Day the World Will Thank Bush for Shaking Up the Arab Region," *The World Today*, February 2013, http://www.chathamhouse.org/publications/twt/archive/view/189203; John Howard, "Iraq 2003: A Retrospective," lecture delivered at the Lowy Institute, Sydney, April 9, 2013, http://www.lowyinstitute.org/publications/iraq-2003-retrospective; Peter Maass, "Did the Iraq War Bring the Arab Spring," *New Yorker*, April 9, 2013, http://www.newyorker.com/news/news-desk/did-the-iraq-war-bring-the-arab-spring; "Iraq, 10 years On: Did Invasion Bring 'Hope and Progress' to Millions as Bush Vowed?" *NBC News*, March 19, 2013, http://worldnews.nbcnews.com/_news/2013/03/19/17325601-iraq-10-years-on-did-invasion-bring-hope-and-progress-to-millions-as-bush-vowed?lite; "Ten Years After the Iraq Invasion," *The European*, March 20, 2013, http://www.theeuropean-magazine.com/stephen-walt--3/6617-ten-years-after-the-iraq-invasion. On the proliferation impact, see "Bombs Without Borders: Perspectives on the Nuclear Proliferation Threat," *Yale Journal of International Affairs* 2:1 (Fall/Winter 2006), 69–76. On China as a beneficiary of the Iraq War, see Matthew Schiazvenza, "Who Won the Iraq War? China," *The Atlantic*, March 22, 2013, http://www.theatlantic.com/china/archive/2013/03/who-won-the-iraq-war-china/274267/. On the question of the erosion of the US international position, see Raymond Hinnebusch, "The Iraq War and

International Relations: Implications for Small States," *Cambridge Review of International Affairs* 19:3 (September 2006), esp. 456–57.

62. Joseph S. Nye, "The Iraq War Ten Years Later," *Project Syndicate*, March 11, 2013, http://www.project-syndicate.org/commentary/the-iraq-war-ten-years-later-by-joseph-s--nye.

63. See Gvosdev, "What Metrics," op. cit.

64. "Summary: A Symposium on Iraq's Impact on the Future of U.S. Foreign and Defense Policy," *Council on Foreign Relations*, October 6, 2006, http://i.cfr.org/content/meetings/Iraq_Symposium_10-6-06.pdf.

65. Michael Hirsch, "The Legacy of the Iraq War? Anti-War Democrats and Rand Paul," *National Journal*, March 18, 2013, http://www.nationaljournal.com/politics/the-legacy-of-the-iraq-war-anti-war-democrats-and-rand-paul-20130318.

66. See, for instance, Anna Dimitrova, "Obama's Foreign Policy: Between Pragmatic Realism and Smart Diplomacy?" (paper presented at the Institute for Cultural Diplomacy Academy for Cultural Diplomacy, June 2011 session), http://www.culturaldiplomacy.org/academy/content/pdf/participant-papers/academy/Anna-Dimitrova-Obama's-Foreign-Policy-Between-Pragmatic-Realism-and-Smart-Diplomacy.pdf;

67. Etzioni, *From Empire to Community*, 100–02.

68. *ibid*, 102.

69. See the discussion, for instance, in Fareed Zakaria, "The Future of American Power: How America Can Survive the Rise of the Rest," *Foreign Affairs* 87:3 (May/June 2008), 18–43; see also David Mason, *The End of the American Century* (Lanham, MD: Rowman and Littlefield, 2009, 2010), esp. 150–52. For a discussion of how to cope with American decline and reverse, which serves as a background for discussions among the Obama administration foreign policy team; see James Mann, "How Obama's Foreign Policy Team Relates to the Vietnam War—or Doesn't," *Washington Post*, June 22, 2012, http://www.washingtonpost.com/opinions/james-mann-how-obamas-foreign-policy-team-relates-to-the-vietnam-war--or-doesnt/2012/06/22/gJQAkVWKvV_story.html.

70. Antonio de Aguiar Patriota, "Brazil and the Shaping of a Cooperative Multipolar Order," *Horizons* 2 (Winter 2015), 224.

71. Etzioni, *Security First*, 1.

72. Interview with Brian Duignan, "Amitai Etzioni on Communitarianism, Civil Rights and Foreign Policy," *Encyclopedia Britannica Blog*, May 16, 2011, http://blogs.britannica.com/2011/05/anita-etzioni-communitarianism-civil-rights-foreign-policy/.

73. Amitai Etzioni, "Security First: Ours, Theirs and the Global Order's," *The National Interest* 88 (March/April 2007), 12.

74. *Ibid*, xiv.

75. Amitai Etzioni, "Sovereignty as Responsibility," *Orbis* 50:1 (Winter 2006), 79.

76. Etzioni, *Security First*, 4.

77. Etzioni, "Sovereignty as Responsibility," 82.

78. Derek S. Reveron, Nikolas K. Gvosdev, and Mackubin Thomas Owens, *US Foreign Policy and Defense Strategy: The Evolution of an Incidental Superpower* (Washington, DC: Georgetown University Press, 2015), 135–36.

79. See, for instance, Kishore Mahbubani, "ASEAN as a Living, Breathing Modern Miracle," *Horizons* 2 (Winter 2015), 147.

80. Lynn Kuok, "Security First: The Lodestar for U.S. Foreign Policy in Southeast Asia?" *American Behavioral Scientist* 51:9 (May 2008), 1428.

81. Carothers, 13.

82. Paul Jackson, "Security Sector Reform and State Building," *Third World Quarterly* 32:10 (2011), 1813.

83. Etzioni, *Security First*, 6.

84. See, for instance, Michael Ladeen's definition, in "Dishonorable Congressman," *National Review Online*, September 10, 2003, http://www.nationalreview.com/articles/207982/dishonorable-congressman/michael-ledeen. Some view Condoleezza Rice's July 2006 press conference, describing the Hezbollah-Israeli conflict as part of the "birth pangs" of a new Middle East, as reflecting this perspective ("What we're seeing here is, in a sense, the growing—the birth pangs of a new Middle East, and whatever we do, we have to be certain that we're pushing forward to the new Middle East, not going back to the old Middle East."). In commenting, Fred Kaplan rhetorically asked, "Does she think it's a sibling of the peaceful, tolerant, democratic Middle East that her president believed would rise up in the wake of Saddam Hussein's collapse?" See "There are Worse Things than the Status Quo," *Slate*, July 24, 2006, http://www.slate.com/articles/news_and_politics/war_stories/2006/07/there_are_worse_things_than_the_status_quo.single.html.

85. Kanan Makiya, "The Arab Spring Started in Iraq," *New York Times*, April 7, 2013, SR7, http://www.nytimes.com/2013/04/07/opinion/sunday/the-arab-spring-started-in-iraq.html?pagewanted=all&_r=0.

86. Etzioni, *Security First*, 52.

87. Amitai Etzioni, *Hot Spots: American Foreign Policy in a Post-Human-Rights World* (New Brunswick, NJ: Transaction Publishers, 2012), 140.

88. James Steinberg, "A Sound Principle, but Not a Playbook," *American Behavioral Scientist* 51:9 (May 2008), 1358.

89. Carothers, 13.

90. Nikolas K. Gvosdev, "For U.S., Middle East 'Moderates' a Fool's Errand," *World Politics Review*, October 15, 2014, http://www.worldpoliticsreview.com/articles/14207/for-u-s-middle-east-moderates-a-fool-s-errand.

91. Even those who support democracy promotion will acknowledge that a "handful of nondemocratic governments still maintain significant legitimacy without elections, whether through cultural norms concerning inherited rule, good economic performance (or at least the reasonably competent distribution of economic largesse from oil revenues), or the mantle of national struggle against foreign enemies." See Carothers, 21.

92. Robert Kagan, "History's Back," *The Weekly Standard* 13:46 (August 25, 2008), http://www.weeklystandard.com/Content/Public/Articles/000/000/015/426usidf.asp.

93. Amitai Etzioni, "The Global Importance of Illiberal Moderates," *Cambridge Review of International Affairs* 19:3 (September 2006), 369–85.

94. W. Gunther Plaut, *Asylum: A Moral Dilemma* (Westport, CT: Praeger Publishers, 1995), 74.

95. Amitai Etzioni, "Obama's Rebalancing: A Fig Leaf," *The Diplomat*, April 26, 2014, http://thediplomat.com/2014/04/obamas-rebalancing-a-fig-leaf/.

96. See the comments in Amitai Etzioni, "MAR: A Model for US-China Relations," *The Diplomat*, September 20, 2013, http://thediplomat.com/2013/09/mar-a-model-for-us-china-relations/.

97. On the idea of Ukraine as serving as such a neutral buffer, for instance, see Stephen Kinzer, "Putin's Push Into Ukraine is Rational," *Boston Globe*, February 25, 2015, http://www.bostonglobe.com/opinion/2015/02/25/putin-reaction-ukraine-about-russian-security/uM3Ipc7lWPgWbpiIWB-JSxI/story.html; Leonid Bershidsky, "Europe Isn't Really Worried About Putin," *Bloomberg View*, February 26, 2015, http://www.bloombergview.com/articles/2015-02-26/europe-isn-t-really-worried-about-putin.

98. Colin Dueck, "Ideas and Alternatives in American Grand Strategy, 2000–2004, *Review of International Studies* 30(2004):513–17.

99. Daniel Drezner, "The Future of US Foreign Policy," *Internationale Politik und Gesellschaft* 15 (January 2008), 28.

100. Nikolas K. Gvosdev, "Communitarian Realism," *American Behavioral Scientist* 48:12 (August 2005), 1591–1606.

101. Amitai Etzioni, "Response," American Behavioral Scientist, 48:12 (August 2005), 1658.

102. Amitai Etzioni, *Winning Without War* (Garden City, NY: Doubleday, 1964), 225.

103. Etzioni, *From Empire to Community*, 4.

104. Etzioni, *From Empire to Community*, 90.

105. Etzioni, *From Empire to Community*, 1.

106. Etzioni, "Response," 1657.

107. Etzioni, *Winning Without War*, 227.

108. Joseph S. Nye, Jr., "American Foreign Policy After Iraq," *Chronicle of Higher Education*, July 27, 2007, http://chronicle.com/article/American-Foreign-Policy-After/9376.

109. Walter Reese-Schaefer, *Amitai Etzioni zur Einfuerhrung* (Hamburg: Junius, 2001), 69.

110. Etzioni, "Response," 1657.

111. Etzioni, *Security First*, 2.

112. Etzioni, *Security First*, 245.

113. Drezner, 27.

114. Walter A. McDougall, "Can the United States Do Grand Strategy?" *FPRI Telegram*, April 2010, http://www.fpri.org/articles/2010/04/can-united-states-do-grand-strategy.

115. Tierney, 27.

116. Jackson, 1813.

117. Comments made at a forum, "The West and Russia: A New Cold War?" Sponsored by the Center for International Relations and Sustainable Development, the Harvard Club, New York, February 18, 2015.

118. Precursors to Etzioni's own findings about the importance of sequencing security first before moving on to other issues—and the impact this began to have on officials handling peace-enforcement and nation-building missions for the United Nations—can be found in Tor Tanke Holm and Espen Barth Eide, *Peacebuilding and Police Reform* (London: Frank Cass, 2000). For the linkages with Etzioni's work, see Barry J. Ryan, "The EU's Emergent Security-First Agenda: Securing Albania and Montenegro," *Security Dialogue* 40:3 (June 2009), 312.

119. Ryan, 311–31.
120. Kuok, 1428–1429.
121. Joshua Kurlantzick, "The Mysterious Opening of Myanmar," *Boston Globe*, December 4, 2011, http://www.cfr.org/burmamyanmar/mysterious-opening-myanmar/p26680.
122. Nikolas K. Gvosdev, "Indecision on Egypt Leaves U.S. Interests at Risk," *World Politics Review*, August 23, 2013, http://www.worldpoliticsreview.com/articles/13184/the-realist-prism-indecision-on-egypt-leaves-u-s-interests-at-risk.
123. Slaughter, "Experts Discuss Global Democracy," op. cit.
124. Joseph S. Nye, Jr., "Security and Smart Power," *American Behavioral Scientist* 51:9 (May 2008), 4.
125. ibid.
126. Robert W. McElroy, *Morality and American Foreign Policy: The Role of Ethics in International Affairs* (Princeton, NJ: Princeton University Press, 1992), 182–84.
127. Jacob Heilbrunn, "The Wise Man," *The National Interest* 136 (March/April 2015), 6.
128. Glyn Morgan, "Security, Stability and International Order," *American Behavioral Scientist* 51:9 (May 2008), 1326.
129. Slaughter, "Experts Discuss Global Democracy," op. cit.
130. Carothers, 25.
131. See, for instance, the roundtable discussion, "Security First Book Club," with Lila Shapiro, Amitai Etzioni, Shuja Nawaz, Stephen Schwartz, Piki Ish-Shalom, Amir Hussain, and Michael Contarino, *Talking Points Memo Café*, September 22–26, 2008, archived at http://aladinrc.wrlc.org/handle/1961/5703.
132. This question over whether the US government must be involved in democracy promotion is a theme explored in "Does Democracy Matter? A Conference Report," *FPRI E-Notes*, December 2014, http://www.fpri.org/articles/2014/12/does-democracy-matter-conference-report. See also the assessment of the Forum for the Future, in James Traub, "A Funny Thing Happened on the Way to the Forum," *Foreign Policy*, January 14, 2011, http://foreignpolicy.com/2011/01/14/a-funny-thing-happened-on-the-way-to-the-forum/.
133. Morgan, 1331, 1337.
134. Morgan, 1337.
135. Jean Bethke Elshtain, "Liberty and Security For All?" *New York Sun*, August 29, 2007, http://www.nysun.com/arts/liberty-security-for-all/6154.
136. See, for instance, "What if the Obama Administration Fully Sided with Iran's Green Movement?" *Washington Post*, June 12, 2010, http://www.washingtonpost.com/wp-dyn/content/article/2010/06/11/AR2010061106014.html.
137. Stanley Renshon, "Security First," *Political Science Quarterly* 123:4 (Winter 2008/2009), 692–93.
138. Thomas L. Friedman, "Democracy is in Recession," *New York Times*, February 18, 2015, A21.
139. Larry Diamond, "Facing Up to the Democratic Recession," *Journal of Democracy* 26:1 (January 2015), 152–53.
140. Renshon, 693.
141. Carothers, 215.

142. Benjamin Reilly notes the "distinctive institutional evolution" that has occurred in the region, suggesting that these features may not be present elsewhere. See his "Political Parties, Electoral Systems and Democratic Governance," *Democracy in East Asia: Prospects for the Twenty-First Century*, eds. Larry Diamond, Marc F. Plattner, and Yun-han Chu (Baltimore, MD: Johns Hopkins University Press, 2013), 16.
143. Carothers, 19.
144. See, for instance, Richard D. Kauzlarich, "The Heydar Aliyev Era Ends in Azerbaijan Not with a Bang but a Whisper," *Brookings Opinion*, January 13, 2015, http://www.brookings.edu/research/opinions/2015/01/13-aliyev-era-ends-bang-whisper-azerbaijan-kauzlarich.
145. Katherine Zimmerman, "Why America's Yemen Policy is Failing," *CNN*, February 13, 2015, http://www.cnn.com/2015/02/13/opinion/zimmerman-u-s-yemen-policy/.
146. Steinberg, 1359.
147. See Kuok, esp. 1429–1431, for a discussion on this problem with regard to US policy in Southeast Asia.
148. Obama was sometimes described as a "progressive realist" or a "hybrid realist."Cf. Steve Clemons, "Failing to Note the Difference When the U.S. Power Tank Is Full or Near Empty," *Foreign Policy*, August 27, 2009, http://foreignpolicy.com/2009/08/27/is-paul-wolfowitz-for-real/; Nikolas K. Gvosdev, "Obama: Wilsonian Idealist or Progressive Realist," *World Politics Review*, November 10, 2008, http://www.worldpoliticsreview.com/articles/2898/obama-wilsonian-idealist-or-progressive-realist.
149. See, for instance, Ryan LIzza, "The Consequentalist," *New Yorker*, May 2, 2011, http://www.newyorker.com/magazine/2011/05/02/the-consequentialist.
150. See Clemons, op. cit.
151. Peter Baker, "Obama Calls for Expansion of Human Rights to Combat Extremism," *New York Times*, February 20, 2015 http://www.nytimes.com/2015/02/20/world/obama-extremism-summit.html?_r=0.
152. McDougall, op. cit.
153. James Gelvin, *The Arab Uprisings: What Everyone Needs to Know*, 2nd ed. (Oxford: Oxford University Press, 2012, 2015), 167.
154. See, for instance, Charles J. Sullivan, "Riding the Revolutionary Wave: America, the Arab Spring, and Autumn 1989," *Washington Review of Turkish and Eurasian Affairs*, April 2011, http://www.thewashingtonreview.org/articles/riding-the-revolutionary-wave-america-the-arab-spring-and-the-autumn-of-1989.html.
155. "Egypt Unrest: US Disowns Envoy Comment on Hosni Mubarak," *BBC News*, February 5, 2011, http://www.bbc.co.uk/news/world-us-canada-12374753.
156. Lizza, op. cit.; see also the discussion found in Hillary Clinton, *Hard Choices: A Memoir* (New York: Simon and Schuster, 2014), 305–13.
157. Nikolas K. Gvosdev and Ray Takeyh, "Decline of Western Realism," *The National Interest* 117 (January/February 2012), 16.
158. David Ignatius, "America is the Ally Egypt Needs," *Washington Post*, February 26, 2015, http://www.washingtonpost.com/opinions/america-is-the-ally-that-egypt-needs/2015/02/26/efe7eeb0-bdfd-11e4-bdfa-b8e8f594e6ee_story.html?hpid=z2.

159. "U.S.-Libyan Relations: The Second Year of Normalization," Remarks by Ambassador Gene A. Cretz at the Carnegie Endowment for International Peace Friday, June 4, 2010, Washington, D.C., http://libya.usembassy.gov/news-events/news-from-the-embassy2/remarks-by-ambassador-cretz-at-the-carnegie-endowment-for-international-peace.html.

160. Gvosdev and Takeyh, 15.

161. Lizza, op. cit.; see also Michael Lewis, "Obama's Way," Vanity Fair, October 5, 2012, http://www.vanityfair.com/news/2012/10/michael-lewis-profile-barack-obama.

162. Helene Cooper and Steven Lee Myers, "Obama Takes Hard Line With Libya After Shift by Clinton," New York Times, March 19, 2011, A1, http://www.nytimes.com/2011/03/19/world/africa/19policy.html?pagewanted=all.

163. Josh Rogin, "How Obama Turned on a Dime Toward War," The Cable (Foreign Policy), March 18, 2011, http://thecable.foreignpolicy.com/posts/2011/03/18/how_obama_turned_on_a_dime_toward_war.

164. Ivo Daalder and James Stavridis, "NATO's Success in Libya," International Herald Tribune, October 31, 2011, http://www.nytimes.com/2011/10/31/opinion/31iht-eddaalder31.html.

165. Helene Cooper and Steven Lee Myers, "U.S. Tactics in Libya May Be a Model for Other Efforts," New York Times, August 29, 2011, A9, http://www.nytimes.com/2011/08/29/world/africa/29diplo.html?pagewanted=all.

166. Amitai Etzioni, "The Lessons of Libya," Military Review 92:1 (January/February 2012), 45–54.

167. Paul Richter and Christi Parsons, "U.S. Intervention in Libya Now Seen as Cautionary Tale," Los Angeles Times, June 27, 2014, http://www.latimes.com/world/middleeast/la-fg-us-libya-20140627-story.html#page=1.

168. Owen Jones, "The War in Libya Was Seen as a Success, Now Here We Are Engaging with the Blowback in Mali," The Independent, January 13, 2013, http://www.independent.co.uk/voices/comment/the-war-in-libya-was-seen-as-a-success-now-here-we-are-engaging-with-the-blowback-in-mali-8449588.html.

169. Mark Mazzetti, Robert F. Worth, and Michael R. Gordon, "Obama's Uncertain Path Amid Syria Bloodshed," New York Times, October 23, 2013, A1, http://www.nytimes.com/2013/10/23/world/middleeast/obamas-uncertain-path-amid-syria-bloodshed.html?pagewanted=all.

170. Gvosdev and Takeyh, 9.

171. Quoted in Richter and Parsons, op. cit.

172. Alan J. Kuperman, "Obama's Libya Debacle: How a Well-Meaning Intervention Ended in Failure," Foreign Affairs 94:2 (March/April 2015), http://www.foreignaffairs/com/print/140292.

173. Kuperman, op. cit.

174. Kuperman, op. cit.

175. Amnesty International, The Battle for Libya (London: Amnesty International, 2011).

176. Yevgeny Primakov, "Russia and China Have Valid Reasons for UN Position on Syria," Russia Beyond the Headlines, February 7, 2012, http://rbth.com/articles/2012/02/07/russia_and_china_have_valid_reasons_for_un_position_on_syria_14329.html.

177. Alex deWaal, "The African Union and the Libya Conflict of 2011," *Reinventing Peace*, December 19, 2012, http://sites.tufts.edu/reinventing-peace/2012/12/19/the-african-union-and-the-libya-conflict-of-2011/.

178. Some commentators speculate whether candidates for office in 2016 who supported both the Iraq War and the Libya intervention may come under scrutiny for those judgment calls. Conor Friedersdorf, "Hillary's Hawkishness Could Cost Her the Presidency," *The Atlantic*, February 19, 2015, http://www.theatlantic.com/politics/archive/2015/02/hillary-clintons-hawkishness-could-cost-her-the-presidency-again/385629/.

179. Rada, 427.

180. Etzioni, *Hot Spots*, 157–58, dealing specifically with the proposals for a "Marshall Plan for the Middle East."

6

Sheathing the Sword of Damocles: Deproliferation

One of the gravest dangers to the security of all states in the international community is the risk that nuclear weapons or other weapons of mass destruction (WMDs) might be used by a rogue state or a terrorist organization. How probable or likely such an attack may be is less critical, because, as Michael Levi argues, "even a small chance of catastrophe is worth worrying about."[1] This is why, in 2009, Mohamed ElBaradei, director of the International Atomic Energy Agency (IAEA), declared, "The gravest threat faced by the world is of an extremist group getting hold of nuclear weapons or materials."[2]

However, the problem is finite and, with effective international cooperation, controllable. When it comes to atomic components, as Graham Allison pithily observes, "It is a basic matter of physics: without fissile material, you can't have a nuclear bomb. No nuclear bomb, no nuclear terrorism. Moreover, fissile material can be kept out of the wrong hands."[3] The challenge is greater with other types of weapons of mass destruction and their delivery systems, but not insurmountable.

Eliminating all weapons of mass destruction—a disarmament strategy—is appealing in theory. But it is seen as impractical in a world where the balance of nuclear arms among a series of great powers is seen as an imperfect but necessary condition for preserving some modicum of global stability and avoiding a destructive great power war.[4] Even if some scholars argue this view is a "myth,"[5] and even if the long-term aspiration of the United States is for nuclear abolition (as outlined by President Barack Obama in his Prague address of April 5, 2009), this belief retains a great hold on the policy community for the short-term.

There are two established tools for dealing with WMDs. The first includes arms control—the effort to regulate the size of arsenals with an eye to limit growth, to freeze numbers, and then to engage in reductions. The second tool is nonproliferation—where the possession of the weapon or the technologies needed for its fabrication and delivery by states that have not yet acquired them is seen as an unconditional negative. With nonproliferation, the minimum standard for success is freezing the status quo, though this floor can be raised to reverse instances where the status quo has been violated.[6]

During the 1960s, Etzioni had seen arms control—freezing the increase in the number of weapons—as a first step, a necessary but incomplete precondition for achieving the ultimate goal of eliminating entire classes of weaponry. Etzioni's interest in forging cooperative mechanisms for first containing and then eliminating weapons of mass destruction, part of his strategy for escaping the trap of the Cold War, gained renewed salience after the September 11, 2001 terrorist attacks. The end of the bipolar world system, and the spread of technology for the fabrication of WMDs and their delivery systems, poses a major risk to world security and to individual nations, both by increasing the probability that such weapons will end up being used (as indeed they were during the Syrian civil war) and heightening the risk that terrorists will be able to access such devices. Etzioni argues that most countries share a common security interest in "removing the access to nuclear arms and the materials from which they can readily be made—first and foremost in unstable and noncompliant states, and only then in all others," a policy he labels "de proliferation."[7] Deproliferation is related to the concept of "counter-proliferation," which focuses on developing military capabilities to successfully employ force against states that have already acquired WMDs. Advances in this area were made by US Secretary of Defense Les Aspin and then-Assistant Secretary of Defense Ashton Carter, who is now the US Defense Secretary. Over time, counter-proliferation has become "code for 'pre-emption of WMD capability.'"[8] Deproliferation does not rule out the possibility that military action might be needed, but looks beyond deterrence to find ways to create incentives for states to give up such capabilities voluntarily.

Nonproliferation is about deincentivizing states from seeking to acquire WMDs, including creating norms against possession of such devices. In addition, it focuses on finding ways to persuade those countries that already possess the necessary technology from passing it along (and, failing that, to interdict any such transfers).[9] Etzioni sees nonproliferation as the first component of a deproliferation approach;

indeed, tighter controls on trade are absolutely necessary. As Kurt Campbell warns:

> Consider the ease with which Pakistan, for example, can develop a nuclear device with assistance from China and place it on top of a ballistic missile purchased from North Korea. The development of transnational trade in WMD and related technologies is a relatively new phenomenon that could exponentially increase the threat of nuclear proliferation.[10]

A two-step deproliferation approach begins with securing existing stockpiles of WMDs and materials and then removing them to safe locations for destruction and dismantling, and ensuring that components that can be used for peaceful means (such as industrial activity or power generation, for instance) have no possibility of being weaponized. Moreover, deproliferation, according to Etzioni's conception, expands on the nonproliferation agenda to move beyond prevention and toward reversal: to create conditions for existing possessors to divest themselves of such devices. Whenever possible, this ought to be encouraged via diplomacy and voluntary action, especially by offering guarantees to regimes that in return for giving up WMDs can obtain binding security guarantees. However, in the case of unstable or belligerent actors, a deproliferation strategy is prepared to contemplate more forcible action to deprive them of such weapons, and the capacity to develop and deploy them.[11] The strategy thus buttresses and augments Graham Allison's own advocacy of the "three nos": "no loose nukes, no new nascent nukes, and no new nuclear states."[12] It also appeals to the self-interest of major powers that want to prevent the spread of WMDs into other states that might be less committed to regional and global stability.[13]

Like nonproliferation—where "international cooperation... requires a shared perception that at least some proliferators are potentially hostile and represent a common danger"[14]—a successful deproliferation strategy requires close and coordinated interstate cooperation and a similar assessment of common threat. Such an assessment buttressed a joint Russian-American operation to remove high-enriched uranium from a research reactor in Vinca, Serbia, and to return it for safekeeping to Russia, as well as plans to develop a facility in Russia to destroy chemical weapons.[15] Indeed, different states are needed to bring different assets to the table. For one, all potential exporters of dangerous technologies must agree to the plan; the experience of the Islamic Republic of Iran, which was able to develop a nuclear and missile industry in spite of severe sanctions imposed unilaterally by the United States, makes this abundantly clear. Some states can be persuaded to give up the infrastructure needed to produce WMDs if offered lucrative economic benefits or provided with alternative technologies (say, to meet the needs of a civilian energy production program). In some cases, other states that are perceived to pose a military threat to the security of the country in question must be prepared to offer binding security guarantees, or otherwise assist the country to fend off possible aggressors.

Etzioni believes that regimes seek out WMDs, in part, out of a sense of insecurity; possession of "the bomb" (or its equivalent) can act as a check on the willingness of other countries to use force, or the threat of force, as a way to exert pressure on a country for its internal policies or external relations. (Vladimir Putin made a similar observation, pointing out in 2013 that this is a driver of proliferation: "Thus a growing number of countries seek to acquire weapons of mass destruction. This is logical: if you have the bomb, no one will touch you."[16]) Commentators who argue that those who aspire to acquire WMDs are only rogue regimes should consider the reality that "nations seek such weapons for a variety of strategic and national interests calculations unrelated to whether they are internally governed as liberal democracies or dictatorships. The cases of Israel and India both pose difficulties for the proposition that autocracies are more inclined to pursue such weapons than democracies."[17]

This is why Etzioni links deproliferation efforts to the search for security and the emergence of reliable regional and global authorities that can give guarantees and act as checks on the most powerful states. A decade ago, Kurt Campbell raised concerns about what factors might drive currently nonnuclear states to reconsider their choice and to seek the option of developing nuclear weapons. These included: fears about US interventionism; a possible withdrawal of the United States from active management of security affairs in key regions; the threat of terrorism; and the reemergence of rivalries over territory, especially between one state with nuclear weapons and one without.[18] Certainly, an emerging Global Safety Authority that could take effective action against terrorism and other destabilizing transnational threats, as well as the employment of the Mutually Assured Restraint paradigm (particularly in East Asia), might work to reduce the perceived need to acquire WMDs for their deterrent capabilities.

Building Blocks for a Deproliferation Approach

Etzioni's ideas have not been proposed in a vacuum but are shaped by an existing network of treaties and institutions set up to deal with nonproliferation. The foundation of this network comprises the three major multilateral agreements: the Nuclear Non-Proliferation Treaty (NPT), which took effect in 1972; the Biological Weapons Convention (BWC), which took effect in 1975; and the Chemical Weapons Convention (CWC), which took effect in 1997. The NPT, which was originally a time-limited accord, was made into an indefinite arrangement in 1995. It relies on the International Atomic Energy Agency (IAEA), an autonomous agency created by treaty that reports to both the United Nations Security Council and the General Assembly . The purpose of the IAEA is to verify that states that have signed the agreement and been designated as non-nuclear states are not diverting any nuclear material from peaceful, civilian programs for military use or to fabricate weapons. The CWC set up an inspection arm, the Organization for the Prohibition of Chemical Weapons, which verifies compliance with the treaty. Efforts to create an ad hoc group to enforce the BWC, however, ran up against logistical difficulties when it tried to create an effective inspections regime, due to the ease with which biological weapons can be produced.[19]

Instead of founding new intergovernmental organizations to handle the tasks of policing nonproliferation, many states have instead opted to create transnational associations to take up different pieces of the proliferation puzzle and to coordinate their national export controls. The principal associations are: (1) the Nuclear Suppliers Group (NSG); (2) the Nuclear Exporters Committee (sometimes referred to as the Zangger Committee after its first chairman, Professor Claude Zangger of Switzerland, who chaired meetings of an informal collection of representatives of states that were exporters of nuclear technology in Vienna during the 1970s; (3) the Missile Technology Control Regime; (4) the Australia Group, set up in 1985 after the use of chemical weapons in the Iran-Iraq War to ensure that controls were in place to oversee the exports of items that could be used as the precursors for chemical and biological weapons; and (5) the Wassenaar Arrangement, which manages export controls on conventional weapons and dual-use technologies. Initially composed of states from the developed West, since the end of the Cold War these groups have expanded their membership to encompass the former Soviet bloc and much of the developing world. For the most part, these export-control regimes "are informal arrangements lacking a treaty basis" but that allow for coordination among states by producing "agreements on common lists of controlled items, targets and procedures for controlling exports." These agreements are then enforced via national bureaucracies (although the Wassenaar Arrangement benefits from having a small secretariat in Vienna). In addition, as a regional association, the European Union also maintains its own set of export controls that are binding on its member-states. Other regional meetings held for the purpose of coordinating exports controls take place in other parts of the world, but without the same binding legal authority that the European Union's own *acquis communautaire* imposes on its members.[20]

In addition, there are nationally sponsored efforts, such as the Cooperative Threat Reduction program (popularly known as Nunn-Lugar after the sponsors of the relevant legislation in Congress, Senator Richard Lugar and Congressman Sam Nunn). This is an American initiative to cooperate in securing nuclear and other WMD material in other states, principally, post-Soviet republics, to lessen the proliferation danger. As discussed in an earlier chapter, Russia and the United States jointly sponsored the development of the Global Initiative to Combat Nuclear Terrorism, and the United States was the motivating force behind the creation of the Proliferation Security Initiative.[21] Yet, while the United States has been a leading force, it cannot dominate these structures; other countries—among them Australia, Germany, France, Russia, and Japan—also have the ability to shape global non-proliferation policy.[22]

These various transnational associations, therefore, have the potential to evolve into a Global Deproliferation Authority. A first step occurred in 2003, when, at the annual plenary meeting of the Wassenaar Arrangement, the national delegates committed to engaging in outreach "to relevant international institutions, e.g. the other export control regimes."[23] As in other areas, the shock of 9/11 galvanized these bodies to take more proactive action and to increase coordination in order to ensure that dangerous materials and even conventional arms would not flow into the hands of terrorists.[24]

President Barack Obama has also taken steps to provide an overarching framework by convening a series of biennial "Nuclear Security Summits" that bring together the main countries involved in nuclear matters. At the first, held in Washington in 2010, the heads of state or government of forty-seven countries agreed to an ambitious four-year plan for securing all fissile material; the subsequent summits in Korea (2012) and the Netherlands (2014) expanded the focus to all radiological sources, and to improve security at nuclear facilities. A key element of this process has been to get countries to eliminate their holdings of highly enriched uranium (from which bombs can be fabricated) and to reduce stockpiles of plutonium.[25] A key strategy has been to encourage individual countries to enact into their national legislation the international guidelines for handling and securing nuclear material; at the close of the 2014 Hague Summit, some thirty-five states had done so.[26]

The Nuclear Security Summits operate on a dual-track basis; the first is to attempt to achieve a general consensus, a minimum standard, that is acceptable to all summit participants and that they are prepared to enforce. The second is to utilize the so-called "gift basket" strategy where states can undertake unilateral commitments that exceed the consensus goals, or where a group of states can agree, on the sidelines of the summit, to more committed or extensive action. The consensus format ensures that no state can be forced to take on obligations beyond its tolerance for action; the gift basket approach, however, allows groups of states to blaze the trail for more comprehensive approaches that, over time, might emerge as the international position.[27]

Tightening up the various networks and improving international coordination via the Nuclear Security Summits are important next steps, given that, in recent years, the "international regimes to combat the proliferation of unconventional weapons face increasing doubts regarding their viability."[28] There are noticeable gaps in the current nonproliferation networks that allow for leakage of technologies, in terms of both capabilities and the political will of different stakeholders to apply them.[29] This effort is vital and necessary but still insufficient. Nonproliferation measures largely impact the "supply" side of the equation, and they cannot completely "stop illicit trade in nuclear material and technology. When there is a determined demand and the price is high enough, there is likely to be a supply."[30] Deproliferation is an attempt to move beyond the prevention of new breakout states in order to address reducing the overall demand for WMDs. Given that forcible counter-proliferation cannot address every case—and, in fact, may spur rather than inhibit efforts to acquire weapons of mass destruction—there must be another way to address the problem. This is what Etzioni's deproliferation proposal is meant to accomplish.

In particular, Etzioni has placed a good deal of faith in the exchange of effective security guarantees for verifiable deproliferation. Under the right conditions, he argues, states like India or Pakistan, whose drive to acquire nuclear weapons was predicated on their insecurities might be persuaded to roll back their programs if they could be persuaded that there were viable non-nuclear options for addressing their concerns.[31]

Deproliferation also ties into other initiatives developed by Etzioni. Defusing the India-Pakistan tinderbox cannot be separated from the larger question of China's role in the world. Etzioni argues that, to the extent that India is seen by the United States as a counterbalance to China, Washington has been willing to overlook India's own nuclear program and ultimately to find ways to increase Indo-American nuclear cooperation, which in turn drives Pakistani insecurity. China has therefore had an incentive to increase its support for Pakistan's own nuclear efforts.[32] Progress in reducing India-Pakistan tensions, therefore, is dependent on the course of US-China relations.

Can Deproliferation Work?

Etzioni maintains that his approach to deproliferation—incentivizing states to give up WMDs rather than using force and threats—has been validated in a number of real-world cases since the end of the Cold War. In July 2008 Etzioni argued:

> There are strong precedents for such a deproliferation approach—i.e., the removal of nuclear arms from Belarus, Kazakhstan, and Ukraine, the successful negotiations with Libya, the (yet-to-be tested) current progress with North Korea, and several elements of the Cooperative Threat Reduction programs and Global Threat Reduction Initiative.[33]

These cases give us a chance to examine the deproliferation thesis in terms of its real-world applicability.

After the breakup of the Soviet Union, the newly independent country of Ukraine, though pledging not to develop new nuclear weapons, considered retaining control of the Soviet arsenal that had been located on its territory, and also initially eschewing the ratification of the 1968 Non-Proliferation Treaty. This would have made Ukraine the world's third largest power. Ukraine also had legitimate security concerns given that a post-Soviet Russia was signaling that it did not necessarily recognize the permanence of Ukraine's borders. A September 1993 effort to produce a bilateral Russia-Ukraine agreement to transfer the Soviet arsenal to Russia did not succeed.[34]

The Trilateral Agreement among Ukrainian president Leonid Kravchuk, US President Bill Clinton and Russian President Boris Yeltsin, signed in January 1994, created the framework to settle the outstanding issues. Ukraine would be given security guarantees in return for transferring the weapons and entering the NPT as a declared nonnuclear state. More importantly, Ukraine was promised hundreds of millions of dollars in additional aid and assistance from the United States, the European Union, and fourteen other Western nations.[35] The so-called "Budapest Memorandum" concluded on December 5, 1994 on the sidelines of the Conference on Security and Cooperation in Europe. It is a political agreement (not a treaty) in which Russia, the United States, and the United Kingdom pledged to ensure the safety and territorial integrity of Ukraine, and to refer any aggression against Ukraine to the United Nations Security Council for international action in return for Ukraine's accession to the Nuclear Non-Proliferation Treaty as a nonnuclear weapons state. China and France also concluded separate bilateral agreements in which they committed themselves to uphold Ukraine's independence. Significantly, the "Ukrainian politicians who had agreed to transfer nuclear weapons in exchange for security had interpreted the Memorandum as a document guaranteeing the inviolability of its borders."[36] In return, over the next two years, Ukraine transferred to Russia all remaining Soviet nuclear arms and gave up the capacity to produce them. The last warhead was transferred in 1996, and the last missile silo on Ukrainian soil was decommissioned in 2001. A mix of security guarantees and economic incentives, per Etzioni's recommendations, had led to a successful deproliferation outcome.

The other two ex-Soviet republics followed similar paths. In Belarus, the government of Stanislav Shushkevich was eager to get rid of Soviet nuclear forces for a variety of reasons. Belarus had been the area most negatively impacted by the Chernobyl nuclear accident in 1986, creating a strong popular dislike of all things nuclear. Moreover, Shushkevich realized that negotiating the removal of the weapons and acceding to the NPT as a nonnuclear state would attract both US attention and, more importantly, economic aid for his small and struggling country. Finally, the Belarusian strategic establishment argued that possession of nuclear weapons rendered Belarus less, rather than more, secure. This reasoning was based on the notion that Belarus would become a target in the event of any sort of conflict between Russia and the West, because of the number of Russian forces that were required to remain stationed in Belarus to maintain the weapons. Returning the nuclear arsenal to Russia in exchange for complete evacuation of Belarus seemed an acceptable bargain. In Kazakhstan, Nursultan Nazarbayev also used the negotiations over his country's nonnuclear status to put Kazakhstan on the US. agenda and to receive aid, but also as a way to cement better relations with Moscow. Removal of nuclear weapons also proved popular given the deadly legacy left by the Soviet atomic testing grounds at Semipalatinsk.[37] It also served to reassure the United States and other governments that had been disturbed by Nazarbayev's initial flirtation with the idea of retaining the country's nuclear arsenal—in the years prior to Pakistan's own successful nuclear tests—on behalf of the entire Islamic world, with the risks that weapons could be transferred to other Arab and Islamic states that sought their own nuclear capacity.[38]

The end of the Cold War, the dismantling of apartheid, and the transition to majority rule also changed South Africa's calculus regarding the costs and benefits of retaining a clandestine nuclear weapons program. In 1991 South Africa joined the NPT, and in 1993 President Frederik de Klerk disclosed the existence of South Africa's nuclear weapons program. He claimed that it had been terminated by 1991; however, that termination took place in secret and without any international verification. South Africa also joined the Nuclear Suppliers Group and the Missile Technology Control Regime, thereby signaling its commitment to abide by nonproliferation norms.[39]

An even more dramatic development was the December 19, 2003 announcement by Muammar Gadhafi "confirming that Libya had decided to abandon its illicit effort to acquire a nuclear bomb, its chemical weapons stocks, and all of its longer-range missiles."[40] Even before the US invasion of Iraq—but in the aftermath of 9/11—the Libyan regime was reevaluating the utility of its WMD programs. The regime focused particular attention on whether the programs enhanced or damaged the country's security, as well as whether Libya would ever be able to produce a credible deterrent. Gadhafi and his advisors—notably, his son Seif al-Islam and his security chief Musa Kusa—came to the assessment that it might be possible to use the programs as a bargaining chip to gain diplomatic recognition and economic relations with the United States and other Western countries. The agreements reached among Libya, the United States, and the United Kingdom committed Tripoli to completely dismantle its WMD programs, to ship the components out of the country, to renounce the use of terrorism as a foreign policy tactic, and—a final critical demand—to the complete cessation of any trade in military equipment or dual-use items with other states that were deemed to be proliferation risks. These states included Iran, Syria, and North Korea. By mid-2004, Libya had been effectively disarmed and had taken on commitments to stop engaging in proliferation.[41] In return, the United States restored diplomatic relations and permitted investment in Libya's ageing energy sectors, thereby signaling that it would no longer back efforts directed at regime change.

Etzioni viewed the 2003 Libya agreement as an important validation of the deproliferation approach. A formerly "rogue" regime had been provided with security guarantees and a pathway to full reintegration with the international community, particularly in economic terms. In return, the regime agreed to complete access to and the dismantling of all sites where WMDs could be produced or deployed, as well as a complete cessation of any support for terrorist organizations. Without firing a shot, what might have become a major source of leakage of dangerous materials that would have threatened global security was eliminated.[42]

Etzioni's longer-term hope was that what, up to this point, had been a series of separate ad hoc deproliferation actions might, over time, become institutionalized (for instance, by expanding to encompass more nations), and so move the international system closer to becoming a true global security community. Some of the technical aspects are already in place. During the 1990s, Russia, the United States, and the IAEA "worked to develop a system for verifying nuclear weapons disarmament, and those who participated concluded that there were no technical obstacles to the implementation of such a regime."[43] There have been other proposals to expand a series of Cold War-era bilateral treaties between Moscow and Washington to become global in scope and nature. If the Intermediate-Range Nuclear Forces (INF) Treaty, for instance, were to become a global ban on all intermediate-range nuclear-capable missiles, it would lead to the complete elimination of an entire class of nuclear-weapons delivery system, not simply regulation of the sale of missile technology as currently occurs under the Missile Control Technology Regime. Multi-lateralizing these agreements might then be a way to jump-start the nuclear disarmament agenda.[44]

Yet, while all of this points to signs that a deproliferation agenda could be a feasible policy option, there are also criticisms. One can begin with Etzioni's 2008 assessment that positive progress toward the removal of all nuclear materials on the Korean peninsula would continue. A year later the Democratic People's Republic of Korea formally announced its possession of nuclear weapons. Estimates in 2015 are that Pyongyang is on track to develop as large a nuclear arsenal as two other undeclared nuclear powers, Israel and Pakistan.[45] Beyond the developments in Korea, there are some larger issues as well with Etzioni's approach.

First, the nations of the world will have to come to some sort of consensus about the very use of nuclear power.[46] As long as countries possess atomic plants and enrichment facilities, there is always the risk that nuclear material could be diverted into a clandestine program or stolen. Under some circumstances, eliminating nuclear power altogether is not feasible. In these cases, alternative proposals have been advanced, such as developing an international nuclear fuel bank. In this scenario, a country receives material and then under careful supervision returns it for processing to a central facility. Such proposals can only work, however, if there is a much tighter and comprehensive system of control and inspections.[47]

Beyond that, some have argued that, in dealing with nondemocratic states and/or countries that are hostile to the United States, diplomacy can only go so far in getting a regime to "freeze" its efforts to acquire WMDs, or to refrain from crossing the threshold to weaponization. But only regime change—even if peaceful and without any sort of overt US support—can bring about any guarantee of true deproliferation.[48] This position maintains that engagement with authoritarian regimes over their WMD programs can, at best, produce a series of limited interim arrangements that stop and monitor, rather than reverse, what progress has already been achieved.

A controversial element of Etzioni's deproliferation strategy is his contention that the United States should support and backstop agreements whereby a country "trades away" its weapons programs in return for assurances that its domestic form of governance will remain unmolested by other states in the international community.[49] On this point, Etzioni has allies. Graham Allison, for instance, argues that in service of the policy objective of achieving a non-nuclear North Korea—one with no weapons that does not proliferate dangerous technologies to other states—the United States and its allies would be prepared to "focus solely on this objective and subordinate all others, especially regime change."[50] This concession would be considered despite the appalling human rights record of the current government. Etzioni, of course, does not propose that any regime that gives up WMDs should be given security guarantees against internal uprisings. This means that a government that deproliferates but then finds itself facing a domestic revolt could not call upon other states for aid in suppressing the rebellion. But the details become murkier as to whether external support for an internal rebellion would constitute a violation of any security guarantees. Etzioni would seem to draw the line at military intervention on behalf of an uprising, although he does contend that "democratization by nonlethal means" and encouragement of evolutionary regime change would not violate the spirit of those security guarantees.[51]

The question of what sort of stick will be wielded to back up deproliferation if diplomacy fails is also problematic. Etzioni recommends reliance on air power and special forces to serve as the tips of the deproliferation spear. These would be used to target, disable, and destroy facilities in noncompliant countries or, if effective intelligence is lacking, to rely on heavier strikes to engage in an effort to change the behavior of the regime. This approach has been criticized as an overreliance "on the twenty-first century equivalent of the silver bullet" that did not take into account the real costs and dangers of using military force as a tool of forcible deproliferation.[52] Etzioni has faith in the effectiveness of a sustained air campaign (perhaps backed up by some use of ground forces) that systematically targets a noncompliant regime's infrastructure and military capabilities until the costs of not negotiating are too high to pay. This idea is part of the larger debate over the very efficacy of airpower; it will find support in some circles while being disputed in others.[53] Nor is it always clear where deproliferation fits in the hierarchy of diplomatic interests. Should pressure on a country to give up WMDs trump the cooperation it may render in other key areas, like counterterrorism? And, if a state chooses to keep its program but demonstrates responsibility and that weapons are being kept under strict control, at what point should a diplomatic démarche give way to military force?[54]

Beyond these issues, there are other challenges that complicate the adoption of a deproliferation strategy. deproliferation does not lead to a guaranteed permanent state but is reversible. A country that has given up WMDs and their delivery systems may still retain the technical knowledge and industrial base to reconstitute programs.[55] Nor are international agreements an ironclad guarantee if a country later openly denounces them or secretly subverts them.

Take the 1987 INF Treaty, which is considered to be a major breakthrough in that it not simply reduced but eliminated an entire class of nuclear weapons delivery systems, and provided for intrusive inspections to verify destruction of the missiles.[56] This agreement is seen as proof that elimination, rather than simple control, of armaments was both possible and feasible. It is also viewed by many as having been an irreversible step. However, in 2007, Russian President Vladimir Putin bluntly raised the question that Russia might denounce the treaty and withdraw from its provisions if it perceived that its security might be at risk. This included the acquisition of middle-range missiles by emerging nuclear powers, or the deployment by the United States of a missile defense system in Europe.[57] Russia cited as a possible precedent the 2001 US withdrawal from the Anti-Ballistic Missile Treaty. In turn, the United States accused Russia in July 2014 of taking actions that amounted to violations of the INF Treaty.[58] Heather Williams, writing for Chatham House, argues that a collapse of the treaty would have negative ramifications in a number of areas. It

> would be a symbolic and practical blow to both nuclear arms control and European security and stability. Arms control efforts heralded the end of the Cold War, and the 1987 treaty - which committed the US and the Soviet Union to eliminate their short and intermediate-range nuclear forces (those with a range of 500–5000 kilometres) - remains of significant normative importance. What made the INF so exceptional were its on-site inspections, which were unprecedented at the time and laid the groundwork for intrusive verification in other agreements, such as the 1991 Strategic Arms Reduction Treaty (START). INF also established a Special Verification Commission to meet and address ambiguities in definitions and questions of compliance. These discussions have historically promoted transparency and allowed states to explain military activities that otherwise potentially could be construed as a violation of a treaty.[59]

Ironically, a second challenge to deproliferation is the current effort to push for nuclear abolition. Since coming into office, Barack Obama has been "determined to reduce the salience and centrality of nuclear weapons in US defense posture, at least in part to help facilitate the achievement of a nuclear weapon-free world."[60] This may seem counterintuitive given that deproliferation ultimately is working for the same aim, but it reflects Etzioni's understanding of the link between WMDs and security. In the absence of both credible, globally applicable security guarantees and clear indications that the United States would engage in a policy of restraint, other powers are much less interested in "accepting the risks of a nuclear weapon-free world in which the United States enjoys a massive conventional superiority."[61] Indeed, Russia and China both view US efforts to develop missile defense systems and to improve conventional global-strike capabilities as a way for Washington to be able to pressure Beijing, Moscow, or any other nuclear power without having to resort to the threat of using nuclear weapons. These efforts are even seen as having the possibility to cripple another country's land-based nuclear forces by conventional means without having to cross the nuclear threshold. None of this engenders much support for complete nuclear disarmament or even deep cuts.[62] Indeed, faced with decline, Russia has become much more reluctant to renounce its nuclear status, fearing that it would become more vulnerable to American pressure.[63]

In addition, a robust deproliferation agenda rests on active and sustained cooperation among the major nuclear powers. The major stakeholders must agree on "what is zero" and what constitutes "complete disarmament"[64]—disagreements that may become more pronounced as negotiations to settle the question of Iran's nuclear program continue. There must also be a shared perception of threat. That has diminished in recent years:

> Few capitals are losing sleep over the prospect, say, of an Iranian or North Korean nuclear weapon detonating on their territories. Most see whatever capabilities Pyongyang and Tehran are acquiring as meant to deter Washington-not to threaten the rest of the world. The feeling seems to be that either there is no threat to the global system, or the threat is containable. We are seeing other countries of the world preparing to live with the realities of a nuclear-armed North Korea and an Iran with a significant nuclear infrastructure at its disposal. And foreign governments are not inclined to take much more decisive measures to ensure the deproliferation of either regime.[65]

Finally, deproliferation will depend on relatively harmonious relations among the great powers. As US-Russia relations deteriorated, there was initial hope that, despite differences over Ukraine, cooperation on nonproliferation and nuclear security could be ring-fenced from turbulence in the bilateral relationship.[66] By early 2015, however, that optimism had vanished. Nearly all US-Russian cooperation in deproliferation efforts, starting with projects to ensure the safety of nuclear material in Russia itself, had come to an end. Moreover, Moscow announced that it would not participate in the last Obama-convened Nuclear Security Summit in 2016. Matthew Bunn sounded the dirge: "A two-decade era in which the United States and Russia worked together to dismantle and secure the deadly legacies of the Cold War appears to have drawn almost entirely to a close. The danger of nuclear bomb material falling into terrorist hands will be higher as a result of this downturn in cooperation—putting U.S., Russian, and global security at greater risk."[67]

This disruption in relations also opens up the possibility that the informal coalition formed by the major powers to deal with deproliferation aims, never a particularly strong alliance, will further erode. Given the worsening ties between Russia and the West, existing fractures over the shape of any likely agreement between the P5+1 (the five permanent members of the UN Security Council plus Germany, with the European Union as a coordinator) and Iran could prevent a final agreement from taking shape. The ideal agreement would guarantee a reversal of Iran's progress toward mastering the technologies needed to fabricate nuclear weapons and to construct their delivery systems, but also prevent consensus on what steps to take next to prevent a nuclear Iran.[68] From a deproliferation perspective, the worst outcome would be a deal that would leave substantial portions of Iran's nuclear infrastructure intact, allowing Tehran to retain a so-called "breakout capability" to quickly move to weaponization.

Etzioni had high hopes that the Libya precedent might serve to advance the cause of peaceful deproliferation in both Iran and North Korea, by demonstrating that it is possible for a country to trade away its weapons programs in return for assurances that its domestic form of governance will remain unmolested by other states in the international community.[69] He was joined in the assessment by others who argued that a series of incentives—including guarantees of regime security—had induced Gadhafi to accept the deal, and that this model could work elsewhere.[70] In the wake of the apparent success in Libya, others began to advocate for policies that resembled Etzioni's concept of deproliferation. President Nazarbayev called on Iran to emulate Kazakhstan's example, noting that

> we must understand that it is not easy for countries to give up their nuclear arsenal or to renounce the intention of developing their own weapons. The truth is that if just one nation has nuclear weapons, others may feel it necessary to do the same to protect themselves. This is why nuclear proliferation is such a threat to the security of us all and leads to greater risk of an illegal, dangerous trade in weapons and material.[71]

He pressed for nuclear-armed countries to give security assurances to those who had given them up, and to create positive incentives in which the decision to renounce nuclear weapons or other forms of

WMDs would bring immediate rewards. Nazarbayev concluded with this appeal: "We must all work hard to create the right conditions in which other countries, too, can make the right choice." Yet events in recent years have called into question whether those "right conditions" can be recreated.

Discrediting Deproliferation? The Fates of Libya and Ukraine, 2011–15

The central component behind Etzioni's deproliferation strategy has been the conscious trade of verifiable, complete, and absolute repudiation of all WMDs on the part of a country in return for the regime receiving binding and ironclad security assurances. Up to the end of 2010, Etzioni could argue that his vision was both realistic and realizable because the examples of Libya and Ukraine showed that it was possible to negotiate a framework by which a state voluntarily gave up its weapons in return for guarantees of its security from attack by external powers.

The start of the Arab Spring, however, challenged those assumptions. After a popular uprising successfully toppled the authoritarian government of Tunisia and significant protests had begun in Egypt, unrest boiled over in Libya against the regime of Muammar Gadhafi. By mid-February 2011, the regime's grip on power was being challenged, particularly in the eastern provinces. Faced with defections from his own military, and confronting not only protestors but armed militias contesting his authority, Gadhafi decided to utilize force to put down what he saw as an insurrection against his rule. By March, pro-Gadhafi forces were retaking ground that had been lost to the rebels, and it appeared that the regime was amassing forces for a major assault to retake the eastern regions, notably, the city of Benghazi. At this point, faced not only with the prospect that a putatively pro-democratic opposition would be eliminated but also that the civilian population of Benghazi would suffer mass, summary reprisals at the hands of Gadhafi loyalists,[72] the United States, and key European countries pushed for a United Nations Security Council resolution (1973) to establish a no-fly zone that would create a safe haven for Libyan civilians. However, the coalition led by the North Atlantic Treaty Organization (NATO) moved beyond creating safe areas to actively targeting the Gadhafi regime. Indeed, Western officials were to quietly acknowledge, as the air campaign progressed, that the no-fly zone was a diplomatic subterfuge and that NATO and the United States were being used to force the regime's surrender.[73]

225

The ultimate overthrow of the regime and Gadhafi's own death at the hands of rebel forces helped to undermine the foundations of the deproliferation strategy. The lesson that a number of governments learned from the Libya events is that "a state without nuclear deterrence capabilities is notably more vulnerable to foreign intervention and internal uprisings."[74] Because it gave up its WMD stockpiles, according to this line of thought, the Libyan regime had made itself an attractive target for American meddling. Indeed, Iran's Supreme Leader Ayatollah Ali Khamenei said of Gadhafi that "this gentleman wrapped up all his nuclear facilities, packed them on a ship and delivered them to the West and said, 'Take them!' . . . Look where we are, and in what position they are now."[75] Pascal-Emmanuel Gobry sums up the consensus view that, as a result of the Libya intervention, other states have learned that "if you have WMDs, you should never give them up, and that the pursuit of WMDs will be a profitable one, because pursuing or stockpiling WMDs gives you enormous deterring power in keeping the West from military intervention in your country."[76]

The loss of the Libya paradigm was joined three years later by the complete collapse of the Budapest Memorandum, which had guaranteed the removal of all nuclear materials from Ukraine. Ukraine's rocky relationship with Russia, particularly after the 2004 Orange Revolution brought a clearly pro-Western government to power, tested the validity of the deproliferation approach. In addition, the change of government led to several disputes with Moscow over the supply of natural gas to Ukraine. But by 2009, the coleader of the Orange movement, Prime Minister Yuliya Tymoshenko, had achieved a shaky *modus videndi* with Russia.[77]

When Viktor Yanukovych was elected president the following year, he made a deliberate decision to return Ukraine to a more neutral posture between Russia and the West. He accommodated several key Russian priorities, among them, the long-term lease of facilities in Crimea for the use of the Black Sea Fleet. With Ukraine removed from the geopolitical chessboard, facilitating the "reset" of relations between the United States and Russia, Moscow's incentive to meddle in its internal affairs diminished.[78] Yanukovych's strategy was to walk a precarious tightrope by promising Ukrainians closer economic ties with the European Union without triggering Russia's anxieties about "losing" its special relationship with Ukraine. Yanukovych miscalculated in concluding the terms of an association agreement with the European Union in 2013 that were perceived in Moscow as pulling

Ukraine into the European sphere, and cutting off its privileged trading relations with Russia. (He may have also been concerned about provisions in the association agreement that would force political and economic reforms in Ukraine that might undermine his own power base.) At the last minute, Yanukovych declined to sign the agreement, triggering the start of massive protests against his government.[79] In February 2014, an EU-troika (comprising France, Poland, and Germany) brokered an agreement between Yanukovych and opposition leaders. The agreement provided for a transition of power—an accord reluctantly accepted by Russia—but the mass of protestors rejected it and opted for pushing Yanukovych from power. The interim government that was formed sent signals that it would seek to align Ukraine with the West, leading Russia to support and foment separatist sentiments in the southern and eastern parts of the country. The Crimean peninsula, where the Russian Black Sea Fleet is based, was effectively separated from the control of the central government. The separation was reached with the assistance of forces that operated without national insignia (the so-called "little green men") and, ultimately, with the help of the Russian military stationed there. In March, the self-proclaimed Crimean Republic petitioned for admission to the Russian Federation. Separatist entities, also proclaimed in Donetsk and Lugansk, have maintained themselves with Russian support.

Whether termed an invasion or an incursion, the actions in Crimea and in southeastern Ukraine are understood to constitute, in the words of Anders Fogh Rasmussen, the NATO secretary general, "a blatant violation of Ukraine's sovereignty and territorial integrity."[80] The Bucharest Memorandum was technically not a binding security treaty mandating that the two supposed remaining guarantors (the United States and the United Kingdom) take action against the other guarantor, the Russian Federation, for its efforts to undermine the territorial integrity and political stability of Ukraine. One could argue, however, that there was a clear moral obligation to do so.[81] Yet the inability of the West to deter the Russians dealt a serious blow to the core proposition of the deproliferation strategy. Many observers now conclude that the "memorandum is nothing but a worthless political declaration."[82] Gobry again sums up the conventional wisdom, as follows: "The lesson of the Ukraine drama is that Ukraine should not have given up its nukes. It's difficult to imagine Putin's military meddling in Ukraine—or the West allowing it—if Ukraine had WMDs. By giving up this deterrent, Ukraine lost much of its ability to self-determine its own future."[83]

227

Former Polish President Alexander Kwasniewski concurs, noting that, in his conversations with Ukrainian officials, "there is a strong belief . . . that there would have been neither the annexation of Crimea nor war in the east of the country had Ukraine remained in possession of a nuclear arsenal."[84] Wolfgang Ischinger, the German diplomat and current chair of the Munich Security Conference, offers a heartfelt dirge for the experiment in deproliferation, noting: "If states end up being punished for relinquishing their weapons of mass destruction, hardly any state will want to follow the Ukrainian example."[85]

The Syrian Exception?

If the fates of Libya and Ukraine have dealt serious blows to the attractiveness of the deproliferation model, does the Syrian case of 2013–14 help to make the case that, under the right sets of conditions, deproliferation makes sense as a strategy for coping with WMDs?

In March 2011, as the revolutionary fervor of the Arab Spring swept across the Middle East, protests began against the authoritarian regime of Bashar al-Assad. The government responded with force to these putative challenges to its rule, leading to wider unrest. By the summer, the tenor had shifted from peaceful demonstration to armed self-defense and then to outright revolt. As the regime lost control of parts of Syria, it began to unleash the full force of its conventional weaponry in an effort to crush the rebellion.

Syria had developed chemical weapons as a poor man's deterrent against Israel's far superior conventional armies and its undeclared nuclear force.[86] Initially, the regime unleashed devastating conventional attacks against revolutionary forces. But as Assad began to lose ground during 2012, there were concerns he might authorize the use of chemical weapons. With intelligence suggesting that the Syrian military was beginning to mix and deploy its chemical arsenal, on August 20, 2012 President Barack Obama issued his fateful warning that "a red line for us is we start seeing a whole bunch of chemical weapons moving around or being utilized. That would change my calculus. That would change my equation."[87]

By the summer of 2013, there were indications, attributable to Syrian government forces, that chemical weapons had been used in the Syrian civil war. The use of poison gas on August 21, 2013 in a Damascus suburb removed all doubt that the line against the use of chemical munitions had been crossed. US military assets were deployed into the Eastern Mediterranean and made ready for strikes against the Syrian regime, and the president told his national security team on August 24th, "When I raised the issue of chemical weapons last summer, this is what I was talking about."[88]

As plans for military action stalled, however, due to a mix of domestic and international factors, the Russian government took advantage of Secretary of State John Kerry's ad lib at a press conference in London on September 9th—that Assad could avoid military action designed to bring about forcible deproliferation if he were to immediately turn over all of Syria's chemical stockpiles.[89] In Geneva between September 12 and September 14, 2013, Russian and American negotiators hammered out a framework agreement that would compel Syria to give up its chemical weapons, and to accede to the Chemical Weapons Convention in return for averting any sort of military strike designed to respond to the August 21st incident.[90] Syria accepted these terms, and the framework was enshrined in UN Security Council resolution 2118, passed on September 28, 2013. The resolution committed Syria to rapid disclosure of its stockpiles and production sites, and to cooperate with the officials of the Organisation for the Prohibition of Chemical Weapons (OPCW)—the institution set up by the signatories of the Chemical Weapons Convention—in the identification, transportation, and destruction of all of Syria's chemical weapons.

By the end of June 2013 the OPCW director-general, Ahmet Uzumcu, was reporting success: all 1,300 tons of the declared Syrian chemical arsenal had been removed from the country. He noted: "Never before has an entire arsenal of a category of weapons of mass destruction been removed from a country experiencing a state of internal armed conflict. And this has been accomplished within very demanding and tight time-frames."[91] The effort had come about because of the extraordinary level of international cooperation—with equipment, ships, personnel, intelligence and monitoring services, and funding being provided by many nations, including the United States, the United Kingdom, Denmark, Norway, Italy, Finland, Germany, Russia, and China.[92] United Nations Secretary-General Ban Ki Moon hailed the mission as "as a model for international cooperation to tackle security risks."[93]

Syria would thus appear to be a *prima facie* case, illustrating that the credible threat of military action can be a spur for a regime to voluntarily give up its WMD stockpiles as part of an overall negotiated settlement that trades full disclosure for immunity from direct strikes. However, there have always been disturbing signs that the Syria deproliferation has not been complete and total, and that the regime has held back on some weapons that were not declared and still may retain the capability to produce new ones.[94] Moreover, there are concerns that chemical agents continue to be utilized by the regime, even if they are in a cruder, nonweaponized form; in February 2015, OPCW "expressed its serious concern" that chlorine has been used against several villages and that such usage would place Syria in violation of its commitments under international law.[95] UN Security Council Resolution 2118, however, contains no automatic provision for enforcement in the event of any violations of its terms. On the reverse side, the agreement to divest Syria of its chemical weapons may have averted an immediate US-led military strike. But it contained no guarantees for the regime and no promise to work for any sort of compromise political settlement that would leave Assad in power. Indeed, US pressure on Assad lessened not because of the deal but because of the rise of the Islamic State. Assad has not bought any sort of immunity by agreeing to this arrangement.[96] Syria thus cannot be claimed as an unequivocal validation of the deproliferation approach, although it does shows that the trading of weapons for some degree of security assurances can produce results.

Concluding Thoughts

Eight years ago, Etzioni was confident that a credible negotiation process for deproliferation, backed by the examples of Ukraine and Libya, could lead to results with North Korea and Iran. Now, the outlook is far less positive. North Korea has essentially ruled out any talks with the United States on its nuclear program.[97] Optimism in 2013 that a combination of diplomacy and sanctions would lead Iran to accept a negotiated solution for deproliferation has now given way to concerns that "a process that began with the goal of eliminating Iran's potential to produce nuclear weapons has evolved into a plan to tolerate and to temporarily restrict that capability."[98] Such an agreement might not pass muster if it does not lead to a clear and verifiable deproliferation outcome.[99]

The real risk to the deproliferation agenda would be a loss of the post-9/11 attitude that the very spread of WMD capabilities to more states—no matter their internal composition or geopolitical alignment—is a threat to the global system. The reemergence of what Etzioni calls the "trusted governments" phenomenon—the willingness to let states that enjoy that status on the part of one of the major powers acquire and retain WMDs—is also problematic.[100] A return to the view that proliferation is acceptable when it benefits one's allies or causes problems for one's competitors increases the risks that such weapons might be used or that they might be stolen or misappropriated.

The first decade of the 2000s raised hopes that there was a feasible pathway to reducing the numbers of WMDs in the world. The deproliferation failures of the 2010s, however, have reinforced the very dangerous idea that possession of WMDs is a better guarantor of regime security than are agreements and treaties—and may "haunt for decades efforts to stem the spread of nuclear weapons."[101]

Notes

1. "How Likely is a Nuclear Terrorist Attack on the United States?" (debate sponsored by the Council on Foreign Relations, April 20, 2007), http://www.cfr.org/weapons-of-mass-destruction/likely-nuclear-terrorist-attack-united-states/p13097.

2. Mohamed ElBaradei, "Looking to the Future," remarks to the Fifty-Third Regular Session of the IAEA General Conference (2009), Vienna, Austria, September 14, 2009, https://www.iaea.org/newscenter/statements/looking-future.

3. Graham Allison, "How to Stop Nuclear Terror," *Foreign Affairs* 83:1 (January/February 2004), http://www.foreignaffairs.com/articles/59532/graham-allison/how-to-stop-nuclear-terror.

4. The so-called "classic" arguments in favor of this approach are to be found in, for example, Thomas C. Schelling, *Arms and Influence* (New Haven, CT: Yale University Press, 1966), and Kenneth Waltz, "The Spread of Nuclear Weapons: More May Better," *Adelphi Papers* 171 (London: International Institute for Strategic Studies, 1981).

5. James E. Doyle, "Why Eliminate Nuclear Weapons?" *Survival: Global Politics and Strategy* 55:1 (February–March 2013), 8.

6. David A Cooper, *Competing Western Strategies Against the Proliferation of Weapons of Mass Destruction: Comparing the United States to a Close Ally* (Westport, CT: Praeger, 2002), 12–13.

7. Amitai Etzioni, "Deproliferation," Bulletin of Atomic Scientists, July 23, 2008, http://thebulletin.org/deproliferation-approach-preventing-nuclear-terrorism-0.

8. Mark Fitzpatrick, "Non-Proliferation and Counter-Proliferation: What is the Difference?" *Defense and Security Analysis* 24:1 (2008), 74.

9. Cooper, 15–19.

10. Kurt M. Campbell, "Nuclear Proliferation Beyond Rogues," *The Washington Quarterly* 26:1 (Winter 2002/03), 9.

11. Amitai Etzioni, *Security First: For a Muscular, Moral Foreign Policy* (New Haven, CT: Yale University Press, 2007), 238.

12. Allison, op. cit.

13. See, for instance, Thomas Graham, "Strengthening Arms Control," *The Washington Quarterly* 23:2 (Spring 2000), 193–94.

14. Cooper, 19.

15. Alan P. Dobson and Steve Marsh, *US Foreign Policy Since 1945*, 2nd ed. (Abingdon, Oxon: Routledge, 2001, 2006), 159.

16. Vladimir V. Putin, "A Plea for Caution From Russia," *New York Times*, September 12, 2013, A31, http://www.nytimes.com/2013/09/12/opinion/putin-plea-for-caution-from-russia-on-syria.html?pagewanted=all&_r=0.

17. Ray Takeyh and Nikolas K. Gvosdev, "Democratic Impulses Versus Imperial Interests: America's New Mid-East Conundrum," *Orbis* 47:3 (Summer 2003), 426.

18. Campbell, 9–15.

19. For a summary, see *The Proliferaton Security Initiative: A Model for Future International Collaboration* (Fairfax, VA: National Institute Press, 2009), esp. 2–4.

20. Michael Lipson, "Transgovernmental Networks and Nonproliferation: International Security and the Future of Global Governance," *International Journal* 61:1 (Winter 2005/2006), 186–87.

21. *Proliferation Security Initiative*, 10, 19, 49.

22. Lipson, 189.

23. Cf. the public statement at the end of the 2003 plenary meeting of the Wassenaar Arrangement, December 12, 2003, http://www.wassenaar.org/publicdocuments/2003/public121203.html.

24. Lipson, 195–96. These steps, imposed by the Wassenaar Arrangement in 2003, included new controls for shoulder-launched missiles, which could be fired against aircraft, and new guidelines adopted by the Australia Group to ensure greater scrutiny of transfers to private entities.

25. Kenneth N. Luongo and Michelle Cann, *Nuclear Security: Seoul, the Netherlands and Beyond* (Washington, DC: SAIS U.S.-Korea Institute, 2013), esp. 17, 18, 28.

26. "Two Thirds NSS Countries: From Guidelines to Law," *National Security Strategy 2014*, March 25, 2014, https://www.nss2014.com/en/news/two-thirds-nss-countries-from-guidelines-to-law.

27. Luongo and Carr, 28.

28. Lipson, 179.

29. Mona Dreicer and Gotthard Stein, *Applicability of Nonproliferation Tools and Concepts to Future Arms Control*, Lawrence Livermore National Laboratory Conference Paper LLNL-CONF-636653 (May 15, 2013), 5.

30. Fitzpatrick, 79.

31. Amitai Etzioni, *Hot Spots: American Foreign Policy in a Post-Human-Rights World* (New Brunswick, NJ: Transaction Press, 2012), 105.

32. Etzioni, *Hot Spots*, 104–106.

33. Etzioni, "Deproliferation," op. cit.

34. Steven Pifer, "The Trilateral Process: The United States, Ukraine, Russia and Nuclear Weapons," Brookings Arms Control and Non-Proliferation Series 6/10 (May 2011), http://www.brookings.edu/research/papers/2011/05/trilateral-process-pifer.

35. See Sherman W. Garnett, "The Sources and Conduct of Ukrainian Nuclear Policy: November 1992 to January 1994," *The Nuclear Challenge in Russia and the New States of Eurasia*, Vol. 6, ed. George H. Quester (Armonk, NY: M.E. Sharpe, 1995), 125–52; and Mitchell Reiss, Bridled Ambition: Why Countries Constrain Their Nuclear Capabilities (Washington, DC: Woodrow Wilson Center Press, 1995), 90–129; also Pifer, op. cit.

36. Alexander Kwasniewski, "Ukrainian-Russian Relations: Lessons for Contemporary International Politics," *Horizons* 2 (Winter 2015), 25.
37. Reiss, 130, 135–36, 149–50.
38. Joshua Kucera, "Why Did Kazakhstan Give Up Its Nukes?" *The Bug Pit (Eurasianet)*, May 15, 2013, http://www.eurasianet.org/node/66967.
39. Matin Zuberi, "The Nuclear Non-Proliferation Regime," in *Weapons of Mass Destruction: Options for India*, ed. Raja Menon (New Delhi: Sage Publications, 2004), 95–96.
40. William Tobey, "A Message from Tripoli: How Libya Gave Up Its WMD," *Bulletin of the Atomic Scientists*, December 3, 2014, http://thebulletin.org/message-tripoli-how-libya-gave-its-wmd7834.
41. William Tobey, "A Message from Tripoli, Part IV," *Bulletin of the Atomic Scientists*, December 7, 2014, http://thebulletin.org/message-tripoli-part-4-how-libya-gave-its-wmd7846.
42. Etzioni, *Security First*, 9–11.
43. Dreicer and Stein, 3.
44. David A. Cooper, "Globalizing Reagan's INF Treaty: Easier Done Than Said?" *Nonproliferation Review* 20:1 (March 2013), 145, 147, 160.
45. "North Korea's Nuclear Ambitions," *Washington Post*, March 7, 2015, http://www.washingtonpost.com/opinions/north-koreas-nuclear-ambitions/2015/03/07/70059198-c1d1-11e4-ad5c-3b8ce89f1b89_story.html.
46. Germany's experience with weaning itself off nuclear power in the wake of the Fukushima accident in 2011 highlights some of the major challenges, including increased fossil fuel usage and higher prices, that may lead other countries not to adopt similar policies. See "The Ups and Downs of German Green Energy," *The American Interest*, July 27, 2014, http://www.the-american-interest.com/2014/07/27/the-ups-and-downs-of-german-green-energy/.
47. Etzioni, *Hot Spots*, 185–94.
48. See, for instance, the arguments raised in James Dobbins, "Coping with a Nuclearising Iran," *Survival* 53:6 (2011), 37–50.
49. Etzioni, *Security First*, 12.
50. Allison, op. cit.
51. See Amitai Etzioni, "Security First: Ours, Theirs and the Global Order's," *The National Interest* 88 (March/April 2007), 15.
52. James B. Steinberg, "A Sound Principle, but Not a Playbook," *American Behavioral Scientist* 51:8 (May 2008), 1358.
53. See, for instance, Robert A. Pape, "The True Worth of Air Power," *Foreign Affairs* 83:2 (March/April 2004), 116–30.
54. Steinberg, 1359.
55. Zuberi, 95–96.
56. See, for instance, Lynn Davis, "Lessons of the INF Treaty," *Foreign Affairs* 66:4 (Spring 1988), 729–29; also Graham, 185.
57. "Russian Threat to Quit Nuclear Treaty over US Shield Plans," *Financial Times*, February 16, 2007, 8.
58. Heather Williams, "Russian Withdrawal from INF Would Threaten Nuclear and European Security," *Chatham House*, July 31, 2014, http://www.chathamhouse.org/expert/comment/15372#sthash.0gbiSOo1.dpuf.

59. Williams, op. cit.
60. Andrew Futter and Benjamin Zala, "Advanced US Conventional Weapons and Nuclear Disarmament: Why the Obama Plan Won't Work," *Nonproliferation Review* 20:1 (March 2013), 107.
61. Futter and Zala, 117.
62. James M. Acton, "Bombs Away? Being Realistic about Deep Nuclear Reductions," *The Washington Quarterly* 35:2 (Spring 2012), 46–47; Futter and Zala, 113–15.
63. Joseph S. Nye, "The Future of Russian-American Relations," *Horizons* 2 (Winter 2015), 40.
64. Dreicer and Stein, 2.
65. Nikolas K. Gvosdev, "The End of Multilateralism," *National Interest*, June 12, 2009, http://nationalinterest.org/article/the-end-of-multilateralism-3142.
66. Rose Gottemoeller, Under Secretary of State for Arms Control and International Security, expressed such a hope during her lecture, "Nuclear Security in the 21st Century," delivered at the Watson Institute, Brown University, Providence, RI, November 5, 2014.
67. Matthew Bunn, "The Real Nuclear Nightmare When It Comes to U.S.-Russian Ties," *National Interest*, January 24, 2015, http://nationalinterest.org/feature/the-real-nuclear-nightmare-when-it-comes-us-russian-ties-12102.
68. James K. Sebenius, "Stepping Stone, Stopping Point, or Slippery Slope? Negotiating the Next Iran Deal," *Harvard Business School Working Paper* 14-061 (January 2014, revised March 2014), http://dash.harvard.edu/bitstream/handle/1/12111353/14-061%20(2).pdf?sequence=3
69. Etzioni, *Security First*, 12.
70. Michael McFaul, Abbas Milani, and Larry Diamond, "A Win-Win U.S. Strategy for Dealing with Iran," *Washington Quarterly* 30 (Winter 2006/2007), esp. 125.
71. Nursultan Nazarbayev, "What Iran Can Learn from Kazakhstan," *New York Times*, March 26, 2012, http://www.nytimes.com/2012/03/26/opinion/what-iran-can-learn-from-kazakhstan.html?_r=3&.
72. Gadhafi's own rhetoric, that the residents of Benghazi could expect "no mercy" if they did not turn against the rebels, contributed to the sense of imminent threat. See Ishaan Tharoor, "Gaddafi Warns Benghazi Rebels: We Are Coming, And There'll Be No Mercy," *Time*, March 17, 2011,t http://world.time.com/2011/03/17/gaddafi-warns-benghazi-rebel-city-we-are-coming-and-therell-be-no-mercy/
73. Greg Jaffe and Karen DeYoung, "In Libya Mission, War Blurs Humanitarian Focus," *Washington Post*, March 31, 2011, http://www.washingtonpost.com/world/lawmakers-batter-gates-on-libya/2011/03/31/AFLSRdAC_story.html.
74. Majid Rafizadeh, "Libyan and Korean Examples Guide Iran's Nuclear Plan," *The National*, April 19, 2013, http://www.thenational.ae/thenationalconversation/comment/libyan-and-korean-examples-guide-irans-nuclear-plan.
75. Quoted in Ramesh Thakur, "Missing Out On an Iran Deal," *The Japan Times*, November 28, 2014, http://www.japantimes.co.jp/opinion/2014/11/28/commentary/world-commentary/missing-out-on-an-iran-deal/#.VMHN1E03PIV.

76. Pascal-Emmanuel Gobry, "How Obama Inadvertently Made an Israeli War with Iran All But Inevitable," *The Week*, September 9, 2014, http://m.theweek. com/articles/443950/obama-inadvertently-made-israeli-war-iran-all-but-inevitable.

77. Andrzej Szeptycki, "The Putin–Tymoshenko Gas Agreement and Political Developments in Ukraine," *ISN*, January 23, 2009, at http://www.isn.ethz. ch/Digital-Library/Publications/Detail/?ots591=0c54e3b3-1e9c-be1e-2c24-a6a8c7060233&lng=en&id=103521http://www.isn.ethz.ch/Digital-Library/Publications/Detail/?ots591=0c54e3b3-1e9c-be1e-2c24-a6a8c7060233&lng=en&id=103521.

78. Nikolas K. Gvosdev, "The Reset Blooms," *National Interest*, October 28, 2010, http://nationalinterest.org/commentary/the-reset-blooms-4309.

79. See, for instance, Lamberto Zannier, "Ukraine and the Crisis of European Security," *Horizons* 2 (Winter 2015), 49–51.

80. "Rasmussen: Russia in 'Blatant Violation of Ukraine's Sovereignty and Territoril Integrity,'" *Kyiv Post*, August 29, 2014, http://www.kyivpost.com/content/ukraine-abroad/rasmussen-russia-in-blatant-violation-of-ukraines-sovereignty-and-territorial-integrity-362587.html.

81. Nikolas Gvosdev, "Ukraine, The Great Powers, Budapest, and Astheneia," *Ethics and International Affairs*, April 10, 2014, http://www.ethicsandinternationalaffairs.org/tag/ukraine-nuclear-weapons-security-guarantees/.

82. Kwasniewski, 25.

83. Gobry, op. cit.

84. Kwasniewski, 24.

85. Wolfgang Ischinger, "The Ukraine Crisis and European Security," *Horizons* 2 (Winter 2015), 96.

86. Flynt Leverett, *Inheriting Syria: Bashar's Trial by Fire* (Washington, DC: Brookings Institution Press, 2005), 119.

87. Mark Mazzetti, Robert F. Worth, and Michael R. Gordon, "Obama's Uncertain Path Amid Syria Bloodshed," *New York Times*, October 22, 2013, http://www.nytimes.com/2013/10/23/world/middleeast/obamas-uncertain-path-amid-syriabloodshed.html?_r=1&hp=&adxnnl=1&adxnnlx=1382536997WQVE9OXdIejP91S/N2ktsw&pagewanted=all&.

88. Adam Entous, Janet Hook, and Carol E. Lee, "Inside the White House, a Head-Spinning Reversal on Chemical Weapons: How the U.S. Stumbled Into an International Crisis and Then Stumbled Out of It," *Wall Street Journal*, September 15, 2013, http://online.wsj.com/news/articles/SB10001424127887323527004579077401049154032.

89. The Russians maintain that the idea of placing Syrian chemical weapons under international control had been raised at the G20 summit in St. Petersburg between Barack Obama and Vladimir Putin, and that the response to Kerry's comment built on those initial conversations. Alexei Anishchuk, "Putin, Obama Discussed Syria Arms Control Idea Last Week: Kremlin," *Reuters*, September 10, 2013, http://www.reuters.com/article/2013/09/10/us-syria-crisis-russia-usa-idUSBRE98901020130910.

90. Michael R. Gordon, "U.S. and Russia Reach Deal to Destroy Syria's Chemical Arms," *New York Times*, September 14, 2013, http://www.nytimes.com/2013/09/15/world/middleeast/syria-talks.html?pagewanted=all&_r=0.

91.   "All of Syria'sDeclared Chemical Weapons Removed, Official Says," *CBS News*, June 23, 2014, http://www.cbsnews.com/news/all-of-syrias-declared-chemical-weapons-removed-official-says/.

92.   Peter Westmacott (the UK ambassador to the United Nations), "Ridding the World of Assad's Chemical Weapons," *The Hill*, July 28, 2014, http://thehill.com/blogs/ballot-box/213379-ridding-the-world-of-assads-chemical-weapons.

93.   "China's Contribution to Destruction of Syrian Chemical Weapons Hailed," *Xinhua*, January 22, 2014, http://news.xinhuanet.com/english/china/2014-01/22/c_133066378.htm.

94.   William Branigin, "Last of Syria's Chemical Weapons Handed over for Destruction, International Body Says," *Washington Post*, June 23, 2014, http://www.washingtonpost.com/world/middle_east/agency-last-of-syrias-chemical-weapons-handed-over-for-destruction/2014/06/23/4eb9a138-fad9-11e3-8176-f2c941cf35f1_story.html.

95.   "OPCW Condemns Use of Chlorine Gas in Syria," *Kuwait News Agency*, February 4, 2014, http://www.kuna.net.kw/ArticleDetails.aspx?id=2423038&language=en.

96.   Paul Pillar discusses the pragmatic reasons why the United States may not push for Assad's removal at the present time, but notes that in the long run, US preferences are still for Assad to leave. "Assad Will Have to Stay for Awhile," *National Interest*, February 4, 2015, http://nationalinterest.org/blog/paul-pillar/assad-will-have-stay-awhile-12186.

97.   Jack Kim, "North Korea Says It Sees No Need to Negotiate with 'Gangster' U.S," *Reuters*, February 3, 2015, http://www.reuters.com/article/2015/02/04/us-northkorea-usa-idUSKBN0L804Y20150204.

98.   "The Emerging Iran Nuclear Deal Raises Major Concerns," *Washington Post*, February 5, 2015, http://www.washingtonpost.com/opinions/the-emerging-iran-nuclear-deal-raises-major-concerns-in-congress-and-beyond/2015/02/05/4b80fd92-abda-11e4-ad71-7b9eba0f87d6_story.html.

99.   See Thomas Nichols, "Enough Is Enough: Time to Ditch the Iran Nuclear Talks," *National Interest*, February 3, 2015, http://nationalinterest.org/feature/enough-enough-time-ditch-the-iran-nuclear-talks-12173?page=show.

100. Etzioni, *Hot Spots*, 188.

101. William Tobey, "A Message From Tripoli, Part V," *Bulletin of the Atomic Scientists*, December 8, 2014, http://thebulletin.org/message-tripoli-part-5-how-libya-gave-its-wmd7848.

7

The Challenges of Building Communities

The proposals contained within the communitarian-gradualist approach (the Security First paradigm) espoused by Etzioni have had some resonance with how the United States has conducted some of its "hard security" policies. However, they have had much less impact on denting the preternatural American optimism that it is possible to rapidly socially engineer societies to become modern, secular, Western-oriented democracies, and to then gather these countries into workable, binding, viable alliances and associations that will be able to take some of the burdens of maintaining the global order off the United States.

Nation-building is the process of constructing a political community that has the primary claim on the loyalty of its citizens and, through the related process of state-building, creating a viable nationwide system of public authority.[1] This process has emerged as a national security concern of the United States, and efforts to become involved in nation-building projects have accelerated since the end of the Cold War. Weak or unstable nations have been seen as security consumers rather than security providers who can spread disorder to their neighbors and negatively impact even the global system.[2] (The 2002 National Security Strategy summed up this line of thinking when it noted that "America is now threatened less by conquering states than we are by failing ones.") Thus, the goal has been not simply to contain any immediate threats that might arise but to utilize American power to bring about fundamental transformation of these societies.[3] This has been seen as the best way to ensure a functional international system—and to also assist in the spread of democracy and liberal values. It is a view that is rooted in confidence in both American capabilities and the attractive power of American values to attract and sustain support for new institutions and organizations. It assumes that "we are builders and have the needed raw material to build regimes following a blueprint we lay out."[4]

Etzioni was always suspicious of assessments that confidently pre-dicted the rapid success of American nation-building and alliance-constructing projects, especially when coupled with a linear view that made progress all but inevitable. Writing in 1963, he counseled: "If we continue to assume that history will follow our most optimistic esti-mates, our Grand Designs are going to be of little use. Only when our critical analysis uncovers the range of possible, and points to the more likely—although not necessarily the most desired—developments will our designs be realistic."[5] In 2004, he warned that

> nation-building . . . by foreign powers can rarely be accomplished and tends to be very costly, not merely in economic resources and those of political capital, but also in in human lives. Hence, for both empirical, social science considerations and on nonnative grounds, foreign powers would be best advised to scale back greatly their ambi-tions and promises. The more these powers focus whatever resources they are willing and able to commit on modest intervention, the more good they will do for the nation they seek to help and for themselves.[6]

Etzioni's concerns have been validated by those who were placed in charge of some of America's recent attempts at nation-building. Gen-eral John Allen, who served in both Iraq and Afghanistan and who was commanding general of the International Security Assistance Force and of all US forces in Afghanistan from 2011 to 2013, commented that "the strategies at use in both Iraq and Afghanistan failed in their tasks (to create modern, effective national governments that could provide security and create conditions for democracy), and that it "was either the wrong approach or just flawed from the beginning."[7]

Understanding How Political Communities Function

Etzioni's sociological investigations into how political communities are formed and gain salience has served to provide an empirical foundation for his policy recommendations. In his 1965 work *Political Unification*, he called attention to the absolute necessity for what he described as "integrating power" for the successful creation of a political entity. Etzioni identified three types of integrating power: coercive, utilitarian, and identitive.[8] Coercive power requires the existence of institutions (e.g., a military or a police force) that are capable of enforcing norms and standards upon those within its jurisdiction. Utilitarian power is generated when the political association generates tangible positive benefits to its members and creates incentives for maintaining the community. Identitive power—often generated by educational and religious institutions, among others—focuses on the creation of a commonly shared identity, which serves as a basis for legitimating policy and for convincing people to accept sacrifice for the good of the whole.[9] Moreover, in the absence of sufficient utilitarian power (and if there is insufficient identitive power), coercive power—and the willingness to use it—can make the difference between the survival and the disintegration of the political entity, particularly at its inception. In short, integrating power is what generates and sustains the buy-in of both key stakeholders and the mass of the population into the legitimacy of any new political construct—be it a national government, a federation, or a transnational association. Over time, force would lose its effectiveness—so the stakeholders would need to develop a common identity and believe that the association was more profitable than separation.

Etzioni also called attention to the importance of what he labeled the "take-off"—the point at which a political "process has accumulated enough momentum to continue on its own." This was not, he stressed, identical with the "initiation" point—the "granting of a charter, the signing or ratification of a treaty, the founding convention . . ."[10] Therefore, even though, to the general public, the public ceremonies announcing the promulgation of a constitution or organization might lead to the impression that the new order had taken shape, there could be a considerable lag until the political structure achieved the necessary buy-in. On the other hand, if the determinants of a successful take-off were missing, then no matter the fanfare at its birth, the resulting political entity would be stillborn. His concerns that people too easily confuse an initiation point with proof that take-off has occurred have been unfortunately been validated in recent years.

In his 1965 work, Etzioni conducted a detailed study of four efforts to undertake what we might today describe as "nation-building" and "association-building": (1) the failed attempts to create the United Arab Republic (UAR) between Egypt and Syria (1958–61); (2) the failed effort to create the Federation of the West Indies (1958–62); (3) the then-ongoing progress of the Nordic Council (the first meeting of which was held in 1953) and (4) the emergence of European Economic Community (created by the Treaty of Rome in 1957)—the latter two seen by Etzioni as possible templates for developing workable transnational communities. Success or failure was directly tied to the presence or lack of integrative power, and to the careful or inattentive matching of political goals and institutions with the realities of what could be supported and sustained. Etzioni's "lessons learned" from these examples can help to create useful typologies that could be applied to recent and current attempts at nation-building and creating new associations.[11]

One of the most critical takeaways from his study is the enduring importance of regional and local identities for the political legitimacy of leaders. The proposed United Arab Republic and the Federation of the West Indies both rest on very solid "identitive" factors. They shared a common language (Arabic or English), as well as political institutions and ideology (pan-Arabism or the legacy of British rule) that, on paper, suggest that the new structures could take root. Yet, there were powerful centrifugal forces at work. Syria and Egypt might claim to be part of "one" Arab nation, but both possess very distinctive identities (as well as different forms of spoken Arabic). This strong sense of distinctiveness and of identification with a defined territory is also true of the various British Caribbean islands, where being Jamaican or Barbadian trumps any sense of collective regional identity. Both of these efforts at nation-building failed, in part, because the assumption that an "Arab" or "West Indian" identity would come to hold greater salience over preexisting ones—and thus support a more centralized state that would privilege the union's interests over those of the constituent parts—was not realized. In addition, proposed political rules in the West Indian case meant that powerful local leaders would have to give up their island power bases if they wished to hold federal posts; this had the impact of dis-incentivizing the most influential figures in the Caribbean, who might have been able to make the Federation of the West Indies work, from running for those offices.

In contrast, the recognition that there was a very weak sense of "Scandinavian" identity—and almost no conception of a "European" identity that trumped existing national ones—meant that the emerging Nordic Council and European Community structures could only succeed by working through, rather than trying to override, the governments and leaderships of the constituent parts. As they proved their worth, a common identity was thus given room to grow, to take root, and to help develop a sense of loyalty to these associations.

This experience highlighted a second observation: the need for the new political construction to be able to demonstrate its benefits to the constituent parts, and to generate support for the sacrifices and compromises that would be needed to sustain the association past its "takeoff" point. In both the UAR and the West Indies examples, it proved impossible to set up a centralized state structure that enjoyed sufficient legitimacy to transfer resources from rich areas to poor ones, to allow for peripheral regions to enjoy more representation and influence at the expense of the core, or to find ways to generate "national" perspectives. In the UAR case, Gamal Nasser eventually resorted to installing Egyptians into key positions in Syria in an effort to ensure loyalty. The largest components of any West Indian Federation, for their case, sought complete independence from Britain as free-standing entities, based on their assessment that the proposed federal structure was too inimical to their political and economic interests.

If such support is lacking, then, in some cases, a certain level of coercion might supply the necessary glue (although too much coercion would backfire). The British, however, were unable and unwilling to force acceptance of the federation on recalcitrant island governments, and threatened neither military force nor economic sanctions. Similarly, Nasser did not want to use a heavy-handed approach in Syria for fear it might forever turn the local population against the idea of joining a larger Arab entity; he was thus willing to let the UAR collapse in order to preserve the chance to try again in the future.

External threats can help to provide incentives for building up new associations. The experience of the Nordic states during World War II, and the reality of being caught between the superpowers, helped to create a rationale for Scandinavian cooperation and mutual assistance even when there would be individual winners and losers. Similarly, the crucible of the Cold War also helped to focus European political leaders on the need for finding effective compromises to make the proposed common market and community structures function. The members of the European Community also saw the long-term benefits from creating a unified market, and the benefits that all would receive even if there would be short-term dislocations that each would suffer (whether in specific industries, in contributing more to the association than would be received back in benefits, and so on).[12] In the absence of the environment created by the Cold War, it is far less likely that the Nordic Council and European Community projects would have been as successful.

Etzioni's four principal case studies, along with a more general survey of successful and unsuccessful unions, led him to make a series of empirical observations. Certainly the most critical was that the greater the amounts of identitive and utilitarian power could be mobilized in favor of the unions and associations, the greater the chance of success, particularly if there was elite buy-in.[13] Beyond that, two other points would prove to be significant in future nation-building attempts. These were the propositions that "the stability of a union is undermined and its growth curtailed when the avenues of political representation are clogged or closed," and that "the amount of power needed to increase the level of integration and to extend the scope of a union tends to be higher than that needed to maintain a given level of integration and scope."[14] These two points were to provide the intellectual foundation for Etzioni's proposal of the "high devolution state," which involved efforts to rebuild countries shattered by conflict or to create new states. To achieve these goals, political power would focus as much as possible on local communities and geographic entities that were accessible and responsive to the population, rather than vested in central political authorities who were more distant and who lacked the ability to mobilize and wield power in a fashion that would be perceived as legitimate.[15]

This would prove to be a critical warning because if the political elite of a community was misidentified, then any program of unification or state-building would be imperiled. Etzioni also called attention to the reality that in any society there would be forces "congenial" to the proposed project and elites and interests that would be opposed. The timing of ensuring that "congenial" factions would be in power (and be able to hold power) long enough for the political community to get off the ground and to solidify would be critical. If and when uncongenial forces took power, their ability to modify or destroy the new political construction would be limited.[16]

In addition, these more accessible leaders might not be politicians but would be important if they wielded "identitive" power that mattered to local peoples. Thus, based on his research, Etzioni stresses that many communities possess

> their own institutions and their own ways of selecting leaders and resolving conflicts. These include tribal councils, community elders, and religious authorities. That is, the people often rely on natural leaders—those who rose to power due to their charisma, persuasive powers, lineage or religious status, but who were not elected in the Western way.[17]

From his domestic policy work on local communities, Etzioni was also very aware that nonpolitical leaders, particularly religious figures, might wield extensive influence. Religion might be a critical source of authority in a community, especially if there had been state collapse or the political system had become dysfunctional.[18]

Etzioni also had a critical piece of advice for external forces that attempted to aid the transition. An outside actor would enhance the success of its efforts only to the extent that the "direction of its application of power coincides with the power structure of the emerging union, and to hinder it the more the application of this power is countered to the emerging structure."[19] Thus, moving beyond reconstruction of the status quo toward the fostering of fundamental social and political change would be a much more complicated and risky operation, particularly if that effort challenged deeply held norms or beliefs. Outside actors could also not rely on being able to convince people directly or to hope that a direct campaign would be sufficient to bypass recalcitrant elites. As he concluded:

> One of the most important findings of sociology is that it is very difficult to reach the masses directly—persuasion flows in two steps: first to leaders and then to their followers. These leaders may include elected officials, heads of civil society bodies from universities or foundations, community leaders, religious functionaries, and (arguably) celebrities.[20]

But because the preference in the United States is to deal primarily with political leaders, especially if the elections process that empowered them was not viewed as completely legitimate, difficulties would ensue if other sources of leadership were to be ignored or excluded.

Hubris Triumphant: The Lure of Transformation

Etzioni's academic research on building political communities, while enhancing his status as a leading scholar in sociology, did not have much impact on American policymakers. For instance, during the Clinton administration, he was consulted on a whole host of domestic-policy initiatives by senior officials, including Cabinet officers. Yet, there is no evidence that he was asked to provide any sort of assessment of various nation- and community-building efforts undertaken by the US government.[21]

During the Cold War, US efforts at nation-, state-, and community-building focused on restoring and reconstructing societies in the aftermath of conflict and on forging ties, primarily for the purpose of mutual security. These efforts were intended to "preserve the status quo" in the wake of the threat posed by the Soviets, rather than to promote "large-scale societal change."[22] Even when—most notably, in the case of occupied Japan after World War II—the United States insisted on promoting reforms or altering political institutions to prevent the return of fascist or militarist powers, this was not done through whole-scale root-and-branch transformation. Instead, the government worked through existing institutions, as far as possible, and by promoting evolutionary change.[23] The reconstruction of West Germany and Japan after World War II is rightfully held out as the "gold standard" of US nation-building efforts.[24] The looming threat of the Soviet Union also provided incentives in both countries to work with the United States to get institutions up and running. Some of the later examples that are usually cited as proof of America's ability to rebuild and reconstruct societies—the Grenada intervention of 1983 and the intervention in Panama in 1989—focused on restoring a preexisting constitutional order and a political system that had been diverted by dictatorial elements.

But the overall record is more mixed, especially when the effort shifted to building up institutions in states far less developed and cohesive than Japan or Germany. The most notable failure was the attempt to create a viable non-Communist, pro-Western regime in southern Vietnam, an effort that was unsuccessful despite a massive influx of resources.[25] US community-building efforts that focused on security were successful in tying together the Euro-Atlantic world in the collective defense of NATO. These efforts built on a high level of preexisting ties and commonalities. However, endeavors in other parts of the world to create a Central Treaty Organization and a South East Asia Treaty Organization ultimately failed.[26]

After the collapse of the Soviet Union, the United States and its European allies were more inclined to intervene "not just to police ceasefires or restore the status quo but to try to transform war-torn societies fundamentally."[27] This often led to a shift in the mission from one of reconstruction to one of development, especially with a focus on creating new institutions—with a corresponding increase in the difficulty and complexity of the effort undertaken.[28] Paradoxically, the end of the Cold War was seen as a boon for these efforts; the idea was that without the distraction of superpower conflict, more focus could be placed on state-building efforts. At the same time, the lack of superpower conflict meant that more attention could be paid to promoting change in favor of liberal democracy and market economies, rather than just setting up a functional administration. There was a great deal of optimism that such efforts could succeed without much risk or major investment, and that Western liberal institutions could be transplanted in a short time.[29] Etzioni set aside his research on the necessary conditions for successful nation- and state-building. Also put off was similar work on conditionality and legitimacy that was being conducted by W.W. Rostow, Karl Deutsch, and Etzioni's own mentor, Seymour Lipset.

Ironically, the lack of an existential conflict meant that it was harder to generate public support for sustained state-building efforts or to accept sacrifices for the sake of creating new transnational communities. Because many of these efforts in the Balkans, Africa, Eurasia, Southern Asia, and the Caribbean during the 1990s were seen as non-vital to the safety and security of the United States, the "reservoir" of public willingness to expend blood and treasure was quite shallow. At the first sign of trouble—as in Somalia—or when costs become prohibitive—as in Haiti—support for continuing such missions collapsed.[30]

The experience of ending the civil war in Bosnia and attempting to reconstruct a Bosnian state that could encompass its Muslim, Croat, and Serb communities highlighted many of the challenges that faced Western nation-builders while validating a number of Etzioni's concerns. After years of fighting, the United States helped to broker a settlement at Dayton in December 1995. The agreement, by devolving power to ethnically based entities, might provide for stability but its provisions worked against the desire to "create a single, democratic, tolerant, and multiethnic state." As Derek Chollet observes, "Like any complex negotiation, the Dayton agreement contained many compromises that were necessary to end the war but made implementing a settlement difficult. Some of these challenges were inherent in the governing structures that the agreement created; others stemmed from the specifics of its implementation."[31]

To end the fighting and stop the humanitarian crisis that the war and massive flows of internally displaced people had caused, the United States and its partners crafted a settlement that created a very weak federal center, yoking together two ethnically defined territorial entities (one itself a further federation of two communities).[32] This was the strongest central "Bosnian" government that key Serb and Croat elites were willing to accept,. While the Muslims wanted a much stronger central government, they were unwilling to risk a purely majoritarian system where, in theory, Bosnian Serbs and Croats could out-vote and veto the preferences of the Muslims. A loose confederation of ethnic cantons existing within the framework of a state called Bosnia—in part because outright annexation of the Serb and Croat portions by Serbia and Croatia would not be permitted by the United States and its allies—was the compromise that ended the war.

This state of affairs posed a real dilemma, however, for Western governments that were committed to not simply ending the fighting but to reforming Bosnian institutions and society along Western liberal lines. This was particularly true, as Sumantra Bose observes, of the continued elevation of ethnic-collective identities in Bosnian politics, trumping the idea of an individually defined pan-Bosnian definition of citizenship.[33] Thus, the West committed itself to undertaking a massive, quite intrusive effort to mold postwar Bosnia more to its liking. This process accelerated after the 1997 meetings in Bonn, Germany, of the "Peace Implementation Council," which was created to oversee the functioning of the Dayton Accords. The creation of the council gave a wide range of new powers to the Office of the High Representative (who acted on behalf of the guarantor countries of the Dayton Accords) to supervise the government; to propose, alter, or even decree legislation; and to remove elected officials from office. The hope was that, based on the reforms the West would implement, a central Bosnian state would both become a more efficient provider of services (Etzioni's utilitarian power) and inculcate a sense of Bosnian identity (identitive power) that would transcend existing loyalties to Bosnia's ethnic communities and to local government administrations.[34]

Chollet described the blueprint for a unified Bosnia as a "maximalist" approach, but lamented that the local governing elites preferred to opt for "minimalist" implementation.[35] Thus, the external actors (the United States and the European Union states) decided to utilize their coercive power to cajole, to prod, and to drag the Bosnian elites to adopt their preferences for how they wanted Bosnia to function—and to back that up with utilitarian power. There were US, NATO, and EU forces deployed to patrol cease-fire lines, to capture war criminals, and to enforce a limited set of mandates. The European Union and the United States had significant levers of influence, notably, the disbursement of aid and the provision of security assistance, as well as the most important incentive of all: the possibility of eventual association with and membership in the European Union.[36] A willingness to use those tools of pressure was critical in getting the postwar Bosnian government to move to enact some of the basic provisions of a unified state: setting up a common currency, issuing common passports and license plates, or having a unified border and customs service. However, it took a decade to centralize one of the most basic state functions (the management of violence) when a united defense ministry and armed forces command were set up to supersede the armed forces maintained by the subunits of the Bosnian state.[37] Yet, there have also been limits. The European Union spent, by one estimate, over 25 billion euros between 1995 and 2010 to maintain and sustain the Bosnian state, but its resources and a willingness to keep spending is not unlimited.[38] Moreover, the United States made it clear that it would impose strict limits on its willingness to use its military forces to implement the agreement. These arbitrary deadlines, which the Clinton administration believed were necessary to sustain support for the deployment of US forces among the general American public, were, in Chollet's categorization

> inherently minimalist and wholly unrealistic. They made sense only if the goal was to create a stable military balance on the ground (which could arguably be done in a year), but not a lasting peace, which would take much longer. The deadline undermined the ability to implement the maximalist parts of the agreement. It gave Dayton's opponents hope that they could simply outwait the international community.[39]

The Dayton Accords did succeed in preventing the war from restarting, but the ambitious plans for creating a new Bosnia have had only minimal success. Key economic and political reforms that would be necessary for Bosnia to move ahead on plans to join the European Union have been stalled for years. Despite the billions spent on aid, Bosnia has one of the highest unemployment rates in Europe, and is considered one of the continent's poorest countries. Twenty years after the Dayton agreement was signed, progress might finally occur in setting up a "coordination mechanism" that would "allow the ethnically-divided country to speak in a single voice in its talks with Brussels and to attract EU funds"[40]—testifying to the ongoing inability to create and to sustain a sense of common statehood and national identity.

When Kosovo detached from Yugoslav (Serbian) control after the NATO campaign in 1999, some of the tensions that were present in how the West undertook nation-building in Bosnia repeated themselves. In particular, it proved difficult to reconcile the "traditional" approach to nation-state building (focusing on using the dominant ethnic group as the basis for the state's national identity, and legitimizing the new construction on majoritarian grounds) with the preference for developing a "post-national multiethnic state" (where a new civic sense of identity would trump existing ethnic, cultural, and religious definitions of identity—and focal points of loyalty).[41] An ambitious Western agenda to create such a state with an identity that would transcend Serbian and Albanian identities ran up against entrenched resistance on the part of local elites and the limits of US and European willingness to use coercive force to defend their vision of what a future Kosovo should look like. Fifteen years after the initial intervention, when a separate Kosovo state was finally proclaimed in 2008, much of the initial agenda—again, despite the expenditure of large amounts of Western resources—has been left unrealized. The frozen conflict between the majority-Albanian south and a Serb-dominated region north of the Ibar River remains unresolved. There is now growing recognition that the Western approach might need to be modified in order to move Kosovo along the lines of what Etzioni would recognize as a "high-devolution state," one where special arrangements that would preserve some juridical links between the Kosovo-Serbian communities and the Serbian state can be negotiated.[42]

Problems in the first wave of post-Cold War nation-building missions led then-candidate Governor George W. Bush to express skepticism of such efforts during the 2000 campaign. While supporting humanitarian assistance, he appeared to rule out more ambitious plans to reconstruct or transform societies using US power.[43] Etzioni's own theoretical framework would have predicted a low probability of success for many of the missions undertaken in the 1990s; empirical evidence was also being collected to suggest that these types of missions are difficult, offering little guarantee of a favorable outcome. In assessing the research, Minxin Pei and Sarah Casper noted: "Few national undertakings are as complex, costly, and time consuming as reconstructing the governing institutions of foreign societies. Even a combination of unsurpassed military power and abundant wealth does not guarantee success, let alone quick results."[44] Moreover, in summing up the historical record, they bluntly concluded:

> The record of past U.S. experience in democratic nation building is daunting. The low rate of success is a sobering reminder that these are among the most difficult foreign policy ventures for the United States. Of the sixteen such efforts during the past century, democracy was sustained in only four cases ten years after the departure of U.S. forces. Two of these followed the total defeat and surrender of Japan and Germany after World War II, and two were tiny Grenada and Panama. Unilateral nation building by the United States has had an

even rougher time—perhaps because unilateralism has led to surrogate regimes and direct U.S. administration during the postconflict period. Not one American-supported surrogate regime has made the transition to democracy, and only one case of direct American administration has done so.[45]

Experiences in places like Somalia, Bosnia, Kosovo, and Haiti have also led to a renewed appreciation for conditions that might assist or impede a nation-building mission, especially if there is a mandate to also construct and maintain a democratic form of governance. Thomas Carothers identifies five conditions that are of "particular importance." These include:

- levels of economic development (a poorer society is more likely to fail than a rich one in the transition process)
- source of national wealth (countries that are impacted by the so-called "resource curse" of deriving revenue from the export of natural resources will have a harder time because authoritarian governments can distribute income to buy allegiance)
- the degree of heterogeneity, since "countries where the population is divided along ethnic, religious, tribal, or clan lines often have a harder time with democratization than more homogeneous societies"
- the extent to which the society has experience with political pluralism, a toleration for dissent, and disagreement over decisions taken by the ruling authority
- the neighborhood ("countries in regions or subregions where most or all of the countries are nondemocratic usually struggle more with democratization than do countries in more democratic neighborhoods")

When several or all of these factors lean decisively in a negative direction, then there is a much lower chance of a successful outcome.[46]

Military action was launched against Afghanistan in 2001 and against Iraq in 2003 to deal with putative security threats against the United States. After those threats were decapitated, the question as to what extent these societies needed to be patched together at a minimal level of functionality versus their transformation into modern liberal democracies was raised in policy circles. Etzioni, for instance, had made it clear that he rejected the so-called "Pottery Barn" rule, reportedly enunciated by then Secretary of State Colin Powell, that if the United States "broke" a country, it would "own" it in terms of being obligated to promote its development and modernization.[47] The only moral duty Etzioni recognized on the part of the occupiers was to return the country to the level of security and development it had enjoyed prior to the

249

conflict. But even those who might have supported a more expansive reconstruction program, to not simply restore conditions but to improve them, might have been taken aback by the daunting nature of the task. Using Carothers's criteria, Iraq—an impoverished country with large oil reserves, significant ethno-sectarian divides, little tradition of political pluralism, and a location in an undemocratic neighborhood—would not have been seen as a promising candidate for rapid transformation. From a conditionality standpoint, Afghanistan, too, would have significant hurdles to overcome. Even armed with nothing else but Etzioni's analysis of the failure of the UAR and the Federation of the West Indies, a policymaker might have reached similar conclusions about the likely fate of ambitious US plans for creating centralized, modernized democratic nation-states in post-Taliban Afghanistan and post-Saddam Iraq.

What is interesting, however, is that the mass of research and analysis, which suggested that nation-building efforts would be difficult with a high probability of failure, was set aside in favor of an optimistic spirit that saw the post-World War II American experience with Japan and West Germany as the norm. These two cases are now upheld as the "paradigmatic" norm of how a determined and focused US postconflict nation-building effort could produce pro-American liberal democracies in a matter of years.[48] President Bush explicitly linked the Japanese and German cases to his proposed efforts to reconstruct Iraq along Western liberal-democratic lines, promising a full and complete commitment of American resources to complete the task:

> Rebuilding Iraq will require a sustained commitment from many nations, including our own: we will remain in Iraq as long as necessary, and not a day more. America has made and kept this kind of commitment before—in the peace that followed a world war. After defeating enemies, we did not leave behind occupying armies, we left constitutions and parliaments. We established an atmosphere of safety, in which responsible, reform-minded local leaders could build lasting institutions of freedom. In societies that once bred fascism and militarism, liberty found a permanent home.

> There was a time when many said that the cultures of Japan and Germany were incapable of sustaining democratic values. Well, they were wrong. Some say the same of Iraq today. They are mistaken. (Applause.) The nation of Iraq—with its proud heritage, abundant resources and skilled and educated people—is fully capable of moving toward democracy and living in freedom.[49]

The Bush administration, therefore, decided to move beyond a minimal Security First-style approach—simply decapitating Saddam Hussein and the Taliban and replacing them with less tyrannical but nondemocratic leaders who could guarantee security—in favor of a more comprehensive transformation.[50]

Pei and Casper, however, writing at the time of the Iraq invasion, tried to dissuade those who argued that Iraq would be just like Germany and Japan, noted instead that it might fall more into the category of a Haiti, where US nation-building efforts had not fared so well:

> Nation building is political engineering on a grand scale. Some nations, such as Haiti, may have social and political attributes (such as deep ethnic fissures, religious animosities, and high levels of inequality) that make them inherently resistant to political engineering by outsiders. Societies that have a relatively strong national identity (such as Japan and Germany), a high degree of ethnic homogeneity, and relative socioeconomic equality are more suitable targets for nation building.[51]

Even though there were expectations that local populations in both Afghanistan and Iraq might indeed welcome US military forces as liberators from existing tyrannies, there were also warnings that if the focus shifted from elimination of tyranny to Western-style nation-building, there might be problems. For instance, a number of specialists had counseled that in such countries, "local identities remain quite powerful and foreign occupations almost always trigger resistance, especially in cultures with a history of heavy-handed foreign interference."[52] Moreover, in societies that lack a high degree of internal cohesion, the risks increased that outside forces would be "dragged into domestic power struggles or manipulated by dueling groups to settle long-standing grievances."[53]

However, the United States committed itself to promoting reforms, especially in postwar Iraq and Afghanistan, that would displace traditional leaders and forms of authority. The hope was that democratic elections would empower a new generation of leaders who would create a modern state capable of dispensing public goods to all citizens regardless of ethnic, territorial, religious, or tribal identity—and that the people would give their allegiance and trust to these new institutions.

A Missed Opportunity in Iraq?

In his initial study, Etzioni points out that an external actor could apply various types of integrative power (including economic assistance and use of military force) to compel different subunits of a proposed entity to come together and to accept new rules of the political game—and to hold that compulsion long enough for the new construction to take root and be internalized.[54]

However, despite making a substantial investment in terms of lives and resources, the United States was never going to devote the degree of coercive power necessary to force through the societal changes necessary to create liberal democracies in both Iraq and Afghanistan. In addition, America underestimated the utilitarian appeal of its proposed reforms as well as the enduring power of culture and religious identity.[55] Indeed, Etzioni's concern was that US efforts to push accelerated transformation would produce governments that would lack legitimacy in the eyes of the populace yet would be too weak to ensure security. Moreover, as Etzioni predicted, the initial flush of enthusiasm for nation-building withered as the costs mounted,[56] while the new regimes constructed were "unable to prevent a high level of interethnic tension and strife."[57]

Etzioni's colleagues Aaron Wildavsky, Michael Thomas, and Richard Ellis developed a series of intellectual tools—most notably, the "cultural audit"—to ascertain what features of a country's existing culture could support and sustain the proposed new institutions, and where resistance to change might be generated. Of particular importance were their observations that "people-changing" might need to precede the creation of new institutions.[58] The cultural audit supported "encapsulation," a concept developed by Etzioni to describe the process by which social interactions (including how transactions are carried out and conflicts are resolved) are limited and defined by a commonly accepted set of rules.[59] Such an approach might look at existing institutions, customs, and laws to determine how they might support evolutionary change.[60] These methods, however, were set aside in favor of what Harold Hongju Koh has characterized as "imposed" democracy promotion (whether by military or nonmilitary means), where a top-down approach is taken.[61] This approach, in turn, depended on either converting existing elites or replacing them, if it was to be successful.

Of course, adopting the top-down approach meant that some of Etzioni's advice would be ignored. This was particularly true of his emphasis on the need to include religious and community leaders in the process of nation- and state-building, and the need to accommodate illiberal but moderate forces in the process. The peril of so doing has been seen most clearly in the experience of the ultimately failed efforts on the part of the US Coalition Provisional Authority (CPA) to determine the shape of post-Saddam Iraq in 2003 and 2004.[62]

When the United States swept aside Saddam Hussein and his regime in spring 2003, Americans had some very clear ideas about the type of Iraq they wanted to reconstruct. L. Paul "Jerry" Bremer, placed in charge of the CPA, has stressed that he had a clear mandate from President George W. Bush to build an entirely new Iraqi political structure—one that would be a model of Western-style liberal democracy for the entire Middle East.[63] Observers noted that what Bremer and the CPA were attempting to do was a "root and branch transformation of the country in our own image."[64] It was going to be a top-down imposition, and CPA officials feared losing control of the transition process. Larry Diamond, who served as an advisor to the CPA on governance issues, notes, the "CPA didn't want anything to happen that they didn't control-and this has been impossible to hide from the Iraqis."[65]

The CPA also tried to encourage American-style separation of religion and politics in Iraq, and was generally uncomfortable with the influence religion exercised in Iraqi life. Bremer made it clear that during his tenure as administrator, he would work to minimize the role of Islam in Iraqi politics, especially in legislation. In this, he was encouraged by both the White House and many members of the US Congress.[66]

In particular, US authorities did not want to involve in the political process the *hawza* (the seminaries of Najaf where the most senior Shi'a Islamic scholars and their students gather and offer guidance to their followers on how to interpret the teachings and principles of Islam). Nor did US authorities want to involve in the process Sayyid Ali al-Husayni al-Sistani, the Grand Ayatollah or the first of the *marja taqlid*, the literal interpretation of which is the "source of imitation." The Grand Ayatollah is understood to be the highest authority when it comes to understanding and interpreting Islamic precepts, at least among the Shi'a, who comprise about 60 percent of Iraq's population. Some compare the structure of authority among the Shi'a in Iraq to the Roman Catholic Church, with Sistani occupying the position of a pope—who is considered to be infallible when issuing decrees touching on faith and morals—and other ayatollahs equivalent to the cardinals.

Sistani was not an advocate of the theses advanced by exiled Iranian Ayatollah Ruhollah Khomeini when he had resided in Najaf. Among Khomeini's beliefs was the novel idea of "guardianship" (*Velayat-e Faqih*). This notion is based on the position that government needs to have a guardian versed in Islamic law who can keep the political administration in line with Islamic precepts, and who has the power to actively intervene to set policy. This concept of guardianship clashed with the more traditional, or "quietist," school of Shi'a Islam, which argues that clerics need to remain outside of politics to serve as moral advisors to society, and should not get involved in the day-to-day affairs of society unless specifically asked to make a ruling (hence the term "quietist," meaning the *hawza* should be quiet and not get involved).

But for Sistani, a rejection of Iranian-style theocracy and direct involvement of the clergy in government did not translate into an embrace of Western liberal democracy. Sistani accepted the premise of the quietist school—that governance ought to be left to the politicians but that the clergy still had a right to provide guidelines for social order (*nizam al-mujama*). In other words, Sistani did not feel that the clergy ought to rule but that the politicians who ran the country's affairs should accept clerical guidance.[67] A phrase that Sistani and other clerics used to justify their involvement in political affairs was "*irshad wa tawjeeh*"(guidance and direction).

Bremer and his staff did not believe that the *hawza* would be particularly supportive of the kind of "New Iraq" they wanted to created— one characterized by a separation between mosque and state and that enshrined a whole host of liberal political and social rights (including women's rights) not found in more traditional Islamic societies.[68] They also did not want to hold early elections that might bring anti-American forces to power and frustrate reconstruction efforts. Because Bremer wanted to emphasize the secular nature of his policies, and to avoid sending any signals that he would compromise with the religious authorities, he made a point of avoiding contact with the *hawza* when on a visit to Najaf in July 2003. As news agencies reported, "In line with this message, Bremer skipped meeting the Shiite clergy here including the powerful Grand Ayatollah Ali al-Sistani, leader of the Hawza, the country's top Shiite Muslim authority . . ."[69]

Therefore, Bremer's initial plan was for the Iraqi constitution to be written first. It would rely on a constitutional committee of appointed (not elected) Iraqis who would be guided by Western advisors. Elections would then be held and sovereignty transferred back to an Iraqi government. The Americans believed that the politicians they had gathered into the Governing Council (*majlis al-hokum*), and the experts who had been appointed to the Iraqi Preparatory Committee that would advise the council, would possess sufficient legitimacy in the eyes of Iraqis to produce a constitution and to set down the broad forms of the post-Saddam political order.

Sistani responded by issuing a short *fatwa* (a legal ruling based on his assessment of Islamic law) on June 26, 2003. It declared that only representatives directly elected by the Iraqi people could draft the constitution, because otherwise "there is no guarantee either that this assembly will prepare a constitution that serves the best interests of the Iraqi people or [that] express [sic]their national identity whose backbone is sound Islamic religion and noble social values."[70]

Sistani emerged as a key figure because many Shi'a look to him to provide authoritative guidance and interpretation of Islamic law, not just about religious practices but on a wide variety of social, business, and political matters. This influence increased in the chaos of post-Saddam Iraq, when people were looking for authoritative leadership. There is a high degree of trust among Iraqi Shi'a in the theological guidance of the Grand Ayatollah to interpret God's will as to the best path forward. Clerics under Sistani reinforced that influence by their ability to deploy what Etzioni would term "utilitarian" power—the foundations that the clerics ran on the basis of voluntary donations made by the faithful, and that enabled them to fund their schools and networks of charitable and social organizations. When secular politicians failed to deliver even on basic services, any of the major Shi'a clerics could organize "social services for the poor, directing his followers to use religious taxes and charitable contributions to set up food banks and health clinics, and provide security, basic schooling, garbage collection and even sewers."[71]

When Saddam Hussein's regime collapsed, therefore, the religious leaders were the best positioned to fill the vacuum. Writing about the situation on the ground in Iraq in April 2003, Middle Eastern studies professor Juan Cole noted that, contrary to the expectations of US officials, "Religious Shiite parties and militias in Iraq have recently stepped into the gap resulting from the collapse of the Baath Party, especially in the sacred shrine cities."[72] George Packard observed that Shi'a clerics "filled the vacuum with energy and organization, taking over hospitals and schools, providing social services to the poor and imposing their Islamic code in daily life, while more secular Iraqis . . . moved about in a daze."[73] Military officers who served on the ground in Iraq rapidly came to appreciate the power and influence of the clergy, turning to them in the early days after the fall of Saddam Hussein to restrain their communities from engaging in looting.[74]

As a result, even the opinion polls conducted by the CPA showed that no secular Iraqi politician could match the approval levels enjoyed by Sistani and other clerics (including the young firebrand Moqtada al-Sadr) among Iraq's Shi'a.[75] Sistani and Sadr both had the capacity to mobilize large numbers of people, in contrast to the political figures that had been selected to sit on the Governing Council.

It soon became clear that the Iraqi politicians selected by the United States to form the Governing Council would not defy the *fatwa*. The exiled Shi'a cleric on the Governing Council, Mohammed Bahr al-Uloum, made it clear that he would not challenge Sistani's authority in this matter. Other politicians were eager to obtain Sistani's blessing and seal of approval. Instead of lecturing Sistani about accepting political realities, they turned to him for guidance and advice. Shi'a politicians made it absolutely clear that they accepted Sistani's views about the clergy having the right to guide and to counsel political leaders. When Ibrahim Jafari, one of the Shi'a members of the Governing Council, took his turn to serve as president of the council, he made a point of traveling to Najaf to meet with Sistani. "We came here to meet Sistani and inform him on what is happening in the Governing Council and take advice from him on all things with the Governing Council," Jafari declared after one such session in August 2003.[76] Even non-Shi'a were affected. At one point Jalal Talabani, the Kurdish leader, went down to Najaf to try and persuade Sistani to withdraw his decree. After visiting with Sistani, Talabani announced to the press, "I see the views of His Grace as logical and reasonable, and I agree with them."[77] Despite their private reassurances to Bremer, the members of the Governing Council not only never publicly disagreed with Sistani, but often endorsed his views. In early 2004, during a visit to Washington, the Shi'a Islamist leader Abdul Aziz al-Hakim told president George W. Bush that Sistani's position on holding direct elections reflected the "view of the entire Governing Council," while Ahmed Chalabi praised Sistani to US Secretary of State Colin Powell as "one of our country's greatest leaders."[78]

The 25-member Iraqi Preparatory Committee, a more technocratic body than the Governing Council, also sided with Sistani. Many of its members were lawyers, judges, and academics; there was also an attempt to foster a balance among its members between Shi'a and non-Shi'a (Arab Sunnis, Kurds, and other ethno-sectarian groups in Iraq). When the committee met on September 8, 2003, it voted 24-0 in favor of Sistani's plan: holding national direct elections for a constitutional assembly. In their meetings, the committee members saw how Sistani's *fatwa* had resonated not only among Iraqi Shi'a, but among non-Shi'a as well, who were concerned about the Americans controlling the constitutional process. Law professor Hikmat Hakim told Sistani when the committee met with him that "his fatwa would be respected" by the committee.[79]

Sistani had backed up his decree not only by appealing to Islamic religious law—making his call for elections a religious obligation for Shi'a—but also by grounding his *fatwa* in a sense of Iraqi nationalism. He believed that Iraqis, not outsiders, should control the political process. With this twin appeal, it was clear to the Iraqi politicians "that the ayatollah had far more legitimacy among the Iraqi people than they did."[80] Sistani showed his political clout in calling Iraqis into the streets in January 2004 to protest in favor of direct elections.[81] In Baghdad alone, more than 100,000 protestors echoed Sistani's call for elections, and it became clear that in contrast to the politicians on the Governing Council, "Iraq's Shiites largely back the position of Grand Ayatollah Ali al-Sistani."[82] Noah Feldman, the law professor who served as the senior constitutional advisor to the CPA, would declare that Sistani proved to have played the "most significant role in Iraqi politics during the period of occupation."[83]

Why were the politicians unable to change Sistani's mind and why were they so afraid to challenge him? Etzioni's work would have suggested that questions of legitimacy were major concerns. As Feldman observed, "Most of the aspiring Iraqi political class succeeded only in revealing the impossibility of jumping from political unknowns to mobilizers of large constituencies. . . . The overambitious attempts of the returnee politicians seemed particularly ineffective because they were closely connected to the wavering and unstable policies for the transfer of power proposed by the CPA."[84]

Bremer's initial plan had been for appointed Iraqi delegates to write the constitution and only then transfer sovereignty back to Iraqi authorities. The inability to convince Sistani to back this proposal forced Bremer to scrap his transition plan. On November 10, he addressed a letter to Defense Secretary Donald Rumsfeld (with copies sent to Secretary of State Colin Powell and National Security Advisor Condoleezza Rice), noting, "I have concluded the time has come to readjust our planned program for Iraq's political transition."[85] In an attempt to mollify Sistani, the Bush administration set June 30, 2004 as the date for the transfer of sovereignty. A provisional government would be selected using a complicated system of regional caucuses—and the CPA would, in conjunction with the Governing Council, draft not a permanent constitution but a "temporary administrative law" (TAL). After agreeing to the plan on November 15, 2003, Iraqi politicians promised Bremer that they could get Sistani to sign on to this new plan.[86]

But this was an empty promise. Sistani opposed many of the elements of the new plan, again reiterating that any government that came to power in Iraq would have to be directly elected. Adnan Pachachi, a Sunni member of the Governing Council who held the presidency in January 2004, was unable to convince Sistani to back the November 15th agreement.[87] Moreover, Sistani asked the Secretary-General of the United Nations, Kofi Annan, to send a mission to Iraq to evaluate whether elections could be held prior to the announced hand-over of power to an Iraqi interim administration—in essence asking the United Nations to arbitrate his dispute with the CPA.[88] In so doing, Sistani reaffirmed that he would "not deal with the coalition on long-term political matters because . . . they are viewed as an occupying force" but that "he will accept the UN team."[89]

When the UN Secretary General sent former Algerian Foreign Minister Lakhdar Brahimi to Iraq as his special representative in February 2004, Brahimi immediately reached out to Sistani to open talks about how the Iraqi transition plan would be structured. Brahimi agreed with Sistani on the importance of elections but also convinced the grand ayatollah that it was critical that "the elections must be well prepared and well arranged and must be done under the best possible circumstances." Brahimi was able to establish a rapport with Sistani and to get him to accept that elections could not be held prior to the transfer of sovereignty planned for June 30, 2004.[90]

Sistani accepted a compromise solution: in return for scrapping Bremer's caucus system, he agreed to the appointment of an Iraqi Interim Government the mandate of which would be to hold elections as quickly as possible; they were held in January 2005.[91] This plan, drawn up largely by Brahimi, was prepared in close consultation with Sistani and his advisors, in contrast to both of Bremer's transition plans—and gave Sistani some input into the composition of the interim regime.

The CPA staff also bowed to the inevitable and began to indirectly consult with Sistani about the shape of the proposed TAL. Although Bremer insisted on installing the whole panoply of Western-liberal civil and political rights, the TAL also cited Islamic religious law as a "source of legislation" and including the proviso that no law in Iraq could contradict the basic tenets of Islam. This formulation was run past Sistani to ensure that it met with his approval.[92] Some of the final language was apparently written by Sistani himself, whose office stayed in satellite telephone communication with the drafters of the TAL.[93] Even with all of this input, however, the Shi'a politicians on the Governing Council were so concerned about receiving Sistani's imprimatur that the signing ceremony for the TAL, which was scheduled for Friday, March 5, 2004, had to be postponed. The Shi'a delegates traveled to Najaf to confer once again with Sistani and to ensure that they had his approval, in part by promising that some features Sistani found objectionable would be modified or deleted altogether from the permanent constitution. The TAL was finally signed on Monday, March 8th.[94] Sistani also played a role in vetting the members of the Iraqi Interim Government and had the opportunity to veto proposed candidates.[95]

In the end, Iraqi Shi'a politicians, far from controlling Sistani, actively sought his endorsement and blessing. Sistani's influence was put to the test at the ballot box in January 2005; the United Iraqi Alliance (UIA) was broadly understood by many Iraqi Shi'a to be the party most in alignment with Sistani, and so enjoyed his tacit blessing. The UIA ended up receiving the largest bloc of votes, and "in this first chance to 'give their voice' most Shi'a had obeyed their religious leaders." In contrast, the more avowedly secular candidates were "stunned" by the lack of support they received from the Shi'a electorate.[96]

Not everyone within the US government ignored the importance of religious and community figures. The State Department's prewar planning for a post-Saddam Iraq included the creation of the "Future of Iraq" project, which brought together Iraqi exiles and US experts.[97] While Sistani was not mentioned by name, there was some recognition of the need to include representatives of the Shi'a clergy as part of the process. A proposal for an "advisory council" also mentioned bringing in tribal and religious leaders from across Iraq.[98] And as events developed on the ground, CPA advisors like Larry Diamond testified as to the importance of bringing people like Sistani into the political process, even if he was, per Etzioni's parlance, an illiberal moderate.[99] As Diamond noted, "No Iraqi commands a wider following of respect and consideration, and has more capacity to steer political developments away from violence and extremism, than Sistani, who insists on free elections as the basis of political legitimacy."[100]

Etzioni counseled that, in places like Iraq or Afghanistan, the United States "must initially tolerate illiberal ideological or religious regimes, as long as the leadership in place helps maintain basic security" and lays the groundwork for a "slow, costly, and imperfect process" of transition toward more liberal forms of governance.[101] This position was at odds with the expectation that, with the destruction of the old regimes, rapid transformation was possible. Etzioni's advice, which ultimately was ignored, was that the US emphasis in postconflict reconstruction should, in the short term, be focused on "detyrannization" and on laying the foundations for a stable and well-governed society, rather than to push for full-fledged democratization.[102]

To some extent, lessons were learned; when conducting policy in Iraq in the future, the United States would not take Sistani for granted as a political force. It is true that he was not able to broker a settlement to end intra-sectarian fighting and that his appeals for peace largely went unheeded, particularly in the bloodletting of 2006–07. Yet, he did not become irrelevant, and Iraqi politicians still took his blessing into account when conducting policy.

In 2008, it was time to negotiate a Status of Forces Agreement (SOFA) with Iraq to provide a new legal basis for the US military presence in Iraq; the UN Security Council mandate contained in the 2005 resolution1546 (subsequently extended by other resolutions) had expired. It was important to get Sistani's approval when negotiating the SOFA, especially given popular discontent with a continued US presence. In the summer of 2008, after being briefed by Iraq National Security Advisor Muwafaq al-Rubaie on the progress of the talks, Sistani refused to endorse the first drafts and laid out his "four conditions" for any agreement: "safeguarding Iraqis' interests, national sovereignty, national consensus and being presented to the Iraqi Parliament for approval."[103]

This time, US officials understood why it was important for senior political figures to get Sistani's blessing. As with earlier major pieces of legislation, "A delegation of Shiite lawmakers and government officials met . . . with Grand Ayatollah Ali Sistani to review" the proposed pact and "the cleric 'gave the Iraqi side the green light to sign it,' according to an official in Sistani's office who spoke on the condition of anonymity."[104] US negotiators, rather than insisting on all provisions of their initial draft, were prepared to make changes and concessions in order to win support for passage of the agreement, which extended the US presence in the country to 2011.

In 2010, Sistani was called in to help mediate disputes between Iraqi political parties that had prevented the formation of a government. In turn, the agreement between the Iraqi National Alliance and the State of Law party not only cleared the way for a new government to be formed in Iraq, but also explicitly guaranteed a role for the senior Shiite clergy for the first time. Grand Ayatollah Ali al-Sistani was named as the final, binding arbiter for any disputes among the members of the governing coalition. In the agreement signed by the parties, "the marjaiya [the assembly of the most senior ayatollahs] has the final say in solving all the disputes between the two sides and its directives and guidance are binding."[105] Now in his mid-80s, this unassuming, reclusive cleric continues to live and work from his small house off an alleyway in Najaf, still helping to shape the destiny of post-Saddam Iraq—exactly the type of community leader Etzioni had predicted would end up playing a key role in the transition.

"Plan Z"

Etzioni would not have been a proponent of the root-and-branch transformational approaches to the building of nations that the United States has undertaken in the last two decades. One of the greatest weaknesses of these nations remains the inability to generate loyalty and commitment on the part of the population to the US-developed institutions and frameworks designed to defend and make sacrifices for them. In Afghanistan, for instance, despite all the money spent and equipment provided to create a national Afghan army, the future of that force is imperiled by high attrition rates.[106] To help fill in the gaps and retain the allegiance of fighters against the Taliban movement, the United States has also turned to supporting tribal and regional militias.[107] In Iraq, large portions of the national army collapsed when faced with the 2014 uprising led by the Islamic State, and the government has been forced to turn to both Shi'a militias and Sunni tribes to help stem and roll back the advance of the Islamic State.[108]

These realities validate Etzioni's observations about finding the focal point of people's loyalty, and the fact that the nation-state may be subordinate to local, religious, or ethnic communities. Faced with major setbacks to American plans to create a unified, centralized Iraqi state that would respect human rights, effectively control its territory, and serve as an ally to the United States, in 2007 Etzioni proposed his "Plan Z" for Iraq and briefed it to members of both the US and UK governments. It is an approach "that tailors the institutions of the state to fit the sociological reality on the ground, rather than trying to force that reality into an imported, precut outfit."[109] Plan Z is based on Etzioni's concept of the "high devolution state," in which a central government devolves significant powers and authorities to local communities and provinces, including regionally defined security forces. In essence, loyalty to the nation would run through the local institutions. The plan would also allow localities to set most of their laws and processes, based on their own preferences, with a central, federal government exercising only those powers necessary to hold the union together. This would help to reassure the different communities, fearful of the prospect of having one group capture control of a highly centralized state, that no one faction would be able to dominate the others. This would be a "bottom-up" approach designed to balance regional and communal interests with national ones—but would only work to the extent that a national government was willing to engage in the necessary devolution of power.[110] That, in turn, would depend on the signals it received from the United States and the extent to which the United States made it clear that movement along these lines was the condition on which future support would be predicated. Plan Z acquired some support within the US Congress, notably from Senator Joe Biden, then the chairman of the Senate Foreign Relations Committee. To some extent, the 2007–08 "surge" of US forces in Iraq, combined with the willingness of American commanders to conclude informal arrangements with tribal leaders, was designed to create the political space for significant changes. These included making constitutional revisions, developing stronger provincial governments, and finding new power-sharing arrangements among the different ethno-sectarian communities of Iraq. The insistence on retaining a strong central government, combined with the unwillingness of Iraq politicians to contemplate greater political devolution, however, doomed whatever short-term breathing room the surge had helped to provide.[111]

The Plan Z approach was grounded in the larger concept of Security First—that attempting a far-reaching overhaul of Iraqi institutions, no matter how well-intentioned, was foolish if it not only failed to bring about basic security but even increased the levels of violence and chaos. Resisting devolution in the name of a preferred utopian end point, or because it would not empower the set of leaders the United States wished to see in control of affairs, was neither a moral approach nor an effective one in terms of guaranteeing security. Etzioni argued that a shift to a high-devolution state would improve security, by both giving sanction to local, tribal, and community forces that could now operate openly and with permission and by reducing the tendency for local groups to resist the central government.[112] In other words, a high-devolution state promotes a form of power-sharing among different elites that can reduce the impetus for conflict.

Under a Plan Z approach, a central government would have far less authority to be able to enforce a whole panoply of rights. In essence, it would shift power to a broader mass of illiberal moderates, who might agree on protecting basic human rights but who would not support the much higher degree of pluralism and individual lifestyle choices that define Western postindustrial democracies. The Plan Z approach would make it far harder for the West to be able to pressure a high-devolution state to enact a liberal agenda, particularly if it were favored by only a small minority of the population.[113]

Etzioni has advanced similar proposals for dealing with Afghanistan. A critical point he made was that US efforts to strengthen a central authority at the expense of tribal communities were ill-advised. As he observed, "Instead of trying to break the tribal authorities and undermine tribal loyalties and structures, we must build upon them and move towards coalition building, which may gradually lead to society-wide commitments and forces."[114] Etzioni did not call for dismantling the efforts taken after 2001 to promote elections and a more effective Afghan central government. However, he felt that the focus on trying to have these new authorities supplant rather than complement the older leadership structures would be counterproductive. Etzioni's ideas are in line with what other development experts and those with a good deal of experience in Afghanistan believe is a feasible way to move forward on improving governance. In testimony before the Senate Foreign Relations Committee in 2009, Claire Lockhart (co-founder, along with Ashraf Ghani, now the president of Afghanistan, of the Institute for State Effectiveness) argued: "A 'light touch' form of governance is possible, where formal structures, including line ministries, can 'mesh' with local and traditional networks and social organizations."[115] Etzioni expects that it is possible to encourage evolution, over time, to more liberal forms of governance and to gain greater acceptance for new structures by which authority is recognized and legitimated in the community.[116] This can be accomplished by working with traditional forms of government, as well as by accepting the creation of much more limited central governments that back away from pursuing a more vigorous democratic agenda. This type of approach also recognizes that many of the functions for the provision of public goods that the West assumes will be delivered by the central state (even when consistent reports suggest that this is not happening[117]) are in fact provided by local, tribal, ethnic, and religious communities.[118] Given this reality, Etzioni argues:

> Given the power and import of communities (often referred to as "tribes"), the issue here is not whether we can or should avoid engaging in nation building, but how we proceed. Do we make our starting point the notion that there is a central national government, whose troops and police we can train as a national force and whose administration of justice and social services we can improve? Or, do we realize that such a center-to-periphery approach is unworkable, and that we need to build from the periphery to the center? This does not mean that we should go find individual citizens to "empower" and work with them. Instead, we should look at places like Afghanistan as lands in which several tribes lie next to each other. (I use the term "tribes" loosely, referring to ethnic and confessional communities whose members have tribe-like ties to one another, ties they do not have to members of other communities.) In other words, there are many societies in which nation building cannot start from the center—and those who insist otherwise pay a heavy price.[119]

One of the problems the US government has with adopting Etzioni's approach is ideological. Americans increasingly are reluctant to view as legitimate any authority that has not received a mandate at the ballot box.[120] Those who Etzioni calls "natural leaders," however, "those who rose to power due to their charisma, persuasive powers, lineage, or religious status, but who were not elected in the Western way" may command more legitimacy and authority.[121] Yet, for a variety of reasons, ranging from statute to preference, American officials are reluctant to work with traditional forms of authority.[122] Etzioni's proposals also require giving up a good deal of control—an approach that, as we have seen in the Iraq case, the CPA was unwilling to countenance in the early days of the post-Saddam transition. The proposals require coming to terms with the idea that expectations may have to be lowered, and that outcomes may come about not through preferred bureaucratic processes but through more informal arrangements involving Etzioni's "natural leaders."[123]

Another difficulty the US government has with Etzioni's approach it that it promotes decentralization. This is often opposed by US and European nation-builders largely because the devolution of power makes it harder to impose a single, central template on the entire country. This reality is ironic given the very strong tradition of states' rights in the US federal experience, and the many inefficiencies it can create.

Several additional criticisms of Etzioni's approach have been advanced, beyond the critique that his recommendations would entrench old authorities resistant to change and reform. Some argue that moving to the high-devolution approach would intensify rather than tamp down insecurity. The rationale is that groups in mixed areas would be incentivized to fight for predominance and devolution, which would lead to de facto partition of a country as regions struggled for even more independence from central authority.[124] Others have noted that devolution to local authorities carries with it no guarantee that security would be enhanced.[125] In addition, power-sharing arrangements of the type Etzioni has discussed run the risk not of promoting good governance but instead of "sharing of the spoils" and entrenching corrupt patronage networks.[126]

Yet, is difficult to conclude that the full-fledged adoption of Etzioni's proposals would have led to worse outcomes. Both Iraq and Afghanistan today are seen as less secure and more violent in the aftermath of the US intervention.[127] The Iraqi elections of 2010 and 2014 and the Afghan presidential elections of 2014 revealed societies that remain deeply segmented along ethnic, religious, and tribal lines, with the democratic process exacerbating rather than tamping down these cleavages. A fragile power-sharing agreement now characterizes the Afghan government. Meanwhile, the divisions along ethnic lines in the Iraqi system have left the country open to the advances of the Islamic State and have brought the country to the brink of fragmentation.[128] These occurrences highlight the problem Etzioni identifies as the "community deficit": despite the existence of a bureaucracy and institutions, the community cannot rely on the loyalty and support of its supposed subjects, who continue to pledge their blood and treasure not to the national construction, but to the regional, tribal, ethnic, or religious communities within it.[129]

Applying Etzioni's Analysis to the Failure of the Democratic Concert

Etzioni's sociological studies also have relevance for explaining the failure of US attempts, both at a global and a regional level, to forge effective leagues, alliances, or concerts of democratic states. These entities would work together to promote liberal democratic ideals, to route around international organizations deadlocked because of the veto power wielded by authoritarian regimes, and to develop more effective transnational associations. More ambitious versions of these proposals call for states to provide each other with mutual assistance and security guarantees.

Yet the two half-hearted efforts that have been initiated—one, a concert of democracies on a Eurasian regional basis (GUAM Organization for Democracy and Economic Development), the other, a global Community of Democracies (CD)—help to illustrate Etzioni's points about the importance of integrative power to the success of such endeavors. These efforts also highlight the dangers that can arise from an overemphasis on the initiation point of an organization as opposed to getting it to its "take-off" point. In addition, the setbacks experienced by both GUAM and the CD call into question the extent to which common values, as opposed to shared interests, can serve as a reliable basis for effective international cooperation.

Created in June 2000, the CD is an initiative of the Clinton administration that was spearheaded by Madeleine Albright, who had served first as US Ambassador to the United Nations and then as Secretary of State.[130] The CD was meant to complement and enhance the work of the United Nations by bringing together a group of market democracies that would be prepared to act in concert to promote and to secure the interest of the world's democratic states.[131] The hope was that democratic states would be inclined to "assist each other, whether in times of relative stability, or when emergencies arise."[132] Three years earlier, with US encouragement, Georgia, Ukraine, Azerbaijan, and Moldova created GUAM as a way to bring together pro-Western, democratizing states for collective action in Eurasia[133]—a test of this concept applied at the regional level.

The CD was created with a great deal of fanfare at its inaugural congress in Warsaw, with more than 100 nations participating, and in 2004 a "Democracy Caucus" was set up under its auspices at the United Nations. Since 2009, there has been a permanent secretariat based in Warsaw. Member-states are supposed to designate a senior official in their governments to serve as liaison and to coordinate the work of the CD across its members. The CD works to coordinate "best practices" in democracy promotion and election monitoring, and to provide assistance for such efforts. Beyond that, however, most observers assess the work of the CD as ineffectual at best and an outright failure at worst. It has been argued that the CD had no clear criteria for defining what states should qualify as a democracy, and as a result it has enjoyed only limited cohesion and no real ability to move on a common security agenda.[134] The lack of a more concrete security or economic agenda to tie together the CD's members means that a "community of democracies is a categorization without much relevant content for international organizations."[135] The "Democracy Caucus" at the United Nations has also not lived up to its promise of serving as a vigorous lobby for human-rights issues. Its effectiveness has been stymied by disputes among the members of the caucus—especially an unwillingness to sacrifice national interests in order to pursue idealistic goals—as well as the suspicion of some members that Washington hopes the group can serve as a front for US interests.[136] Regional caucuses (of both democracies and nondemocracies) at the United Nations have proven their effectiveness to lobby on issues of concern for states that share a common geography, highlighting the importance of Etzioni's observation about the importance of what he termed "ecological" factors in pushing states to closer action.[137] But the proposal for the "Democracy Caucus" to develop a common position prior to UN votes on behalf of democratic states has not taken root. Instead, observers have pointed to the lack of solidarity among members and the reality that "developing-world democracies like South Africa, India and the Philippines have often voted against Western states on human rights issues at the United Nations."[138] While the caucus still exists, it is described by some as "largely moribund."[139]

It was expected that the creation and expansion of the CD would be driven by the same set of challenges that Etzioni predicted would push the nations of the world toward Global Authorities;[140] that did not turn out to be the case. Apart from rhetorical commitments about shared values, the CD has not been able to develop itself into a more effective body based on shared interests.[141] Moreover, some countries that are part of the CD have raised the question as to whether such efforts could be successful without the participation of the major nondemocratic states as well—and have worried that the CD would end up undermining other, fragile attempts at promoting greater global governance.[142] In the end, the CD remains largely a "debating society"—a forum for ideas and discussion—because that is the role that most of its members are comfortable with.[143]

GUAM has also had a troubled history. First created as a consultative forum in October 1997, the group expanded to encompass Uzbekistan in 1999 and established a charter and institutions at its Yalta summit in June 2001. In 2003, the group pledged to create mobile antiterrorist units to guard energy infrastructure from attack, to create a joint security center, and to set up a parliamentary assembly to connect the legislatures of the member-states, while increasing trade and business contacts among the members. Then-Ukrainian President Leonid Kuchma proclaimed that GUAM had established "a sufficient foundation to secure a new quality of collaboration." Moreover, the United States used some "integrating power" of its own, both diplomatic encouragement and economic aid, to encourage GUAM's institutionalization. Then-Georgian President Eduard Shevardnadze declared that "without the support of the Americans it would be difficult to resolve the issues" that still divided the members.[144] Yet, institutionalization of this organization proved to be problematic, as national parliaments failed to ratify agreements or to take steps to support the strengthening of the organization.[145] Uzbekistan suspended its membership in 2002 and withdrew from the group in 2005, and, as with the other members, Etzioni's observations about the importance of having "congenial factions in power simultaneously"[146] were borne out. Changes in governments among the different members led to inconsistent stances on the importance and utility of the organization. This was especially noticeable in Moldova and Ukraine; when more pro-Russian administrations took office, interest in promoting GUAM declined. No government was willing to put national interests—including the possibility of improving trading and political relations with Russia—ahead of supporting other members when they encountered difficulties with Moscow. Thus, a major opportunity to deepen the identity of the bloc or to show its cohesion by adhering to a single position.[147]

Unlike the CD, GUAM member-states share a number of linked interests—resisting Russian pressure, seeking to develop access to energy sources that bypass Russian control, and searching for a closer relationship with the Euro-Atlantic world.[148] Yet they did not always see collective action as the best way to achieve these ends. Despite its shared values, the group was unable to develop joint peace-keeping forces for the bloc with an eye to deploying them to members who faced separatist conflicts.[149] GUAM, as a group, was reluctant to openly support Georgia when it was forced to cope with a Russian intervention in 2008.[150] Similarly, while expressing full support for Ukraine's position in its current conflict with Russia, other members of GUAM have kept their response to Moscow quite muted.[151]

There are proponents of the view that shared values can form the basis of effective regional and international organizations, and that democracies, by virtue of similar forms of domestic governance, will have similar views on foreign policy issues.[152] This group must confront other factors that Etzioni predicts will have more influence on whether the group will survive and thrive, or wither away. As long as the democracies of the world do not view themselves as forming a distinct and connected group of states—not sharing a common "ecology"—it is difficult for them to take on collective obligations, particularly when it comes to security.[153] Indeed, when it comes to the Community of Democracies, an organization with global scope, "the more likely regional considerations will trump democratic solidarity."[154] Even a regionally defined organization like GUAM was hampered by the fact that its members were noncontiguous, and were divided into two wings by the Black Sea—an "unsettling" factor for helping to promote consolidation, according to Etzioni.[155] More importantly, the governing elites have to believe that the benefits of collective action will outweigh the costs of remaining separate. One of Etzioni's conclusions is that the "impact of supranational institutions is largest when other conditions for unification are favorable and least when they are not favorable."[156] If the utilitarian and identitive factors backing a proposed association are weak—and certainly, in the case of the CD, they were—the impact of setting up the CD and its associated structures are lessened. A shared commitment to Westernization and a common suspicion of Russia proved to be insufficient to sustain a move for greater political, economic, and military integration among the GUAM members. This was especially true when individual members of the group found that they could achieve a better deal from Russia or the West by defecting from the collective. Finally, neither the CD nor GUAM ever reached a clear take-off point; in particular, GUAM was susceptible to being overdependent on the personal relationships between the individual presidents of its members rather than internalizing the group within the national bureaucracies of its members. Similarly, the CD never occupied the prime attention of most of its members' foreign-policy process.[157] Moreover, neither GUAM nor the CD ever attempted to convince the populations of their member-states that they were indeed part of a larger community—an effort that Etzioni believes is essential for the success of any transnational venture.[158]

The failure of both of these US-sponsored initiatives—failures that could have been predicted based on Etzioni's criteria—is important as the United States considers further modifications it may wish to propose for the international order. Simply building new architectures is no guarantee that other states will buy in.[159] A new security and economic grouping of Pacific Rim democracies, for instance, will not gain traction if more attention is not paid to the different sources of integrative power. Such sources include whether there is sufficient identitive grounds in a commonly shared Pacific identity and in the mythos of shared values, and whether such an association would generate sufficient utilitarian benefits to cause the elites of different prospective members to accede to such an association. The European Union is now experiencing difficulties as a result of its community deficit; the demands it makes upon its member-states and their citizens are not buttressed by a sufficient basis of common identity to generate enthusiastic support when times are difficult. Given this situation, it will be important not to overestimate the ease with which getting such an important and far-reaching association off the ground will be.[160] Etzioni has provided a useful checklist for the policymaker in gauging the steps that have to be taken to get a new association or political union up and running.

Concluding Thoughts

In the aftermath of what seem to be failed attempts at nation-building in Iraq and Afghanistan, Joseph Nye concludes that it is very unlikely that the United States will attempt another long-term effort designed to bring about major social and political transformation of another society.[161] The United States is now faced with the possibility that both Iraq and Afghanistan will completely fragment after the departure of Western forces. This is occurring at the same time that the country is trying to hold together disintegrating states like Syria or South Sudan. Add to this the witnessing of the failure of revolutions in places like Egypt to produce sustainable democratic regimes, and it appears likely that the focus of U.S. nation-building efforts is likely to shift in favor of Etzioni's Security First paradigm. This approach seeks to generate regimes capable of providing security, and, in so doing, to create the possibility for a longer-term transition to more liberal forms of governance.

Moreover, despite the hopes of some in the US foreign-policy establishment that shared values could produce a lasting foundation for transnational cooperation, the difficulties the United States has had in creating new post-Cold War international groupings also suggests that countries are more likely to work together on the basis of what Etzioni has described as "transactional" relationships geared to ensuring their security.[162] Whether a particular country or an international organization can help provide safety from different sorts of threats—from terrorism and disorder to ecological and economic disaster—will take precedence over concerns about its internal forms of governance. Etzioni notes that nation- and institution-building efforts, as a result, "would focus first on security, but then expand to attend to other human needs."[163] Over the last decade, the effort to build states that can both provide security to their own citizens and regions and serve as beacons of liberal democracies has ended up producing constructions that can do neither. Consequently, this does not sound like bad advice.

Notes

1. Reinhard Bendix, *Nation-Building and Citizenship: Studies of Our Changing Social Order* (Berkeley, CA: University of California Press, 1964), 1, 3.
2. Francis Fukuyama, "Nation-Building and the Failure of Institutional Memory," *Nation-Building Beyond Afghanistan and Iraq*, ed. Francis Fukuyama (Baltimore, MD: Johns Hopkins University Press, 2006), 2.
3. James Dobbins et al., *America's Role in Nation-Building: From Germany to Iraq* (Santa Monica, CA: RAND Corporation, 2003), xiv.
4. Amitai Etzioni, "Bottom Up Nation Building," *Policy Review* 158 (December 2009/January 2010), http://www.hoover.org/research/bottom-nation-building.
5. Amitai Etzioni, "A Grand Design? A Review," *Journal of Conflict Resolution* 7:2 (June 1963), 162. This is a review essay examining Joseph Kraft's *The Grand Design* and Walter Lippmann's *Western Unity and the Common Market*.
6. Amitai Etzioni, "A Self-Restrained Approach to Nation-Building by Foreign Powers," *International Affairs* 80:1 (January 2004), 1.
7. Quoted in Michael Hirsch, "The Legacy of the Iraq War? Anti-War Democrats and Rand Paul," *National Journal*, March 18, 2013, http://www.nationaljournal.com/politics/the-legacy-of-the-iraq-war-anti-war-democrats-and-rand-paul-20130318.

8. Amitai Etzioni, *Political Unification Revisited* (Lanham, MD: Lexington Books, 2001), 37.
9. Etzioni, *Political Reunification Revisited*, 38–39.
10. ibid, 51.
11. ibid, 97–284.
12. See, for instance, *Together or Apart: The Nordic Council and the EU*, eds. Karina Jutilla and Terhi Tikkala (Helsinki: Think Tank E2, 2009), esp. 33–34; Werner Kamppeter, *Lessons of European Integration*, report issued by the International Policy Analysis Unit of Internationale Politik, April 2000, http://www.fes.de/analysen/kamppeter1_1.html.
13. Etzioni, *Political Unification Revisited*, 94.
14. ibid, 95.
15. The "high-devolution state," presented as an option for postwar Iraq, was discussed by Etzioni on Capitol Hill on June 18, 2007. For a perspective on the proposal and the event, see James W. Riley, "Break Up to Make Up," *National Interest*, June 19, 2007, http://nationalinterest.org/commentary/break-up-to-make-up-1633.
16. Etzioni notes, for instance, the importance of getting the European Community off the ground at a time when similar political movements held power in the constituent countries. *Political Unification Revisited*, 26.
17. Amitai Etzioni, "Mission Creep and Its Discontents: The Afghanistan Conflict," *Middle East Quarterly* 18:2 (Spring 2011), http://www.meforum.org/2879/afghanistan-mission-creep.
18. Amitai Etzioni, "Religion and Social Order," *Policy Review* 148 (April/May 2008), 60.
19. Etzioni, *Political Unification Revisited*, 94.
20. Etzioni, "Religion and Social Order," 65.
21. Nikolas K. Gvosdev, "The Communitarian Foreign Policy of Amitai Etzioni," *Society* 51,4 (2014), 372.
22. Rebecca Patterson, *The Challenge of Nation-Building: Implementing Effective Innovation in the U.S. Army From World War II to the Iraq War* (Lanham, MD: Rowman and Littlefield, 2014), 29.
23. See, for instance, the description of the guiding principles of the occupation of Japan, in Gavin Long, *MacArthur* (London: B.T. Batsford, 1969), 180.
24. James Dobbins, Michele A. Poole, Austin Long, and Benjamin Runkle, *After the War: Nation-Building from FDR to George W. Bush* (Santa Monica, CA: RAND, 2008), xiii.
25. Patterson, 29–30.
26. Derek S. Reveron, Nikolas K. Gvosdev, and Mackubin Thomas Owens, *US Foreign Policy and Defense Strategy: The Evolution of an Incidental Superpower* (Washington, DC: Georgetown University Press, 2015), 5, 28.
27. Dominique Vidal, "A Guide to Nation Building," *Le Monde Diplomatique*, December 10, 2003, http://mondediplo.com/2003/12/10rand.
28. The distinction between reconstruction and restoration missions—rehabilitating a preexisting set of institutions—versus creating new constructions is one drawn by Francis Fukuyama, "Nation-Building and the Failure of Institutional Memory," *Nation-Building: Beyond Afghanistan and Iraq*, ed. Francis Fukuyama (Baltimore, MD: Johns Hopkins University Press, 2006), 5.

29. Howard J. Wiarda, *Dispatches from the Frontlines: Studies in Foreign Policy, Comparative Politics and International Affairs* (Lanham, MD: University Press of America, 2014), 168.

30. Gary Dempsey and Roger W. Fontaine, *Fool's Errands: America's Recent Encounters with Nation Building* (Washington, DC: The Cato Institute, 2001), 168–69.

31. Derek Chollet, "Dayton at Ten: A Look Back," *The Tenth Anniversary of the Dayton Accords and Afterwards: Reflections on Post-Conflict State- and Nation-Building*, ed. Nida Gelazis (Washington, DC: Woodrow Wilson Center, 2006), 23.

32. Philip Spencer and Howard Wollman, *Nationalism: A Critical Introduction* (London: SAGE, 2002, 2003), 140.

33. Sumantra Bose, *Bosnia After Dayton: Nationalist Partition and International Intervention* (Oxford: Oxford University Press, 2002), 91–94.

34. Timothy Donais, "Bosnia," *The Handbook of Political Change in Eastern Europe,* ed. Sten Berglund, Joakim Ekman, Kevin Deegan-Krause, and Terje Knutsen (Northhampton, MA: Edward Elgar Publishing, 2013), 494–96.

35. Chollet, 26.

36. Gerard Toal, "'Without Brussels There Can Be No Bosnia-Herzegovina?' Managing BiH's Geopolitical Challenges," *Tenth Anniversary of the Dayton Accords,* 39–40.

37. Chollet, 25.

38. T. David Curp, "Human Rights and Wrongs in Failed States: Bosnia-Herzegovina, the International Community and the Challenges of Long-Term Instability in Southeastern Europe," *Failed States and Fragile Societies: A New World Disorder?* eds. Ingo Trauschweizer and Steven M. Miner (Athens, OH: Ohio University Press, 2014), 33.

39. Chollet, 26.

40. "EU Hails Bosnia Reform Pledge," *Agence France Press,* February 23, 2015, https://uk.news.yahoo.com/eu-hails-bosnia-reform-pledge-200406633.html#tg0lv9f.

41. Barry J. Ryan, "Policing the State of Exception in Kosovo," *Kosovo, Intervention and Statebuilding: The International Community and the Transition to Independence,* ed. Aidan Hehir (Abingdon, Oxon: Routledge, 2010), 115.

42. Gerard M. Gallucci, "What Next for Kosovo Serbs?" *TransConflict,* February 26, 2015, http://www.transconflict.com/2015/02/what-next-for-kosovo-serbs-262/.

43. See the transcript of the second presidential debate between Vice President Al Gore and Governor George W. Bush, October 11, 2000, archived by the Commission on Presidential Debates at http://www.debates.org/?page=october-11-2000-debate-transcript.

44. Minxin Pei and Sarah Casper, *Lessons from the Past: The American Record on Nation Building* (Washington, DC: Carnegie Endowment for International Peace, May 2003), 1.

45. Pei and Casper, 1.

46. Thomas Carothers, "The Sequencing Fallacy," *Journal of Democracy* 18:1 (January 2007), 24.

47. Amitai Etzioni, *Security First: For a Muscular, Moral Foreign Policy* (New Haven: Yale University Press, 2007), 66.

48. Noah Feldman, *What We Owe Iraq: War and the Ethics of Nation Building* (Princeton, NJ: Princeton University Press, 2004), 7.

49. "Full Text: George Bush's Speech to the American Enterprise Institute," *The Guardian*, February 27, 2003, http://www.theguardian.com/world/2003/feb/27/usa.iraq2.

50. Feldman, 18.

51. Pei and Casper, 4.

52. Stephen M. Walt, "Top 10 Lessons of the Iraq War," *Foreign Policy*, March 20, 2012, http://foreignpolicy.com/2012/03/20/top-10-lessons-of-the-iraq-war-2/?wp_login_redirect=0.

53. Pei and Casper, 4.

54. Etzioni, *Political Unification Revisited*, 94–96.

55. Amitai Etzioni, *Hot Spots: American Foreign Policy in a Post-Human-Rights World* (New Brunswick, NJ: Transaction Publishers, 2012), 140.

56. Amitai Etzioni, *From Empire to Community* (New York: Palgrave Macmillan, 2004), 78.

57. Etzioni, *Security First*, 78.

58. This is discussed in Nicolai N. Petro, "A Russian Model of Development: What Novgorod Can Teach the West," *Civil Society and the Search for Justice in Russia*, eds. Christopher Marsh and Nikolas K. Gvosdev (Lanham, MD: Lexington Books, 2002), 45–48, drawing from Michael Thomas, Richard Ellis, and Aaron Wildavsky, *Cultural Theory* (Boulder, CO: Westview Press, 1990).

59. See the discussion in Gerard Fairtlough, *The Three Ways of Getting Things Done: Hierarchy, Heterarchy and Responsible Autonomy in Organizations* (Axminster, UK: Triarchy Press, 2005, 2007), 103–04. For how this concept can be applied in political contexts, see, for instance, Li Pang-kwong, "Executive and Legislature: Institutional Design, Electoral Dynamics and the Management of Conflicts in the Hong Kong Transition," *Political Order and Power Transition in Hong Kong*, ed. Li Pang-kwong (Hong Kong: Chinese University of Hong Kong, 1997), 70–71.

60. Etzioni, *Hot Spots*, 121.

61. Harold Hongju Koh, "America's Jekyll-and-Hyde Exceptionalism," *American Exceptionalism and Human Rights*, ed. Michael Ignatieff (Princeton, NJ: Princeton University Press, 2005), 127.

62. This section draws on a case study, Nikolas K. Gvosdev, "The Ayatollah Versus the Ambassador: The Influence of Religion on Politics in Post-Saddam Iraq," *Case Studies in Policy Making*, 12th ed, eds. Hayat Alvi and Nikolas K. Gvosdev (Newport, RI: Naval War College, 2010), 289–308.

63. L. Paul Bremer (with Malcolm McConnell), *My Year in Iraq: The Struggle to Build a Future of Hope* (New York: Simon and Schuster, 2006), 12.

64. George Packer, *The Assassins' Gate: America in Iraq* (New York: Farrar, Straus and Giroux, 2005), 186–87.

65. Larry Diamond, "What Went Wrong in Iraq," *Foreign Affairs* 83:5 (September/October 2004), with text archived at http://www.mtholyoke.edu/acad/intrel/iraq/diamond.htm.

66. "Bremer Will Reject Islam as Source for Law," *Associated Press*, February 16, 2004, http://www.msnbc.msn.com/id/4276149/.

67. Ahmed S. Hashim, *Insurgency and Counter-Insurgency in Iraq* (Ithaca, NY: Cornell University Press, 2006), 245.

68. Rajiv Chandrasekaran, *Imperial Life in the Emerald* City (New York: Alfred A. Knopf, 2007), 186.

69. "Bremer Reaches Out to Iraqi Shiite Heartland," *Agence France Presse*, July 9, 2003.

70. A copy of the *fatwa* is available in Feldman, 140.

71. Vali Nasr, *Forces of Fortune: The Rise of the New Muslim Middle Class and What It Will Mean for Our World* (New York: Free Press, 2009), 170.

72. Juan Cole, "Shiite Religious Parties Fill Vacuum in Southern Iraq," *Middle East Report Online*, April 22, 2003, http://www.merip.org/mero/mero042203.html.

73. Packard, *Assassins' Gate*, 168.

74. Lawrence Rothfield, *The Rape of Mesopotamia* (Chicago, IL: University of Chicago Press, 2009), 103.

75. Michael Hirsch, "Grim Numbers," *Newsweek*, June 15, 2004, http://www.newsweek.com/id/53862.

76. "Governing Council President Meets Iraq's Top Shiite Cleric," *Agence France Presse*, August 6, 2003.

77. Chandrasekaran, *Imperial Life*, 205.

78. Bremer, 283.

79. Chandrasekaran, "How Cleric Trumped," op. cit.; Chandrasekaran, *Imperial Life*, 186–87.

80. Chandrasekaran, *Imperial Life*, 190.

81. Kirk Troy, "Iraqi Ayatollah al-Sistani Exerts Powerful Influence in Shaping New Government," *Voice of America*, February 25, 2004. Cited at http://payvand.com/news/04/feb/1185.html.

82. Howard La Franchi, "US Seeks Global Aid for Iraq," *Christian Science Monitor*, January 21, 2004, 1.

83. Feldman, 36.

84. Feldman, 42.

85. Chandrasekaran, *Imperial Life*, 198.

86. Chandrasekaran, "How Cleric Trumped," op. cit.

87. Bremer, 272.

88. Chesterman, 110.

89. Brian Uruqhart, "New Demands and Old Constraints: The Role of the United Nations in the International System," *Brown Journal of International Affairs*, 11:1 (Summer/Fall 2004), 228.

90. See "ARABS-UN—Feb. 12—Brahimi Meets Sistani," *APS Diplomat Recorder*, February 14, 2004.

91. Troy, "Iraqi Ayatollah," op. cit.

92. ibid, 296.

93. Rod Nordland and Babak Dehghanpisheh, "What Sistani Wants," *Newsweek*, February 14, 2005, http://www.newsweek.com/id/48896/page/1.

94. Bremer, 302–06.

95. Reuel Marc Gerecht, "Democratic Revolution in Iraq?" *AEI Outlooks and On the Issues*, June 21, 2004, http://www.aei.org/issue/20774.

96. Packer, *Assassins' Gate*, 439.

97. This report was largely ignored by the Department of Defense and has come under criticism for not providing concrete blueprints for action. Nevertheless, many CPA officials later found the project to be of use, with one describing it as "our Bible coming out here." See the reactions to the project at "New State Department Releases on the 'Future of Iraq' Project," *National Security Archive*, September 1, 2006, http://www.gwu.edu/~nsarchiv/NSAEBB/NSAEBB198/index.htm.

98. "The Future of Iraq: The Iraqi Component." It should be noted that the redacted version of the report takes the section dealing with Khoi and Uloum and notes, "Too soon to start naming candidates." A copy of the report can be found at http://www.gwu.edu/~nsarchiv/NSAEBB/NSAEBB198/20020005.pdf.

99. We can see this in differing understandings of what constituted "democracy." Bremer told the Governing Council during its meeting of November 6, 2003 that "democracy is majority rule with protection of minority rights." For many of the Shi'a clergy, democracy was the mechanism for transforming Shi'a majoritarianism into control of Iraq's government. Bremer, 213.

100. Testimony of Larry Diamond, "Iraq's Transition: The Way Ahead," Senate Foreign Relations Committee, 108th Congress (2nd session), May 19, 2004, http://www.au.af.mil/ay/awc/awcgate/congress/040519diamond.pdf.

101. Etzioni, *Security First*, 30.

102. Etzioni, *From Empire to Community*, 80.

103. "Grand Ayatollah Ali Sistani rejects SOFA," *UPI*, July 8, 2008, http://www.upi.com/Emerging_Threats/2008/07/08/Grand-Ayatollah-Ali-Sistani-rejects-SOFA/UPI-69541215548391/#ixzz2xl3kny8y.

104. Mary Beth Sheridan, "Iraq Head, Top Cleric Back 2011 Exit by U.S.," *Washington Post*, November 16, 2008, http://www.washingtonpost.com/wp-dyn/content/article/2008/11/15/AR2008111500679_pf.html.

105. See Nikolas K. Gvosdev, "Mosque and State," *The National Interest*, May 14, 2010, http://nationalinterest.org/commentary/mosque-and-state-3598.

106. Gary Owen, "The Real Reason the US Military Was So Secretive About Afghanistan," *Vice News*, February 2, 2015, https://news.vice.com/article/the-real-reason-the-us-military-is-suddenly-so-secretive-about-afghanistan.

107. Alan Taylor, "Afghanistan, February 2013: Anti-Taliban Militias," *The Atlantic*, March 6, 2013, http://www.theatlantic.com/photo/2013/03/afghanistan-february-2013-anti-taliban-militias/100468/.

108. Borzou Daragahi, "The Front-Line Fight Against Isis," *FT Magazine*, March 6, 2015, http://www.ft.com/cms/s/0/cfe12b08-c2ae-11e4-a59c-00144feab7de.html#axzz3Tcn29cZy.

109. Amitai Etzioni, "Plan Z for Iraq," *The National Interest* 92 (November/December 2007), 44.

110. Hall Gardner, *Averting Global War: Regional Challenges, Overextension, and Options for American Security* (New York: Palgrave Macmillan, 2007), 269.

111. See, for instance, Zachary Keck, "History's Judgment: The Iraq Surged Failed," *The Diplomat*, June 13, 2014, http://thediplomat.com/2014/06/historys-judgment-the-iraq-surge-failed/.

112. Etzioni, "Bottom Up Nation Building," op. cit.

113. Etzioni, *Hot Spots*, 146–47.
114. Etzioni, "Bottom Up Nation Building," op. cit.
115. Testimony before the Senate Foreign Relations Committee, September 17, 2009, http://www.foreign.senate.gov/imo/media/doc/LockhartTestimony090917a1.pdf.
116. Etzioni, *Security First*, 52.
117. In Afghanistan, for instance, consistent reporting suggests that most Afghans view the central government as "weak, corrupt, and unresponsive to [the] core needs" of the population. Cited in Robert McMahon, "The Brave New World of Democracy Promotion," *Foreign Service Journal*, January 2009, 35.
118. Howard J. Wiarda, *Cracks in the Consensus: Debating the Democracy Agenda in U.S. Foreign Policy* (Washington, DC: CSIS, 1997), 47.
119. Etzioni, "Bottom Up Nation Building," op. cit.
120. Wiarda, 35, 44, 47.
121. Etzioni, "Bottom Up Nation Building," op. cit.
122. Etzioni, *Security First*, 173.
123. See, for instance, the discussion in Nathan Pino and Michael D. Wiatrowski, "Implementing Democratic Policing and Related Initiatives," *Democratic Policing in Transitional and Developing Countries*, eds. Nathan Pino and Michael D. Wiatrowski (Aldershot: Ashgate, 2006), 122.
124. Stephen Schwartz, "Partition Iraq? No," *The Weekly Standard*, June 19, 2007, http://www.weeklystandard.com/Content/Public/Articles/000/000/013/793qobod.asp?page=1.
125. James W. Riley, "Break Up to Make Up," *National Interest*, June 19, 2007, http://nationalinterest.org/commentary/break-up-to-make-up-1633.
126. Wiarda, 48.
127. Gian Gentile, "America's Nation-Building at Gunpoint," *Los Angeles Times*, August 13, 2013, http://articles.latimes.com/2013/aug/13/opinion/la-oe-gentile-army-colonel-gives-iraq-and-afghanis-20130813.
128. Barah Mikail, "Avoiding Iraq's fragmentation," *Open Democracy*, June 18, 2014, http://www.washingtonpost.com/world/afghanistans-new-president-hold-me-accountable/2014/09/29/0f229a14-47c0-11e4-b72e-d60a9229cc10_story.html. https://www.opendemocracy.net/arab-awakening/barah-mikail/avoiding-iraq%E2%80%99s-fragmentation; Sudarsan Raghavan, "Ghani, Abdullah Sworn in as Part of Afghanistan's Power-Sharing Arrangement," *Washington Post*, September 29, 2014.
129. Etzioni, *From Empire to Community*, 187.
130. Henry R. Nau, *Perspectives on International Relations: Power, Institutions, and Ideas* (Washington, DC: CQ Press, 2015), 476.
131. Tony Smith, "Wilsonianism After Iraq: The End of Liberal Internationalism?" *The Crisis of American Foreign Policy: Wilsonianism in the Twenty-first Century*, eds. G. John Ikenberry, Thomas J. Knock, Anne-Marie Slaughter, and Tony Smith (Princeton, NJ: Princeton University Press, 2009), 60.
132. Madeleine K. Albright, "Sustaining Democracy in the Twenty-First Century," The Rostov Lecture Series, School of Advanced International Studies, Johns Hopkins University, Washington, DC, January 18, 2000, http://www.state.gov/1997-2001-NOPDFS/statements/2000/000118.html.
133. Mike Bowker, *Russia, America and the Islamic World* (Aldershot, Hampshire: Ashgate Publishing, 2007), 140.

134. Aidan Hehir and Eric A. Heinze, "The Responsibility to Protect: 'Never Again!' for the Twenty-First Century?" *Human Rights, Human Security, and State Security: The Intersection*, ed. Saul Takahashi (Santa Barbara, CA: ABC-CLIO, 2014), 18.

135. Arthur A. Stein, "Incentive Compatibility and Global Governance: Existential Multilateralism, a Weakly Confederal World, and Hegemony," *Can the World be Governed?: Possibilities for Effective Multilateralism*, ed. Alan S. Alexandroff (Waterloo, Ontario: Centre for International Government Innovation and Wilfrid Laurier University Press, 2008), 74.

136. Edward R. McMahon and Scott H. Baker, *Piecing a Democratic Quilt?: Regional Organizations and Universal Norms* (Bloomfield, CT: Kumarian Press, 2006), 28–29.

137. Etzioni, *Political Reunification Revisited*, 27.

138. McMahon, 37, 38.

139. George Modelski, "Preventing Global War," *The Ashgate Research Companion to War: Origins and Prevention*, eds. Hall Gardner and Oleg Kobtzeff (Farnham, Surrey: Ashgate Publishing, 2012), 607.

140. James M. Lindsay, "The Case for a Concert of Democracies," *Ethics & International Affairs* 23:1 (Spring 2009), https://www.carnegiecouncil.org/publications/journal/23_1/roundtable/002/.

141. Stein, 74.

142. Modelski, 607.

143. Charles A. Kupchan, "Minor League, Major Problems: The Case Against a League of Democracies," *Foreign Affairs* 87:6 (November/December 2008), 97.

144. Taras Kuzio and Sergei Blagov, "GUUAM Makes Comeback Bid With US Support," *Eurasianet.org*, July 7, 2003, http://www.eurasianet.org/departments/insight/articles/eav070703.shtml.

145. Alexander Nikitin and Marc Loucas, "Peace Support in the New Independent States Different From the Rest," *Peace Operations: Trends, Progress and Prospects*, ed. Donald F. C. Daniel (Washington, DC: Georgetown University Press, 2008), 246.

146. Etzioni, *Political Unification Revisited*, 26.

147. Janusz Bugajski, *Dismantling the West: Russia's Atlantic Agenda* (Washington, DC: Potomac Books, 2009), 84.

148. Kornely Kakachia, "The Ukraine Crisis: Repercussions for Georgia," *PONARS Eurasia Policy Memo* 349 (September 2014), 2; see also Taras Kuzio, "GUAM as a Regional and Security Organisation," National Security and Foreign Policy of Azerbaijan Conference, St. Michael's College, University of Toronto, March 28, 2008, http://www.taraskuzio.net/conferences2_files/GUAM_Azerbaijan.pdf.

149. Tatiana Zhurzhenko, *Borderlands into Bordered Lands: Geopolitics of Identity in Post-Soviet Ukraine* (Stuttgart, Germany: ibidem Press, 2014), 72–73.

150. Bugajski, 84, Zhurzhenko, 72.

151. Kakachia, 4.

152. Robert Kagan, "The Case for a League of Democracies," *Financial Times*, May 13, 2008, at http://www.ft.com/cms/s/0/f62a02ce-20eb-11dd-a0e6-000077b07658.html#ixzz3RmUj32UA.

153. Nikolas K. Gvosdev, "NATO is Regional for a Reason," *Atlantic-Community. org*, September 21, 2007, http://www.atlantic-community.org/app/index. php/Open_Think_Tank_Article/NATO_Is_Regional_For_A_Reason.
154. Kupchan, 102.
155. Etzioni, *Political Unification Revisited*, 28.
156. ibid, 302.
157. According to Etzioni, a transnational group or political union will command greater loyalty and exercise more authority as the level and scope of integration increases. Etzioni, *Political Unification Revisited*, 94.
158. Etzioni, *Hot Spots*, 199.
159. Kupchan, 107.
160. Etzioni, *From Empire to Community*, 187.
161. Joseph S. Nye, "The Iraq War Ten Years Later," *Project Syndicate*, March 11, 2013, http://www.project-syndicate.org/commentary/the-iraq-war-ten-years-later-by-joseph-s--nye.
162. Etzioni, *Security First*, 245.
163. ibid, 248.

8

Hot Spots: Meeting the Challenges of the Twenty-First Century

As Amitai Etzioni looks at the current international landscape, he is not confident that current trends, if left unaddressed, will lead the world to greater peace and stability. States are coming under increasing pressure, and new disruptive technologies and capabilities are being diffused beyond governments into the hands of nonstate actors. A series of what he defines as "hot spots" are emerging to challenge the status quo; these could imperil the global economic system upon which the prosperity and security of so many nations now depends. At the same time, the traditional arrangements upon which the United States has relied to manage global and regional disorder are breaking down.[1] In his assessment, Etzioni is joined by others—the Skoll Global Threats Fund, for instance, has identified five principal challenges to the global order that require concerted international effort to be solved or the mitigation of their consequences. These challenges are: "nuclear proliferation, Middle East conflict, climate change, water scarcity, and pandemics."[2]

In particular, the United States has depended on a close partnership with the nations of the European Union in order to help maintain an international system that provides for easy communication, free trade, and security that is resilient enough to contain these problems. First, a strong trans-Atlantic relationship has enabled the United States and Europe to set the global agenda, particular in international institutions, and to cooperate in providing security for the global commons— "those spaces no nation controls but on which all rely for security and prosperity."[3] Europe has been the traditional comanager, with the United States, of key global organizations (such as international financial institutions), and collectively the two countries have worked to set universal standards and norms.[4] Second, the United States has worked to contain instability in the Middle East from spilling out into the larger global environment, and to ensure that there is unimpeded access to the vital energy resources of the region. To accomplish this, Washington relied on a network of partnerships with Israel, Sunni Arab monarchies, and a series of presidential dictatorships to define the regional security architecture.[5] US alliances in Asia, together with China's traditional inward focus on its own modernization, allowed the West to generally set the agenda for both regional and international issues without facing serious and sustained objections.[6]

In 2015, however, all of these arrangements are under pressure. The Arab Spring has upended the traditional balances in the Middle East and is releasing pent-up forces that were kept bottled up and under control for decades. Indeed, the Middle East is now on a trajectory to become an exporter of instability for decades to come.[7] The European project is under major strain, calling into question whether an effective trans-Atlantic partnership can continue to define the global agenda. Moreover, America's European allies are increasingly not maintaining the capabilities that enabled them to work with the United States in helping to secure the global commons.[8] At the same time, China's rise is presenting more robust challenges to a Western-defined international order and its rules. As Europe falters, can a rising China take its place as a coguarantor of the current global system, especially when it has shown that it remains "quite content with the U.S. bearing the costs and risks of building stable governments in the Middle East, securing the flow of oil, and otherwise managing the global commons."[9] Finally, the United States is under intense pressure to reduce its budgetary outlays, particularly in the areas of defense and national-security spending, and to proceed with cuts even if other states do not guarantee that they will fill in any gaps that may open.[10]

At the same time, as a result of globalization, the security and prosperity of almost all countries (with the few exceptions of those who have attempted to cut themselves off from intercourse with the larger world) is now dependent on a series of transnational economic, security, and political networks that transfer capital, technology, know-how, goods, and services across borders.[11] (Generally, the global commons are understood to encompass "the maritime, outer space, and cyber-space domains, which carry the flows of goods, data, capital, people, and ideas on which globalization rests.")[12] A much higher percentage of both American and Chinese gross domestic product (GDP) is now generated as a result of cross-border commerce and interaction than was true even thirty years ago. Some 45 percent of global GDP in total is generated from international trade.[13] More than 90 percent of global trade, in turn, is carried out in the maritime domain, which requires guarantees that shipping lanes can be kept open and safe for transit.[14] Air travel, space systems, and cyberspace are also important parts of the web of connectivity that binds nations together and permits the flow of ideas, technologies, and capital. Yet, while these networks have come to be of vital importance to nations around the world, they contain much vulnerability and their "fragile indefensibility imparts exceptionally high risk for nations and organizations."[15] For instance, a vast majority of the world's cybertraffic is carried on a series of undersea cables that, particularly at their entry points onto land, are quite vulnerable to accident or deliberate sabotage. A 2008 incident in which three of the fiber-optic cables that link Egypt to Italy (and thus connect Europe with the Middle East and South Asia) were cut disrupted connectivity and data access in a number of countries.[16] The persistence scourge of piracy—particularly around the Horn of Africa, the Straits of Malacca, and the Gulf of Guinea—has been estimated to cost the global economy between $7 billion and $12 billion per year and encompasses everything from losses and insurance costs to the detrimental impacts on local economies.[17] Finally, the rapid spread of disease facilitated by global networks means that the outbreak of a pandemic can negatively impact the labor forces of many countries while shutting down supply networks. Thus, some estimates predict that a pandemic, depending on its severity, could reduce global GDP by 2 percent to 6 percent.[18]

Yet, an increasing number of observers—some drawing on Etzioni's own work—are coming to the conclusion that current approaches to safeguarding the international system and the global commons are insufficient.[19] Reliance on US power to do the job is no longer an option, as the capabilities of other states rise and as the overall share of American power decreases.[20] In his analysis of the new global order, former CIA Director Michael Hayden echoes Etzioni's concerns about a series of multiple hot spots that cannot all simultaneously be contained by US. He highlights, in particular, three current trends. The first is what he calls the "new malevolence," and the threat posed by nonstate actors to the global commons by means of terrorism, transnational crime, and cyber challenges. The second trend is the "impermanence of things we thought permanent, such as the breakdown of existing architecture (and even some of the states) we have relied on in the past to manage global disorder. The third trend is the "perilous trajectory of

U.S.-China relations," and the fact that mismanagement of that relationship will imperil the global order.[21] These challenges are simultaneous and overlapping, which makes it impossible to prioritize power and attention at a time when the existing international system is breaking down. This diffusion of challenges concerns former National Security Advisor Brent Scowcroft, who worries about conditions being created for drift and disorder within the international system.[22]

One option for dealing with the reality of this "new global disorder" is to trust that states and other organizations that depend equally on the global commons will voluntarily restrain any of their own activities that might damage those fragile networks and domains, and will be prepared to take action to neutralize other threats that might emerge.[23] This requires a good deal of faith in the willingness of countries and of nonstate actors to take those steps out of a sense of shared responsibility, and to entrust a significant amount of their economic and military security to the belief that others will do the "right" thing. Yet, it does not seem prudent that decision makers will accept major risks arising out of the vulnerability of the current global networks as an operating principle of their national security strategy. This reluctance increases the incentive for states to free ride on the assumption that another country will step up to take on the responsibilities of keeping the system functioning.[24] So far, because major disasters have been avoided, there has been no pronounced push for stronger international cooperation to address these issues, not even on the same level as emerged after 9/11. Yet, as Joseph Nye has pointed out, these challenges "can do damage on a scale represented by a terrorist use of a weapon of mass destruction," and the impacts can be mitigated only by closer international cooperation.[25] However, as a recent Carnegie Europe report concluded, the problem is that "interdependence is racing far ahead of national and global governance."[26]

Will the European Union Snap Back?

Much of the assessment of the coming global disorder is based on predictions that the European Union is faltering. Some believe that it cannot live up to its early promise of knitting together the states of Europe into a transnational association that would be the equivalent of a superpower—in terms not only of its economic potential, but its ability to wield military and diplomatic power and to then effectively partner with the United States to maintain the existing system. Others have argued that a rejuvenation of the European project might yet occur, and that this, in turn, would revitalize the Euro-Atlantic pillar as a "dissuading force against transnational coercion and disorder."[27] In this scenario, Europe would (1) assume its place as the world's "second superpower"; (2) be able to undertake a "division of labor" with the United States for each to defend and extend zones of order and prosperity around the world; and (3) in tandem with America's formidable military capabilities, deploy its cadres to improve health and development around the world.[28] Once the European Union came through the current crisis, it would be able to take the lead in dealing with some of these issues.

Etzioni is not confident that this vision can be realized. He notes "that if the EU is unable to engage in much stronger community-building—if there is no significant transfer of commitment and loyalty from the citizens of the member nations to the evolving supranational community—the EU will be unable to sustain the kind of encompassing state-like shared governance endeavor it attempts to advance."[29] In other words, the EU grew too quickly and did not generate a sufficient sense of community among its constituent parts to sustain its political claims. This development has not been helped by the tendency of EU institutions to meddle "in a lot of matters better left to the Member States themselves."[30] Etzioni credits the fall in support among the populations of many European countries to a deepening European integration and the growing divergence of the European Union-level elite from the national societies of its member-states.[31] This reinforces predictions made by the late Samuel Huntington of a growing gap that would emerge between a national population and a transnationally focused elite.[32]

Former Danish Prime Minister Per Stig Moller agrees with Etzioni's diagnosis. Etzioni argues that because the first steps in the creation of the EU brought clear benefits to the citizens of the member-states, there was a greater willingness to accept or at least tolerate EU institutions.[33] Now, with the European economy "stuck in a coma," these institutions are not able to generate the growth that helps to give legitimacy to the claims of the EU. This has been the catalyst for the rise of parties and political movements that either wants to get out the EU altogether put a halt to its further development. Speaking to Etzioni's point about community-building, Moller laments that growing numbers of young people are disillusioned with the European project and do not feel engaged in Europe.[34] Similarly, despite the stabilization of the global economy and the international system that has occurred since the crisis of 2008–09, Thierry de Montbrial, the president of the French Institute of International Relations, sees increased skepticism on the part of the citizens of EU member-states about its value. This, along with rising nationalism and continued problems that threaten the viability of the single currency, impacts Europe's ability to function as a dynamic player in the world community.[35]

None of this means that the European Union is on the verge of dissolution. But, as Etzioni predicts, the "EU is more likely to scale back" and "retreat to being only a free trade zone enriched by numerous legal and administrative shared arrangements."[36] In other words, Europe would remain a single market, with those administrative and legal institutions necessary to keep that market functional—but it would not become a society.[37] This would make it much harder to fulfill the ambitious vision of the EU as the world's second superpower, helping to underwrite the global order to. Moreover, the temptation is rising for European states to retreat to a "Fortress Europe," and to disengage from an ambitious effort at projecting a common foreign policy.[38]

Moller raises a second issue—that of Europe's ability to contribute to its own security.[39] In the past, the reigning assumption of US national security planners was that Europe faced no internal threats to its well-being, and so could cooperate with the United States to extend a security zone across a wider portion of the globe. In addition, planners believed that the United States could deal with pressures to cut its own defense budget by reducing its commitments to Europe in favor of the rebalance to the Asia-Pacific.[40] Those assumptions are now being challenged by recent developments in Europe and the Middle East, which suggest that even as the United States enters into a new age of budget austerity, it will have to deploy a set of scarcer resources back to areas of the world that it assumed were quiet and secure.[41]

For all of these reasons, even those who are strong proponents of the notion of a revitalized trans-Atlantic partnership taking the lead in securing the global commons and the international order acknowledge "that the traditional model of the EU and the United States acting as Western stewards of global order is reaching its limits."[42] The rising tide of nationalism within the EU countries that Etzioni has charted will make these governments more inward-looking and less likely to embrace the commitments and the sacrifices needed to sustain the global order. As European states cut back on the checks they are willing to write to pay for global public goods, there is no guarantee that the United States will pick up the shortfall.

Pragmatism in the Midst of Middle Eastern Turmoil

One of the reasons Moller identifies for the pullback in the interests of European states to contribute to globally defined missions in favor of defending their borders has been the aftereffects of the Arab Spring— the breakdown of the old regimes that kept order, that limited migration flows across the Mediterranean, and that cracked down on radical movements. Rising instability in the greater Middle East, including the very real possibility of state collapse, jeopardizes global economic and political security since the region still remains "the world's most important source of energy and the key to the stability of the global economy."[43] Hopes that there would be a rapid consolidation of new regimes once the initial revolutionary wave passed have given way to the sinking realization that the "Middle East . . . has entered a period of extreme instability that will surely have negative economic impacts both regionally and globally."[44]

In particular, the old regimes that could deploy a successful mix of coercive and utilitarian power to contain and channel unrest have found those resources to be both more limited and less effective. Moreover, the ability of outside powers to fund these efforts have begun to run short.[45] Large amounts of US aid were sent to Hosni Mubarak's regime in Egypt, in part to gain the government's support for the peace treaty with Israel and to continue security cooperation between Cairo and Washington. Yet, the steady increase in food prices, with aid levels unable to keep up, helped to fuel popular anger at the government and to encourage people to support the protests in 2011.[46] Ironically, the last major spike in food prices was the proverbial straw that broke the backs of the governments in Tunisia and Egypt and that led to protests throughout the region. This spike was due to two occurrences. The first was a major drought in China and less than optimal weather conditions in Russia and Canada, which in turn led to greater pressure on wheat supplies. The second was the growing demand for energy on the part of the rising powers, which impacted both the price of fertilizers, and, more importantly, saw a steady diversion of agricultural products into biofuel production.[47]

With global energy prices now dropping, the oil producers of the region have less income to spend to continue to bribe restive populations in their own countries, or to prop up friendly regimes among their neighbors. Moreover, as Etzioni himself noted, there is no prospect of a massive reconstruction package for the region along the lines of the post-World War II Marshall Plan that jump-started the economies of Western Europe, in part because of continued pressures for budget austerity in the West.[48] If this is the case, the United States and its allies can no longer rely on utilitarian power to ensure some degree of compliance with the needs of the international order. As Ambassador Murat Özçelik, who served as Turkey's special envoy to Iraq has noted, the focal point of efforts must shift to prophylactic measures designed to seal off the trouble spots of the region while trying to mitigate the consequences of fighting and conflict: "The immediate objective for the Western and regional actors should be to block the mobility of jihadists, degrade their fighting capability, and facilitate humanitarian efforts."[49] This task is made more significant by the partial disintegration of the Iraqi and Syrian states, and with it, the creation of zones where groups like the Islamic State can control territory, access revenue streams, and enjoy safe havens. In turn, this attracts supporters from all over the world: dozens of Chinese citizens have found their way to Iraq to join the jihad,[50] while groups like Boko Haram in West Africa have pledged their allegiance to the Islamic State.[51] The challenge facing the United States is how to ensure that the resources of the Middle East upon which the "international trading system and the global economy are largely dependent" can continue to flow, while finding ways to contain and isolate the regional sources of instability from destabilizing the rest of the world.[52] This is why Ambassador Özçelik advises the United States and its allies to adopt a pragmatic approach to the region that emphasizes long-term sustainability.[53]

Meanwhile, the Chinese approach (mirrored by some of the other rising powers) is to concentrate on a different sort of pragmatic politics. The approach taken emphasizes economics over politics, and signals that Beijing is willing to offer utilitarian power (markets, loans, investment, technology, and even weapons) to any state in the region that is, in turn, prepared to be responsive to Chinese interests. Indeed, observers are struck by China's pragmatic stance of being prepared not only to deal with every country in the Middle East but also to reach out to different factions within states as part of this effort to make connections to safeguard China's equities.[54] To some extent, the Chinese have adopted Etzioni's recommendations to be prepared to deal even with theocratic factions, and do not have any ideological limitations that prevent them from developing close ties with all sorts of governments as long as they show that they can keep order.

Yet both approaches remain reactive to developments in the Middle East. Etzioni would prefer a more proactive stance toward the region's hot spots, especially since there have already been several warning eruptions indicating that there could still be a massive explosion. This would have profound negative consequences for the international order.[55] Etzioni has proposed greater involvement in and management of problems in this region. These proposals include the deployment of effective peace-enforcement forces at several trigger points to help provide security guarantees, and the willingness to develop and enforce a great power consensus on the Iranian nuclear program that could address Iran's legitimate national security concerns but also reassure neighbors who are concerned about its efforts to expand its influence.[56] Yet, Etzioni's proposals do not resonate. There seems to be little enthusiasm, at present, for a desire on the part of the United States to make China a coequal guarantor of Middle Eastern stability, or for Beijing to even want to take on such commitments. Indeed, China's State Council has yet to issue any sort of "White Paper" that would encapsulate a strategy toward the Middle East.[57] China has indicated a willingness to play a more involved role in the region only when US action (or the lack thereof) threatens core Chinese economic interests. Beijing sent its own vessels to carry out antipiracy operations off the coast of Somalia to supply drones to both the Iraqi central government and the Kurdish regional government in their struggle against the Islamic State. This decision indicates a preference for complementing rather than supplementing Western activity, with the United States still expected to take on the lion's share of the burden in stabilizing the region.[58] But there is nothing that suggests efforts at closer coordination among the United States, Europe, China, and other key powers in support of a common strategy for preventing instability from the Middle East from spilling over and negatively impacting the global system.

This is especially clear when considering what steps have been taken to prepare for the worst-case scenarios surrounding what Etzioni describes as "the hottest spot" in his constellation of problems that beset the world. He refers here to the future of Pakistan, especially the risk of state weakness or even collapse, which would open up its nuclear arsenal to being seized by extremist and even terrorist organizations.[59] Yet, in the context of its ongoing strategic conversations with the United States, China has been quite reluctant to "engage in open, extensive dialogue and cooperation with the United States on Pakistan, perhaps for fear of alienating allies in Islamabad or appearing aligned to the (often unpopular) Americans." Western worries have been expressed by Etzioni, by Daniel Markey, and by others about the chances that Pakistan could become a failed state, and there has been a corresponding push to try to place its nuclear weapons under reliable control. This contrasts with what appears to be an almost "cavalier" Chinese "lack of concern about the potential for terrorist attacks and unauthorized access to radioactive materials" that might result if there were to be a loss of control over that force.[60] Even with the increased instability in the region, there appears to be no consensus around the advisability of considering a concerted international effort to engage in forcible and verifiable deproliferation should there be the prospect of state failure in Pakistan.

Securing the Global Commons: A Central Organizing Principle?

A wait-and-see approach to coping with possible contingencies arising from a major shock in the Middle East may be understandable, but leaving the infrastructure of the global commons vulnerable to disruption seems to be needlessly inviting a major risk. In theory, the rising powers have critical incentives to join with the West in maintaining the current system. As Li Yan has observed:

> A fundamental interest is to maintain secure, open and stable access. For cyber security issues, both have to deal with problems like hackers, cyber terrorism and cyber crime. In outer space, maintaining non-militarization and dealing with space trash are of mutual interest. For the maritime common, both countries need to confront threats from pirates, and they have already collaborated in doing so in the Gulf of Aden.[61]

Indeed, Henry Kissinger has expressed confidence that dealing with this set of common issues could lay the foundations upon which a much improved Sino-American relationship could be built—specifically highlighting energy, the environment, and proliferation as three of the main issues where Chinese-American collaboration will be critical.[62]

There have been some promising beginnings. The Proliferation Security Initiative and the antipiracy mission in the Indian Ocean demonstrate that, when faced with a common threat that negatively impacts the security and prosperity of many states, it is possible to forge effective transnational collaboration to address the problem. Regional responses to pandemics and extremist activity on the part of the members of Association of Asian Southeast Nations (ASEAN), working not only among themselves but also with China, the United States, Korea, Japan, and Australia, show that even states that are very jealous of their sovereign prerogatives can find mechanisms for collective action.

Yet, in tackling the larger questions of the global commons—and the type of international order that is needed to sustain them—there is much less commonality, in both identifying the problems and agreeing upon what constitutes acceptable risk and adequate solutions.[63] Moreover, it can be difficult to determine what constitutes equitable concessions and sacrifices that different countries ought to make in support of a common effort, whether it is in cutting greenhouse gas emissions or contributing forces and funds for peacekeeping and peace-enforcement missions.[64] A perennial suspicion of China, India, and other rising powers, for instance, is that efforts to promulgate universal standards are ways for the West to lock in its advantages and to hold them back.[65]

The first option for moving forward—either that China and other rising powers will simply adopt *in toto* Western standards and agree to fund Western initiatives at the levels the West finds acceptable, or that they can be compelled to do so—is not practical nor likely.[66] Indeed, when the European Union proposed that the Council of Europe's "Convention on Cybercrime" set the global standard for identifying and defining such behavior, China and Russia promptly countered with the standards in use by the Shanghai Cooperation Organization, while other countries like Brazil and India flatly refused to even consider this proposal on the grounds that the European standards had been formulated without any input from or consultation with states from the global South.[67] In addition, many of the existing negotiations on issues dealing with the global commons and the international order use a binary format that does not leave much room for third-way options: proposals are advanced as total packages and generally reflect the interests of specific sectors of the global economy or regions of the world. This has solidified, rather than ameliorated, some of the gaps between the global North and West versus the global South and East, and has made it that much harder to reach agreement on setting binding rules and standards for issues pertaining to the global commons and the international system.[68]

This leaves dialogue as the only feasible option. Such a dialogue would need to have two main components. The first would be to discuss a formula for burden-sharing that would require China (and other rising powers) to contribute far more than would be their preference. Nina Hachigian, who now serves as the US ambassador to ASEAN, has observed that even if the West remains wealthier (on a per capita basis), it is the rising powers—with China in the lead—that increasingly has the capacity and resources.[69] The second component, as Yuan Peng, director of the Institute for American Studies at the China Institutes of Contemporary International Relations, lays it out, would be the discussion on how China, the United States, and other major powers jointly would reshape the international order and set down new rules for governing the commons.[70] This would have to be a dialogue—a joint effort with give and take—not a monologue defined to impose a set of predrafted Western rules. This call for dialogue, taken straight from the Etzioni playbook, has also been endorsed by other observers of global governance issues. Stewart Patrick, who served on the State Department's Policy Planning staff during the Bush administration, with particular oversight for these issues, has called for "the United States to forge agreement among like-minded nations, rising powers, and private stakeholders on new rules of the road" to lead not to a perfect solution but "good enough" global governance.[71]

The goal would have to be, as G. John Ikenberry pointed out in his debate with Etzioni about the future of global rules in the twenty-first century, to find "ways for states to navigate the turbulent waters of economic and security interdependence."[72] The problem is that when it comes to the global commons, different powers have different perspectives, advantages, capabilities, and interests, which makes the search for "common rules" more difficult.[73] The United States is committed to maintaining open access to maritime, cyber, and space domains, and so looks for ways to regulate or limit the acquisition of capabilities by others that could be used to impede access. Other countries, beginning with China, remain reluctant to cede so much trust that the United States will not seek to use its preexisting advantages in the commons to negatively impact their interests; Washington is not inclined to accept limits on its freedom of maneuver.[74] There is also a critical ideological divide. Neo-Westphalian states like Russia and China want access to the commons, particularly the cyber domain, to run clearly through nodes controlled and policed by the nation-state. They also worry about the disruptive impact of the new technologies on the social orders they have created.[75] The West wants the commons to promote the free flow of goods, services, and ideas. However, it also charges some of the rising powers with attempting to subvert the open nature of the commons in order to gain national advantages (whether it be relying on cyberespionage or advancing claims to significant portions of the undersea shelf and offshore maritime domain).[76] In essence, the United States feels threatened by the efforts of other powers to develop the systems that challenge America's ability to manage the commons.[77] At the same time, rising powers like China feel threatened by the continuing American dominance of the commons, which they see as a threat to their security.[78] The claim of the United States that it is seeking to keep the global commons open is, in turn, interpreted by China and others as an American attempt to exercise control over the commons.[79] Thus, as Frédéric Ramel concluded:

> The security dilemma in terms of the global commons comes from the perception of the possibility to access them (or not). The motivation comes from the fact that these spaces are vital for States to function, or to cite Rousseau, for their "political bodies", irrespective of the nature of the regime. The United States, Russia and China draw elements from these spaces that are fundamental to their own economic development, i.e. vital for the functioning of the political body itself.[80]

As Li Yan has noted, this reality should serve as a driver for "the formulation of international 'norms', or practices, related to the global commons. The lack of norms in cyberspace and outer space is partly responsible for the mutual insecurity and suspicion on both sides. So it is imperative to formulate governance systems acceptable to the international community to regulate the behaviors of all nations."[81] Li's proposals echo Etzioni's own call for sustained diplomatic engagement to define such "new international rules."[82] Etzioni believes, for instance, that in terms of developing an effective code of mutual conduct in cyberspace, that the "International Code of Conduct" submitted by China, Russia, Tajikistan, and Uzbekistan to the UN General Assembly in September 2011 might serve as the basis for such a dialogue. As some Chinese interlocutors have suggested, this might be augmented by incorporating well points found in the Tallinn Manual developed by Western experts working under the auspices of the NATO Cooperative Cyber Defense Center of Excellence.[83] Even given the very clear flaws of the Chinese-Russian-Tajik-Uzbek proposal, echoing Etzioni, other observers urge the United States to utilize this opening, since it demonstrates that "China agrees that international rules for cybersecurity concerns are desirable, and ... appears willing to facilitate international cooperation in setting new rules for cyber security."[84]

293

When it comes to issues of the global commons, Etzioni's advice is to look for accommodation—a solution "that satisfies the interests of both parties."[85] To escape the security dilemma Ramel identified, reassurance through verifiable and binding restraint would be the best option. This would include: (1) transparency in ship and plane deployments and in space launches; (2) limits (or even bans) on different types of antiaccess and cyber weaponry; and (3) guarantees that, in return for unimpeded access for merchant shipping to coastal maritime zones or the free and secure flow of information along the Internet, countries would not send military or intelligence vessels along those same routes or push for regime change.[86]

The main stumbling block, however, is that many nations—especially the United States—do not have "a clear understanding of what kind of international legal regime" that would govern different domains of the global commons "would best serve their long-term national interests."[87] Neither the Chinese nor the Russians, for instance, have shown a willingness to quietly accept international legal precedents that might question their claims to parts of the Arctic or the South China Sea, for instance.[88]

The cyber issue raises additional problems. When it comes to cyberattacks, there have been enormous improvements in forensics that allow for a greater chance that the ultimate source of an attack or disruption can be traced and identified. However, there is still sufficient murkiness in being able to assign unimpeachable responsibility that it "raises significant doubts about whether the international community can effectively enforce cyber-security treaties" and that, in the absence of countries willing to create "an enforcement system that features an elite professional staff, cutting-edge technology, and a robust international network," any treaty that is signed will be unenforceable.[89] Indeed, major powers may be quite unwilling to create the necessary enforcement provisions because of a desire to be able to retain the option to use cyberweapons as an alternative to being forced to employ more open and kinetic options.[90] This is why a number of legal experts have argued "that insufficient alignment of powerful nations' respective interests will prevent them from crafting an effective treaty on cyber security."[91] For countries like China or the United States, the question as to whether the utility of employing cyberattacks because of the intelligence gain or the ability to disrupt an adversary's plans is outweighed by the dependence on computer networks for running the country's economic and security infrastructure, and the vulnerability of those systems to attack.[92] When it comes to other new technologies that could be used for intelligence-gathering or for attack—including different types of drones—none of the major powers have shown much interest in any sort of preemptive ban on being able to deploy such systems.[93] However, the risk is run that a familiar pattern will be observed: the United States resists a formal, binding treaty that limits a US capability in the commons as long as the United States possesses an overwhelming advantage. This sets the stage for other countries to try to catch up and to eschew signing any agreements that might preclude their own efforts, and, in so doing, increases the risks to the global commons.[94] The lack of clear frameworks also increases the possibility for accidental clashes. This was discussed, in Chapter 3 of this book, with regard to disputes between Washington and Beijing over the freedom to navigate within the maritime areas claimed by China as part of its exclusive economic zones. The concern is that the absence of understandings and demarches that apply to other domains of the global commons runs the risk that the "red lines" of different countries will remain unclear and opaque and could lead to an unintended conflict.[95]

Most observers believe that a robust Sino-American bilateral dialogue on key issues related to the global commons would produce a consensus upon which a more multilateral architecture could be built that would, at the beginning, also encompass the European states, India, and Russia.[96] This led Robert Manning, a former senior counselor to Undersecretary of State Paula Dobriansky during the George W. Bush administration to propose that "for Sino-US ties, a step forward might be active dialogue on prioritizing strategic issues relating to the global commons. Both the US and China need open areas, such as online and in space, for their economies and militaries to function. Discussing codes of conduct makes sense."[97]

Given the problems with a treaty-based approach to regulating affairs in the global commons, the Obama administration has offered to explore the creation of nonbinding international codes of conduct that would help to establish norms.[98] Yet, the American preference for offering vague guarantees rather than considering binding and enforceable treaties runs up against a growing suspicion that the United States still seeks to preserve its advantages in order to be able to dominate other states. Vitaly Churkin, the ambassador of the Russian Federation to the United Nations, recently noted that the abrogation by the United States of the Anti-Ballistic Missile Treaty in 2001, and its replacement with a set of loose promises that the United States would not deploy any sort of ballistic missile defense that would negatively impact Russian security, has proven, from Moscow's point of view, to be unsatisfactory, and that this model would not be acceptable in other areas.[99] In turn, the apparent unwillingness of the United States to consider binding treaty language for banning capabilities that could be deployed in cyberspace or outer space reinforces the interpretation that the US aim is dominance over, rather than the securing of, the global commons.[100]

Chinese President Xi Jinping has signaled an interest in making progress with the Obama administration on these issues, by displaying an "openness to cooperative, rather than confrontational, steps forward toward shaping international . . . norms."[101] One area where dialogue among the United States, Europe, Russia, China, and other powers is becoming essential concerns the determination of what actions in the global commons, particularly in outer space and in the cyber realm, rise to the level of acts of war. James Lewis, in highlighting this as an area for possible discussion, notes: "This could be defined as any action that produced an effect equivalent to an armed attack using kinetic weapons. One fundamental question is whether a cyber exploit must produce physical damage and casualties to be regarded as the use of force or whether intangible damage can be considered a use of force and an act of war."[102] Indeed, Lewis takes a page from the gradualist approach: rather than approaching these issues in their entirety, he recommends breaking them apart into more discrete pieces, since "focused agreements on specific issues are more achievable."[103]

Moving forward, rather than any broad sweeping agreements, we are likely to see "incremental accumulation of customary international law resulting from the actions and statements of nations in response to events as they unfold."[104] A still-theoretical threat emanating from mismanagement of the global commons does not yet have enough power to motivate governments to take stronger action, especially when there are other more immediate pressing needs. Stewart Patrick concurs with his Lewis's recommendation "to lower expectations and start with the necessary and possible" in trying to forge codes of conduct for the commons.[105]

This may perhaps be the reason behind Etzioni's much more realistic assessment of the prospect of achieving any sort of wide-ranging international accord on combating climate change. An urgency to produce a comprehensive accord surrounded the December 2015 Paris climate conference. Yet, the environmental damage that is expected to be caused by pollution is still not going to have its most devastating impact for decades. The push of the European Union for legally enforceable targets on emissions suffers from its inability to guarantee that developing countries will receive funding to compensate for the losses they would incur by accepting these new standards. India and other rising powers (including, as quietly echoed in political circles, the United States) have clearly indicated that no enforcement mechanism that has the result of limiting economic growth will be accepted.[106] Accepting that no major multilateral deal is possible, given political realities in countries around the world, Etzioni has advised shifting resources and attention to finding technological solutions that can mitigate the damage that has already occurred, as well as finding ways to permit the rising powers to enjoy the fruits of economic development without inflicting further strain on the environment.[107] Recent US initiatives undertaken with both China and India to expand cooperation on clean energy and to pursue other such solutions are first steps along the recommendations that Etzioni has laid out.[108]

No direct challenge arising from a disaster attributed to a breakdown of one of the domains of the global commons has, as of yet, been the equivalent of a 9/11 terrorist attack. Therefore, while theoretically compelling, these problems have not yet activated the same level of immediate concern and have thus not served as a goad for forming stronger Global Authorities. Hacking and cybercrime have been annoyances, but no cyber attack—either by a state actor or a terrorist group—has yet succeeded in destroying infrastructure or inflicting large amounts of fatalities. Arguments about indirect causation arising from unaddressed problems, such as a combination of drought and energy prices creating conditions for the Arab Spring, remain too abstract to serve as the basis for immediate policy reactions. Piracy has been the issue that has come closest, and this is where we have seen the most progress in developing a transnational response, as outlined in Chapter 4. Etzioni thus maintains that the best way to habituate states to closer cooperation and to forge a greater sense of community is to concentrate on the immediate "hard security" issues, the "clear and present dangers."[109] As the security situation improves, it might be possible to make much more rapid progress toward dealing with these issues of the commons, because there might be more of a basis for mutual trust. An example of this would be if an approach styled along the lines of a Mutually Assured Restraint, as discussed in Chapter 3, were to come to define the Sino-American relationship and to decrease existing tensions.[110] There is also the possibility of taking an infrastructure developed to deal with a security threat and finding a dual use for it; for instance, the same measures that can be used to track and to isolate terror suspects, or to respond to a massive terrorist attack involving chemical or biological weapons, can be repurposed to cope with the spread of an infectious disease and to deal with the outbreak of a pandemic.[111]

Thus, for Etzioni, it is the primacy of direct kinetic threats that still exert the most influence over governments and that provide the impetus for closer cooperation. An interesting test, therefore, is whether the revival of terrorist groups with global reach will restart the cooperation of the mid-2000s and strengthen Etzioni's nascent Global Authorities in a way that could then be broadened to deal with other challenges. Given the partial collapse of the Middle East state system, this could very well be the catalyst for a new round of a global war on terror.

Etzioni has always argued that closer international cooperation is forged when there is an immediate security threat that must be addressed. This is what compels countries (and their publics) to sacrifice some sovereignty and take on burdens that, in the absence of the problem, they would refuse.[112] The 2015 Global Risks report released by the World Economic Forum at its yearly conclave in Davos showed a marked shift away from the focus in recent years on the longer-term challenges (income disparity and climate change) to immediate geopolitical challenges. Among these are the risks of interstate conflict, the inability of governments to provide security, and the collapse of states. The Ukraine crisis and other regional flash points, along with the resurgence of terrorist organizations, starting with the Islamic State, must be resolved. If they are not, immediate threats to human security—disease, disorder, and chaos, and even the use of weapons of mass destruction—will be heightened. Meanwhile, an expected economic slowdown has reduced the resources that countries, most notably the developed industrial democracies of the West, can spare.[113] Under such conditions, we return to the fundamental question that lies at the heart of Etzioni's Security First paradigm: "If we realize that we are much less powerful than we tend to assume, which threats deserve the most urgent attention?"[114] Basic, immediate security rises to the top of the list. Etzioni remains confident that keeping the focus on these core issues will produce the habits of cooperation that, in time, can tackle a wider range of issues.

Notes

1. Amitai Etzioni, *Hot Spots: American Foreign Policy in a Post-Human-Rights World* (New Brunswick, NJ: Transaction Publishers, 2012), vii–viii.
2. Gregory F. Treverton, Erik Nemeth, and Sinduja Srinivasan, *Threats Without Threateners? Exploring Intersections of Threats to the Global Commons and National Security*, Prepared for the Skoll Global Threats Fund (Santa Monica, CA: RAND, 2012), iii.
3. Stewart Patrick, "The Unruled World," *Foreign Affairs* 93:1 (January/February 2014), http://www.foreignaffairs.com/articles/140343/stewart-patrick/the-unruled-world.
4. See the contributions made by Radek Sikorski, John Hulsman, Hans Binnendijk, and Richard Kugler to a symposium, "Can NATO Survive Europe?" *American Enterprise Institute*, March 15, 2004, http://www.aei.org/publication/can-nato-survive-europe/print/.
5. Nikolas K. Gvosdev and Ray Takeyh, "The Decline of Western Realism," *The National Interest* 117 (January/February 2012), 9–11.
6. See the testimony by Sheila A. Smith, "U.S. Alliances in Northeast Asia: Strong Partners with Deep Divisions," at the "Hearing on U.S. Alliances in Northeast Asia," before the Foreign Relations Subcommittee on East Asian and Pacific Affairs, United States Senate (113thCongress, 2nd session), March 4, 2014, as issued by the Council on Foreign Relations, http://www.cfr.org/asia-and-pacific/us-alliances-northeast-asia/p32533.
7. "Is the Middle East Fighting a New Thirty Years War?" *The American Interest*, July 27, 2014, http://www.the-american-interest.com/2014/07/27/is-the-middle-east-fighting-a-new-thirty-years-war/.
8. Denitsa Raynova and Ian Kerns, "The Wales Pledge Revisited: A Preliminary Analysis of 2015 Budget Decisions in NATO Member States," *European Leadership Network*, February 26, 2015, http://www.europeanleadershipnetwork.org/the-wales-pledge-revisited-a-preliminary-analysis-of-2015-budget-decisions-in-nato-member-states_2472.html.
9. Amitai Etzioni, "MAR or War?" *The Diplomat*, October 17, 2013, http://thediplomat.com/2013/10/mar-or-war/.
10. David Alexander and Andrea Shalal, "Budget Cuts to Slah U.S. Army to Smallest Since Before World War Two," *Reuters*, February 24, 2014, http://www.reuters.com/article/2014/02/24/us-usa-defense-budget-idUSBRE-A1N1IO20140224.
11. Robert O. Keohane and Joseph S. Nye, Jr., "Globalization: What's New? What's Not? (And So What?)" *Foreign Policy* 118 (Spring 2000), 106–07.
12. Patrick, op. cit.
13. "Global Shipping: A Dynamic Market," *World Ocean Review* 1 (2010), http://worldoceanreview.com/en/wor-1/transport/global-shipping/.
14. Scott G. Borgerson, *The National Interest and the Law of the Sea*, Council on Foreign Relations Special Report 46 (May 2009), http://www.cfr.org/oceans/national-interest-law-sea/p19156.
15. Paul S. Giarra, "Assuring Joint Operational Access," *Conflict and Cooperation in the Global Commons: A Comprehensive Approach for International Security*, ed. Scott Jasper (Washington, DC: Georgetown University Press, 2012), 145.

16. Paul Saffo, "Disrupting Undersea Cables: Cyberspace's Hidden Vulnerability," *The Atlantic Council*, April 4, 2013, http://www.atlanticcouncil.org/blogs/new-atlanticist/disrupting-undersea-cables-cyberspaces-hidden-vulnerability.

17. *Maritime Piracy*, (Broomfield, CO: One Earth Future Foundation, December 2010), 25.

18. Harvey Rubin, "Future Global Shocks: Pandemics," report prepared for the OECD/IFP Project on "Future Global Shocks," no. IFP/WKP/FGS(January 14, 2011), 31–32.

19. See, for instance, Janet McIntyre-Mills, *Transformation from Wall Street to Wellbeing: Joining Up the Dots Through Participatory Democracy and Governance to Mitigate the Causes and Adapt to the Effects of Climate Change* (New York: Springer, 2014), 171.

20. Patrick, op. cit.

21. Michael V. Hayden, "Understanding the New Global Disorder," keynote address delivered at the FPRI annual dinner, Philadelphia, PA, November 19, 2014, and published in FPRI E-Notes, December 2014, http://www.fpri.org/articles/2014/12/understanding-new-global-disorder-three-tectonics.

22. Brent Scowcroft, "A World in Transformation," *The National Interest* 119 (May/June 2012), 7–9.

23. See, for instance, the assumption that countries, guided by such an understanding, would refrain from destroying satellite networks, in Michael Krepon, "Space and Nuclear Deterrence," *The Space* Review, September 16, 2013, http://www.thespacereview.com/article/2367/1.

24. Treverton, Nemeth, and Srinivasan, xi.

25. Joseph S. Nye, Jr., "Security and Smart Power," *American Behavioral Scientist* 51:9 (May 2008), 5.

26. Daniel Keohane, Stefan Lehne, Ulrich Speck, and Jan Techau, "A New Ambition for Europe: A Memo to the European Union Foreign Policy Chief," *Carnegie Europe*, October 28, 2014, http://carnegieeurope.eu/publications/?fa=57044.

27. Michael Hikari Cecire, "Whither the Euro-Atlantic Space? Redefining Euro-Atlantic Security in a Post-Post-Cold War Era," *e-cadernos ces* 19 (2013), http://eces.revues.org/1613.

28. See, for instance, Alexander Wolf, "The Rise of China: Implications for the Transatlantic Relationship," AIGCS Advisor, May 7, 2012, http://www.aicgs.org/publication/the-rise-of-china-implications-for-the-transatlantic-relationship/; Andrew Moravscik, "Europe, the Second Superpower," *Current History* 109 (March 2010), 91–98.

29. Etzioni, *Hot Spots*, 214.

30. Per Stig Moller, "Russia and Other Quandaries: Europe's Uncertain Future," *Horizons* 2 (Winter 2015), 105.

31. Etzioni, *Hot Spots*, 208–09.

32. Huntington foresaw problems because this elite would "have little need for national loyalty, view national boundaries as obstacles that thankfully are vanishing, and see national governments as residues from the past whose only useful function is to facilitate the elite's global operations." Samuel P. Huntington, "Dead Souls: The Denationalization of the American Elite," *National Interest* 75 (Spring 2004), 5.

33. Etzioni, *Hot Spots*, 205.
34. Moller, 104.
35. Thierry de Montbrial, "The Ugly Crisis: Ukraine, the West and Russia," *Horizons* 2 (Winter 2015), 74.
36. Etzioni, *Hot Spots*, 214.
37. Moller, 105.
38. Keohane, Lehne, Speck, and Techau, op. cit.
39. Moller, 105.
40. Nikolas K. Gvosdev, "Venezuela, Ukraine Challenge Assumptions Behind Defense Cuts," *World Politics Review*, February 28, 2014, http://www.world-politicsreview.com/articles/13598/the-realist-prism-venezuela-ukraine-challenge-assumptions-behind-defense-cuts.
41. Anthony H. Cordesman, *Chinese Strategy and Military Power in 2014: Chinese, Japanese, Korean, Taiwanese, and US Perspectives* (Washington, DC: CSIS, 2014), 23–24.
42. Keohane, Lehne, Speck, and Techau, op. cit.
43. Gal Luft, "Dependence on Middle East Energy and Its Impact on Global Security," Energy and Environmental Challenges to Security, eds. Stephen Stec and Besnik Baraj (Houten, Netherlands: Springer, 2009), 198.
44. MichaelSpence, "The Global Security Deficit," *Project Syndicate*, July 25, 2014, http://www.project-syndicate.org/commentary/michael-spence-warns-that-political-instability-and-conflict-are-now-the-main-threat-to-the-global-economy.
45. Shadi Hamid, "The Struggle for Middle East Democracy," *Cairo Review of Global Affairs* 1 (2011) 18–29, http://www.aucegypt.edu/GAPP/CairoReview/Pages/articleDetails.aspx?aid=20.
46. Jess Zimmerman, "How Food Prices Can Fuel Revolutions Like Egypt's," *Grist*, February 1, 2011, http://grist.org/article/2011-01-31-how-food-prices-can-fuel-revolutions-like-egypts/.
47. Sophie Wenzlau, "Global Food Prices Continue to Rise," *WorldWatch Institute*, April 11, 2013, http://www.worldwatch.org/global-food-prices-continue-rise-0; Troy Sternberg, "Chinese Drought, Wheat, and the Egyptian Uprising: How a Localized Hazard Became Globalized," *The Arab Spring and Climate Change: A Climate and Security Correlations Series*, eds. Caitlin E. Werrell and Francesco Femia (Washington, DC: Center for American Progress, 2013), 7–14.
48. Etzioni, *Hot Spots*, 166.
49. Murat Özçelik, "The Two Radical Sources of Instability in the Middle East," *Global Memo*, August 15, 2014, http://www.cfr.org/councilofcouncils/global_memos/p33347.
50. Zachary Keck, "China Created ISIS, Too," *The Diplomat*, September 15, 2014, http://thediplomat.com/2014/09/china-created-isis-too/.
51. "Nigeria's Boko Haram pledges allegiance to Islamic State," *BBC News*, March 7, 2015, http://www.bbc.com/news/world-africa-31784538.
52. Paul Haenle and James Jeffrey, "Political Instability and U.S. Strategy in the Middle East," *Carnegie-Tsinghua Center for Global Policy*, May 29, 2013, http://carnegietsinghua.org/2013/05/29/political-instability-and-u.s.-strategy-in-middle-east/gkcj.
53. Özçelik, op. cit.

54. Gabriel Domínguez and Ju Juan, "Soft Power—China's Expanding Role in the Middle East," *Deutsche Welle*, February 2, 2015, http://www.dw.de/soft-power-chinas-expanding-role-in-the-middle-east/a-18233271.

55. See, for instance, Heba Qudsi, "Christine Lagarde: Conflict in Iraq Can Trigger Higher Global Oil Prices," *Asharq Al-Awsat*, October 5, 2014, http://www.aawsat.net/2014/10/article55337218/imfs-christine-lagarde-conflict-in-iraq-can-trigger-higher-global-oil-prices.

56. Amitai Etzioni, "Shifting Sands," *Journal of International Security Affairs* 20 (Spring/Summer 2011), 87–97; Amitai Etzioni, "Rethinking the Pakistan Plan," *The National Interest* 117 (January/February 2012), 55–65.

57. Charles W. Freeman, "The Middle East and China," remarks prepared for (but not delivered to) a conference of the United States Institute of Peace and Georgetown University, Washington, DC, February 17, 2015, http://chasfreeman.net/the-middle-east-and-china-2/.

58. Freeman, op. cit.

59. Etzioni, *Hot Spots*, 95.

60. Daniel Markey, "Pakistan Contingencies," *Managing Instability on China's Periphery*, eds. Paul B. Stares, Scott A. Snyder, Joshua Kurlantzick, Daniel Markey, and Evan A. Feigenbaum (New York: Council on Foreign Relations, 2011), esp.49, 52.

61. Li Yan, "Securing the Global Commons, a New Foundation for the Sino-US Relationship," *ChinaUSFocus*, March 19, 2012, http://www.chinausfocus.com/peace-security/securing-the-global-commonsa-new-foundation-for-the-sino-us-relationship/#sthash.G5wbb4Rp.dpuf.

62. "Secretary of State Henry Kissinger Reflects on the Establishment of Diplomatic Relations with Beijing and the US-China Relationship Today," interview conducted by Susan Johnson for the Association for Diplomatic Studies and Training Foreign Affairs Oral History Project, July 25, 2012 and published by the American Foreign Service Association, September 2012, http://adst.org/wp-*content*/uploads/2012/09/Kissinger-Henry.pdf.

63. For instance, different countries, particularly between the industrialized West and the developing South and East, may have varying standards of what constitutes acceptable limits on air pollution or of how air quality should be interpreted. See, for instance, Adrian Fernandez, Miriam Zuk, and Leonora Rojas-Bracho, "Applications of Guidelines in Policy Formulation," *Air Quality Guidelines: Global Update 2005* (Copenhagen: World Health Organization, 2006), 174–79. Etzioni himself has used the example of Iran—that while all the major powers agree that Iran obtaining a nuclear weapon would be an undesirable precedent, different countries may ascertain the risk of that eventuality in different ways. Etzioni, *Hot Spots*, 37.

64. See, for example, Chinese claims vis-à-vis the United States in climate policy, in Gorild Heggelund, Steiner Andresen and Inga Fritza Buan, "Chinese Climate Policy: Domestic Priorities, Foreign Policy, and Emerging Implementation," *Global Commons, Domestic Decisions: The Comparative Politics of Climate Change*, eds. Kathryn Harrison and Lisa McIntosh Sundstrom (Cambridge, MA: Massachusetts Institute of Technology, 2010), 244–45.

65. China, India, and other rising powers have begun to pull masses of their populations out of poverty into the middle class, but using methods that

do put the global environment and climate at greater risk. Cf. Treverton, Nemeth, and Srinivasan, 1.

66. Etzioni, *Hot Spots*, 25–40.

67. James A. Lewis, "Multilateral Agreements to Constrain Cyberconflict," *Arms Control Today*, June 4, 2010, https://www.armscontrol.org/act/2010_06/Lewis.

68. The formal structure of multilateral talks has caused some states to default to a position of refusal because the possibility of conditional agreement (but with modifications or reduced time frames) is not always an option. See Treverton, Nemeth and Srinivasan, 28.

69. Yuan Peng and Nina Hachigian, "Global Roles and Responsibilities," *Debating China: The U.S.-China Relationship in Ten Conversations*, eds. Yuan Peng and Nina Hachigian (Oxford: Oxford University Press, 2014), 108.

70. Peng and Hachigian, 105.

71. Patrick, op. cit.

72. G. John Ikenberry and Amitai Etzioni, "Is China More Westphalian Than the West?" *Foreign Affairs* 90:6 (November/December 2011), 176.

73. Peng and Hachigian, 105.

74. Patrick, op. cit.

75. See Michael Swaine, "Chinese Views on Cybersecurity in Foreign Relations," *China Leadership Monitor* 42 (Fall 2013), 4, for Chinese commentary on the need to bring the Internet "into line with state administration" and the recognition that, left unsupervised, cyberspace transcends and breaks national boundaries and can lead to internal disruption.

76. Some of the back-and-forth can be seen in Amitai Etzioni, "China Might Negotiate Cybersecurity," *National Interest*, March 14, 2013, http://nationalinterest.org/commentary/china-might-negotiate-cybersecurity-8222.

77. See, for instance, Ashley J. Tellis, "Does China Threaten the United States in Space?" Testimony prepared for the House Armed Services Subcommittees on Strategic Forces and Seapower and Projection Forces, January 28, 2014, with additional commentary provided by the Carnegie Endowment for International Peace, http://carnegieendowment.org/2014/01/28/does-china-threaten-united-states-in-space. For a sense as to how China's efforts to pursue capabilities beyond what is perceived by the United States as necessary for China's security and for defense are evaluated, see Elbridge Colby, "Why China's Growing Defense Budget Matters," *Real Clear Defense*, March 9, 2015, http://www.realcleardefense.com/articles/2015/03/09/why_chinas_growing_defense_budget_matters.html.

78. Nathan Gardels, "Cyberwar With China: Former Intelligence Chief Says It Is Aiming at America's 'Soft Underbelly,'" *Huffington Post*, April 9, 2010, http://www.huffingtonpost.com/nathan-gardels/cyberwar-with-china-forme_b_452639.html.

79. Li Yan, "The Global Commons and the Reconstruction of US-China Military Relations", *Asia Paper*, March 2012, 16.

80. Frédéric Ramel, "Access to the Global Commons and Grand Strategies: A Shift in Global Interplay," *Etudes de l'IRSEM*, 2014, 28, https://hal-sciencespo.archives-ouvertes.fr/hal-01087574.

81. Li, "Securing the Global Commons," op. cit.

82. Etzioni, "China Might Negotiate Cybersecurity," op. cit.

83. Xu Longdi, "Obama Intensifies Cybersecurity Measures," *ChinaUSFocus*, April 5, 2013, http://www.chinausfocus.com/peace-security/obama-inten-sifies-cybersecurity-measures/.
84. Jyh-An Lee, "The Red Storm in Uncharted Waters: China and International Cyber Security," University of Missouri-Kansas City Law Review 82:4 (2014), 963.
85. Ramel, 28.
86. See, for instance, Amitai Etzioni, "MAR: A Model for US-China Relations," *The Diplomat*, September 20, 2013, http://thediplomat.com/2013/09/mar-a-model-for-us-china-relations/; Etzioni, *Hot Spots*, 45–60.
87. Phillip A. Johnson, "Is It Time for a Treaty on Information Warfare?" *International Law Studies—Volume 76 Computer Network Attack and International Law*, eds. Michael N. Schmitt and Brian T. O'Donnell (Newport, RI: Naval War College, 2002), 453.
88. Patrick, op. cit.
89. Lee, 964.
90. What may prove to be an unanswerable question is whether the alleged use of cyber weapons by the United States to disrupt aspects of Iran's nuclear program, achieving destruction of equipment in "what until then could be accomplished only by bombing a country or sending in agents to plant explosives" sufficiently delayed Iran's efforts to give diplomacy more time and helped to restrain Israel from launching airstrikes of its own. If so, then making it harder to use such options would not be something that a US administration would be eager to sign up for. Cf. David E. Sanger, "Obama Order Sped Up Wave of Cyberattacks Against Iran," *New York Times*, June 1, 2012, A1, http://www.nytimes.com/2012/06/01/world/middleeast/obama-ordered-wave-of-cyberattacks-against-iran.html.
91. Lee, 964.
92. Sanger, op. cit.
93. John Frank Weaver, "Asimov's Three Laws Are Not an International Treaty," *Slate*, December 1, 2014, http://www.slate.com/articles/technology/future_tense/2014/12/autonomous_weapons_and_international_law_we_need_these_three_treaties_to.html
94. For a discussion of this development vis-à-vis drones, see Peter Bergen and Jennifer Rowland, "A Dangerous New World of Drones," *CNN*, October 8, 2012, http://www.cnn.com/2012/10/01/opinion/bergen-world-of-drones/.
95. Christopher P. Twomey and Xu Hui, "Military Developments," in *Debating China*, 168.
96. Lee, 964.
97. Robert A. Manning, "Beijing and Washington Can Swerve Off Collision Course," *The Atlantic Council*, August 21, 2014, http://www.atlanticcouncil.org/publications/articles/beijing-and-washington-can-swerve-off-collision-course.
98. Patrick, op. cit.
99. Comments made at a forum, "The West and Russia: A New Cold War?" Sponsored by the Center for International Relations and Sustainable Development, the Harvard Club, New York, February 18, 2015.
100. Lewis, op. cit.
101. Lee, 966.

102. Lewis, op. cit.
103. Lewis, op. cit.
104. Johnson, 453.
105. Patrick, op. cit.
106. "EU Wants Paris Climate Deal to Cut Carbon Emissions 60% by 2050," *The Guardian*, February 23, 2015, http://www.theguardian.com/environment/2015/feb/23/eu-wants-paris-climate-deal-to-cut-carbon-emissions-60-by-2050; Jeff McMahon, "India Lowers Expectations for Paris Climate Talks," *Forbes*, February 20, 2015, http://www.forbes.com/sites/jeffmcmahon/2015/02/20/india-lowers-expectations-for-paris-climate-talks/.
107. Amitai Etzioni, "Climate Change? Don't Hold Your Breath," *Huffington Post*, February 5, 2013, http://www.huffingtonpost.com/amitai-etzioni/climate-change-dont-hold_b_2623037.html.
108. See the "Fact Sheet: U.S. and India Climate and Clean Energy Cooperation" released by the White House on January 25, 2015, http://www.whitehouse.gov/the-press-office/2015/01/25/fact-sheet-us-and-india-climate-and-clean-energy-cooperation; and the "Fact Sheet: U.S.-China Joint Announcement on Climate Change and Clean Energy Cooperation," released by the White House on November 11, 2014, http://www.whitehouse.gov/the-press-office/2014/11/11/fact-sheet-us-china-joint-announcement-climate-change-and-clean-energy-c.
109. Amitai Etzioni, *From Empire to Community* (New York: Palgrave Macmillan, 2004), 171.
110. Amitai Etzioni, "For a New Sino-American Relationship," *Amitai Etzioni Notes*, September 24, 2013, http://www.amitaietzioni.org/2013/09/for-a-new-sino-american-relationship.html.
111. On the repurposing of a structure dealing with intercepting WMD components (the PSI) to other tasks, see Amitai Etzioni, "Tomorrow's Institution Today," Foreign Affairs 88:3 (May/June 2009), http://www.foreignaffairs.com/articles/64976/amitai-etzioni/tomorrows-institution-today. On how the apparatus set up to deal with bioterrorism can also be used to cope with pandemics, see Amitai Etzioni, "Progressive Security and Conserving Rights," *Huffington Post*, July 6, 2009, http://www.huffingtonpost.com/amitai-etzioni/progressive-security-and_b_211975.html.
112. Etzioni, *From Empire to Community*, 171.
113. A summary of the report's conclusions can be accessed at http://reports.weforum.org/global-risks-2015/part-1-global-risks-2015/introduction/.
114. Amitai Etzioni, *Security First: For a Muscular, Moral Foreign Policy* (New Haven, CT: Yale University Press, 2007), xviii.

Epilogue: The Advisor's Advice Ignored?

Etzioni's communitarian realism—his emphasis on a Security First paradigm that creates conditions for gradual reform, and evolution toward a more effective global community that can safeguard human rights—can sound appealing. But is the US political system willing to put this approach into practice? To what extent can Etzioni's recommendations shape policy to deal with current crises, and what impact may they have in affecting the thinking of future candidates for office? After all, we consistently hear themes about the need for a more humble, focused, less ambitious, prioritized foreign-policy approach. In theory, this perspective is fertile soil for Etzioni's approach to take root. But often "the change proposed amounts to not much more than playing the same tune—on a different instrument."[1] Indeed, as Adam Garfinkle observes, the first tendency of the US policy establishment is "to try and shove events, movements, forces and foreign peoples into familiar cognitive grids where they just won't go."[2]

For these and other reasons, Etzioni's recommendations run into problems in being accepted and implemented by a US presidential administration. In addition to being neither reliably "conservative" nor "liberal," making it more difficult for a partisan candidate to be able to endorse the entire platform, Etzioni's approach is also gradualist in nature. It breaks apart policy initiatives "into numerous limited steps" to be implemented over a long period of time.[3] This puts it at odds with the general American preference (of both decision makers and the general public) for comprehensive solutions that can be rapidly implemented within the time frame of a single administration or even within a single electoral cycle.[4] Indeed, within the US national security apparatus, as James Steinberg admits, "the urgent often crowds out long-range planning," with most attention placed on the short term.[5] Moreover, Etzioni's observation that there are "no magic keys" and that a "more acceptable international system will have to be pieced together from such small and in themselves limited measures"[6] clashes with the preferences of many US presidential administrations for signature legacy accomplishments in foreign policy.[7] When coupled with a political culture that emphasizes "quick results," Etzioni's emphasis on a long-term, evolutionary perspective for policy makes it less likely that politicians will embrace the communitarian label or its program *in toto*. Moreover, the extended time frame of Etzioni's approach serves as the basis for recommendations that seem to require unpalatable short-term compromises. For instance, Etzioni advises the United States to partner with so-called "illiberal moderates" and authoritarian regimes that are prepared to take constructive steps in the international arena. An example of this is supporting deproliferation of weapons of mass destruction, even if it means lifting pressure for immediate liberal-democratic reform. This is a stand that is difficult for many Americans (particularly liberal internationalists) to accept, but it is one that Etzioni feels is justified if it helps to bring about a "safer and better world."[8] In the long run, such a stand may in fact strengthen the trend toward more open societies. In addition, Etzioni's own frank assessment is that most policy choices are not "between the best and the second-best" but that "the brutal international reality often requires following [what] might be called a 'second-worse' course in order to avoid having to negotiate the worst one."[9] This assessment helps to explain why he is often consulted and his ideas are always given a respectful hearing, but without much follow-through. In some ways, Etzioni is like a doctor who makes a diagnosis and devises a plan for recovery that requires significant lifestyle changes, only to find that the patient then rejects that course of treatment in the hope that the odds can be beaten by sticking with a more familiar regimen.

It is difficult for American politicians to accept least-worst options and the compromises they entail rather than holding out for optimal preferences, especially when there is no sense of imminent peril. One weakness of Etzioni's approach is that it is based on the false assumption that US policymakers will accept that the rise of challenges is too great for any one state to solve. This forces a greater degree of cooperation and the recognition that there are limits to what US power can achieve in the world. In June 2007, Etzioni testified before the Iraq Commission, an independent fact-finding body in the United Kingdom that is analogous to the US Iraq Study Group that was established to examine options for British policy.[10] He discussed his expectations that the setbacks the United States experienced as a result of the Iraq War—a series of "dominoes" that would fall—would help to generate a reassessment of the goals and aims of US foreign policy. The dominoes not only included the failure to set up a stable, democratic, pro-American government in Iraq itself, but the idea that instability in Iraq would spread and destabilize other countries in the Middle East. Moreover, Etzioni anticipated that the American failure in Iraq would: (1) embolden challengers, (2) distract the United States from other pressing challenges, (3) give countries like Iran and North Korea the time and breathing room to make tremendous progress on their nuclear programs, and (4) make it harder for the United States to forge effective partnerships with other states. Certainly, Etzioni's warnings touch on what would happen if Iraq had been validated by recent events, notably the rise of the Islamic State (IS) and the major setbacks experienced by the Iraq military in 2014.[11]

Part of the problem, of course, is that in American political culture the mistakes and failings of the past are not seen as collective failures but as attributable to a specific presidential administration. Indeed, a major feature of both successful and failed presidential campaigns in recent years has been the assertion that setbacks experienced in US foreign policy are not the result of fundamental flaws in the approach, but mistakes in programming and execution by a specific national security team.[12] This is because there is still an unwillingness to accept that the exercise of American power for a good cause might not produce exemplary results, and that it could end up hurting more than helping. In addition, there is a lingering sentiment that exercising restraint and seeking compromise in order to form global coalitions represents a betrayal of American ideals.

Etzioni had likewise assumed that the setbacks encountered by the Obama administration—particularly in the Middle East after the Arab Spring, the apparent failure of the reset with Russia, and the risk of a clash with China—would set the stage for a reassessment. He was looking for signs that US policy would pivot toward a more realistic idealism at the start of the second term.[13] Yet the absence of a sense of urgency remains a critical reason why Etzioni's recommendations still have not acquired any sort of critical mass. Indeed, there has been a lack of progress in addressing nuclear proliferation and environmental degradation—not to mention the rise in great-power tensions between the United States and Russia and also with China. In addition, the efforts of nuclear powers—including newer ones like India and Pakistan—to upgrade and modernize their arsenals have stalled. This lack of development caused the *Bulletin of the Atomic Scientists* to advance the hands of their "doomsday clock" to an unprecedented (for the post-Cold War era) position of 11:57 PM, or "three minutes to midnight." (By point of comparison, the clock was set to 17 minutes to midnight in December 1991.) Highlighting the sense of urgency, Kennette Benedict, the executive director of the *Bulletin*, observed, "We are not saying it is too late to take action but the window for action is closing rapidly. We move the clock hand . . . to inspire action."[14]

Nor have fears about the prospect of a major clash among the great powers led the Obama administration to make significant course corrections in policy. Proposals that have been advanced that parallel Etzioni's concept of "Mutually Assured Restraint" (MAR)—among them Richard Gowan's call for paying "renewed attention to various forms of 'big-power buffering' in high-value trouble-spots like Ukraine and the Western Pacific"[15]—have largely fallen on deaf ears.

Despite the talk of a "new model of great power relations," the tensions that could spark into open conflict remain largely unresolved. Limited progress toward a climate agreement that was reached between China and the United States at the summit meeting between Xi Jinping and Barack Obama in Beijing in November 2014 was overshadowed by concerns over US support for protestors in Hong Kong, and warnings against American meddling in Chinese domestic affairs.[16] Nor has the United States altered its plans to rebalance its military posture toward the Far East. Indeed, by 2020, some 60 percent of US naval and airpower is scheduled to be based in the Asia-Pacific theater, and new systems are being developed "to check an increasingly assertive China."[17] Moreover, there are calls for the United States to establish a "series of linked defenses along the first island chain" as a way to deter Beijing. This approach would be designed to establish a "formidable conventional deterrent" through closer US military cooperation with, and basing of, components in countries like Japan and the Philippines.[18] To the extent this approach is sustained in the coming years, it represents a rejection of the MAR principles outlined by Etzioni in favor of a strong forward presence along the Chinese periphery. This runs the risk of creating flash points for conflict between the United States and China rather than tamping down areas of possible controversy.

In spring 2014, a crisis in Ukraine flared up after Ukrainian president Viktor Yanukovych was deposed by a protest movement that had arisen from his last-minute refusal to sign an association agreement with the European Union. His refusal, under pressure from Russia, led to a series of events that escalated the sudden chill in relations between Russia and the West. Among these events was Crimea's detachment from Ukrainian control, the taking control of some territories in southeastern Ukraine by Russian-backed separatists, and the placement of Russia under economic sanction by both the European Union and the United States. Yet there seemed to be no interest in using the MAR principles for defusing the Ukraine crisis between Russia and the West. Would it have been possible, to paraphrase Etzioni, to find a reasonable compromise that would require Russia to acknowledge Ukraine's desire for some degree of integration with Europe while the United States would accept a certain degree of Russian predominance in the Eurasian space? In the first months of the crisis, elements of MAR could be found in proposals advanced by both former Secretary of State Henry Kissinger and former National Security Advisor Zbigniew Brzezinski to create a degree of geopolitical space in Ukraine, and to search for ways to tamp down points of conflict.[19]

The Maidan movement that took power in Ukraine, however, was not interested in abandoning a westward orientation. Moreover, the Russian seizure of Crimea and support for separatists in southeastern Ukraine diminished Western interest in finding any sort of compromise solution that would require Ukraine to give up its aspirations. Even if a MAR-style solution for Ukraine would be the "ideal equilibrium," as Ian Bremmer notes, "recent events have made that exponentially harder to achieve."[20] With proposals for US forces to deploy to Ukraine to begin training the Ukrainian military (albeit to the western portions of the country), the possibility for a direct confrontation between Russia and the United States increases.[21] In addition, there is now significant opposition to any sort of proposal for the neutralization of Ukraine. Former NATO Supreme Allied Commander Admiral James Stavridis and former German Defense Minister Karl-Theodor zu Guttenberg sum up what is becoming a consensus view among Western policymakers that any sort of "Finlandization" of Ukraine is not an acceptable solution: "Rarely confronted with the question of whether it would be enough for countries like Ukraine or Georgia to "only" refrain from pursuing their security and economic interests to the fullest, or if further significant sacrifices would be a precondition for taming Russia."[22] Ukraine has now emerged as a zero-sum conflict. Moreover, as the crisis is prolonged, cooperation between the United States and Russia in other areas—seen as vital for the preservation of global security—has been negatively impacted. As Robert Legvold has lamented:

> As a result, when US-Russian leadership is needed more than ever to cope with the instability of nuclear proliferation and the militarization of space, they are allowing the arms control regime painfully constructed over the last 40 years to die a slow death. As adversaries, they're unlikely to work well together to counter cyber warfare, climate change and catastrophic terrorism. The temptation will be to use these, and other titanic changes such as China's rise, against each other. Rather than sponsoring enhanced European security, they are leading the charge in re-militarizing Europe's core.[23]

Etzioni had assumed that a sustained, persistent threat of terrorism with a global reach could tamp down such geopolitical rivalries among the United States, China, and Russia, and would hold together a coalition of states that would form an embryonic Global Safety Authority. Al-Qaeda survived and was transformed into a looser collection of regionally based franchises, and the IS rose to take control of portions of Iraq and Syria. The IS thereby acquired the territorial and resource base to bolster its range, influence, and capabilities. This should have revitalized the post-9/11 anti-terror coalition, especially given the fact that these groups continue to target not only US and Western interests but also those of China, Russia, and other emerging powers—not to mention the existing governments of the Middle East. Yet the struggle against the Islamic State and Al-Qaeda 2.0 has not served to fully reunite the coalition. It has enhanced the cooperation among existing sets of allies, principally between the United States and key countries in Europe,[24] but has been insufficient to restore some of the levels of coordination, particularly in intelligence sharing, among a wider set of countries. In particular, disagreements over whether the current regime of Bashar Al-Assad in Syria and the Islamic Republic of Iran are partners in this struggle or obstacles that must also be removed, as well as differences of opinion on how the campaign ought to be carried out, has prevented consolidation of efforts.[25]

Especially disturbing has been, since early 2015, the failure of countries to coordinate their military strikes against IS, or even to confer in advance before taking action.[26] There is also a lack of coordination when it comes to providing outside assistance to the government of Iraq to combat the IS; Iranian support requested by the Iraqi government is kept separate from interaction with the US-led coalition that provides air support and training. Nor has the fight against the IS provided a basis for a US-Iran working relationship.[27] These problems of uncoordinated action call into question the applicability of the Proliferation Security Initiative model and the SHADE process for coordinating the antipiracy campaign off the Horn of Africa, or for coping with future transnational security challenges. This runs the risk that the fight against the IS and other such groups, rather than helping to forge a common approach, will be splintered and separate, weakening its overall effectiveness while doing little to contribute to an improved global security architecture.

There are hopes that finding a diplomatic solution to the Iranian nuclear question might clear the way for closer US-Iranian cooperation in the fight against the IS—although, of course, this could alienate other coalition partners.[28] Yet, all of the variants of a solution now fail to focus on an exchange of security guarantees for deproliferation; this option is now seen as utterly unfeasible, especially after the Ukraine crisis. Instead, the focus is on the freezing by Iran of its nuclear activities in return for sanctions relief, with monitoring activities in place to ensure that any Iranian decision to pursue weaponization can be detected and stopped, either by diplomatic or military means.[29] Rather than focusing on a glide path to giving up the tools that could be used to fabricate weapons and their delivery systems, the diplomatic approach is on the extent to which Iran can retain some of its nuclear tools as long as there are reasonable guarantees that they would stay "boxed," and that Iran would not attempt to achieve breakout capability.[30]

In addition to the ongoing challenges posed to the deproliferation agenda by the search for an agreement with Iran, Barack Obama's visit to India in January 2015 set back further the realization of Etzioni's hopes for reducing the number of nuclear-weapons states. Additional cooperation between the United States and Indian nuclear establishments, part of the strategic gamble that India may help in serving as a counterweight to China (alongside the previously discussed military rebalance), has had two negative deproliferation effects. The first has been to further erode the Non-Proliferation Treaty framework designed to forestall the spread of nuclear weapons technology; the second, the ramping up by Pakistan of its own production of nuclear warheads, increasing the risks that a weapon might be stolen or used.[31]

The short-term prognosis may be that Etzioni's various recommendations are not only not being heeded but are being actively disregarded in the formulation and execution of US foreign policy. The long-term trends, however, suggest that there will be an inexorable shift back toward the vision Etzioni has laid out, particularly as the ongoing aftereffects of recent major operations such as Iraq and Libya continue to have negative repercussions. As W. James Antle III has observed, speaking about those two conflicts, "the two most recent preventive wars fought by the United States would end up achieving nearly the opposite of their original aims."[32]

The United States may still be the most powerful nation in the world. But staying on its current course, it can either exhaust its power by trying to solve global issues (e.g., serve as "the world's policeman") or it must of necessity (for fiscal reasons, if nothing else) allow problems to remain unaddressed. This lack of attention means that future threats that would endanger the United States could metastasize. Etzioni provides a blueprint to aid the United States in reshaping the global order of the 21st century in a way that can husband the country's strength and secure its interests while remaining true to its values. James Steinberg, Deputy Secretary of State in the first term of the Obama administration, contends that Etzioni's writings provide a principle to inform, rather than a playbook to guide, the policymaker. Nevertheless, he notes that Etzioni offers an alternative framework "within which to address the challenges and trade-offs facing policy makers as they struggle to make what Etzioni calls the 'second worst choice.'"[33] In some cases, these recommendations require major alterations to the US foreign-policy status quo. With a growing belief that the approaches that have defined the last three presidential administrations—for instance, the interventionist application of US power to force positive change—are no longer sustainable, yet a continued unwillingness to countenance the large-scale withdrawal of the United States from global affairs, Etzioni's communitarian realism may yet find new adherents within the American foreign-policy community.

Notes

1. Amitai Etzioni, *Security First: For a Muscular, Moral Foreign Policy* (New Haven, CT: Yale University Press, 2007), xii.
2. Adam Garfinkle, "What the MSM Is Failing to Tell You," *The American Interest*, January 29, 2015, http://www.the-american-interest.com/2015/01/29/what-the-msm-is-failing-to-tell-you/ .
3. Amitai Etzioni, *Winning Without War* (Garden City, NY: Doubleday, 1964), 219.
4. For some of the domestic political pressures, including those of the electoral cycle, see Kevin H. Wang, "Presidential Responses to Foreign Policy

Crises: Rational Choice and Domestic Politics," *Journal of Conflict Resolution* 40:1 (March 1996), 68–97.

5. James Steinberg, "The Intellectual Challenge of Mid-Range Strategy and Planning," panel presentation, Strategy and Policy Planning Workshop of the project, Wielding American Power: Managing Interventions After September 11, co-sponsored by the Woodrow Wilson Center and the Triangle Institute for Security Studies, February 14–15, 2005 at http://tiss.sanford. duke.edu/research/power/Panel1_000.htm.

6. Etzioni, *Winning Without War,* 236.

7. See, for instance, Albert R. Hunt, "Obama's Final Legacy to Be Set by Foreign Policy," *Bloomberg,* February 8, 2015, http://www.bloombergview.com/ articles/2015-02-08/obama-s-legacy-will-be-set-by-foreign-policy.

8. Amitai Etzioni, *The Hard Way to Peace: A New Strategy* (New York: Crowell-Collier Press, 1962), 13.

9. Amitai Etzioni, *Security First: For a Muscular, Moral Foreign Policy* (New Haven: Yale University Press, 2007), 3.

10. The Iraq Commission testimony was broadcast by Channel 4. Etzioni appears in the first episode of the Commission, on June 5, 2007, which can be accessed at http://www.channel4.com/player/v2/player.jsp?showId=6883.

11. See, for instance, "Islamic State Was Fueled By 'Epic American Failure In Iraq,' Reporter Says," *Fresh Air (National Public Radio),* September 10, 2014, http://www.npr.org/2014/09/10/347391620/islamic-state-was-fueled-by-epic-american-failure-in-iraq-reporter-says.

12. Nikolas K. Gvosdev, "Ghosts of Iraq," *National Interest,* May 20, 2013, http:// nationalinterest.org/commentary/ghosts-iraq-8491; Nikolas K. Gvosdev, "How the GOP Lost National Security," *National Interest,* December 13, 2012, http://nationalinterest.org/commentary/how-the-gop-lost-national-security-7842.

13. Amitai Etzioni, "Obama's Foreign Policy: Three Stages of Hope," *Huffington Post,* January 17, 2013, http://www.huffingtonpost.com/amitai-etzioni/ obama-foreign-policy_b_2426868.html.

14. Megan Gannon, "Doomsday Clock Set at 3 Minutes to Midnight," *Scientific American,* January 24, 2015, http://www.scientificamerican.com/article/ doomsday-clock-set-at-3-minutes-to-midnight/.

15. Richard Gowan, "Big-Power 'Buffering' Mechanisms Needed to Manage Era of Disorder," *World Politics Review,* November 10, 2014, http://www. worldpoliticsreview.com/articles/14400/big-power-buffering-mechanisms-needed-to-manage-era-of-disorder.

16. Mark Landler, "Fruitful Visit by Obama Ends With a Lecture From Xi," *New York Times,* November 13, 2014, A6, http://www.nytimes.com/2014/11/13/ world/asia/china-us-xi-jinping-obama-apec.html?_r=2.

17. Andrew F. Krepinevich, Jr., "How to Deter China: The Case for Archipelagic Defense," *Foreign Affairs* 94:2 (March/April 2015), http://www.foreignaffairs. com/articles/143031/andrew-f-krepinevich-jr/how-to-deter-china.

18. Krepinevich, op. cit.

19. Both, for instance, have called for Russia to accept some degree of association with the European Union, and to cease interference in Ukraine's domestic affairs but also for NATO not to expand to include Ukraine and for Ukraine to accommodate some of Russia's legitimate security and

economic interests. See Henry Kissinger, "To Settle the Ukraine Crisis, Start at the End," *Washington Post*, March 5, 2014, http://www.washingtonpost.com/opinions/henry-kissinger-to-settle-the-ukraine-crisis-start-at-the-end/2014/03/05/46dad868-a496-11e3-8466-d34c451760b9_story.html; Zbigniew Brzezinski, Excerpts from "Mutual Security on Hold? Russia, the West, and European Security Architecture," presentation at the Woodrow Wilson Center for Scholars, Washington, DC, June 16, 2014, http://www.atlanticcouncil.org/blogs/natosource/brzezinski-the-west-should-arm-ukraine.

20. Ian Bremmer and Harry Kazianis, "The Ukraine Nightmare: Five Questions for Ian Bremmer," *Real Clear Defense*, March 4, 2015, http://www.realcleardefense.com/articles/2015/03/04/the_ukraine_nightmare_5_questions_for_ian_bremmer_107696.html.

21. Paul McLeary, "US Soldiers Readying for Ukraine Deployment," *Defense News*, March 3, 2015, http://www.defensenews.com/story/defense-news/blog/intercepts/2015/03/03/ukraine-russia-putin-war/24327263/.

22. Karl-Theodor Zu Guttenberg and James Stavridis, "Who is to Blame?" *Horizons* 2 (Winter 2015), 69–70.

23. Robert Legvold, "Why the New Cold War Matters," *CNN Money*, January 15, 2015, http://money.cnn.com/2015/01/15/news/economy/davos-cold-war-opinion/.

24. Patrick Tucker, "'Dramatic Improvement' in US and European Intel Sharing Because of ISIS," *Defense One*, February 11, 2015, http://www.defenseone.com/technology/2015/02/dramatic-improvement-us-and-european-intel-sharing-because-isis/105120/.

25. Maria Sidelnikova, "Veronica Krasheninnikova: There Are No Reasons to Talk About Loss of U.S. Interest in the South Caucasus," *Vestnik Kavkaza*, February 17, 2015, http://vestnikkavkaza.net/interviews/politics/66507.html.

26. Nancy Youssef, "U.S. Won't Back Egypt's Attacks on ISIS," *The Daily Beast*, February 19, 2015, http://www.thedailybeast.com/articles/2015/02/18/u-s-won-t-back-egypt-s-attacks-on-isis.html; Noah Rotman, "U.S. Is Pretty Concerned About Egypt, UAE Taking Fight to ISIS in Libya," *Hot Air*, February 18, 2015, http://hotair.com/archives/2015/02/18/u-s-is-pretty-concerned-about-egypt-uae-taking-fight-to-isis-in-libya/.

27. Jim Michaels, "U.S. Fears Iran Military Influence is Growing in Iraq," *USA Today*, March 2, 2015, http://www.usatoday.com/story/news/world/2015/03/02/iraq-operation-tikrit/24246965.

28. David Ignatius, "America is the Ally Egypt Needs," *Washington Post*, February 26, 2015, http://www.washingtonpost.com/opinions/america-is-the-ally-that-egypt-needs/2015/02/26/efe7eeb0-bdfd-11e4-bdfa-b8e8f594e6ee_story.html?hpid=z2.

29. Aru Pande, "Obama: Iran Must Freeze Sensitive Nuclear Activity for at Least a Decade," *VOA News*, March 2, 2015, http://www.voanews.com/content/obama-iran-must-freeze-sensitive-nuclear-activity/2665473.html.

30. David Ignatius, "A Compelling Argument on Iran," *Washington Post*, February 24, 2015, http://www.washingtonpost.com/opinions/a-compelling-argument-on-iran/2015/02/24/8062ec44-bc76-11e4-b274-e5209a3bc9a9_story.html?tid=HP_opinion?tid=HP_opinion.

31. Amitai Etzioni, "The Darker Side of the U.S.-India Nuclear Deal," *The Diplomat*, February 13, 2015, http://thediplomat.com/2015/02/the-darker-side-of-the-u-s-india-nuclear-deal/?utm_source=WhatCounts+Publicaster+Edition&utm_medium=email&utm_campaign=The+Darker+Side+of+the+U.S.-India+Nuclear+Deal&utm_content=The+Diplomat.

32. W. James Antle III, "Iran Talks at a Crossroads," *The American Conservative*, March 2, 2015, http://www.theamericanconservative.com/articles/iran-talks-at-a-crossroads/.

33. James B. Steinberg, "A Sound Principle, but not a Playbook," *American Behavioral Scientist* 51:8 (May 2008), 1361.

Index